COLUMBIA COLLEGE LIBRARY
600 S. MICHIGAN AVENUE
CHICAGO, IL 60605

American Composer Zenobia Powell Perry

Race and Gender in the 20th Century

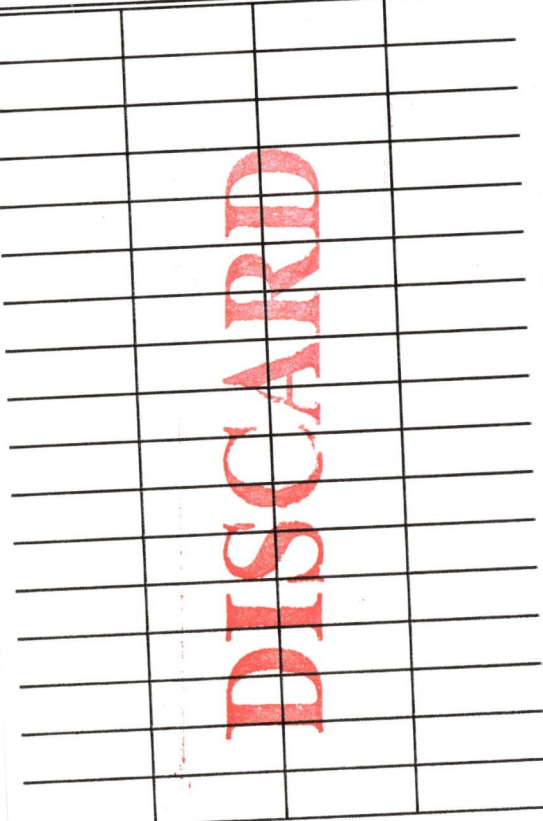

American Composer Zenobia Powell Perry

Race and Gender in the 20th Century

Jeannie Gayle Pool

The Scarecrow Press, Inc.
Lanham, Maryland • Toronto • Plymouth, UK
2009

SCARECROW PRESS, INC.

Published in the United States of America
by Scarecrow Press, Inc.
A wholly owned subsidiary of
The Rowman & Littlefield Publishing Group, Inc.
4501 Forbes Boulevard, Suite 200, Lanham, Maryland 20706
www.scarecrowpress.com

Estover Road
Plymouth PL6 7PY
United Kingdom

Copyright © 2009 by Jeannie Gayle Pool

All rights reserved. No part of this publication may be reproduced, stored in a retrieval system, or transmitted in any form or by any means, electronic, mechanical, photocopying, recording, or otherwise, without the prior permission of the publisher.

British Library Cataloguing in Publication Information Available

Library of Congress Cataloging-in-Publication Data

Pool, Jeannie G.
　American Composer Zenobia Powell Perry : race and gender in the 20th century / Jeannie Gayle Pool.
　　p. cm.
　Includes bibliographical references and index.
　ISBN-13: 978-0-8108-6376-7 (pbk. : alk. paper)
　ISBN-10: 0-8108-6376-6 (pbk. : alk. paper)
　ISBN-13: 978-0-8108-6377-4 (ebook)
　ISBN-10: 0-8108-6377-4 (ebook)
　1. Perry, Zenobia Powell, 1908–2004.　2. African–American women composers—United States—Biography.　3. Creek indians—Biography.　I. Title.
ML410.P29533P66 2009
780.92—dc22
[B]　　　　　　　　　　　　　　　　　2008033403

♾™ The paper used in this publication meets the minimum requirements of American National Standard for Information Sciences—Permanence of Paper for Printed Library Materials, ANSI/NISO Z39.48-1992.
Manufactured in the United States of America

Book designed by Beverly Simmons.

Contents

Foreword by Donald Rosenberg	vii
Acknowledgments	ix
Illustrations	xi
Musical Examples	xiii
Sidebars	xv
Introduction	xvii

CHAPTERS

1.	Zenobia Powell Perry: Articulate Link to American Culture of the 1920s and '30s	1
2.	Song and Verse in Boley: A Lifetime of Inspiration for an American Composer	13
3.	"Lift Every Voice and Sing": Booker T. Washington; Boley, Oklahoma; and the Political Reality for Blacks	27
4.	Distinctively American: Race and Music	39
5.	The Hidden History: Blacks and Native Americans' Cultural Implications	55
6.	Mentors, Allies, and Supporters: Crucial for Musical Development	67
7.	Dett, Reece, and Dawson: Role Models for Careers in Black Music	79
8.	Zenobia Powell Perry: An "Ambiguous Woman"	95
9.	Professional Teaching Career and Graduate School	109
10.	Becoming a Composer: Studies with Milhaud and Willman	123
11.	Analysis of Musical Style and Selected Works	143

CONTENTS

APPENDICES

A.	Chronology	181
B.	List of Compositions	185
C.	Inventory of Documents Related to the Life and Career of Zenobia Powell Perry	195

Notes	215
Bibliography	247
Index	257
About the Author	277

Foreword

Donald Rosenberg and Zenobia Powell Perry.
Photo by Beverly Simmons.

Most composers have at least some hopes for their music. The creative process is a means to an end—the realization of ideas in performance, when musicians finally share the composer's messages with an audience.

So, what are we to make of the unusual and inspiring saga of Zenobia Powell Perry? The black Creek Indian composer never sought the artistic limelight. She began to compose in earnest only in her forties. And she was content essentially to provide works for students and friends, without a thought that her music would ever be published.

FOREWORD

As Jeannie Pool states in her fascinating study of Perry: "She knew what all composers know: that the reward is found in the moment of writing." Pool weaves the story of Perry's life from humble beginnings in Oklahoma to a position of respect and admiration in Ohio and elsewhere through the eyes and ears of a keen musician.

The tale is almost hard to believe: how a black female pianist came to the attention of such eminent figures as Eleanor Roosevelt, who provided financial aid for her graduate studies, and Darius Milhaud, who guided her through the thickets of composition, made her his assistant at the Aspen Music Festival, and encouraged Perry to cherish her musical instincts, with roots going back to spirituals of African slaves.

But we believe. Despite numerous hardships, Zenobia Perry remained a nurturing teacher and productive composer to the end of her life in 2004 at the age of ninety-five. In the months preceding her death, she was celebrated in a series of concerts focusing on her skillfully crafted and affecting chamber music.

Perry, who also wrote orchestral pieces, art songs, and an opera, was in the audience for these programs to hear music she never imagined would go beyond a devoted circle of friends and colleagues.

Pool's passionate advocacy of Perry, partly through astute analysis of the composer's music, could go a long way in helping to change perceptions about what it means to contribute to society without concern for mainstream expectation.

—*Donald Rosenberg*
July 2008

Donald Rosenberg is classical music critic of *The Plain Dealer* (Cleveland). He earned a bachelor of music degree from the Mannes College of Music and master of music and master of musical arts degrees from the Yale School of Music as a French horn major. He participated in the Aspen and Marlboro music festivals and performed with the New York String Orchestra. He played under such conductors as Pablo Casals, Robert Shaw, William Steinberg, Pierre Boulez, Aaron Copland, Georg Solti, Herbert Blomstedt, John Nelson, and Otto-Werner Mueller. He has covered fourteen international tours of the Cleveland Orchestra and is author of *The Cleveland Orchestra Story: Second to None* (Cleveland: Gray & Co., 2000). He has written for *Gramophone*, *Opera* (London), *Opera News*, *Musical America*, and many other publications. He served two terms as president of the Music Critics Association of North America.

Acknowledgments

Many thanks to Beverly Simmons, who designed and edited this book. Her support, diligence, expertise, and steadfast friendship have made the publication of this biography possible. I would also like to acknowledge others who contributed to this book, including: Michael Kilbourne, John Triplett, and Ruth Yellowhawk at WYSO Radio in Yellow Springs, Ohio, who provided facilities and technical support to record a major interview of Zenobia Powell Perry; Vincent A. Lenti, who provided information and insight about the Eastman School of Music in the 1920s and '30s; Suzanne Flandreau, Center for Black Music Research; Anne Simpson; Lance Bowling; my mother, Betty Pool (1933–2000); Stephen M. Fry; Beverly Grigsby; Deon Nielsen Price; Marilyn Wilson; Jack Crotty; Beatrice O'Rourke, professor emerita, Central State University; Marilyn Sandness; Joanne Brooks; Ruth Petrie; Grace D. Wiley; and Miss Davis, University of Arkansas at Pine Bluff; Jane Gallante, an expert on Darius Milhaud; Dominique René de Lerma; Dr. Charles James Bate of Tulsa, Oklahoma; Emmett Chisolm of the University of Wyoming; The National Archives in New York City; Quintin Jones, Meharry Medical School Archivist; Mrs. Henrietta Hicks of The Boley Museum; John Frizzell of the Newspaper Archives of the Oklahoma Historical Society; Randy Roberts, librarian of Pittsburg State University, for sending a copy of Velma Dolphin-Ashley's thesis on Boley, Oklahoma; Jo Ann Haycraft, for sharing her research on Allan Willman; Clark County (Springfield,

ACKNOWLEDGMENTS

Ohio) Public Library; University of California, Los Angeles Music Library; Betsy Furth, Aspen Music Festival and School; Mary Heady, archivist, Lincoln University of Missouri; Mary Linscome, archivist, University of Northern Colorado; Betty R. Black at Langston University; Enid Douglass of Claremont; Berkeley Price; Darryl Taylor; and Robert Bornstein. Many thanks to my dissertation advisors at Claremont Graduate University: Nancy van Deusen, Gwendolyn Lytle, and Katherine Hagedorn. Thanks to Gregg Nestor for help with the musical examples. I also would like to thank the PatsyLu Fund of the Open Meadows Foundation for their support of my work to promote Zenobia Perry's music. Thanks to Erik Vorkink who continues to host the web site: www.zenobiapowellperry.org. Also many thanks to David Zea (1931–2006) and the F. Eugene Miller Foundation for their financial support of this biography. At Scarecrow Press, I am grateful for the guidance and support of Sally Craley and Stephen Ryan.

Knowing Zenobia Powell Perry for more than two decades was a true joy and privilege. I hope that you will get to know, through this book, what an amazing woman she was. I encourage you to listen to and perform her music. I offer this work as another piece of the puzzle in our attempt to understand the multi-faceted and geographically decentralized musical life of our time in the United States.

Finally, I offer my gratitude to Zenobia Powell Perry and her daughter, Janis-Rozena Peri, for sharing their lives and music with me. Zenobia demonstrated a profound act of faith and trust when agreeing to work with me on this biography. I am genuinely moved by her generosity.

—*Jeannie Gayle Pool*
May 2008

Illustrations

Unless otherwise noted, all illustrations are courtesy of the Zenobia Powell Perry Estate.

Donald Rosenberg and Zenobia Powell Perry	vii
Zenobia Powell Perry at age 95	xvi
Zenobia Powell Perry at the Paul Laurence Dunbar House	xx
Performers at Trinity Cathedral in Cleveland	xxii
"'Boley March Song,' or the Negroes' Home of the Free"	15
Boley Town Council, c.1910	16
Boley Grammar School	18
Calvin Bethel Powell, M.D.	19
Medical, Dental, Pharmaceutical Faculty Graduates, Meharry Medical Department, Central Tennessee College, 1894	21
Birdie Lee Thompson Powell	23
Zenobia Powell at age 15	26
Zenobia Powell at age 17	26
Children of Dr. C. B. Powell and Birdie Thompson Powell	26
Convention of Black Medical Care Providers, c.1920	34
Boley Grammar School Activities, c.1916	38
Zenobia Powell Perry at the piano in the early 1950s	53
Zenobia Powell Perry, c.1992	54
Zenobia Powell, c.1923	66
Hazel Harrison	68
Mr. and Mrs. Cecil W. Berryman, April 11, 1930	73

ILLUSTRATIONS

R. Nathaniel Dett, c.1928	80
"William L. Dawson and Zenobia Powell Perry Embrace at Columbus, Ohio Concert"	87
Concert program from Langston University, July 12, 1939	94
Jimmie Rodgers Perry	103
Lemuel Powell Perry	103
Zenobia Powell Perry and Kelton Lawrence, Duo-Piano Team	121
Dr. Allan Willman, c.1947–48	124
Darius Milhaud with students at the University of Wyoming, 1949	130
Charles Jones, Aspen Music School Faculty, at home in New York	133
Zenobia Powell Perry in front of the house she built in Wilberforce, Ohio	137
Professor Emerita Zenobia Powell Perry, 1985	140
Janis-Rozena Peri, 2008	146
Program, *Tawawa House* premiere, May 1987	180
Zenobia Powell Perry on her 95th birthday, 2003	184
Zenobia Powell Perry, honored by Mu Phi Epsilon	194

Musical Examples

All musical examples are published by Jaygayle Music (ASCAP), unless otherwise noted.

1.	"Threnody," page 1	148
2.	"Benediction," page 1	149
3.	"Arioso," page 1	152
4.	"The Cottage," page 1	153
5.	"Drizzle," page 1	154
6.	"O de Angels Done Bowed Down," page 1	160
7.	"Ah Got a Home in a Dat Rock," page 1	162
8.	"Sound Patterns," page 1	165
9.	"Ships That Pass in the Night," page 1	168
10.	"Tempo," page 1	170
11.	*Echoes from the Journey*, page 1	172

Sidebars

Zenobia Powell Perry 95th Birthday Concert Tour	xix
"Music in Community Living" by Zenobia P. Perry	141
Poets Set to Music by Zenobia Powell Perry	147
"Gifts of God" by Zenobia Powell Perry	164
Synopsis of *Tawawa House*	177
"A Wish" and "The Sea Waves" by Zenobia Powell Perry	214

Zenobia Powell Perry at age 95.
Photo by Floyd R. Thomas, Jr., courtesy National Afro-American Museum and Cultural Center, Wilberforce, Ohio.

Introduction

The year 2008 marks the one hundredth anniversary of the birth of American composer and music educator Zenobia Powell Perry. This biography was written when Zenobia was in her nineties and was completed in April 2002, with her invaluable assistance and approval.[1]

I met Zenobia's only daughter, Janis-Rozena Peri, in New York in the late 1970s. When she discovered that I was doing research on women composers, she proudly told me that her mother was a composer in Ohio and lived less than twenty miles from my parents' home. We became friends. I met Zenobia Perry in 1980 at the Conference/Workshop on 20th-Century String Quartets by Women Composers in New York City. We met for the second time in March 1981, when I had the privilege of presenting her daughter in a recital of works by black American women composers. At the same conference, Zenobia Perry was included at a monumental session on black American women in music at the First National Congress on Women in Music at New York University, chaired by Raoul Abdul. As founder and coordinator of the International Congress on Women in Music, I had produced both of these events.

My research on Zenobia Perry began in July 1993, with a lengthy oral history interview, recorded at WYSO Radio in Yellow Springs, Ohio. I used

INTRODUCTION

that interview, along with recorded performances of Zenobia's music to make a radio documentary, which was broadcast on WYSO, as well as on KPFK Los Angeles 90.7 FM, on my weekly program, *Music of the Americas*.[2] As opportunities permitted, I also programmed her works on concerts and festivals that I produced over the years. In choosing a doctoral dissertation topic, a biography of Zenobia Perry seemed a timely choice.

As difficult as it is to write a biography about a living person, it was crucial to have had access to Zenobia for so many years and to have been able to ask questions as my understanding of times, places, and events deepened. In order to make both of us comfortable, we needed to negotiate our terms. I cared so much about her that I did not want to hurt her or seem critical of her in any way. Yet I was determined to tell the whole truth, as best as I could. I have taken great care to present a clear picture of what I learned about her life and, as much as possible, to allow Zenobia to speak for herself.

When I finished the dissertation, I sent her a copy to read. It was months before she responded. Finally, she called to say, "Jeannie, I just don't understand it. How did you figure out all these things about my life? No one knows these details; not even my daughter. It is like you were there all the time." As biographer and musicologist, I could not have wished for a greater compliment from her. I asked if there were things I should correct or change and she responded, "No, you've got it right." That was good to hear, because I had already received my degree!

In the last years of her life, she continued to be honored. Thursday, July 11, 2002, was "Zenobia Perry Day" in Xenia, Ohio, declared by the City of Xenia and the Golden Age Senior Center. Mayor John T. Saraga, Golden Age Senior Center staff, and Zenobia's colleagues and friends organized the day to recognize and celebrate her lifetime accomplishments and contributions to the Dayton area.[3]

In order to promote Zenobia Perry's music, I created a web site[4] in 2003, which included a chronology, brief biography, and list of works. Through the site, it is possible to order editions of her music, as well as a compact disc,[5] which I produced in 2002.

On August 7, 2003, at the Centennial Convention of Mu Phi Epsilon International Fraternity in Cincinnati, a special session was held in honor of Zenobia Perry's 95th birthday. It included my interviewing her, followed by a performance of her music by pianist Deon Nielsen Price,[6] clarinetist Berkeley Price,[7] tenor Darryl Taylor,[8] and her daughter, soprano Janis-Rozena Peri.[9]

INTRODUCTION

With these same performers, arts administrator Beverly Simmons and I co-produced a concert tour throughout Ohio, October 1–5, 2003, to celebrate Zenobia Perry's 95th birthday.[10] Joining the artists from the Mu Phi Epsilon program was pianist John ("Jack") Crotty.[11] The tour—presented in cooperation with the National Afro-American Museum and Cultural Center of Wilberforce, Ohio, and sponsored in part by a grant from the Ohio Arts Council—included concerts in Cleveland, Columbus, Dayton, Cincinnati, and Wilberforce. Additional support was provided by Mu Phi Epsilon Music Fraternity Foundation, Culver Crest Publications, and Jaygayle Music.

ZENOBIA POWELL PERRY 95TH BIRTHDAY CONCERT TOUR

Wednesday, October 1, 2003
11:30 AM   Lecture by Jeannie Pool, on the music of Zenobia Powell Perry.

12:10 PM   Brownbag Concert, opening the 25th anniversary season of Music & Performing Arts at Trinity, Trinity Cathedral, Cleveland.

Thursday, October 2, 2003
12:30 PM   Interview of Janis-Rozena Peri on WYSO, Yellow Springs.

8:00 PM   Concert at Riley Concert Hall, Otterbein College, Columbus.

Friday, October 3, 2003 *(Zenobia Powell Perry's 95th birthday)*
1:00 PM   Recital in Sears Recital Hall, University of Dayton.

8:00 PM   Concert in Kelly Hall, Antioch College, Yellow Springs, sponsored by the Office of Multicultural Affairs; followed by a reception.

Saturday, October 4, 2003
11:00 AM   Recital at Paul Laurence Dunbar House, 219 Paul Laurence Dunbar Street, Dayton, featuring Zenobia Perry's *Song Cycle Based on Poetry of Paul Laurence Dunbar*.

3:00 PM   Concert at Mount Auburn Presbyterian Church, Cincinnati. Music by Zenobia Perry, Deon Nielsen Price, H. Leslie Adams, Jeannie Pool, Florence Price, and Margaret Bonds. Free-will offering to benefit the Mallory Center for Community Development; reception honoring Zenobia Perry and former Senate Majority Leader William Mallory, Sr. (ret.), on the occasion of his 72nd birthday.

Sunday, October 5, 2003
10:30 AM   Service at Christ Episcopal Church, Xenia, featuring spirituals arranged by Zenobia Perry, sung by Darryl Taylor and Janis-Rozena Peri, accompanied by Deon Nielsen Price and John Crotty.

INTRODUCTION

3:00 PM   Concert at Paul Robeson Cultural & Performing Arts Center, Central State University, Wilberforce, followed by a reception at the National Afro-American Museum and Cultural Center.

Zenobia Powell Perry at the Paul Laurence Dunbar House in Dayton.
Photo by Beverly Simmons.

Because of a preview article in the *Cleveland Plain Dealer*,[12] a huge crowd attended the opening concert at Trinity Church, launching the tour with enthusiasm. Zenobia attended every event and talked with audience members, who adored her and listened raptly. She enjoyed every moment, as did the producers, sponsors, and performers. She was honored and celebrated that week like no other time in her life. Although it was evident that she was not feeling well, she was elated and gratified.[13]

In January 2004, she was diagnosed with liver cancer. Her health failed quickly and, on January 17, 2004, she died in a Xenia nursing home, surrounded by her daughter and close friends. She could leave this world, knowing that her story would be told and that her music would be performed.[14] Her memorial on January 24, 2004, at Christ Episcopal Church in Xenia, was attended by more than two hundred people. That same year, Janis-Rozena Peri lost her father, whom she hardly knew.

INTRODUCTION

This biography is based on innumerable interviews, phone calls, personal visits, letters and other documents, over a twenty-year period, including Zenobia Perry's own unpublished autobiographical essay. Many of her personal papers and scores, along with digital copies of the oral history interviews and other items used in the preparation of this book, have been deposited in the Archive of the Center for Black Music Research at Columbia College in Chicago.

When available, I have used Zenobia Perry's own words to tell her story, either transcribed from interviews or from her writings. Her voice reveals much about her life and philosophy, her unique way of viewing the world. For this reason, I have in some places left the grammar and dialect as originally presented.

Performers at Trinity Cathedral in Cleveland, applauding Zenobia Powell Perry *(left to right)*: Jack Crotty, Berkeley Price, Janis-Rozena Peri, Deon Nielsen Price, Darryl Taylor.
Photo by Beverly Simmons.

1. Zenobia Powell Perry
Articulate Link to American Culture of the 1920s and '30s

Composer and pianist Zenobia Powell Perry was born on October 3, 1908,[15] to a well-educated, middle-class family. Her father, Calvin Bethel Powell, was a black physician, and her mother, Birdie Lee Thompson, was Creek Indian and black. Originally trained in piano by a local teacher, Mayme Jones, who had been a student of black pianist-composer R. Nathaniel Dett, Perry went, in 1931, to study music with Dett in Rochester, New York. Brief studies with Cortez Reece at Langston University in Oklahoma encouraged her to think seriously about composition. Later she went to Tuskegee Institute in Alabama, where she assisted the famous black choir director, arranger, and composer William L. Dawson. After completing her degree, she headed a black teacher-training program, supervised in part by Eleanor Roosevelt, who became a friend, ally, and mentor and sponsored her graduate studies in education in Colorado. Additional studies in composition were with composers Darius Milhaud, Allan Willman, and Charles Jones at the University of Wyoming and the Aspen Conference on Contemporary Music in the late 1940s and '50s.

Her first university faculty position was at Arkansas Agricultural, Mechanical and Normal College ([A. A. M. & N.] later called University of Arkansas, Pine Bluff), from 1947 to 1955. From 1955 until 1982, she was a faculty member and composer-in-residence at Central State University, Wilberforce, Ohio, where in 1985 she was named faculty emerita.[16] Her compositions have been performed by the Cleveland Chamber Symphony, the Detroit Symphony, West Virginia University Band and Orchestra, and other performing ensembles, as well as by many singers. Her opera, *Tawawa House*—based on the history of Wilberforce, Ohio, and completed with a commission by the Ohio Arts Council/Ohio Humanities Joint Program—was premiered in 1987.[17]

Zenobia's hometown, the all-black town of Boley, Oklahoma, provided a lifetime of inspiration and material for her work as a composer, long after the town—known for its black ownership, self-governance, and autonomy—had been destroyed by Jim Crow politics. The history of Oklahoma and, in general, the history of the United States in the early twentieth century, as it related to race relations, had a tremendous impact of Zenobia Perry's life. The philosophical outlook and political activism of Booker T. Washington, with whom she had a life-long family connection, was a major influence in her life and the institutions where she studied and served as faculty and administrator.

Zenobia Powell Perry's life story highlights a need to re-evaluate what factors determine a successful career as a composer in the United States in the twentieth century. She was not born into a family of musicians; she was not a child prodigy; and she never lived in a major urban center. Her being black, Creek Indian, Midwestern, and female contributed to a fascinating combination of factors that make her music reflective of a unique perspective, full of originality and inventiveness. Although she never sought fame as a composer, her goal was to serve her community as a musician.

Perry began composing seriously in her forties. Although encouraged to compose when she was a young woman by her teacher, R. Nathaniel Dett, she did some arranging as an accompanist and faculty at Tuskegee Institute, but did not study theory and composition until she was well into her thirties.[18] She would never be considered one of the leading-edge composers of our time, because her success was limited and her reputation thus far extends only to a small community of people who hold a long-term interest in black American music and women composers.[19] She was modest about her accomplishments and not aggressive in promoting her music. She is nevertheless an important black American woman composer of concert music.

In many ways, Zenobia Perry lived a blessed life: often seemingly in the right place at the right moment, always taking advantage of even the smallest of opportunities presented, and always meeting challenges with a "can do" attitude. As a young woman, she was abandoned by her first husband while pregnant, and then suffered the death of her eleven-year-old son. Married a second time during World War II, she divorced again when her second child was a preschooler. She successfully raised her daughter, Janis-Rozena Peri, who is not only a fine musician in her own right, but also a singer with a strong spiritual outlook and social conscience.[20] Zenobia Perry raised her daughter while pursuing advanced degrees in music, including studies in composition and orchestration, and while fulfilling her responsibilities as a college music instructor and administrator.

In addition to her extensive responsibilities as the eldest sibling in her immediate family, she supported her elderly mother for many years and helped raise her brother's children. For these and other accomplishments, Zenobia Powell Perry offers an extraordinary role model for women who hope to achieve success in their music careers, while being mothers and/or involved family members. Not only did she have a successful career in music, she was also active in the civil rights movement, as a member of the NAACP since 1962.

Perry received numerous honors and awards, particularly after her retirement in 1982, related to her teaching, composing, and volunteer community work. But the most significant tribute is the continuing performances of her works by a devoted group of musicians, many of them former students, and by those who have recently discovered her works. To date, only one piece has been published, although her name is beginning to appear in reference books, as well as in publications about black American composers and women in music.[21]

Through the years, Perry demonstrated resourcefulness, determination, and perseverance. She knew how to get what she needed and pursued music throughout her life, despite her father's lack of encouragement, two marriages, two divorces, and two children. She would tell the story of how she decided to follow R. Nathaniel Dett to the Eastman School of Music, to continue her studies with him. She took the funds deposited by her parents (required for all students) at Hampton Institute for her return ticket to Oklahoma and used it to settle in Rochester. Only afterwards did she contact her father to ask for his support.[22] She was a woman who, once she knew what she wanted and needed, obtained it.

Perry's music presents a fresh, clear, individual voice of a woman who lived a life of substance and breadth, a woman who carried with her the love and strength of her own very proud and distinguished parents and the keen guidance of her musical mentors. She was the beneficiary of an extraordinary network of friends, colleagues, and former students, including several generations of music students. She cultivated these protégés with care, and, especially after her retirement, was continuously asked for advice, reassurance, and recommendations.

Zenobia Powell Perry is a precious and articulate link to a special moment in American culture of the 1920s and '30s. This was a period when black American composers and musicians were beginning to be recognized for their unique contributions to the country's musical life. This influence extends worldwide in all kinds of music through the experiences of her teachers R. Nathaniel Dett and William Dawson, reaching back to the pre-Civil War black American music of African slaves. She is linked to a musical tradition born of early African-American life, particularly the spirituals. Among her colleagues have been black American musicians of earlier generations, some of whom made a living as virtuoso traveling performers with international concert careers.

Furthermore, her studies with the French Jewish composer Darius Milhaud and white American composer Allan Willman brought her into contact with the international contemporary music community of the 1940s and '50s, allowing her to expand her musical language and make contacts among many first-rate performers and composers. Their encouragement and support were critical in propelling her from a performance career to composition as the focus of her musical life. Both Milhaud and Willman knew, respected, and appreciated many successful women composers (including the famous French composition teacher Nadia Boulanger) and both were interested in black American music.[23]

Perry was also influenced by black American and Native American folklore, music, language, and poetry, traditions that are richly reflected in her own compositions—both instrumental and vocal—and in her original poetry. Poised between both traditions, she teaches us much about the nexus where black American and Native American experiences converge. In this sense, her story is a uniquely American story, richly dense in substance, and steeped in the hopes of each generation of minorities in this country, as they have pursued creative expression.

Zenobia Perry lived a simple, healthy, modest life, deeply rooted in Midwestern ways and common sense. Her values embodied the highest sense of right and wrong, just and unjust, fair and unfair, and a commitment to fight for what is right. At the core of black rural American life, these values have enabled several generations to survive and prosper in a country that has been prejudicial and often hostile. She had control over her life and work by owning the roof over her head and the tools of her trade. She managed to provide for herself, her daughter, her mother, and others throughout her teaching career. Yet she had resources beyond what most of us have, in terms of a fortified soul and a loveliness of being, which particularly enabled her as one of the splendid teachers of our time.

Giving back to her community, to repay what she received over the years, was of paramount importance to her. She taught quilting at a senior citizen home, served as secretary of the local NAACP chapter, and often spoke in local schools. She was active in her church and a member of the Greene County Women's History project, which is documenting the achievements of outstanding women in her area of Ohio.

There are many reasons to review the compositions of Zenobia Powell Perry.[24] For many years, particularly in the late 1950s and '60s, not many contemporary composers wrote tonal music or music with clear, classic, melodies—two aspects that characterize her works. Her compositional style is deeply rooted in singing traditions, reflected in its melodic integrity, and in the length and balance of her phrasing. Beginning in the mid-1980s, many composers using a more traditional tonal resource began to receive wider acceptance, although an international contemporary atonal idiom still prevails, to a certain extent, particularly among composers in academia. Zenobia Perry always found support for her music in black colleges, where the black American singing traditions and the training of amateur singers have been carried on within choral programs. Accordingly, she continued to write in one style that satisfied her own creative aspirations. Despite not fitting into the stylistic mold of the academic American composer of her generation, she never felt compelled to follow the criteria of the contemporary music community's taste. Rather, she composed to please herself and the performers for whom she wrote, and thereby always found an audience that appreciated her very personal, even intimate, expressions of emotion. Much of her music is straightforward and direct, yet elegant and profound.

Some may speculate that, had she been more widely performed, she may have gravitated to the atonal, more "modern," compositional style of her peers. However, her ambition was never to be a famous composer, but rather to express herself through her music, while serving her community. There are many gems in this body of work, each of which shines, even glitters, on its own, meriting repeat performances. Rather than complain that, as a composer in America in the late twentieth century, she had to teach to support herself, Perry found great joy in her teaching and was motivated to compose by her students and academic life.

Perry also found constant inspiration in her love of poetry and deep admiration of several poets, both past and present: notably, Paul Laurence Dunbar (1872–1906), Donald Jeffrey Hayes (no dates available), Claude McKay (1890–1948), Frank Horne (1899–?), R. H. Grenville (no dates available), and Thomas Hardy (1840–1928). Her profound love of language and keen ear for the many voices of her lifetime are apparent in the texts she used for her own compositions.

Thus, she stands rightfully alongside other black composers of her generation: Julia Perry (1924–1979), Ulysses Kay (1917–1996), Hale Smith (b.1925), Thomas Jefferson (T. J.) Anderson (b.1928), Margaret Bonds (1913–1972), Undine Smith Moore (1904–1989), Eva Jessye (1895–1992), George Walker (b.1922), Evelyn La Rue Pittman (1910–1992), Betty Jackson King (b.1928), and Arthur Cunningham (1928–1997), among others. Yet major scholars and researchers who have tried to document the history of African-American composers of the twentieth century have overlooked her, and she is only mentioned briefly in the literature.[25] Among the few black American women writing concert music in recent decades—Dorothy Rudd Moore (b.1940), Jeraldine Herbison (b.1941), Regina Harris Baiocchi (b.1956), Tania Léon (b.1944)—Perry was the most senior.[26]

"Composing a Life"

Before continuing with the details of Zenobia Powell Perry's life and career, let us look at some of the contemporary issues related to biography, specifically biographies of black American composers and biographies of women. Samuel A. Floyd, Jr., and Marsha J. Reisser, in their introduction to *Black Music Biography: An Annotated Bibliography*,[27] write:

> Biography is "life writing." To be effective, it should provide insight into and information about a musical subject's personality and character, trials and accomplishments, preferences and prejudices, and in the case of a musician, his/her musical influences, education, tendencies, uniqueness, achievements, and impact, weaving all of this into a narrative that tells the story of a subject's life. Such works, to be used successfully as research resources should offer even more: bibliographies, discographies, photographs, chronologies, and indexes are all important features of definitive biographies. From our point

of view, good biographies have both immediate and far-reaching applications and implications; they are both literary and scholarly, musically competent, and appreciable by both scholars and laymen.

Floyd and Reisser describe aspects of some biographical and autobiographical works that are explored in greater detail in their book, making the point that most of the biographical work on black musicians is lacking depth and detail, and that

> many of the subjects warrant better treatment, especially those in the field of concert music. But biographical studies of many significant figures are yet to appear, while the lives and works of still others will forever remain obscure, because the informants and the documents needed for the chronicling and illuminating of these latter lives no longer exist. The possibility remains that good life-works can be written about William Grant Still, James P. Johnson, and Howard Swanson, individuals whose stories would make splendid biographies but whose lives still remain largely un-delineated. Some lives are too impalpable, or information about them is too meager, to yield solid biographies.[28]

More than two decades have passed since this was written, and the only black American concert music composers who have biographies published about them are R. Nathaniel Dett and Harry T. Burleigh (1866–1949),[29] although Floyd's *International Dictionary of Black Composers* (published in 1999)[30] is a major advance in the field of black music biography. Several dissertations that are biographical studies are available through University Microfilm Service in Ann Arbor, Michigan. Rae Linda Brown completed a doctoral dissertation on Florence B. Price but, without adequate documents and interview informants, has had difficulty revising her original dissertation for publication.[31] The works on William Grant Still (1895–1978) include his wife Verna Arvey's memoirs[32] and two anthologies of biographical articles about Still,[33] but a biography has not yet been accomplished, despite the fact that he is perhaps the most famous black American composer of his generation.

Only recently have complete biographies of twentieth-century American women composers been published: Judith Tick's remarkable biography of Ruth Crawford Seeger (1901–1953);[34] Adrienne Fried Block's biography of Amy Beach (1867–1944);[35] Catherine Parsons Smith and Cynthia S. Richardson's book on Mary Carr Moore (1873–1957);[36] Virginia Bortin's biography of Californian Elinor Remick Warren (1905–1991);[37] and a German biography of Ruth Schonthal (b.1924).[38] Many biographical articles on American women composers appear in journals, like the International Alliance for Women in Music's *IAWM Journal* and its annual publication, *Women and Music: A Journal of Gender and Culture.* There is much work to be done. Certainly biographies of several American black women composers of concert music should be on the list of priorities, including biographies of Undine Smith Moore, Julia Perry, and Margaret Bonds.[39]

A basic career summary of Zenobia Perry conforms to traditional musicological models of achievement for an American composer of her generation: a long and successful career in academia, performances, commissions, and awards. Perhaps she is not well-known as an American composer because of several key factors: she was Midwestern, black, female, underpaid, underfunded, humble, and she never sought notoriety. The lack of fame does not mean she is an unworthy composer, nor even that she is a minor or inconsequential composer. Many who are well-known today were not only accomplished composers, but also either were good publicists, hired publicists, or obtained support from institutions or commercial entities that had a financial stake in the pursuit of such promotion. However, to concentrate on the evidence of Perry's success, in terms of the traditional model for achievement, would fail to develop a thorough and complete picture of her life and the depth of her achievements. Perhaps with such a limited approach, the very essence of her individual genius—as a composer, educator, pianist, poet, advocate, role model, colleague, friend, daughter, mother, sister, and aunt—would elude us.

Mary Catherine Bateson, in her book *Composing a Life: Life as a Work in Progress,*[40] writes about the "composition of our lives. Each of us has worked by improvisation, discovering the shape of our creation along the way, rather than pursuing a vision already defined."[41] This is particularly true when there are few role models for what one hopes to become. She writes in a life-affirming way about life "as an improvisatory art, about the ways we combine familiar and unfamiliar components in response to new situations, following an underlying grammar and an evolving aesthetic."[42]

Bateson's work is useful when considering Zenobia Perry's life. It would seem, at first glance, that Perry was diverted from her career path many times in her life, if her original goal had been to become a composer. Although she had learned about composers and composition as a child, and found a strong role model in R. Nathaniel Dett, her goal was to become a better musician and to have a life in music. Like many other composers, she did not know early on that she wanted specifically to become a composer. She was not acquainted with black women composers, only with pianists and singers. However, everything she did in her early years that may seem off the career path for becoming a composer, served to prepare her for the breadth of the career she later developed in music.[43]

Bateson suggests that, typically, in pursuit of biography, we do not "look at problems in terms of the creative opportunities they present," but instead are "overfocused on the stubborn struggle towards a single goal rather than on the fluid, the protean, the improvisatory. We see achievement as purposeful and monolithic... rather than something crafted from odds and ends, like a patchwork quilt, and lovingly used to warm different nights and bodies."[44] The women's history movement and the black history movement have sought to make the invisible visible and to provide role models. "The process starts with the insistence that there have been great achievements by women and people of color. Inevitably, it moves on to a rethinking of the concept of achievement."[45] Zenobia Perry's story challenges, in the most fundamental ways, mainstream musicological thinking about achievement in composition, particularly in the black community.[46]

Bateson warns that "there is a pattern deeply rooted in myth and folklore that recurs in biography and may create inappropriate expectations and blur our ability to see the actual shape of lives."[47] She reviews "the image of quest" on which most biography is written, "assumptions [which] have not been valid for many of history's most creative people."[48] She writes of a "set of discontinuities"[49] that "require us to continually refocus and redefine our multiple commitments and goals." She writes, "*Fluidity* and *discontinuity* are central to the reality in which we live. Women have always lived discontinuous and contingent lives."[50] Furthermore, "Continuity is the exception in twentieth-century America... constancy is an illusion."[51] "A composite life poses the recurring riddle of what the parts have in common—what are the more abstract underlying convictions that have held steady, that might never become visible without the surface variation?"[52] These concepts are presented in Bateson's introduction, which she titled, "Emergent Visions." The book is a collection of comparative biographies of five women. At the time of its publication, the author was living in Cambridge, Massachusetts, and was a professor of anthropology and English at George Mason University in Fairfax, Virginia.

What Mary Catherine Bateson suggests is that one needs to go beyond studying an individual's resilience or perseverance when faced with adversity and discontinuity, which often becomes the overriding theme in some biographies, the standard "profiles in courage." She emphasizes that biographers must examine how one composes one's life by refocusing and redefining one's multiple commitments and goals, as a way to see achievement in new terms. Bateson challenges us to see what the parts of a *composite* life have in common, as a way of identifying the underlying convictions that characterize that life and work. This addresses the very issue of why one writes biography. If biography is a way to inspire others and ourselves in the pursuit of fully realizing a person's true gifts and talents, then it needs to present the truth of how people have turned the discontinuities into opportunities. These convictions, these values, in Zenobia Perry's life are independence, self-reliance, justice, equality, and service to one's community.

Zenobia Perry came of age between the two world wars, in a generation of American blacks for whom physical survival was not guaranteed. Poverty, racial discrimination, violence—including lynchings, and other hate crimes—dominated life in many black communities, especially in the 1920s and '30s, and especially for women. Achieving physical safety was a major goal, when making choices about where and how to live. The Great Depression disproportionately affected the lives of black Americans. In spite of these circumstances—or perhaps because of them—many blacks chose education, "enlightenment," and community service.[53]

Perry served her community for more than fifty years by writing music. It is clear that many of her pieces were written for particular performances and for specific performers who needed new music: students for recitals, colleagues and friends for special occasions, and college performing groups for educational purposes. She did not set out to write new, innovative music, using techniques never before imagined, to impress upon her fellow composers the uniqueness of her talents. She did not think about composing as a path to immortality. She wrote music for immediate use and made it as useful and as appropriate for the occasion as possible. Always pragmatic, she wrote music to meet the needs—and limitations—of the performers who requested the pieces. Unlike many of her fellow composers—who seemingly only wrote for one another and were more concerned with innovation than the performer's possibility for accurately realizing a composition—she enjoyed many performances of her work in her community, presented by those who appreciated her willingness to serve. She was not paid as a composer; in fact, until she joined ASCAP in 2002, she did not receive even performance rights payments.

Does this make her less than a professional? Not at all, but it does make her convictions clear. Was she frustrated by a lack of widespread acclaim or fame? No, she had a very satisfying musical life and was grateful for the opportunities that she had, unlike many fellow composers of her generation who publicly decry the lack of recognition. Many of them are resentful of the fact that their entire careers were in academia, whereas Perry appreciated academia as a safe harbor, which provided a steady, although modest, income. She agreed with black American composer Undine Smith Moore's self-assessment: "I am a teacher who composes," whose service to her community was her greatest calling.[54]

The public has grown accustomed to biographies of *great* men composers who lived tortured artistic lives of extreme pain and defeat, yet who experienced *great* personal triumph through the creation of music. Psychoanalytical portraits of great men composers have been very popular in recent years, beginning with Maynard Solomon's biographies of Beethoven and Mozart or Joan Peyser's biographies of Leonard Bernstein and George Gershwin. I recall, as a graduate student, being discouraged by a faculty advisor from writing a biography of the American composer Amy Beach, precisely because she had lived a normal, well-adjusted, altogether uninteresting life, despite her successful career as a composer. There was neither attempted suicide, divorce, debilitating illness, vice, extramarital affairs, lesbian alliances, nor nervous breakdowns. Apparently, there was not enough *pathos* in Beach's story for my advisors to approve doctoral-level examination. Zenobia Perry, too, had a successful and "normal" life, yet she offers fascinating insight into the life of a black woman composer of our time.

Often the assumption has been that women could not be *great* composers because of the discontinuity in their lives, necessitated in part by biology and tightly constricted societal rules.[55] Indeed, many women who wanted to be composers avoided marriage and childbirth altogether, due to a belief that such commitments would ruin their lives and careers. On the contrary, it may be more logical to assume that having children could enhance one's strengths as a composer, provide new musical material, and even serve to expand one's career.[56] Zenobia Perry's own daughter, Janis-Rozena Peri, has commissioned and premiered her mother's works, to excellent critical review.[57]

Bateson writes: "Once you begin to see these lives of multiple commitments and multiple beginnings as an emerging pattern rather than an aberration, it takes no more than a second look to discover the models for that reinvention on every side, to look for the followers of visions that are not fixed but evolve from day to day."[58] Zenobia Perry's life is a series of "reinventions"—as musician, composer, educator, daughter, sister, mother, and community volunteer. The ways in which she balanced the

CHAPTER 1

discontinuities and "reinvented" her life reveal her individual and unique character, and immense creative gifts. The microcosm of Zenobia Perry's life reveals the shape of her own lyric commentary on the world, as she knew it. She constructed a life filled with music that was her own metaphor for thinking about the world. It was not a parable or allegory, but a constant improvisation.[59]

This biography:

- begins with a history of Perry's hometown of Boley, Oklahoma, which provided inspiration and material for her compositions throughout her life;
- examines the political reality for blacks in the early twentieth century, in the context of the philosophy and accomplishments of Booker T. Washington, with whose family Perry had a life-long association;
- discusses the issues of race and music and the need to identify musical elements that are "distinctively American" in American music;
- reviews the hidden history of black and Native American in the United States and how this history reveals connections to the origins and development of American music previously unconsidered;
- looks at the mentors, allies, and early supporters who were crucial for Perry to reach her goal of becoming a professional musician;
- profiles her musical mentors and their profound impact on her life: R. Nathaniel Dett, Cortez Donald Reece, William L. Dawson, Allan Willman, and Darius Milhaud;
- discusses gender issues and how Perry's life exemplifies the challenges faced by women composers of her generation;
- surveys the highlights of her teaching career;
- provides an analysis and general description of her musical style and compositional output; and
- discusses Perry's place in the contemporary musicological canon and proposes that music advocacy and basic training in composition be added to the canon.

It is hoped that this book offers insight into the question of why there have been so few black women composers in American music, while revealing just what a marvelous role model Zenobia Powell Perry offers for those who want to become composers.

2. Song and Verse in Boley
A Lifetime of Inspiration for an American Composer

Say, have you heard the story,
Of a little colored town,
Way over in the Nation
On such a lovely sloping ground?
With as pretty little houses
As you ever chanced to meet,
With not a thing but colored folks
A-standing in the streets?
Oh, 'tis a pretty country
And the Negroes own it, too
With not a single white man here
To tell us what to do—in Boley.

—Uncle Jesse of Arkansas, town poet[60]

This chapter examines the history of Boley, Oklahoma, and its founders, including Zenobia Perry's parents, whose values, commitment, and determination to succeed in family and community life shaped every aspect of her life, providing a solid foundation for her career in education and in music. She grew up in a home filled with music and the love of words. Her memories of the early days of Boley and its struggles proved an endless source of inspiration for her own music and poetry. An understanding of the early history of Boley and its people is essential to understanding her life, music, and poetry.

The all-black town of Boley, founded in 1905, inspired poetry, song, and splendid oratory. It inspired Zenobia Perry as a poet, and as a composer, in writing two of her largest works: *Echoes from the Journey* for voice and orchestra (1990), which traces the history of black American life through song, and her opera, *Tawawa House* (1985), about slaves, the Underground Railroad, and building a black community in Wilberforce, Ohio.[61] Her early life in Boley influenced her choice of poetry to which to set her music, and motivated her to commit herself to the education of black youth. Zenobia's Creek Indian mother loved to sing and recite poetry, while her physician father was a politically savvy and well-read man, who loved literature and drama, especially Shakespeare.

Boley was described in the "'Boley March Song' or the Negroes' Home of the Free," composed by F. M. Liston and published by the Boley Music Publishing Company in 1913:

> Be courageous brother and forget the past,
> The great and mighty problem of the race is solved at last
> Boley is the salvation of the Negro race
> They're many and they're mighty,
> But for you there is a place.
>
> *(Chorus)*
> It's time for you to look around
> And take a trip to Boley town
> For we'd have you understand
> It's the best place in the land
> There the Negro rules supreme
> You would think it was a dream
> Come to the land of Canaan
> To the Negroes' home of the free.
> Stars and stripes forever
> for you I'll explain
> You see the stars when you're striped,
> I am sure you've felt the pain
> So why do you linger?
> We'd not have you wait
> The sun is swiftly sinking
> and the day is growing late.[62]

"'Boley March Song,' or the Negroes' Home of the Free,"
cover and page 1.

From the moment it was founded, eloquent words and music were essential to the life of the town, permeated by a special brand of exhilaration, including poetry regularly found in the local newspapers, written by locally and nationally known poets. Poetry readings, dramatic recitations, classical music performances, and good public speaking were highly regarded by Boley civic organizations and public schools. Entire speeches were published in the newspapers and widely discussed. The grand Masonic Temple of Boley was built for just such community presentations.

The work of black American poet Paul Laurence Dunbar (1872–1906) was well known to the Powell family; his poem "The Poet" describes the role of the poet in the community. Later in life, Perry set this poem as part of a song cycle of poems by Dunbar.

The Poet

He sang of life, serenely sweet,
With, now and then, a deeper note.
From some high peak, nigh yet remote,
He voiced the world's absorbing beat.
He sang of love when earth was young,

CHAPTER 2

And Love, itself, was in his lays.
But ah, the world, it turned to praise
A jingle in a broken tongue.[63]

Being born in Boley in 1908, when it was a thriving all-black town, cited as a model for American blacks, had a profound influence on Zenobia Perry's life. Based on land speculation, Boley was a profit-making venture, representing at the beginning of the twentieth century the highest hopes and aspirations of black Americans who wanted to live full lives, unimpeded by prejudice and bigotry.

Boley was established with a "can do" spirit of blacks and black Indians from the South, Midwest, and Texas. This "can do" spirit sums up Zenobia Perry's outlook throughout her life and sustained her through good times and bad. Boley's musical life was not extraordinary for the times, particularly when compared to the musical life in American cities like Cincinnati, Chicago, Kansas City, or New Orleans, where black musicians were in sufficient numbers and of such impressive talents as to have significant impact on the musical lives of those cities in the period 1890–1910. But Boley's commitment to education and advancement of the citizenry supported the development of a rich cultural environment, nonetheless.

Boley Town Council, c.1910:
Dr. C. B. Powell is in the back row, second from the left.
Courtesy of Oklahoma Historical Society, Oklahoma City.

Along with some twenty-five to thirty other all-black towns in the state at this time, Boley was a bold social experiment. In the early days of the city, blacks functioned fully as citizens, voters, property owners, business owners, educators, and professionals, without hindrance or interference from a dominant white community. Blacks invested fully in all aspects of their community life and held high expectations for its success. Many blacks throughout the United States watched the development of such all-black towns, to see if they might offer a viable alternative to second-class citizenship experienced by blacks in the northern cities, and degrading and hopeless conditions of blacks throughout the South, where the goals of Reconstruction were foiled. The 1890s in the United States were a period of tremendous hopefulness for Americans, but also a period of extreme economic volatility. Blacks in the northern cities and in California were finding opportunities for education and employment, but blacks from the southern and border states were still looking for places to settle. They were looking for places where they could own land, start businesses, educate their children, and enjoy the prosperity that resulted from their own labor and ingenuity. No one should underestimate how serious blacks of that generation were about creating a home where they could live free and unharassed, as promised in the Emancipation Proclamation, but still elusive for most.

The Establishment of Boley

A black man, Edwin P. McCabe, is often credited with having started the movement to create black towns in Oklahoma. All-black towns were not a new idea—Nicodemus, Kansas, was founded in 1877, and Mount Bayou, Mississippi, was founded in 1887. However, during McCabe's twenty years in the Oklahoma territory, some twenty-five black communities were established and the black population increased 537 percent to 137,000.[64]

In September 1904, the Fort Smith and Western Railroad laid its tracks through Boley, seventy-two miles east of Guthrie.[65] According to one account of the town's founding, Boley was established on eighty acres of land owned by Abigail Barnett, a young black Choctaw Indian woman.[66] Organized in September 1904, and incorporated on May 11,

CHAPTER 2

1905, it was named Boley in honor of surveyor J. B. Boley, who worked for the Fort Smith and Western Railway Company as roadmaster and surveyor.[67] By 1915, it had 4,200 people.[68]

Boley was established by "a biracial trio of townsite speculators," whose major objective was profit. The company was established by two white men, Lake Moore and "Captain" William Boley, who then brought in Thomas M. Haynes, a black man, "to front for the creation and the initial promotion of Boley," and to serve as the town's resident manager.[69] Moore was a federally appointed commissioner to the Indian tribes. Despite the company's name, the Fort Smith and Western Townsite Company had no official affiliation with the railroad. James Barnett, a widower and descendent of a black Choctaw former slave, was able to obtain four 160-acre allotments through the federal government's Dawes Act.[70] The 160 acres used for the Boley townsite had little agricultural value and were held in the name of his six-year-old daughter, Abigail Barnett.[71] An amendment to the Dawes Act in 1906 (called the Burke Act) allowed Indians the right to sell any land held adjacent to railroad stations.

Several factors led to the company's decision to develop Boley as an all-black town: it was located between the already established white railroad towns of Paden and Castle; conditions in the former Confederate states were causing blacks to seek homes in Oklahoma; and the nearest black town, Langston, was seventy miles away and had no railroad station. The company's principal interest was the quickest possible profit from land speculation, so they developed a promotional campaign to recruit blacks from Denison, Forth Worth, Sherman, Houston, Paris, and Texarkana.[72]

Boley Grammar School

SONG AND VERSE IN BOLEY

Calvin Bethel Powell, Father

Calvin Bethel Powell, M.D.

It is not clear how Calvin Bethel Powell came to settle in Boley,[73] although a brief announcement in the *Boley Progress* on December 14, 1905, helps pinpoint his year of arrival: "Dr. Powell of Southern Ill. has located in the town of Boley. We welcome Dr. Powell and hope for him a hardy success."[74] In an article entitled, "Proceedings of the Town Council," which appeared in *The Boley Beacon*, on March 12, 1908, Dr. C. B. Powell is mentioned as the town's health officer: "Dr. Powell, health officer, reported no contagious diseases and recommended that the town be cleaned up for health precautions."[75]

C. B. Powell had clinics in various small towns throughout eastern Oklahoma, traveling from one to another and back to Boley. It is clear that he was one of the black elite of his generation, having been educated at Roger Williams College and Meharry Medical College. He also had experience living outside of the United States, in Africa, which many American blacks had not had. Zenobia believed that her father had finished his "standards" in London, England, equivalent to an American high school education.

CHAPTER 2

According to the archives at Meharry Medical College, C. B. Powell was born in 1863.[76] He always said he was born on the fourth of July, probably because he had no idea of his actual birth date. He was African American but raised in Somaliland, a region of East Africa that includes Somalia, Djibouti, and parts of eastern Ethiopia.[77] When he was a boy, American and British missionaries had a settlement there, although Somaliland was actually a colony of Italy.[78] At some point, the family lived in England, and later returned to Mound City, Illinois.[79] By the time Calvin Powell settled in Boley, he was estranged from his immediate family because of religious differences.[80]

Being the youngest child raised in a Christian missionary family serving in Africa had a major impact on Calvin's life. After finishing high school in Mound City, he taught there until he went to teach at Walden College in Tennessee, and later enrolled in the medical school of Central Tennessee College, the Meharry Medical Department. But the enrollment records at Meharry show he attended Roger Williams University in Nashville.[81] The Nashville Normal and Theological Institute (later called Roger Williams University) was founded in 1864 to provide classes for local Negro Baptist preachers. It was known as the Negro Baptist College and was financed by local clergy, northern contributors, and local Baptist churches. Northern white Baptists controlled the school, which focused on teaching fundamentals to students, whom wanted to go into ministry or teaching.[82] Education and developing professional careers were a focus of the lives of Calvin Powell and his siblings.[83]

According to a family story,

> When [Calvin Powell] first went to the campus of Meharry, he was wearing trousers that the English people were wearing. They were green velvet and he said that everybody laughed at this man coming up with green velvet pants. He said, after awhile, he finally got to the place where he could wear his green pants at medical school without being laughed at.[84]

There are no doubts that he stood out among his black American classmates, and not just because of his clothing; he spoke with a British accent.

Graduating from Meharry Medical College made Powell into one of the "black elite." Lovett, in his book, *The African-American History of Nashville, Tennessee, 1780-1930*, describes the black elite as not only "defined by the romanticism of their white counterparts' habits and behavior, but by their own influence, affluence, and skin color. In culture and mannerisms, mulattos and elite blacks often reflected the tastes and attitudes of elite whites and not that of lower-class white persons."⁸⁵ Many of the black elite desired racial assimilation and acceptance of upper-class blacks into white society. But with legalized racial segregation, elite blacks instead became closer to the masses and eventually led the civil rights movement, "promoted progressive reform, social organizations, cultural and literary movements, the idea of a clean and healthy community, and a respectable society among Negroes."⁸⁶ Lovett describes the black elite as "men and women who enjoyed some economic independence, sometimes a greater degree of wealth, better education, and some influence in the community."⁸⁷

Medical, Dental, Pharmaceutical Faculty Graduates,
Meharry Medical Department, Central Tennessee College, 1894.
C. B. Powell is in the second to top row, just left of center.

After graduating from Meharry in 1894,⁸⁸ Calvin was sent by missionaries to Minnesota to do his internship among the Indians. Then he moved back to Mound City, where he married his first wife, a mathematician, with whom he had two sons, both of whom died in infancy. Zenobia Perry recalls, "He had pictures of these little boys in caskets. Why do people take pictures of dead children? One was a baby and the other lived to be two years old. Because his own mother died in childbirth, this was particularly hard for him to take."⁸⁹

CHAPTER 2

After his first wife died, Dr. Powell moved to Boley in 1905. He is shown in a photograph of civic leaders from Boley's early days, well known among Oklahoma historians.[90] Later Calvin Powell became Mayor of Boley[91] and was involved in the politics of the region. Zenobia Perry provided a description of the town of her childhood:

> Boley's businesses included: a bank, a lumber yard, three cotton gins, a grist mill, a photography and ice cream parlor, a shoe shop, coffee shop, hotel, and the Creek-Seminole Business College and Agricultural Institute, as well as the usual businesses, e.g., drugstore, hardware, dry goods, ready-to-wear, grocery, and newspaper. *Boley Progress*, a bimonthly news bulletin, was distributed throughout the South where possible future residents lived. Every Boleyite could greet you with the boast of living in a black town with the tallest building between Okmulgee and Oklahoma City.[92]

Boley was the site of the State Masonic Temple for Negroes, where blacks from throughout Oklahoma gathered for celebrations, including the annual Grand Lodge Meeting and barbecues.[93] Many speeches, lectures, and other performances were presented there.

As one of the physicians in Boley, Dr. Powell treated all kinds of patients in the area. "He was a doctor who used to make house calls in a horse-drawn wagon, or a horse-drawn sled when it snowed."[94] According to a family story, repeated often over the years, Dr. Powell went to visit a sick girl who had pneumonia, and "he said that she was the prettiest little thing that he had ever seen. So he wanted to get her in marriage instead of some other gift for getting her well."[95] Birdie Thompson and Calvin Powell were married in a double wedding ceremony on Christmas Eve at the church in Boley, probably in 1906 or 1907.[96]

A Toast

> Here's to your eyes,
> for the things I see drowned in them,
> Here's to your lips,
> two livid streaks of flame.
> Here's to your heart,
> may it ever be full of love, of loving,
> Here's to your body,
> a lithesome hilltop tree,
> Swaying, swaying,
> to a spring morning's breath,
> Here's to your soul
> as yet unborn.
>
> —*Frank Smith Horne* (1899–1974)[97]

SONG AND VERSE IN BOLEY
Birdie Thompson Powell, Mother

Birdie Lee Thompson Powell.

Birdie Lee Thompson was 18 or 19 when she married Dr. C. B. Powell; there was a 26-year age difference between them. Birdie was born in Hope, Arkansas, but the family moved to Blossom, Texas, when she was an infant, and then to Flat Rock, Oklahoma. Birdie's mother's name was Luticia.[98] An Indian bride may have been considered a status symbol for Dr. Powell.[99]

Birdie's parents had a farm; her grandfather was a black slave to a Creek master. "He knew a great deal about the law in Blossom, Texas, and often told his family about being sent by his master to pick up legal documents."[100] There were eight children in Birdie's immediate family: four boys, then four girls—Birdie was the eldest girl. The brothers were: Clem, Merridy ("Uncle Mudd"), Frank, and Ed; the sisters: Birdie, Artee, Nora, and Neva. Birdie studied bookkeeping at the Creek Seminole College.[101] The oldest son, Clem, continued to farm the land with his father for several decades.[102] Zenobia Perry has vivid memories of their eighty-acre farm and farmhouse in Oklahoma:

> They lived in Flat Rock, Oklahoma, on a farm and it looked like two log houses put together. Mamma and the girls stayed in one and all the boys stayed in the

CHAPTER 2

other. They had one great big room with four beds for the boys. They grew sugar cane; they always had molasses, and a little cotton, but not too much cotton, and beans, probably soybeans, and peanuts.[103]

Zenobia was the first of four children born to Birdie and Calvin. She was delivered by a midwife, Mrs. Strickland, who lived across the street, because Dr. Powell was away caring for his patients. C. B. delivered his other three children. The four children were born within five years: Zenobia in 1908, Cleolla [Thelma] in 1910, Calvin in 1912, and Douglass in 1913.[104]

Zenobia's earliest memories were of hearing her mother sing:

> My mother was always singing; in fact, her name was Bird because she was always singing. . . . I don't think I ever heard her sing jazz songs, but she sang folk songs, she sang spirituals, she sang things that I think she made up herself. She sang Creek songs. She sang all the time. When Mamma wasn't singing, we wondered what was wrong, because we knew we were in trouble, even when we didn't know what.[105]

> Because she sang all the time, whenever our father was baby-sitting us when she had to go off and do something else, he would sing and we'd always laugh. Papa's singing to himself sounded awful. He used to sing English folk songs and hymns. I used to tell Mamma, "All Papa can sing is 'I had a bird that sang to me, Saw my bird on a yonder's tree; birdie went peep peep peep peep peep peep, fill-I-fee, fill-I-fee.' . . . That's all he knows," I said.[106]

Among the songs he sang were: "Oranges and Lemons," "The Bells of Saint Clement's," "You Owe Me Five Farthings," "A Ring, A Ring O' Roses," "Ash-a" (imitating sneezing), and "I Had a Bird and The Bird Fed Me."[107] Both parents sang in church choirs from time to time. "Papa's medical practice caused him to be absent frequently but on occasions his voice added to the carrying power of the bass line."[108]

> My mother was always singing, and if she wasn't singing she was reciting poetry. She had my father buy her many books of poetry and she would memorize them and go about her housework and we'd follow her around to hear her poetry or her singing.[109]

Zenobia Perry recalled one time when her mother recited in public:

> I remember her saying that she was never going to recite in public, but then someone asked her to recite "The Organ" and she dressed up. I didn't know Mamma when she came out onstage. She had on such a peculiar looking thing [costume]. "The organ gave a whistle and the woman gave a grin and that old man was a singin' by himself." It brought the house down, but she wouldn't do it again.[110]

Everyone was encouraged to recite poetry, give speeches, and perform in dramatic presentations, often in costume with props. It was an integral part of community life and entertainment.

Poet and novelist Langston Hughes visited Boley, as did the poet Chauncy Hill.

> Papa was an almost insatiable reader. There was no family room in our house but there was a well-furnished library where we spent most of our evenings. Mamma and Papa read to us from the time we were born. My sister, brother, and I were reading before we were old enough to attend school.... Papa read all the time. As soon as he would get his dinner and look us over and play with his kids a time or two, he'd read. He sat in a rocking chair, closest to a lamp. So I had to have a rocking chair, closest to a lamp, to sit down by him, so every time he started to read, I had to read, too. He read every day. He read the classics, a habit he developed when being educated by the missionaries as a young man.[111]

In this environment where books, poetry, song, and oratory prevailed, Perry learned to love words and music. She observed first-hand the courage and dedication of a community of blacks who yearned to live in freedom and prosperity.

Perry's opera, *Tawawa House* (1985), for which she wrote both music and libretto, opens thus:

> Let the knowing speak,
> Let those who were oppressed speak of their countless fears
> Their chartless path of sorrows,
> Road of travail.
> Let those who blazed a trail for the hopeful
> speak.
> They were wont to wear their human dignity.
> They marched forth at dawn
> to hail their destiny;
> and from their days we learn:
> to search for truth;
> to love all humankind,
> and to cherish freedom,
> freedom.
>
> Seeds of hope, they were planting;
> shields of strength, they were wearing;
> cheerful songs,
> songs of dauntless faith

Sung in the opera by runaway slaves on the Underground Railroad, which had a stop in Wilberforce, Ohio, these words are also about her parents and the people of Boley, Oklahoma, "who blazed a trail for the hopeful." Boley, a western cow town turned black cultural, intellectual, and educational center, inspired poetry, music, oratory, and opera.

Boley was a unique town in the American West, because of the courage and commitment of these pioneers. The distinction of being a child of this unique social experiment of black Americans yearning to be free, independent, and successful, was a continuous source of inspiration and material for Zenobia Perry's music.

Zenobia Powell at age 15 *(left)* and age 17.

The children of Dr. C. B. Powell and Birdie Thompson Powell *(left to right)*: Douglass, Thelma, Zenobia, and Calvin, Jr.

3. "Lift Every Voice and Sing"
Booker T. Washington; Boley, Oklahoma; and the Political Reality for Blacks

Lift every voice and sing, till earth and Heaven ring,
Ring with the harmonies of liberty;
Let our rejoicing rise, high as the listening skies,
Let it resound loud as the rolling sea.
Sing a song full of the faith that the dark past has taught us,
Sing a song full of hope that the present has brought us;
Facing the rising sun of our new day begun,
Let us march on till victory is won.

Stony the road we trod, bitter the chastening rod,
Felt in the days when hope unborn had died;
Yet with a steady beat, have not our weary feet,
Come to the place for which our fathers sighed?
We have come over a way that with tears has been watered,
We have come, treading our path through the blood of the slaughtered;
Out from the gloomy past, till now we stand at last
Where the white gleam of our bright star is cast.

God of our weary years, God of our silent tears,
Thou Who hast brought us thus far on the way;
Thou Who hast by Thy might, led us into the light,
Keep us forever in the path, we pray.
Lest our feet stray from the places, our God, where we met Thee.
Lest our hearts, drunk with the wine of the world, we forget Thee.
Shadowed beneath Thy hand, may we forever stand,
True to our God, true to our native land.[112]

—*James Weldon Johnson (1871–1938)*

CHAPTER 3

Zenobia Powell Perry's life was enormously influenced by Booker T. Washington's philosophical outlook, political strategy, activism, and the black college he founded, which has served as a model for black higher education to this day. Although Perry met him once when she was seven years old, her father knew him well, and the whole Boley community was built upon his values and commitment. Boley, in fact, thrived because of Washington's nationally published endorsement. Zenobia Perry had a life-long personal connection to the Washington family that began when she recited the Tuskegee hymn for Booker T. Washington when he came to Boley in 1915. He told her parents, "Well, that's going to be a Tuskegian!" Zenobia remembered, "For some reason I was afraid of Booker T. Washington. He didn't have dark eyes . . . they were gray and I hadn't seen gray eyes before. He was kind of reddish. He wasn't dark and he wasn't light. His granddaughter, Edith Johnson, looks very much like him. I'll never forget his eyes." Edith Johnson, who lived most of her life in Wilberforce, was a close personal friend of Zenobia's until Edith's death in January 2002. In addition, Perry studied piano with Washington's daughter, Portia Washington Pittman, and his niece, Hazel Hooligan, both concert artists and faculty members at Tuskegee in the 1930s.[113]

It is important to understand Booker T. Washington's vast and dynamic impact on life for American blacks in the late nineteenth and early twentieth centuries, with regard not only to Perry's individual development and career path, but also to the values and commitment of her family and the Boley community. Washington's perspective was widely debated in his lifetime, and although criticized and ultimately rejected by the Pan-African and black national movements of the 1920s, nevertheless it laid the foundation for many blacks in the United States to be lifted up and out of poverty into self-sufficient and better lives. Not only did the Powell family have direct contact with Booker T. Washington, but also the whole town of Boley developed with Washington's support and endorsement. Furthermore, Zenobia and her brother Calvin, Jr., attended the Tuskegee Institute, founded by Washington. Tuskegee became the model of black higher education for the country, combining academic pursuit with the development of hands-on skills that would guarantee its graduates employability. The program provided remedial studies for students who lacked sufficient educational background to succeed in other university programs. It provided financial aid, including some innovative work-study arrangements, to help students of poor and struggling families. After graduating from Tuskegee, Zenobia taught in Tuskegee's teacher training school, and then served on the faculty of several black colleges modeled after Tuskegee, including Arkansas Agricultural, Mechanical and Normal College (A. A. M. & N.), in Pine Bluff, and Central State College in Wilberforce, Ohio.

An educated ex-slave, Booker T. Washington (1856–1915) became the spokesman for moderate black America in the late nineteenth century. He had graduated from Hampton Institute in Virginia, a Negro Vocational College, founded in 1865. He believed that Negroes should receive training in farming, handicrafts, home economics, and carpentry, in order to advance themselves. Agricultural chemist George Washington Carver joined its faculty in 1896 and contributed significantly to the success of the school. Washington developed many friendships with prominent whites and convinced philanthropists Andrew Carnegie and George F. Peabody to endow Tuskegee.

Washington also was deeply concerned about preserving and promoting the Negro folk culture and traditions, particularly related to music and the other arts. Students of Tuskegee often were asked to demonstrate certain arts and crafts, ranging from tailoring to tatting. Because Washington insisted that all Tuskegee students learn the "plantation melodies," William L. Dawson, who later taught at Tuskegee after being educated there himself, became a leading black American arranger of spirituals. Under Dawson's direction, the Tuskegee Institute Choir became world-famous for their performances of this music. The fact that students from Tuskegee have promoted and taught spirituals all over the United States in schools and churches has guaranteed the survival of the repertoire in living performances to this day.[114]

Many questioned the long-term success of Washington's efforts on behalf of his race. Black craftsmen could not find decent jobs and black farmers could not escape debt or sharecropping. Lynchings continued, as did rampant discrimination against blacks. Other prominent black leaders, like northern-born and Harvard-trained William E. B. Du Bois (1868–1963), advocated that blacks seek full equality. The National Association for the Advancement of Colored People (NAACP) was founded in 1909 to seek legal remedies for victims of race riots, lynchings, and Jim Crow politics. Its first victory was in 1915, when the U.S. Supreme Court nullified Oklahoma's grandfather clause, holding that blacks and Native Americans could not vote. By the end of the nineteenth century, black churches were the focal point for Reconstruction, and became the most important community organizations. Many churches held very conservative views, including the belief that blacks must accommodate themselves to white prejudices instead of challenging them. Washington was one of the leading spokesmen for this position.

Dr. C. B. Powell met Booker T. Washington during one of Washington's visits to Boley. He first came in 1905, and the residents hoped his visit would advance their plans to incorporate and to publicize the community to attract new settlers. He spent at least a week in the "twin territories," spoke at the Guthrie Opera House, and conferred with A. W. Sango, a prominent Muskogee politician, who was head of the Tullahassee Mission. His speeches in Oklahoma were published in the local papers. Upon his return to Alabama, he sent an article entitled, "Boley: A Negro Town in the West," to the nationally distributed black publication, *The Outlook*.[115] In the article, Washington repeated a story often told about the founding of Boley, which involved an argument between two white men in Weleetka over the potential for black self-government.

At the time of his visit, Washington was studying Native American culture, in the hopes of instituting Indian education at the Tuskegee Institute. According to Norman L. Crockett, Washington

> asked to meet a number of natives. To his surprise, he was always introduced to a black person. In time he discovered that the term native referred to ex-slaves of the Creeks, blacks emancipated by the Reconstruction treaties following the Civil War. Because of their command of English and their ability to communicate in the Creek language, a few blacks rose to important positions in the tribes—negotiators they were called.[116]

Although Washington's story in *The Outlook* had some misinformation about Boley, his endorsement encouraged many to settle there.

On August 22, 1915, Washington returned to Boley, as head of a delegation of the National Negro Business League that was meeting in Muskogee. He spoke at the Boley city park, where "he advised blacks to cease their mobility." Referring to Alfred Sam, an Akim Chief from the Gold Coast, who was organizing a back-to-Africa movement in Okfuskee County, Washington counseled his audience to remain in Oklahoma and, as he had stated in the Atlanta Exposition speech many years earlier, "to cast down your bucket where you are."[117]

Washington had conflicting feelings about the creation of all-black towns. He opposed the northward migration of blacks, because he felt they should remain in the South. He saw black towns as places where people could learn self-government and develop leadership skills, but thought that, if black towns were taken to the extreme, blacks would suffer for their lack of contact with whites and there would never be integration.

Few anticipated the political and economic reality of the all-black towns that did not receive proportionate shares of tax revenues for roads, bridges, schools, or other infrastructural improvements. Solidly Republican in 1906, Boley held the balance of power in the county, because the white towns were evenly divided between Democrats and Republicans. However, after statehood in 1907, blacks and Indians were disenfranchised; blacks were denied the right to vote and Jim Crow laws were instituted. Crockett also points out that

> the idea of building a viable agricultural service center in 1905 ran counter to the major economic trends of the period. Thousands of rural white communities, unhampered by discrimination, failed to compete in the national economy at the same time. Boley merchants found it difficult to obtain the capital necessary to extend credit to area farmers who desperately needed it. As a consequence, both farmers and merchants became insolvent. Running counter to national economic trends, Main Street was dying, not just in Boley, but in the entire country.[118]

Many thought that Washington was naïve, as were the blacks who felt Boley could offer an independent, separate alternative for black life in America. Others were well aware that the viability of an agricultural service center in 1905 was far from certain. Blacks did not have access to capital and they underestimated their enemies, both white and Indian. Historian William Loren Katz also describes the problems faced by Boley:

> When Oklahoma moved toward statehood, black leaders looked forward to a decisive voice in the new government and to black representatives in Congress. During Booker T. Washington's visit to Boley, the Western Negro Press Association, meeting in Muskogee, asked President Theodore Roosevelt not to admit Oklahoma until he was given assurances that it would not pass Jim Crow laws. The fear of the journalists was well taken. The President did not respond and no such guarantees were requested by Congress when Oklahoma entered the Union in 1907. Moreover, three years later Oklahoma enacted a grandfather clause that disenfranchised its black citizens on the basis that their grandfathers, as slaves, had not voted. What law failed to accomplish in ending black independence, power and manhood rights, whites achieved through fraud and violence. The black enclaves of Oklahoma fell victim to the white supremacy they had fled. The black dream of Oklahoma became another southern nightmare.[119]

Although Dr. Powell was committed to an all-black town as an alternative for blacks in America, when the town began to fail economically, he shifted his focus to efforts to obtain suffrage and civil rights for blacks in Oklahoma. In those years, he carried a weapon for self-defense:

CHAPTER 3

> I remember my father would go to the station and he would say, "I'll have to have Zenobia Perry and Calvin come and go with me because I'm taking my guns to the train because I don't know what kind of reception I'm getting from here to the train." Then we'd take the guns back home. And then when he was coming back from Guthrie, we'd meet the train to give him his gun.... [Boley] was built over a whole pool of oil so whites tried to run the blacks out of the county so they could get to the oil. I think that was what all the pressure was on my father.[120]

In spite of all the difficulties facing Boley, some very special qualities of the town persisted. Velma Dolphin-Ashley made the following observation about Boley in 1940:

> The various schools, churches, clubs, and lodges of the town have given it a greater cultural value because they have been conducted as they have. The disturbances in these various social units have definitely contributed to the molding of civic pride and loyalty with the community. By their disturbances they have learned the importance of cooperation which is immediately manifested when the town or any of its citizenry is exposed to abuse.[121]

Boley was successful, in part, because of its citizens' enthusiasm, a "can do" spirit, although the main reason for its initial success was immediate acquisition of the rail line,

> in tandem with the acceptance of a black nationalist ideology by the black upwardly mobile class and those who aspired to become members of that class. ... The black nationalist ideology created widespread acceptance of the black-town's separatist stance and, by encouraging wealthy blacks to assist poorer ones, increased the targeted market of blacks willing and able to relocate in a town with only black citizens. Boley's promoters continued to capitalize on these two phenomena until World War I, when new opportunities began to attract black workers to northern cities.[122]

There is no doubt, however, that the residents of Boley faced decades of hard times, despite their collective talent, energy, and enthusiasm.[123] Throughout the twentieth century, when blacks said, "I'm from Boley," others responded, "Ah, yes, Boley," recognizing the name and what it symbolized. Former residents of Boley have become civic, business, and educational leaders in black communities throughout the United States. To be a Boleyite is to be a member of a special brother/sisterhood.

"LIFT EVERY VOICE AND SING"
National Focus on Black Culture

After World War I, there was a strong interest nationally in what was termed "the Negro problem." White novelists and playwrights used Negro themes and stories; white composers turned to Negro folk music and jazz. Blacks themselves became more interested in learning about themselves and their history and became more involved in advocacy. The race riots of the summer of 1919 made the country aware of the depth of discontent in the black community. Various national black organizations developed more vigorous programs to secure rights for black citizens. Marcus Garvey's Back-to-Africa movement had the support of hundreds of thousands of blacks.

The Harlem neighborhood of New York City was considered by many to be the capital of Negro intellectual life. The flowering of black artistry in the 1920s—among writers, poets, musicians, and artists to protest the life of blacks in American—was called "The Harlem Renaissance." Many books and periodicals were published and widely distributed; there was national impact.

Although he lived in Oklahoma, Zenobia Perry's father had many friends among the emerging black American intelligentsia. Both of her parents followed the major national black publications with keen interest. In 1921, the first of a series of Negro revues, *Shuffle Along*, made its appearance, with dancers Josephine Baker and Bill Robinson. The 1920s emerged as the Jazz Era, with Bessie Smith, Louis Armstrong, and Duke Ellington on phonograph records and radio broadcasts. Perry's father and mother took keen interest in the development of this movement and knew some of its proponents.

Growing up in a black town, one was not so aware on a daily basis of the prejudices against blacks that permeated American life, and it provided a secure environment.[124] Zenobia Perry said,

> The first time I saw a bunch of white people together was when I went with my father by train to Guthrie. Before that I was not aware that there were so many white people anywhere and I said to him, "What's wrong with all these people? They're all sick. None of them have any color." He said, "Oh, my. That's the way they are." I said, "Are they sick? Are they lepers?" He said, "No, they are not lepers." He told my mother and he was laughing as he said, "Poor child, she'll find out later." When I got to graduate school where I had a mixed class, I never felt intimidated like the other blacks in the class did. I never did.[125]

CHAPTER 3

Boley's steady decline actually began around 1915, the year of Washington's death. This was the time of the Great Migration, when hundreds of thousands of African Americans moved from the South to northern cities. The reason for the creation of all-black towns led to their demise. Blacks gained political rights and new jobs in northern cities, not in southern or southwestern towns. Racial insulation ultimately proved to be restrictive for subsequent generations of blacks, although it had been very attractive to their parents. Originally, these black towns were monuments to blacks' quest for liberty, dignity, and self-sufficiency, but more opportunities for advancement developed in northern cities.

Convention of Black Medical Care Providers, c.1920.
Dr. C. B. Powell is in the back row *(fifth from left)*, wearing a bow tie.
Courtesy of Henrietta Hicks, The Boley Museum.

During the 1920s, blacks in Boley began to have problems with whites who wanted the land and oil rights. Dr. Powell, along with others in Boley, was engaged in a difficult political battle to secure Boley and its citizens' rights. Political unrest and violence intensified, to the point that Mrs. Powell, who was often alone with the children, while her husband was on the road, decided she wanted to leave Boley. Dr. Powell wanted to stay in Boley, because the education was good and his medical practice continued to thrive. However, when a race riot in Tulsa in 1921 left twenty-one whites and sixty blacks dead, fear among blacks throughout the state increased.

C. B. Powell and the other community leaders were under immense pressure. The family returned from church one evening to find their house on fire. The flames were immediately extinguished and the house was saved, but Perry believed that it had been set in retaliation for some of her father's political work.

> Late in 1924, Marian Anderson, the celebrated contralto, came to town to sing. About half way through the concert the city fire alarm rang briefly. A few men left the auditorium including the undertaker, Mr. Bradley, and my father. As the alarm did not ring again everyone else stayed put. When the concert was over Mamma gathered us together and we went to the Bradley home to meet Papa. Within sight of the house we saw the bedroom, kitchen and hall lights were on. We walked into the kitchen. There sat Mr. Bradley and Papa talking quietly. When they saw us, Mr. Bradley made light of the situation saying, "Settin' here in all de muss, thank de Laud hit Anita no woos."
>
> Someone had gotten through the open bedroom window and set fire to the carpet in the room and to the cabinet and table in the kitchen. There was more smoke damage than actual destruction by fire. When we reached home that night my father first went through the house with flashlight and gun before he allowed us in.
>
> That summer we went to Lawton, Oklahoma, but Mamma didn't like Lawton. My sister was sent to Ardmore where she was boarded with the Owens family until she finished high school. More than half of Boley's high school graduates did not return to their hometown for employment. The political climate in Oklahoma worsened as KKK activities became more flagrant.[126]

These were difficult years for the Powell family. Given the troubles in Boley at that time, it is clear that Dr. and Mrs. Powell did everything they could to protect their children and shield them from the political unrest and violence. The younger sister and brothers were sent away to complete high school, because of conditions in Boley. Along with others, Dr. Powell discussed Marcus Garvey's ideas and considered going back to Africa.[127]

Marcus Garvey (1887–1940) founded the United Negro Improvement Association, which promoted racial pride and a vision of black nationalism, and called upon blacks to abandon hope for integration, and instead to create a separate independent black nation in Africa. By the early 1920s, the UNIA had a million members in thirty-eight states, including Oklahoma, and forty-one foreign countries. Garvey's newspaper, *The Negro World*, had 200,000 subscribers. However, in 1924, he was arrested and convicted for mail fraud and in 1927, was deported back to Jamaica.[128]

Several groups in Oklahoma during these years were involved with the back-to-Africa movement. Alfred Charles Sam, who claimed to be an African tribal leader, born in the interior of the Gold Coast and ruler of a town in West Akim, lived in Oklahoma during this time; he was called "Chief Sam." He recruited sixty people from the back-country cotton farms in eastern Oklahoma—mostly from Okfuskee County where Boley is located—to go back to Africa. On August 21, 1914, the S. S. *Liberia* left from the Port of Galveston, Texas, bound for the Gold Coast Colony, British West Africa, arriving there January 13, 1915. An intriguing book by William Elmer Bittle and Gilbert Geis, *The Longest Way Home: Chief Alfred C. Sam's Back-to-Africa Movement*, details Chief Sam's "turbulent upheaval of local life."[129] According to the authors, "This story is an amazingly poignant one which illustrates again the desperate hopes of an utterly desperate group of people."[130]

In her history of Boley, Dolphin-Ashley provides interesting details about the Chief Sam affair:

> First, the Akim Trading Company sent a Congregational minister to Boley in 1915 to encourage the people to return to their native Africa and build up that country for the Negro race. The minister was so passionate in his appeal that many of the people believed him. Later, Chief Sam, the nominal head of the company, came to Boley and added his voice to the appeal. The result was that literally hundreds of the people left; they withdrew their money by the thousands from the banks. Some had stores of one sort or another, others had farms; but they left regardless of property. An attempt was made to show the people that it was all a hoax but they did not listen to reason. So many people joined the movement that the city officials had Chief Sam arrested and brought to trial. He proved that he had a right by charter to solicit money and people for his movement. This satisfied the county officials and Chief Sam was released. The people followed him and with them went a fair third of Boley's population and wealth.[131]

Bittle and Geis state that "the Sam movement illustrates an ultimate stage of passivity: not utter resignation, but the final and extreme, the most vigorous and only feasible protest—the emigration to a distant, fictionalized homeland, the rejection of an American residency."[132] Before this, there had been numerous efforts of African Americans to return to Africa, beginning as early as 1714. In fact, repatriation was an important component of Abraham Lincoln's original plan for American Negroes—as important as emancipation.[133]

The Chief Sam saga provides insight into what blacks in eastern Oklahoma faced when Zenobia Perry was a teenager. Bittle and Geis describe the white hostilities towards Negroes, which "led to widespread discontent among Blacks."[134] They trace the political struggles in Boley that escalated into violence. By 1910, it was clear, "there would be no Negro autonomy in Oklahoma, no Negro dignity, no Negro peacefulness. There would be no growing respect and admiration from white neighbors and no industrial and agricultural prosperity. Nothing had been changed during the long fight; nothing had been bettered."[135] Blacks had two choices in Okfuskee County: acceptance or escape. According to Bittle and Geis, "Acceptance became the solution for those who were now too tired, too timid, or too cynical to re-create a new dream. It also became the solution for those who still entertained hope of bettering the situation and who refused to face the reality of their position."[136] Chief Sam's group supported escape. The Powell family chose acceptance, since a middle-class lifestyle was available to them because Dr. Powell's medical services were sorely needed in the area. Besides, the doctor was already in his fifties, with his second family, and his second attempt to put down permanent roots in a community.

Many felt that Booker T. Washington and his large mass of supporters had sufficiently protected black Americans, although he had managed to set up separate and autonomous black institutions and organizations throughout the United States that continue to serve black Americans to this day. In the long run, the attempt to extend this experiment to the twenty-five black towns in Oklahoma failed. However, Booker T. Washington's philosophical outlook and positive achievements affected every aspect of black American life, as can be seen clearly in Zenobia Perry's life. Not only was she educated at Tuskegee, the educational institution Washington founded, but she taught at several black colleges that were modeled after it. Washington's message to blacks about becoming self-sufficient, self-governing, and putting down roots in communities, encouraged such experiments as Boley and guided the efforts of black community organizations throughout the twentieth century, including the NAACP, with whom Zenobia Perry was affiliated beginning in the 1950s. Her parents taught these basic values to their children, values that were reinforced in the community and in the schools. Zenobia, in turn, taught these values to her children and students and modeled them in her work as an educator, administrator, and community volunteer.

Boley Grammar School Activities, c.1916.

4. Distinctively American
Race and Music

Wer sich selbst und aldre kennt	One who knows oneself and others
Wird auch hier erkennen:	Will also recognize that
Orient und Okzident	Orient and Occident
Sind nicht mehr zu trennen.	Can no longer be separated.
Sinnig zwischen beiden Welten	I admit consciously to living
Sich zu wiegen laß ich gelten:	In both worlds;
Also zwischen Ost- und Westen	Indeed one is best enjoined to travel
Sich Bewegen sei zum Besten!	Between the two worlds of East and West!

—Johann Wolfgang von Goethe, 1826[137]

In the United States, "one who knows oneself and others recognizes that" black and white can no longer be separated and we are "best enjoined to travel between the two worlds." However, in American music, a composer's race still has a considerable impact on his/her career and musical style. Why does our society continue to hold certain expectations for composers of particular races, depending on the musical style? If a black American composes, why is he or she expected to write in a so-called black American musical style or idiom? If a black composer does not write in a "black" musical style or idiom, what are the consequences, personally and professionally? What if one is of mixed race, e.g., black and white, or black and Native American? What are society's expectations about the kind of music that composer should or could write? How are such expectations, bound by race, gender, ethnicity, or place of national origin, the antithesis of the very process of musical composition? Mixed-race composers "are damned if they do and damned if they don't" write what society expects of them.

The political reality for blacks in this country, regardless of the actual racial and ethnic heritage/identity of the individual "black" person, has been determined by the "one drop rule." This is the same barbaric rule that dictated who must abide by Jim Crow laws—with one drop black blood, one is considered a black. But what about the tremendous diversity among black Americans and how it is expressed in the wide variety of musics? In recent decades the call for honoring our multi-cultural roots has still not resulted in a new definition of what it means to be an American at the beginning of the twenty-first century.[138]

Examining Zenobia Perry's personal history, her mixed racial background, and her musical style, reveals a clearer delineation of the issues at hand, and how they are exemplified in the life of an American composer. These complex issues are so volatile that their very discussion inflames what many have identified as the culture wars raging in American society today. On the other hand, such insight and historical overview may provide new understanding and a possible path for resolution. Zenobia Perry has always been considered a black American composer, but perhaps she would be more accurately described as a black Indian American composer or black Native American composer? Yet, the contemporary Native American cultural community has little interest in concert music, so no support would be gained from that society by promoting her Native American heritage.[139] On only one occasion in her long career was she included on a concert of the National Association for the Advancement of Native American Composers and Musicians; that was in 1961.[140]

This neglect has been true for other composers of mixed black and Indian heritage, as well. Perry's music, however, is grounded in what musicologists consider a "black" American musical tradition, which is generally considered in musicology to be a combination of European and African musical elements. However, most histories of black American music begin with chapters on African music, in an attempt to demonstrate that what is "black" in black American music originates in African music. This approach is based on a political decision born out of the 1920s Pan-African movement and solidified in the 1960s black pride and power movement. While this may illuminate the political realities of being black in America, it does a disservice to American music, its composers, and the art of composition.[141] Racism and racial conflict between blacks and Indians prevent the open exploration of the intersection of these two traditions; that is, if they are even to be considered separate traditions.

According to distinguished black music historian Eileen Southern, "Afro-American music" is a term applied to the music of black Americans,

> which is characterized by a style which fuses African and European musical elements; this fusion has resulted in certain unique stylistic features, though it is primarily African in tone and conception. No basic dichotomy exists between Afro-American folk music and art music, since the black composer draws freely upon folk elements; indeed, a large body of Afro-American music, including that for theater and dance as well as popular music and religious concert music, falls between the two poles of art and folk music.[142]

She provides a detailed description of what are commonly identified as fundamental characteristics of Afro-American music:

> The most distinctive trait of Afro-American music is its rhythms. The early music generally has duple meters and syncopation; modern blues and gospel in slow tempos typically employ triplets overlaying the basic pulse, and dotted rhythms are frequent. The music is always polyrhythmic, with strong cross-accents, and occasionally may be polymetric, as in piano rag. . . . Strict unison singing is rare, but polyphonic textures are more often heterophonic (i.e., elaborations on the melody) than truly harmonic in nature; the "barbershop" triadic harmonies often attributed to black music belong to popular rather than folk music. Pieces generally consist of small units (e.g., the 12-bar blues . . . and the 16-bar spiritual . . .) repeated many times. Improvisation prevents monotony, ensuring that no unit is identical with another.

> Modes and pentatonic scales are common in early music and in present-day rural music, while the more sophisticated urban 20th-century musicians generally prefer the blues scale (though this also occurs in early spirituals). The only stable notes of the blues scale are the first, second, and fourth (using the major scale as a pattern); the rest of the scale is handled freely, and a single melody can include lowered and natural thirds, fifths, sixths, or sevenths, or any combination of these. The altered notes do not fit the European chromatic scale but sound slightly below the pitch.[143]

Southern also points out that "since the mid-19th century there has been a continuous absorption of Afro-American music into the mainstream of American music, so that in many instances, for example, jazz, the two have become indistinguishable. Thus it is important to focus on the identifiable origins of the various genres of Afro-American music and on its role as catalyst in the history of American music."[144]

Identifying the origins of various elements of black music has been the focus of much recent scholarship in black music studies and in ethnomusicology. However, there is much work to be done to determine how these origins have served as a "catalyst in the history of American music."[145] At what point do we stop trying to identify and isolate the origins of African-American music and begin to embrace those traditions and musicians as being central to contemporary American musical life? By dwelling on the speculative process of determining the origins, we continue to perpetuate the separate treatment of "black" in music as a static concept that does not yield to integration.

Ingrid Monson, in her introduction to *The African Diaspora: A Musical Perspective*, describes "the importance of placing the emotional and spiritual dimensions of music within the context of concrete historical and social practice" and the need to "reject the idea of a static African essence in favor of a more continuously redefined and negotiated sense of cultural authenticity that emerges from generation to generation in response to large geopolitical forces."[146] She points out how "the very point of cultural pride also serves to fuel stereotypical notions of the essential black subject, whose 'natural' intuitive, emotional, and rhythmic gifts define her or his possibilities."[147]

In *The Black Atlantic*,[148] Paul Gilroy points out that—rather than describing certain musical elements as being identifiable as the core of the centrality of black music—what emerges instead is that the centrality of black music is in the fact that "the self-identity, political culture, and grounded aesthetics that distinguish black communities have often been constructed through their music."

A leading expert in Native American music, Charlotte Heth, points out that the voice is the most important instrument in this tradition. Vocal music can be solo or responsorial, can involve unison choral singing or multi-part songs, and can be accompanied with rattles, drums, or whistles. The songs are often in Native American languages, but also in vocables (i.e., non-translatable syllables). They vary in words, number of repetitions, nature of instrumental accompaniment, and how the singers work together. She concludes that all Native American music "come[s] from a particular world view and depend[s] largely on the dance or ceremony being performed."[149]

One also must wonder what relationship Native American music has to the elements described as African-American musical elements? It is well known that most of the Native American music documented by ethnographers and ethnomusicologists has been music for social occasions, e.g., dances, love songs, ceremonial events, or powwows, rather than sacred music. Little has ever been written about the sacred music traditions among Native Americans, so it is difficult to tell if they have any bearing or relationship on what is identified as African-American musical elements or characteristics.[150] However, it is clear from the above descriptions that African-American music and Native American music have many elements in common, particularly related to the predominance of vocal music and the use of vocal music for religious rituals and sacred expression. Both traditions involve percussive instruments in accompaniments with distinctive rhythms.

The recent scholarship on both African American music and Native American music focuses on how "the self-identity, political culture, and grounded aesthetics" that distinguish these cultures "have been constructed through their music,"[151] but little has been published regarding the similarities of the two musical cultures. Ingrid Monson's statement in connection to black music—"the very point of cultural pride also serves to fuel stereotypical notions"—also applies to Native American musicians, "whose 'natural' intuitive, emotional, and rhythmic gifts define her or his possibilities."[152] These are only two examples of common elements shared by both cultures, which require further examination and study.

"An Inner-Fusion Takes Over"

A cursory look at the relationship of blacks and Native Americans—and their respective musical traditions—is required for a better understanding of Zenobia Perry's life and music. Distinguished black American composer William Grant Still had a "mother [who] was of Negro, Spanish, Indian and Irish ancestry, and in whose father's veins flowed Negro, Indian and Scotch bloods. The son of this union naturally came into life with a heritage that was truly American in all its aspects."[153] In this sense, Zenobia Perry is also "truly American"; yet, aspects of her life story and music raise questions about what this means. She describes her musical style:

> As a composer I have been exposed to and influenced by the variety of musical styles floating around in these United States. Choosing one and eliminating the others would be painful to me because then I could not express my interaction to life. An inner-fusion takes over: intricate or free-

> flowing rhythm, the complex yet subtle inflections of melodic lines, or occasional emphasis on color, use of modes and pentatonic successions combine in various ways to shape the ancestral music deep inside my soul. So, no matter how conventional or unconventional my music appears or sounds the subtleties are always there.[154]

Today we identify all kinds of American musics, undoubtedly the dominant influence in musical culture around the world. Black American music is principally understood to mean black popular music—rhythm and blues, jazz, bebop, Motown, funk, soul, gospel, rap, and hip-hop. Spirituals are considered to be the art song of the black musical tradition.[155] Native American music, in the minds of most people, including Native Americans, is music involving drums, flutes, rattles, and vocals, often heard at powwows. Zenobia Perry's music does not fit into any of these categories, because she wrote music for the concert stage and for performance in churches (although she did arrange several spirituals). In some circles, this may mean she was "not black enough" or that she failed to fully embrace her "African-ness." Her music is rarely programmed on concerts of contemporary music with other blacks, whites, Latinos, and Asians. Most of her performances have been on concerts of African-American music, a continued kind of segregation. Black concert artists complain bitterly that they are usually hired only during Black History Month (February) and only asked to perform black music. Likewise, black composers receive most of their performances in January and February.[156]

When asked if blacks brought any distinctive qualities to classical music, Perry said:

> Perhaps the rhythms are a little suggestive of black rhythm . . . a syncopation that comes on the after beat of the downbeat of most measures. . . . This characterizes almost every phrase of music that is associated with blacks. . . . This didn't originate in Africa. It originated here in America, among American blacks. If you go to Africa, you'll find they don't syncopate. They have a number of cross rhythms. . . . One person will take one rhythm and another will take still another, and you may have four or five rhythms going on. But it isn't syncopated as such: it's cross rhythms. I find this very interesting because we think syncopation is African. It isn't. It originated here . . . and I think it was a matter of putting emphasis on things that were not emphasized in the music one (usually) heard. For instance, when we think of all the rhythms we know, the moving parts of a theme, moving parts of a melody . . . If they don't go the way we expect, we pay more attention to them. . . . It was taken up by the jazz performers, but first it was called "rag" because the rhythm didn't fit the patterns: it was kind of ragged—that's where the word came in—rags. From that, of course, we began to adopt it in a number of ways.

This man said [to me], "You know, I like to perform your music, but I would be happy to know that blacks really knew what harmony was all about," and I said to him, "I think the problem is we don't emphasize the same type of harmony . . . the emphasis comes on something else, and so you say we have a different harmony. It isn't [different]. The closer you get to what is contemporary . . . the more you find this type of harmony has been taken over by almost everyone who writes. *So, we can't say it's distinctive to a race, it's distinctive to America.*"[157]

"White" music in America is considered to include country western music, big band jazz, music for film and television, and "classical" music, all of which have been immensely influenced by what are often identified as African-American musical elements. For example, the 12-bar blues form is often used in so-called white country western music. Rock music grew out of blues, gospel, doo-wop, and R & B. Elvis Presley was "invented" in the 1950s, by white record labels, to prevent the "race labels" from taking over the entire market.[158] Many black music idioms have found their way into film and television music, mostly composed by white composers.[159] In what rational or reasonable way does one determine what is *white* and what is *black* in American music today? Rap and hip-hop music is such a commercial success, because its audience and its creators cut across all racial barriers. Granted, this is a gross oversimplification of the history of American music in the past century, but it may help us to think for a moment. The problem of defining what is *American music* lies in the difficulty in defining what is *American*.

Essential to any discussion of what is "American" in American music, is the question of rhythm, in particular syncopation. Syncopated rhythms—originating in jazz and folk idioms and then working their way into the concert music realm—are believed to be the artistic link between low and high art in American music and to be the single most important element that "produces a genuinely American music."[160]

Musical scholarship of recent decades has emphasized the differences among Americans composers and their music, rather than their common experiences, characteristics, and values. Well aware of the price of these divisions, William Grant Still called for reconciliation and a new definition of what it means to be an American. The collection of essays about his life, *William Grant Still and the Fusion of Cultures in American Music,* edited by his daughter Judith Anne Still, challenges many concepts applied to American music. It identifies a deep fear of fusion, because we are afraid of being lost as individuals and individual "cultures" and yet also afraid of being isolated because of our individual identities.

But this actually describes what has happened in recent years. Narrowly defining American music—an unspoken mission that has predominated in American musicology from 1940 to 1970—has led to the loss and exclusion of many worthy composers, including Zenobia Powell Perry. Musicologists split hairs, when it comes to delineating the differences among American composers and musical styles, to the extreme point that it *excludes*, under the guise of being *inclusive*. For example, to classify Perry as a black Native American woman composer puts her in such a small group that she is, in effect, excluded and isolated, rather than being embraced by the overall general group of American composers. This kind of categorization forces Zenobia Perry, and others like her, to remain in the margins of American cultural life. The fact is that American concert music itself—written by a wide and diverse group of composers of both sexes, of all races and ethnic backgrounds—is already marginalized; concert music constitutes a very small percentage of all music in America today. This is, in part, because it has been generally held and promoted as being a "pure" European (white) music, making it a distortion of twentieth-century European concert music, as well as a distortion of what makes up the diversity in contemporary American concert music. This approach has limited its appeal and eroded its audience.[161]

Composer, teacher, educator, and American music advocate Howard Hanson (1896–1981) wrote:

> William Grant Still's place in music history as the dean of America's Negro composers is assured. It is a proud distinction, but it is not enough. For Still is, above all, an American composer, interpreting the spiritual values of his own land through his own brand of personal genius.... His music does what, I believe, most of us feel music should do, it communicates.... All of which tends to prove that music which has its roots deep in the human heart is the most personal, the most national, and also, the most universal.[162]

Robert Bartlett Haas observed, about Still's personal development as a composer, that his

> first course was to take up the Negroid idiom and elevate it to symphonic form—not the folk themes but the idiom. Then he branched out to use in his music all the ethnic strains which combine in his own background. Thus he reached a distinctive personal idiom which has traced out the fusion of musical cultures in America.... In the earlier part of his life Still was not acquainted with the Negro idiom at all. He had to learn it as he learned other things.... And, although at one time he did something with this Negro idiom, he used it as he used everything else, then left it behind, shutting out nothing new. Still went into popular music to learn what he could, but never let it control him. The European and American *avant-gardists* tried to claim him,

but he is an independent thinker, not a musical faddist. He has always spoken for himself. He doesn't disclaim the right of others to do what they want, but for him the consistent path was devoted craftsmanship, form, melody, beautiful sounds—and the exploration of the racial strains which fuse in his own background. Father: Scotch, Negro and Choctaw Indian. Mother: Negro, Indian, Spanish and Irish. On his own (on occasion) he has added the Creole idiom of French Louisiana and the Hebraic as he learned it through his commission undertaken for the Park Avenue Synagogue.

Because of Still's encompassing perspective and personal security, the "Black" music movement, the "soul music" tradition, hasn't diverted him. *He sees it as limiting and essentially racist.* The militants claim he is writing "Eur-American," not "Afro-American" music, but this is not an historically accurate statement.[163]

This concept, which has been applied to black American music, stems from a racist history of segregation and is determined by the "one drop" rule. It has confined and dictated the careers not only of minority composers, but also of all composers in this country. These essentially racist views have allowed the wholesale dismissal of talented, insightful composers of all races—composers of "music that has its roots deep in the human heart [which] is the most personal, the most national, and also, the most universal."

"Racial Strains That Fuse"

All that a composer desires is to be taken seriously. Still's process, "the consistent path . . . devoted [to] craftsmanship, form, melody, beautiful sounds—and the exploration of the racial strains which fuse in his own background," is the process of all composers. To limit someone to being a *black* composer implies confining that person to the exploration of the black strains in his/her own background; or a Native American composer confined to the exploration of the Native American strains. To confine or limit a composer's world to musical material of his/her own racial background is racist.[164] For all composers, all musical material is "fair game" and should be used as Still did: "as he used everything else, then left it behind, shutting out nothing new." All music becomes part of a composer's background as soon as s/he hears it, regardless of whether or not a composer uses that material in his/her composition. Zenobia Perry challenged us to begin to identify elements of black music as being "not distinctive to race... but distinctive to America."

This is the insidious nature of the racial prejudice in composition, as in all other fields. Illogical and based on stereotypical understandings and perceptions, it reveals as much about the perpetrator's ignorance of the nature of musical material as it does about an ignorance of the very process of composition. To lump all black composers and their compositions together is racist. As black American composer Ed Bland points out, "The injustice of racism is that blacks aren't looked at individually."[165]

Ronald Radano understands how the boundaries of black music are born of the nation's racial boundaries:

> Black music's invention within the American cultural landscape emerged as a consequence of the nation's racial boundaries. Its exclusivity and power derive from contradictions inherent in racial ideology that defines black music as something at once Other and constituted within the social Same. Accordingly, musical qualities of difference that took shape in a circumstance of intercultural familiarity supplied the paradoxical symbols of racial particularism and nationalism: black music could simultaneously define slavery and represent the sonic embodiment of America. By the twentieth century, the rising presence of black music had a profound impact on the public understanding of race and music, to the point of influencing the evolution of scholarly engagement. The language of the musicologies, together with the experience of music overall, would continually operate in constant contact with this fundamental racial dynamic.[166]

The evolution of scholarly engagement on these issues seems long in coming, particularly in the way these oppressive stereotypes have influenced the careers of individual black composers. Such notions are identified as part of a racial ideology, which are "the very point of cultural pride also serv[ing] to fuel stereotypical notions"[167] about black music. Such stereotypes, like the notion that black music cannot be easily notated, need to be re-examined and exposed for their damaging implications.

Christopher Small, in his book *Music of the Common Tongue: Survival and Celebration in Afro-American Music*, attempts to show that,

> by any reasonable reckoning of the function of music in human life, the Afro-American tradition is the major music of the west in the twentieth century, of far greater human significance than those remnants of the great European classical traditions that are to be heard today in the concert halls and opera houses of the industrial world, east and west.

> To this purpose, I need to carry on two discussions simultaneously: first, an examination of the various aspects of the Afro-American tradition in both its contemporary and its historical forms, in an attempt to show them all as

aspects of the one great and coherent culture, and, second, a study of what seem to me some important aspects of the art of music in general, in an attempt to understand something of what it is that gives Afro-American music its power in the lives of so many people across the whole world in our century.[168]

He goes on to say that it is difficult to write about Afro-American music traditions:

> perhaps because *as a music that does not in the main rely on written or printed notes*, it is not only decentralized but it also does not reveal itself in that linear manner which is characteristic of the notation-dependent tradition of European classical music. Blues, jazz, rock, and so on, are not separate musical categories, however much the analytical temper of Europeans would have it so, but are constantly shifting and interacting facets of the great tradition, meeting and flowing into one another, grouping, and regrouping with dizzying rapidity, and without regard for the labors of specialists or archivists.[169]

On the contrary, "blues, jazz, rock, and so on" are separate musical categories precisely because of class differences in the black community and in America on the whole: to think otherwise is to reveal naïveté about the history of American life. These are separate musical categories, because there are only a few musicians who would be considered by practitioners of that group, to be capable of performing convincingly in more than one of these genres.[170] Small's outlook is also based on a misconception that the black music tradition is one "great tradition." It glosses over the specific differences within the African-American community, historically and today, and assumes that blacks live separately from the rest of society. Full consideration of this diversity within the African-American community mandates the perspective that this music is "distinctive to America" and not to a race. It fails to recognize all of the musical elements present in the United States and how they have nurtured and fed one another—so much so that any attempt to declare one element as being the sole venue, property, or legacy of one race or another is in itself a racist act. It perpetuates segregation and the centuries of inequities based on race.

Small is not the only African-American music *aficionado* to make this point. But why do he and others insist on separating African-American music from "the great European classical traditions that are to be heard today in the concert halls and opera houses of the industrial world, east and west" and all other musics rooted in American soil? Why not think of the music that is "distinctive to America" as being born of a mixture of all the musical traditions of this soil: black, Native American, European classical, Spanish, etc.? Why is this such a difficult concept? Is it because racism has propagated this separation? Is it because institutionalized racism has instilled an irrational and illogical separation of people of color from whites?

Many black American musicians had wanted to study "the great European classical traditions" in order to develop a solid music craftsmanship, but were denied opportunities because of institutionalized racism. Black music was considered "a music that does not in the main rely on written or printed notes, it is not only decentralized but it also does not reveal itself in that linear manner which is characteristic of the notation-dependent tradition of European classical music." Such an attitude has prevented many musicians in this tradition from receiving a complete education in music, including learning both to read and to write music. Can we somehow justify the past exclusion of blacks from music theory and compositional training by thinking that what was truly original about their musical contribution to American culture could not or did not need to be notated? In fact, it has been notated, but only for the financial gain of people other than the creators of the music. This injustice continues to this day.

Like many minority musicians, Zenobia Perry wanted a complete music education—performance training, theory, and composition—which included learning how to notate the music, so that she could "own" her own music and benefit from its creation, publication, and distribution. She was in her twenties before the idea of such an education was even suggested to her and she was in her late thirties before she found a mentor-teacher in theory and composition in the person of Darius Milhaud. Her extensive training as a pianist and violinist did not include learning to write music, only to read and interpret it.

Those who possess the skill of notating music and composing music must have the conviction that their students deserve this level of music training. Many teachers and institutions believed in the past that blacks and women were not worthy. Had it been otherwise, there would now be many more black and women composers, or at least they would be in the same proportion of all musicians as among white men. Those few blacks and women who gained access to such instruction were the ones fortunate to have exceptional, unprejudiced teachers. White men who taught theory and composition to blacks and women were rare and unusual. Even today, many black colleges do not have theory and composition programs, but continue to concentrate on vocal, piano, and choral singing (although some have jazz programs where education in theory and composition is a by-product of the performance program).[171] Many still do not have programs for the study of orchestral instruments.

Black musicians have often suffered economically because they were not able to write down their own music. There are countless examples in popular music of white musicians who wrote down compositions by black musicians, copyrighted them, and collected the royalties and other benefits of publication.[172] The idea that black music, by its very nature, "does not in the main rely on written or printed notes," is "decentralized," or "does not reveal itself in that linear manner," excludes black music from the centuries-old laws, stating that intellectual property, if not written down, is not "composed." Only in 1978 did the U.S. government amend the copyright law to make it possible to copyright a recorded performance of music, with the same protection and benefits afforded notated music. This may have been an honest attempt to afford rights and privileges for "composers" of unnotated music—particularly jazz and blues—but the immediate benefit of such an amendment went to composers of electronic and computer music, who had difficulty notating synthetic sounds and "musique concrète." A professional copyist in Los Angeles recently remarked that the number of black composers in Los Angeles—one of the major commercial music centers in the world—who could notate their own works still totals only a handful.[173]

Teaching music notation and music diction is difficult and requires both patience and a clarity of method.[174] Furthermore, notating music demands a high level of precision, a rigorous thought process, and the ability to hone skills and musical thinking. Just as writing prose is a way of teaching and developing thinking, notating music is a way of teaching and developing musical thinking.[175] Failing to learn this skill can be a hindrance to any musician's individual development, regardless of whether s/he desires to become a composer.[176] Insistence that blacks or women (or any musicians) do not need to know how to write music down is based on a misconception about composition. In the case of improvised musics, it exposes a misconception about improvisation. As Ed Bland points out, "Jazz musicians always know what they are going to play before they play it. They have it all worked out. They might as well write it down, if they haven't already. Most competent jazz performers have no need to write it down."[177]

The story of Zenobia Perry's quest for a complete music education, particularly for training in theory and composition, provides a clear picture of how blacks and women have been excluded from the possibility of becoming composers. The discrimination was based on both race and gender.

CHAPTER 4

On the surface, the focus of a study of Zenobia Perry's life in music might appear to be the mixing of her black and Creek Indian heritages. Although her ancestors included both black and Creeks, she is considered to be a black composer; she always lived in black communities, and taught at predominantly black colleges. She did not choose to confine her life as a composer to the black community, yet, in fact, she was grateful for the support and success she had within that community. But she was painfully aware of how little opportunity she or any American composer, regardless of their racial backgrounds, had to develop and thrive as a composer. Those who care about composition as an art form should be banding together to create a supportive and nurturing environment for all composers, instead of splitting hairs over racial backgrounds and distinctions.

Yes, her situation was more complex because of the mixed racial heritage, because she was a woman, because she was Midwestern. But what does it have to do with the music she wrote or the very musical materials she chose to work with? It has much to do with her lack of opportunities to pursue training in music theory and composition and the lack of support from her family and community for her desire to become a composer. One cannot help but wonder what it is about the history of black and Native Americans in the United States that affected the course of her life, the development of her career. Why are black Indians not widely discussed or singled out as a cultural group in this country, when blacks and Indians as separate racial groups have commanded such attention in American history? Because blacks and Native Americans in the United States have had a fascinating interrelation since African slaves were brought to the Americas, the simple answer—if there is such a thing—is that it is a story of racism on top of racism.

Zenobia Perry, like many in this country, was forced to disregard some of her roots, in favor of other roots, in order to survive (and potentially thrive) in a racist, segregated society—a society that historically pitted one minority against another and established a pecking order on degrees of "whiteness" and "Indian-ness." All of this served to keep the dominant group in power in society, both economically and culturally. Perry's career was spent primarily at two black colleges that tended to dictate and limit the development of her musical style. Colleagues and students, called upon to perform her music, resisted her efforts to push them to perform her more adventuresome works—works more interesting to her as a composer, in a more "international" concert music style, which she learned in her studies with Milhaud and through her other contacts with colleagues working

RACE AND MUSIC

outside of black colleges. To complain about this resistance, however, would have been to appear ungrateful for the opportunities that were presented to her through black academic life.

However, Zenobia Perry's life story and music require a re-examination of the categories in black American music and its stylistic elements that have served to segregate and marginalize this music. Her music and her life story argue forcibly for a new consensus of what is "distinctively American" about contemporary music in this country.

The next chapter discusses Zenobia Perry's mixed black and Native American ancestry, in the context of the history of blacks and Native Americans in the New World. A closer examination of this complex history further intensifies the discussion about race and musical style.

Zenobia Powell Perry at the piano in the early 1950s.

Zenobia Powell Perry, c.1992.

5. The Hidden History
Blacks and Native Americans' Cultural Implications

At the piano Zenobia Perry played a melody from one of her compositions and was asked, "Is that from a spiritual?" "No," she answered. "It is based on a Creek Indian lullaby. Many of my melodies are Creek songs." Zenobia Perry's grandfather Charlie Thompson (born c.1839) was a black Creek Indian slave, whose master was a Creek Indian slaveholder. Just as many Americans feel ambivalence in their relationship to whites who held blacks as slaves, so blacks feel about Indians who held blacks as slaves. Some Native Americans held Africans as slaves into the early decades of the twentieth century in the Indian Territories.

Historically, the U.S. government policies towards Indians have been substantially different than U.S. government policies about blacks and these differences continue to be pronounced in our own time.[178] This intense complexity involved with European and American events and policies still leaves many serious questions about Native Americans unanswered.[179] This chapter reviews this history to establish why many black Americans do not claim their Native American heritage and *vice versa*, why Native Americans do not claim their black heritage.

This complexity explains why the inter-relationships and connections between black and Native American music traditions have not been explored or widely discussed in either community or in the nation's music community as a whole. Such a discussion has not yet taken place in ethnomusicology or in black music studies. This complexity is the reason Zenobia Perry has wavered between her mother's ambivalence and pride about her own mixed racial and cultural heritage. In her later years, she has felt more comfortable about her "Indianness." At certain times in her life, it was not discussed because she was trying so hard to "fit in." One sees her new level of comfort in her hairstyles, costuming, and in her willingness to discuss her mixed heritage with young people in the community. The path to reconciliation requires that we begin to focus on what is "distinctively American" in American music.[180]

According to William Loren Katz,

> The 1920s estimate that a third of African Americans have Indian blood requires new research. Today just about every African-American family tree has an Indian branch. Europeans forcefully entered the African blood stream, but Native Americans and Africans merged by choice, invitation, and love. This profound difference cannot be understated—and it explains why families who share this biracial inheritance feel so much solace and pride.[181]

This may be true for some relationships between Indians and blacks, but the issues seem to be more complicated since many Indians were holders of African-American slaves. Until recently the intertwined histories of blacks and Indians have not been discussed and have not been taken up in most history of black Americans or Native Americans. Descendants of these mixed unions either considered themselves to be black or Indian, but not black Indians or Indian blacks. The reasons for this are many and complicated. For the purpose of this discussion, it is necessary to review some of this history.

There are many accounts related to black Indians going back to the sixteenth century, the results of relationships between Africans and Indians. Generally it is well known that African slaves found haven in Native American communities before the Civil War, but the relationship between Indians and Africans goes back to the sixteenth century. Native Americans were sold into slavery by the British to the Spanish West Indies, and many were taken to Europe. But as disease and physical abuse decimated the Indian population, Europeans went to Africa for manpower. In the sixteenth century, the Portuguese had brought more than 50,000 Africans to Europe; some of these became the crews of the explorers' ships sent to the New World. Eventually more than 12 million Africans were taken there. The mixing of Indians and Africans began immediately because of the policies of the slave traffickers.

Because they believed men were better suited for heavy work but women were more likely to survive the Middle Passage, slavers customarily loaded their ships with two African men to each African woman. And because they thought that Native American men were more dangerous and more likely to escape than Native American women, they reversed the ratio for these slaves: two Indian women to each Indian man. As a consequence of these practices, enslaved Indian and African populations intermingled more quickly.[182]

The Trail of Tears

For the U.S. government, problems presented by Native Americans in the eastern states were "solved" by the Indian Removal Act of 1830 which provided for mass deportation of Indians of the Five Civilized Nations from the southeast. Sixty thousand Native Americans and blacks were moved to lands in Arkansas and Oklahoma—land that whites considered uninhabitable. For Cherokees, this removal became known as the "Trail of Tears." Among the 14,000 Cherokees, 1,600 were identified by the U.S. government census as "black Indians"; only 10,000 Cherokees survived.[183]

Government "Indian" agents sent from Washington to this new Indian Territory encouraged slave holding. "'Mixed bloods' owned slaves and usually had some white ancestry. Though a minority, they felt both of these facts made them superior, fit to rule. This also meant the amount of 'white' blood was a positive, as much as the amount of 'black' blood was a negative. 'Full bloods' formed a majority, but because they had no white blood and held no slaves, they had little power."[184] According to Katz, "By 1860 Cherokees had 2,511 slaves, Choctaws 2,344, Creeks 1,532 and Chickasaws 975. Slavery had become the major economic and political factor in these nations."[185] According to some accounts, Indians may have practiced a milder form of bondage and whites were generally upset by the leniency of Indian slaveholders.

> To the extent that some Native Americans adopted a mean-spirited, profit-hungry slavery urged on them by whites and Indian agents, they faced the same rebelliousness that marked the southern states. But, despite the inducements and pressures, most rejected that foreign standard and followed their own gentler instincts. This simple decision stands as yet another example of a treasured independent spirit by Native Americans. The beneficiaries were the

CHAPTER 5

Afro-Americans whose slave years were spent with people who found it very difficult to treat other human beings as pieces of property.[186]

The American Civil War

During the Civil War most Native Americans had become allies of the Confederacy. When the Confederacy was defeated, many existing treaties were abandoned, and a large portion of the Indian Territory was taken from the Five Nations and given to the Plains Nations, Shawnees, and Delawares. The U.S. government demanded that all slaves of Indians become free and equal. Then the U.S. government embarked upon a massive land redistribution campaign. African slaves of Indians in Indian Territory were not freed.

Within the Indian Nations, black Indians faced years of efforts to win citizenship rights, land, education, and equality of opportunity. According to Katz, "The black effort in the Indian Territory reflected their wider and less successful campaign for equality during this era of Reconstruction in the southern states."[187] To Katz, the difference for blacks living in Indian Territory or in the United States lies in the fact that "whatever unfairness they felt among their Indian friends could not match what they would experience among whites. They knew this and stayed. Here were a people who would never lynch or brutalize their sons and daughters."[188] Among Creeks, Seminoles, and Cherokees, blacks that were ex-slaves made tremendous economic strides, far surpassing what blacks among whites could achieve. However, blacks who fought for the Union during the Civil War were denied full membership in the Indian nation.

In the introduction to *The WPA Oklahoma Slave Narratives* the editors offer the following perspective:

> Twenty-eight of the 130 informants were actually in servitude in present-day Oklahoma as slaves of American Indians who were members of the Creek, Cherokee, Chickasaw, or Choctaw nation....
>
> One of the most intriguing aspects of the Oklahoma slave narratives is that some of them record a detailed inside view of slavery among the so-called Five Tribes. The Cherokees, Creeks, Chickasaws, and Choctaws, all had taken from the Euro-Americans the practice of black slavery, while the Seminoles chose to adopt blacks into their bands. When the federal government expelled these groups from their traditional homes in the southeastern United States, they

took with them their black slaves. The Indians had a reputation for showing more humanity to their slaves than the whites, although these narratives illustrate a wide range of relations between the groups. The enculturation of the blacks into the tribes was so great that some slaves knew only Indian languages until after emancipation. . . .

Indian Territory in the eastern half of present-day Oklahoma was divided in sympathies during the Civil War, with members of Indian tribes fighting on both sides during the conflict. . . . After the Confederate surrender at Appomattox in 1865, the Five Tribes were forced to negotiate new treaties with the victorious United States government, which insisted that they make the former slaves full legal members of the tribes. This took place for the Cherokees, Creeks, Choctaws, and Seminoles, but the Chickasaws refused to accept their former slaves as full tribal members. To this day there are many African Americans who receive full benefits of membership in four of the Five Tribes.[189]

This complexity of black Indians as being former slaves or descendants of former slaves of Native American masters led many blacks to deny their mixed heritage, just as white ancestry was disavowed or played down.

At the time of Wounded Knee (1890), one of the most famous massacres between Indians and the U.S. military, most surviving Indian tribes had moved onto reservations.[190] There were 25 reservations in Indian Territory, now Eastern Oklahoma, and 75 throughout the rest of the country. The Bureau of Indian Affairs (BIA), developed as a branch of the Interior Department, was in charge of running the reservations, through a network of agents, teachers, clerks, traders, and supply contractors. The BIA handed out annual benefits, food, blankets, education, and religious "guidance."

Under the Dawes Act of 1887, communal lands of the reservations were divided into small parcels and distributed to Indians as private property, the purpose being to break down tribal unity and to "civilize" the Indians. This proved disastrous to Native Americans and within four decades Indian land went from 138 million acres to 48 million acres. By 1910, the Native American population was only 250,000 compared to the estimated 800,000 in the days of Columbus.[191]

The black population in Oklahoma in 1910 was 137,000.[192] Blacks worked hard to try to prevent Oklahoma from becoming a segregationist state and formed several organizations to fight for equal rights. However, "Black Indians called the black newcomers to their region 'state Negroes.' It is unclear if either black population moved toward making common cause."[193] This conflict between black Indians, Indians, and newly arrived

CHAPTER 5

blacks may have been one of the causes that Oklahoma became a "Jim Crow" state. Some have speculated that unity among them may have prevented it. But unity was impossible given that Indians had held Africans as slaves—some still did after 1907—just as unity in Southern states between whites and blacks was impossible.

Oklahoma Statehood

When Oklahoma entered the Union as the 46th state in 1907, black Indians could not vote and African Americans faced violent intervention if they tried to vote. After statehood, the Democrats moved the capital from Guthrie (a Republican stronghold) to Oklahoma City. Most blacks were Republicans in those days, the party of Abraham Lincoln. Schools, public buildings, railroad cars were segregated and Oklahoma had the distinction of being the first state to segregate telephone booths. It became another white supremacist state. The dream of Oklahoma being a good place for blacks and Indians to live was destroyed. Many blacks left Oklahoma for points east, including major northern urban centers. Some even tried to obtain passage back to Africa.[194]

By the time Perry's father had settled in Oklahoma as a doctor, blacks and Native Americans were already so intermixed and integrated that a black Creek woman marrying a black (African) man did not seem so unusual. Many of the blacks already living in the Oklahoma territory before the land rush were part Indian, maybe as many as 30–40 percent. According to Perry, no one even thought about who was black and who was Indian and who was mixed; it was not an issue. "We never thought about that. We weren't taught that. We were interested in what a person could achieve—what was his worth as far as betterment of the whole community. We never thought about race. No one said this was a black woman, a white woman, or an Indian woman."[195]

By 1871 most tribes had relinquished ancestral lands and in 1887, the government changed its policies with the General Allotment Act. The goal was to turn individual Indians into landowners and they were offered parcels in 160, 80, or 40 acre plots. Indians lost some 90 million acres by legal and illegal means. The Dawes Act caused "thousands of black Indians to seek formal tribal membership to obtain land allotments and payments previously offered only to Native Americans."[196] But tribal lands not distributed to Native Americans under the Dawes Act were opened to whites and to blacks for settlement.

According to Kim Dramer:

> The first large parcel of land in Indian Territory opened to outside settlement was the former territory of the Creek and Seminole tribes. On April 22, 1889, the day the law took effect, approximately 100,000 settlers crowded onto the land to stake claims. By the end of the day the entire area had been parceled out. About 10,000 of these settlers were what Native Americans would eventually call "state blacks"—former slaves and African Americans from other areas of the country, who wanted to settle on the cheap land available in Indian Territory. In order to qualify as tribal members, black Indians were required to distinguish themselves from state blacks.
>
> Qualifying as a member of a Native American tribe became more difficult after the government established the Dawes Commission in 1898. Until 1914, the commission officially determined who qualified as a tribal member. The process was lengthy and involved—the average applicant waited three to five years, regardless of his or her color or race, to be accepted as a tribal citizen. And citizenship was far from guaranteed; in fact, because ownership of Indian land reverted to the government, the United States profited by refusing citizenship. Blacks who were born slaves were required to prove that they had been owned by Native Americans. Usually an Indian would testify at a special hearing on behalf of the applicant. For this reason, granting tribal citizenship to former slaves was sometimes called "adoption of freedmen."[197]

The result is that some black Indians received allotments of land and money, while others did not.[198]

The U.S. government system of recordkeeping perpetuated the problems. Many freedmen and their descendants are listed as black in the 1900 federal census of the Indian Territory. In the 1910 census, after Indian Territory had become the state of Oklahoma and these families had been officially admitted into Native American tribes, they are listed as Indian. In the 1920 census, they are once again classified as black.[199]

In 1920, the United States Census Department discontinued its separate category for mulattos, or people of mixed black and white heritage. A mulatto had been defined as a person "having some proportion or perceptible trace of Negro blood." But the category was inconsistently applied—in the 1910 census, for example, many Native Americans were counted as mulatto.[200]

> Classifying mixed-blood American of Native American and African-American heritage as black rather than Indian was motivated in part by economic interests. Native Americans held legal claims to land or annual government payments according to various treaties they had established with

federal authorities. By reclassifying Americans of mixed heritage as black, authorities were not only able to deny their claims in order to save money and gain access to desirable land; they were also able to apply Jim Crow laws.[201]

Dramer points out how arbitrary the rules were and into what position this forced many people:

> In 1930, a person of mixed Native American and African-American heritage was counted in the national census "as a Negro unless the Indian blood predominates and the status as an Indian is generally accepted in the community." And as late as 1940, any person of mixed heritage was classified as a "Negro" unless his or her Native American ancestry "very definitely predominates and he [or she] is universally accepted as an Indian." Such sleight of hand gave rise to the popular assumption that Native Americans were vanishing or were already extinct. Land speculators and parsimonious politicians were particularly eager to espouse this view, since it would free more land and require less financial support from the government. But the reclassification also yielded unexpected results. By the 1890s, some of the country's most celebrated artists, poets, and musicians were, by government standards, black. A growing sense of pride among African Americans led to a movement known as Pan Africanism, in which black people around the world were urged to unite against oppression. Nowhere was this sense of unity and pride more evident than in Harlem.[202]

In Booker T. Washington's report on his visit to Boley, Oklahoma, in 1908, he wrote:

> During the course of my visit I had an opportunity for the first time to see the three races—the Negro, the Indian, and the white man—living side by side, each in sufficient numbers to make their influence felt in the communities of which they were a part, and in the Territory as a whole. . . . When I inquired, as I frequently did, for the "natives," it almost invariably happened that I was introduced, not to an Indian, but to a Negro. . . . I was introduced later to one or two other "natives" who were not Negroes, but neither were they, as far as my observation went, Indians. They were, on the contrary, white men. "But where," I asked at length, "are the Indians?"
>
> "Oh! the Indians," was the reply, "they have gone," with a wave of the hand in the direction of the horizon, "they have gone back!"
>
> . . . There are still, I am told, among the "natives" some Negroes who cannot speak the English language, and who have been so thoroughly bred in the customs of the Indians, that they have remained among the hills with the tribes by whom they were adopted. But, as a rule, the Negro natives do not shun the white man and his civilization, but, on the contrary, rather seek it, and enter, with the Negro immigrants, into competition with the white man for its benefits.[203]

A national black leader, Booker T. Washington, was trying to sort out who was whom by skin color and facial features, and not by actual power relationship. The issue of black Indian slaves did not enter his mind, only "adoption." Some blacks who spoke only Indian languages who "remained in the hills," continued to be held as slaves into the early years of the twentieth century although black slaves had been emancipated in the United States with the Civil War.

Urban migration of blacks (and black Indians) in the teens and twenties offered new opportunities for jobs and education and a growing sense of pride led to the Pan Africanism that urged all blacks to unite against oppression. Several efforts, including Marcus Garvey's back-to-Africa movement and the NAACP, evolved into the civil rights movement of the 1940s, '50s, and '60s. Perry's parents left Boley for the larger city of Bartlesville (near Tulsa), abandoning the dream of Boley and black autonomy. The children of the Boley pioneers moved to various locations—thriving black communities throughout the country. Native Americans continued to battle U.S. government Indian policies and the B.I.A., which in the 1950s resettled some 35,000 Native Americans to large cities.[204]

William Loren Katz in his book *Black Indians* points out, "Children of the black awarenesss of the 1960s have rarely cared to mention an Indian ancestry because this might be seen as a denial of their African origins and the value of blackness. All this is part of the racial nightmare we have inherited."[205] Among blacks, the racial make-up of the father determined how the family would live—black father meant life in the black community; Indian father meant life among Native Americans. Many of the liaisons were between black men and Indian women and therefore these unions were considered to be black families. Because social status was determined by the amount of white blood one had, the pecking order was as follows: whites/Indians with white blood/pure blood Indians/Blacks with white blood/Blacks with Indian blood/Black who appeared neither Indian or white blooded. "Among biracial couples I remember prominent Indian families with surnames of Rainwater, Blue Feather, and Dilly Hunter," remembers Perry. She feels pride over her Native American and black heritage, although her mother, who worked hard for upward mobility for her children, was hard pressed to even admit she was Creek Indian.[206]

Janis-Rozena Peri said that her grandmother Birdie Thompson

> was actually kind of embarrassed about it [her Creek heritage]. Also her mother's side was Creek Indian. I don't think Luticia [Birdie's mother] was entirely all Creek. I think there was a white relative somewhere because one day somebody came to the door—both my mother and grandmother mentioned this to me—and it was an embarrassing tale for her. There evidently were

CHAPTER 5

people who were looking up their roots and they were white and they had discovered they had these black relatives. I'm fascinated that they actually wanted to investigate it and that they came to the door. My grandmother talked to them through the screen door and would not let them in.[207]

Twenty-First Century

So, who are we as we enter the twenty-first century in America? Surely any family who claims to have lived on this soil for 150–200 years could very well be of mixed racial heritage, regardless of what parents and grandparents may claim. DNA testing and racial/ethnic profiling now make it scientifically possible to determine with amazing precision one's racial/ethnic identity. One woman, involved with genetic testing for Kaiser Hospitals in Los Angeles, said the hardest part of her job is to meet with a family to disclose to them a disease or condition a child faces related to a hidden racial history: for example, telling a Filipino-American family their child has Tay-Sachs disease, passed down from Sephardic Jewish ancestors (probably from Spain) who settled in the Philippines. The Catholic family often denies a mixed Jewish heritage as a possibility and attempts to reject the hospital's accurate diagnosis of the child's condition. She has had to explain to "white" families how it is that their child has sickle cell anemia. Such testing is routinely done at HMOs, but the results are not disclosed to patients unless a medical condition develops. But should not who we are depend on our values, not on skin color or facial features? Our values are reflected in our culture. This seems so simple, yet so difficult at this moment in American history.[208]

At conferences on black American music, Zenobia Perry has often heard from other participants: "Sister, why do you dress like an Indian? You aren't an Indian!" When she explains that she is black and Creek, they often just shake their heads and walk away.[209]

She adds, that on the other hand, "Sometimes I get this kind of comment: 'You know, if it weren't for your native strain, I don't think your music would be nearly as interesting.' 'Well,' I say, 'I'm just me. What comes out, is me.' And I think that happens to every composer."[210]

Zenobia's daughter, Janis-Rozena, summarized this complicated issue:

> The minute you [as a black person] claim that other part of your heritage, then you are automatically disassociating yourself from the African-American

heritage. This is part of the schizophrenia. Logic tells you we couldn't look like we do if there wasn't a lot of mixing, but the emotion, the craziness of it—the lack of logic, says that. For instance, at our family reunion someone will bring up the fact that we have Native American heritage and invariably when that comes up someone will say, "I'm just plain African American, just a plain black," just to make it clear "I know where my loyalties lie." This is a political issue. It is a loyalty issue.[211]

When Zenobia Perry claimed her Indian heritage, the proverbial "feathers" were ruffled, in both the black and Indian communities. Instead, her story should stimulate wider discussion of how the mixing of black, white, and Indian is exemplified in American music and resulting in those elements that are "distinctively American." We are still collectively in denial of the reality of this nation's history and insist on perpetuating cultural segregation. But segregation fails to provide an environment conducive to a vibrant, flourishing concert music tradition involving composers of both genders, and of all racial and ethnic groups, not to mention a cohesive, productive society.

Zenobia Powell, c.1923.

6. Mentors, Allies, and Supporters
Crucial for Musical Development

"Music was indelibly stamped on my being."

—*Zenobia Powell Perry*

Crucial to the development of a musical career is support from parents, siblings, friends, mentors, colleagues, and community. Rarely will a musician enjoy unconditional support from all those constituencies, but support from at least one camp is essential. In a society that generally disapproved of women becoming composers and where few black women in the late nineteenth and early twentieth century even attempted composition, role models for Zenobia Perry were not readily available to encourage and support her desire to pursue composition.[212] However, the black women pianists, singers, and music teachers in her community were encouragement enough to get her started in music. This chapter examines the early mentors and allies who offered the musical support Zenobia needed as a child, which led her to choose music as a profession. It discusses the musical life of Boley, Oklahoma, in the 1910s and '20s, and what kind of music education was available in the schools and through private instruction.

CHAPTER 6

Concert Pianist Hazel Harrison

Hazel Harrison,
from a 1947 concert program.

For the young Zenobia, seeing a live concert performance as a child was so magical an experience as to steer her toward musical training. Neither of her parents were professional musicians, so she only heard amateur music-making in the home and in her church. For her, the pivotal moment—when she knew she wanted to become a musician—came during a performance of black American concert pianist Hazel Harrison in Boley, when Zenobia was nine or ten years old. Harrison, who had just returned from Germany, was on one of her many U.S. tours. Zenobia recalled the details of that experience as if it had only been yesterday:

> I remember it was a winter night, because my mom, sister, and I got all bundled up to walk the four or five blocks to the Masonic Lodge where she was playing. Some of the streets were paved with bricks then, but most were just covered with sand. I was wearing my purple, imitation fur coat with a black collar and a nice matching imitation fur hat. Children always got to sit in the first row, so that's where my sister and I sat, with my mother in the seat behind us. I looked up to that bright stage, the polished wooden floor and that fancy grand piano, and there was Hazel Harrison, with her hair all pretty and curled up on the top of her head, wearing this sky-blue dress with beads that just shined all over the place. I'd never seen anything like it.
>
> And when her fingers started going up and down on the piano—all the beautiful noise coming out of her hands—shivers ran up and down my

spine. She played Strauss's "Beautiful Blue Danube Waltz," "Prelude no. 10," Schubert's "Military Polonaise," and I don't recall what all else.[213]

> I was so excited, I couldn't sleep. Finally, she [mother] put the light out on me and I was afraid of the dark so I went to bed, clothes and all. I didn't even pull off my shoes. Somebody undressed me. But from that time on, I knew I wanted to be in music.[214]

The day after the concert, Hazel Harrison visited the Boley Elementary School and told the students about her studies in Germany and about her life as a concert pianist. She described how she had had to eat potatoes three times a day while studying in Germany, because that was all she could afford. The image stayed with Zenobia, who was deeply impressed with the idea that if you were going to have a life in music, you must be willing to have a limited income and make sacrifices.[215] She immediately asked her parents for piano lessons.

Hazel Harrison (1883–1969) was the first American black woman musician to establish an international concert career as a pianist. She had received her early music training in her native Laporte, Indiana, then in Chicago, with Victor Heinze. Before World War I, she had studied with Ferruccio Busoni and his pupil and assistant Egon Petri in Italy, returning to the U.S. at the outbreak of World War I. She made her Chicago début in 1919 and her New York début in 1922 and taught at the Chicago University of Music, Tuskegee Institute, Howard University (1958–1963), and Alabama State University (1958–1963). Among Harrison's friends were Harry T. Burleigh, E. Azalia Locke, Frederick Hall, Abbie Mitchell, William Dawson, Roy Tibbs, Camille Nickerson, Todd Duncan, and Louise Burge.[216]

Piano Teacher Mayme Jones

Zenobia Perry's first music lessons were on the violin, with a music teacher in the public schools, on an instrument purchased by Grandmother Thompson. Her father did not like the violin, and agreed to purchase a piano. Eventually she was allowed to study with Mayme Jones:[217]

> The town's piano teacher wanted to start me in the study of piano but my father was reluctant. He was sure that a scientific preference would take center stage later on. . . . [M]y father was a proud man, a very cultured man who loved Shakespeare and the theater—he thought piano playing might lead me

CHAPTER 6

astray or into the saloons or some place he didn't want me to be. One day as he was coming home, he saw me picking peaches in Mayme Jones's yard. Mayme was the music teacher in Boley, and my father got it in his head that I was picking those peaches for free music lessons. So he went ahead and offered to pay for them.

The private lessons were reinforced by the public school music program:

By the time I reached fifth grade, I fell in love with the music classes and the Jackson sisters. Minneola, who was in charge of general music and the high school chorus, and her sister Veola, who was a first grade teacher but came to the high school chorus sessions to sing difficult solos, such as soprano solos from *Messiah* by Handel and *Rigoletto* by Verdi. Mr. Langrum played violin and was in charge of the orchestra. He was after three years replaced by a woman, Inez Scott.

Music was taken with the same seriousness as reading and math. It was imperative that every high school graduate could identify the most popular "World Classics" when we heard them, e.g. *Messiah* by Handel; *Eine kleine Nachtmusik* by Mozart; Symphony no. 40 by Mozart; Symphony no. 5 by Beethoven; *Hungarian Rhapsodie* by Liszt; *Juba Dance* by R. Nathaniel Dett; and *Maple Leaf Rag* by Scott Joplin. Elocution, interpretive dance, handicrafts and music were taught after regular school hours and on Saturdays by devoted teachers. Most often my piano lessons were taught after school.[218]

There was also plenty of music in the Powell home. According to Zenobia, "Mr. Mathonican [her father's closest friend] and I always had a lot of things to do and we'd surprise my father. He played the Jew's Harp and he would play while I played piano and we would serenade my father."[219]

So my father ordered me a piano, an upright Kingsbury, if I'm not mistaken. And in three weeks it arrived in Boley by train from Chicago. My father hoped to get it in time for my 11th birthday, but it came a week late. We took it home with Mr. Evans' two mules and wagon. My father, Mr. Evans, and his brother and a Mr. Callaghan helped unload it.

I practiced on it all the time, at least three hours a day. My brothers and sister would complain about all the noise I'd be making, but my mother always supported me and my music, and she'd say to them, "Put some cotton in your ears if you don't want to hear it."[220]

When my piano arrived from Chicago and it was unpacked I could hardly wait for the tuner to finish his work so that I could play my piano. As soon as I awoke every morning I ran to the parlor to see my piano and play it. In this way I formed the habit of practice immediately upon rising every morning. At times Mamma pinched me away from the piano to get dressed and started on my daily chores. During the second year of piano lessons I won the Junior Pianists State Contest and played in concert for the State Teachers' Association. That preparation became a family project. My mother sewed my wardrobe for the trip; my sister and older brother chose the luggage my father bought for the adventure and we all practiced travel etiquette, except my father who seemed only mildly amused.[221]

Mayme Jones had studied with R. Nathaniel Dett when he was teaching at the Lincoln Institute in Jefferson City, Missouri, a black music school.[222] Mayme Jones also directed a choral club in Boley that staged a pageant in the Silver Springs Park at Easter time.[223] Her sister was a singer and taught the first grade in Boley and had sung opera in Missouri.

According to Zenobia Perry, when Nathaniel Dett came to Boley, at Mayme Jones's invitation, he stayed in the Powells' home. Over the years, he became a very good friend of Zenobia's father.[224] Often Dett came alone, but a couple of times he brought his wife and two daughters.[225] Perry learned to play Dett's piano music from Mrs. Jones[226] and when he visited, he coached her. Thus, she knew from a very young age that there were black composers who were taken seriously and had been published.

> I had accompanied the high school chorus and served as first chair in the violin section of the orchestra. At almost every special assembly program I was programmed to play a piano solo. My repertoire contained popular classics that showed my "clean performance" of fast difficult passages, e.g., *Harmonious Blacksmith* by Handel; *Solfeggietto* by C. P. E. Bach; *Prelude in C Minor* by J. S. Bach; *Rondo Capriccioso* by Mendelssohn; and *Menuet in G* by Paderewski. Three black concert pianists came to Boley in my high school days: James Reese, R. Nathaniel Dett, and Blind Boone. Blind Boone had the reputation of immediately duplicating the performance of any pianist he heard.[227] My teacher asked me to play [Ignacy Jan] Paderewski's *Menuet* for the blind man. After my performance he sat down and played the piece exactly as I had done. The feat upset me emotionally and I cried.[228]

At the school there was always some kind of opera or operetta production under way, which Zenobia always accompanied. Once they practiced so late that her mother went to the school with a lantern and a blanket to make a point with the teacher. After that, all the practices were over before dark.[229]

Regarding popular black music, Perry recalled, "We knew about jazz and blues, but my mother, of course, did not accept this. My father did, but she didn't. So we knew about it, so often when she would go to church and we'd come back before she would get dinner ready, we'd go off on jazz and she'd say, 'That's enough of that now. When dinnertime comes, you've got to play real music.' She didn't call that real music."[230]

The Powell family had a radio at home, but never played it until her father came home; they often listened to radio dramas together. Her mother was enthralled with *Tales of Hoffman* by Jacques Offenbach. "She thought it was so weird and so beautiful that a woman would sing herself to death. We always listened to *Tales of Hoffman* whenever it came over the radio."[231] They also had a Victor record player, with a cone-shaped horn, and all kinds of records, including music, plays, and opera.[232]

This was the rich musical environment found in Boley, Oklahoma, and in the Powell home that stimulated Zenobia's imagination and gave her a foundation in musicianship. After finishing high school, she stayed home to help her family, while working part-time for a barber. She continued to practice the piano and have occasional lessons. She wanted to study music more seriously, but her father objected. "My father often said, 'I wouldn't give you a red dime to go anywhere to study music.'"[233] He sent her to nursing school, but she dropped out due to ill health and returned to Boley, adamant in her desire to study music.

The Cecil Berryman Conservatory, Omaha

Zenobia's mother knew how miserable she was for not continuing her music education, so in 1929 Birdie Powell sent her daughter to live with her brother Frank and his family in Omaha. Frank was a musician at a theater there,[234] and he introduced Zenobia to the Berrymans. She attended their music school, earning a certificate for piano performance. The following spring, she played the Grieg piano concerto with orchestra, under the direction of Cecil Berryman.

About that performance, Zenobia recalled:

> It was so funny. I remember that the piano was such that he was standing up higher. But instead of standing there, when it was time for me to start, he came around and peeked down and all the audience laughed because he was looking to see if I was at the piano because I was so small.[235]

Cecil Wells Berryman was born in Central City, Nebraska, in 1888. He studied piano, composition, and theory with Wager Swayne and Emile Schwartz at the Paris Conservatory. He concertized in Europe and in the Eastern and Midwestern United States and wrote articles for *Etude* and *Musical Observer*. He also composed works for piano, a concerto, a violin sonata, and songs. For several years, he headed the department of piano and theory at the University at Omaha.

MENTORS, ALLIES, AND SUPPORTERS

His wife, Alice Virginia Berryman, was born in 1889 in North Platte, Nebraska, and also studied in Paris with Swayne and with Rudolph Ganz. She made her New York début in 1915 at the Princess Theatre, and also concertized extensively. At one time, she was head of the piano normal training department of the University Conservatory of Omaha. They married in 1916 and had three children. They set up their own piano studio, called the Cecil Berryman Studio and later the Cecil Berryman Conservatoire.[236]

Mr. and Mrs. Cecil W. Berryman, April 11, 1930.
Courtesy of Omaha Public Library.

From Omaha, Zenobia returned to Boley to work in a barbershop. She also played in a local church and assisted teachers at the elementary school. Dett had visited Boley that year and encouraged her parents to send her to Hampton Institute, where he had held a faculty position since 1913. Because he had two daughters, Josephine and Helen, Zenobia's mother felt that he could be trusted to look after young Zenobia. It is clear that throughout her life, Zenobia Perry's mother was the chief supporter of her desire to study music. So, finally, plans were made for Zenobia to go east to study music with Nathaniel Dett.

These stories about Zenobia Perry's efforts to study music reveal a young woman who knew her own mind and heart. She was fortunate to find some local teachers who could get her started, and fortunate to have had her mother's support. Her father's opposition continued to be a hindrance in fulfilling her dream, but she was determined to find a way. These mentors, allies, and supporters—so critical to her musical development—helped her formulate an image of the artist she would like to become.

Before examining Perry's musical mentors, it may be instructive to consider her education as a child in Boley, Oklahoma. The values of that community, inspired by Booker T. Washington, among others, gave her the firm foundations in academics and in life skills that were to serve her so well.

Education for "Lives of Creative Makeshift and Improvisation"

In *Composing a Life*, Mary Catherine Bateson points out that "the recognition that many people lead lives of creative makeshift and improvisation surely has implications for how the next generation is educated and what we tell our sons and daughters."[237] Given the instability experienced by most black Americans of Zenobia's parents' generation, there was a clear understanding in the family and within the community about what children needed to know to prepare them for "lives of creative makeshift and improvisation."

Bateson elaborates, "Ancient walls covered with ivy [found in colleges and universities] are more lovely than tents and trailers, but we need to teach the skills for coming into a new place and quickly making it into a home. When we speak to our children about our own lives, we tend to reshape our pasts to given them an illusory look of purpose. But our children are unlikely to be able to define their goals and then live happily every after. Instead, they will need to reinvent themselves again and again in response to a changing environment."[238] Black parents at the beginning of the twentieth century understood this clearly and endeavored to provide such training and education. Zenobia's own background illustrates this.

These parents made sure that their children learned a wide variety of skills; any class deemed "uplifting" would attract one or more of the Powell children. A family friend tutored them in mathematics, reading, nature study, and needlecraft. She also taught crochet, tatting, and embroidery. Both daughters learned to design and sew clothes, including tailoring of men's suits, skills that served them throughout their lives. They learned quilting from grandmother Luticia Thompson; their mother often quilted "mostly for the company of the other women."[239]

Life in Oklahoma at the beginning of the twentieth century was hard for most people. Many families in Oklahoma did not have houses, but lived in dugouts, often with a wooden door and a window in front, but the rest constructed of clay.[240] As the family of a doctor, the Powells enjoyed a higher quality of life than most in Boley. The Powell children were made well aware of the additional comforts they enjoyed as a middle-class family and saw for themselves the conditions under which others not so fortunate lived. Zenobia's parents had a strong sense of pride and wanted the children always to look nice and to be clean and neat in appearance.[241] Birdie Powell had household help;[242] however, she taught her children how to do all the household chores. These basic life skills not only served Perry throughout her life, but paved the way for her to become an outstanding educator.

Because the Boley community had a serious commitment to a well-rounded education for its students, from its earliest days the schools in Boley were the town's major selling point. Local newspapers published photographs of teachers and administrators, with detailed biographies that focused on their educational training.

According to Henrietta Hicks, president of the recently established Boley Museum, the Boley Public School System began in 1904 when Miss M. T. Duke was brought there to teach. The next year, U. S. White became principal and a "two-room box house was built at a cost of $200.00." The principal was paid $40 per month and the teacher $35. By the second year, there were 127 children enrolled. A new school building was built in 1909, at the cost of $15,000. By 1914, the four-year high school had been accredited and had eleven teachers and 429 students; by 1921, there were thirteen teachers and 539 students. The new high school, built in 1926, is still used as the city's high school. A Works Progress Administration grant in 1936 allowed Boley to add a Vocational Agriculture Building to the campus and another WPA grant in 1940 for $17,000 covered the costs of adding the Athletic Stadium.[243]

Zenobia Perry learned French from her neighbors, "The O'Dorseys, who spoke French as well as English. In playing with their children I learned to speak French. And when the time came for a second language

CHAPTER 6

in high school, I took French." Of her primary school days, she said,

> In the next block facing the O'Dorseys was Boley's school, housed in two structures. The primary school (grades primer through third grade) was housed in a large rambling frame structure all on one floor. Grades four through twelve were housed in a large two-story red brick building. Each teacher in the primary school was responsible for all activities of the grade to which she was assigned. There were no male teachers assigned to primary grades. On special occasions the principal, who was always male, visited the primary grades but most often the primary grades were marched into the second story auditorium of the red brick building with the rest of the school for assemblies, special programs, and commencement activities.[244]

Many guests visiting Boley stayed in the Powells' large comfortable home, but the family also opened up their home to local children on "snow days." She remembered:

> Since our house was near the school, families living in surrounding rural areas often arranged for their children to stay at the Powell residence during inclement weather until they could be picked up by their parents. Some winters were very stormy. We enjoyed having the many visitors but I am sure that extra children made heavy responsibilities for Mamma. Emergency rations of canned goods stored at school in the domestic science pantry by the PTA furnished some food items in prolonged storm periods. While dinner was being prepared children were required to study their lessons. After dinner those who had not been rescued gathered around the piano and sang songs we learned in school and Sunday School. Often a neighbor, Mrs. Alice Barron, was called to our house to help. Children who spent the night were in bed no later than nine o'clock.[245]

Perry also remembered, "We had one big church in the town and the various denominations would take turns having their services." The Catholics had services early in the morning, after which they would remove all their statuettes for the next service. Her family attended Episcopal services, because her father considered himself a member of the Church of England, in communion with the Archbishop of Canterbury.[246]

In 1940, Velma Dolphin-Ashley offered the following description of Boley's religious life:

> Boley's religious life is interesting and baffling. For almost two years from 1904 to 1906 the citizenry worshipped together. Methodists, Baptists, Christian Scientists and all other religious sects were represented in the town at that time. Into the community a group of "closed communion" Baptists filtered, advancing the idea that it was a sin for the Baptists to worship with the other sects. So the Baptist Church was begun. It was called Antioch Missionary Baptist Church. Before many years passed there was a split in the church

over the discharging of a minister. Those displeased set up a Second Baptist Church in Boley.

There are three Methodist churches in town that have been there since 1907: The Congregational Methodist Episcopal, the African Methodist Episcopal and the traditional Methodist Episcopal.

The C.M.E. Church has the largest church building in town while the Antioch Baptists have the most permanent structure and the largest congregation in town.... In 1918 the Saints Church was built.... In 1919 The Church of God in Christ was organized.... The [Catholic] church was built in 1915....

Religious differences have not caused any outstanding civic or social strife in Boley. The school board was accused once of hiring teachers who were Baptist or influencing them to become Baptists after they were hired, but this accusation was without accurate foundation. The city officials have belonged to practically every church in town.... The people in Boley accept leadership regardless of church denomination.[247]

Zenobia Perry said her family was a member of the Antioch Missionary Baptist Church,[248] which, according to Dolphin-Ashley, was not built until 1927.[249]

Perry told a story of going to the local Catholic church to hear the organ, in the hopes that she could have piano lessons from the organist:

One of the Sisters was Lowena Davis and she played the organ. I went over to see if she would let me hear her play the organ. I went over there and I said, "Sister Lowena, do you love potatoes?" She said, "Yes." I said, "Well, if I bring you some potatoes would you let me listen to you play the organ?" She said, "You don't have to bring me potatoes. Just come on in and listen." I got my mother to let me go over there and listen. After awhile I got to the place where she would show me how you play the keyboard. Finally she came up and told my father, "You know, Zenobia is ready for her first communion," and that's when my father said, "No, she's not going to be a Catholic. I'll get her a piano and she can practice at home from now on." And that's how I got to have a piano.[250]

Mamma was very active in the Parent Teachers Association of Boley's school system, the Women's Federated Arts and Reading Club, and the Spring Rose Chapter of the Order of Eastern Star. Also Mamma and an older staunch member of the church organized the Children's Star Light Band of Antioch Baptist Church. In later years the Band was chaperoned by Mamma and another mother of children belonging to the Antioch Baptist Church. Often the group included playmates of the Powell children and Sunday school attendants from other churches.[251]

Perry remembered, as well, that "whenever we went out to play, she'd come too. She was always the pitcher when we played ball."[252] Dr. Powell often told his partner, Dr. Young, "You see, I have five children."[253] Her father worked all day, every day, without stop. "Once in awhile, she'd say, 'You know, when you get married don't marry someone older than you, like your daddy is to me. Why? Because you'll always be trying to live up to his expectations and won't pay too much attention to what you want yourself.' She said, 'If I had it to do over I wouldn't have done it quite the same way.'"[254]

It is clear that there was much formality in the household. According to Perry, "I'll never forget when my mother was ill and my father wouldn't go into the kitchen unless he had on his apron and cap." Janis-Rozena Peri also remembered that her grandmother always referred to her husband as "Dr. Powell," even years after his death.[255]

> Often my father would take us [by train] to St. Louis. He wanted us to hear the legitimate stage and to hear some Shakespeare. We were not exposed to Shakespeare in our little town. We would read some Shakespeare, but that is nothing like the actual stage production. So he'd get tickets once a year we'd . . . hear a Shakespearean play and some other type of drama and possibly an opera. We came to Cincinnati once to see the opera and we were very elated that here they were having opera in a zoo. Half the time when the artists were singing, and they were making a certain type of note, one of the animals would answer. We thought that was so funny.[256]

The combination of the Boley community's excellent schools and the Powell family's cultural enrichment provided an environment conducive to the intellectual, academic, and cultural development of its young people. This solid foundation served Zenobia Powell Perry throughout her life and offered a model for her own teaching and institution building.

7. Dett, Reece, and Dawson
Role Models for Careers in Black Music

Mary Catherine Bateson emphasizes a need in education for multiple role models, not a single role model, "so that it is possible to weave something new from many different threads."[257] As an adult, Zenobia Powell Perry had five significant musical mentors: R. Nathaniel Dett (1882–1943), Cortez Donald Reece (1910–1974), William Dawson (1899–1990), Allan Willman (1909–1989), and Darius Milhaud (1892–1974). From them, she learned a wide variety of musical skills, from composing and arranging to conducting and piano pedagogy; more importantly, however, she learned first-hand how to build a successful career in music. Each offered "different threads to weave something new" in her own life. She worked with Dett, Reece, and Dawson in the 1930s; Willman and Milhaud in the 1940s and '50s. All five men were composers and arrangers; Dett and Dawson were choral conductors. Dett, Reece, and Dawson were black; Willman and Milhaud were white and Jewish. This chapter focuses on the three black men who mentored Zenobia Perry in the 1930s and '40s; chapter 10 focuses on Allan Willman, Darius Milhaud, and Perry's studies at the University of Wyoming and the Aspen Music Festival and School, in the next decades.

CHAPTER 7

R. Nathaniel Dett

R. Nathaniel Dett, c.1928,
from a Hampton Institute concert program.

In the fall of 1931, Zenobia Perry went alone by train to Hampton, Virginia, to study with R. Nathaniel Dett, with hopes of enrolling as a full-time college student at the Hampton Institute.[258] Hampton Institute was a popular choice for many blacks seeking higher education and job training, particularly in the 1920s and '30s. It is possible that Zenobia Perry's father still hoped that she would prepare for a medical career there.

With Jim Crow laws demanding separate train cars for non-whites, Perry recalls the friendly, cordial black porters who looked out for her on the journey. She wondered if her father had had a special word with them. Black composer William Grant Still described train transportation for blacks in those days, from his experiences touring the country with W. C. Handy's orchestra: "Our traveling was done in Jim Crow cars, which were usually only half cars. They offered very little that was comfortable or desirable: cinders, smoke, unpleasant odors, and the feeling of humiliation."[259] Non-whites could always be moved from their train seats to make room for whites.[260]

When Perry arrived at Hampton Institute, she tried to enroll, "but Mrs. Quick [Dean at Hampton] told my father that I wasn't ready for Hampton," and suggested that she enroll in the Preparatory Division. Mrs. Quick told her, "My dear child, you should be home on your mother's knee."[261] Soon after her arrival, she learned that Dett was leaving Hampton for Rochester, to complete his master's degree at the Eastman School of Music. She took the money her father had deposited at Hampton for her return ticket to Oklahoma and used it to go to Rochester. Once she was settled in Rochester, she telegraphed her father to ask him to continue his financial assistance and support.[262] She had witnessed some mistreatment of Dett at Hampton and decided she would not go to school there.[263] She was horrified to see some students pour buckets of water on Dett's head from a second-story window as he walked by the building. Although it was a black college, Hampton had a predominantly white faculty; she was aware of the tension there.[264]

In Rochester, Zenobia encountered even more complications, because it was in the middle of Eastman's semester (around Thanksgiving) and too late to enroll. She could not stay in the dormitories. Dett was only a graduate student, with limited clout. He made arrangements for her to stay with Mrs. Brockman,[265] who was the wife of the postmaster and who thought that Perry was a very gifted child. Given her small size, many assumed that she was younger than she actually was: at times this worked to her advantage. Perry remembered one friend named "Bailey" from Kansas, who played trombone. "She and I would have lots of fun. She didn't stay at the dormitory either. We'd always have lunch together and we'd practice."[266]

The fact that Perry followed Dett to Rochester without consulting her parents reveals how determined she was to continue her music education. She would not risk her father's reprimand and she could not bear the embarrassment of once again "failing," like she had at nursing school. She did not want to go back home to her parents. She needed a musical mentor and Dett was available to play this role in her life. She often mentioned how similar Dett was to her own father in appearance and how she found it reassuring that Dett knew her father and mother. "I don't know how they got to be friends," she said. "They were both about the same size and they kept you laughing the whole time."[267]

Zenobia Perry felt comfortable with Dett. He was aware of her father's opposition to her career choice, yet he encouraged her musicianship just the same. Perry said, "I was a messed-up kid at that time. When this woman [at Hampton] told me I should be home on my mother's knee and I thought I was a college student—well, that really floored me. It really upset me. Dett was going to Eastman, so I went to Eastman. I thought he was wonderful because he knew my father."[268]

R. Nathaniel Dett was born in Drummondsville, Ontario, on October 11, 1882, and died at Battle Creek, Michigan on October 2, 1943. In 1908, he became the first black to receive a Bachelor of Music degree from the Oberlin Conservatory. He continued his studies at Columbia University, the University of Pennsylvania, the American Conservatory in Chicago, Harvard University (where he studied with Arthur Foote), and in France with Nadia Boulanger.[269] He published his first composition in 1900, while still a teenager. He developed the Hampton Institute Choir, which toured the United States and Europe and was heard on national radio broadcast, into one of the finest college choirs in the country. In 1919, he helped to found the National Association of Negro Musicians (NANM), for which he served as President from 1924 to 1926. His more than one hundred compositions include works for orchestra and chorus, including three oratorios; suites for piano; motets and part songs; and arrangements of spirituals. Publicly, he spoke often of the importance of black folk music.[270]

To be sure, these were difficult times for Dett. After teaching at Hampton Institute for nearly two decades (from 1913 until 1931), and having just returned from a triumphant tour of Europe with the Hampton Institute Choir,[271] he was in some kind of trouble with the Institute's administration. According to his biographer, Anne Key Simpson, the president of Hampton had asked for Dett's resignation in July 1931, which humiliated and angered Dett. There was a meeting of the NANM at Hampton, August 22–26, 1931, during which the Hampton Choir sang "I'll Never Turn Back No More," Dett's daughter Josephine played Louis Brandt's *Tarantella* for piano, and other students performed works of Dett's. The timing of this thirteenth annual meeting ironically was just as Dett was encountering problems at Hampton. He was given a leave of absence with pay for the school year 1931–32, which enabled him to spend a year at Eastman. Mrs. Dett and their daughters remained at Hampton during that year.[272]

Dett enrolled in Eastman School of Music in Rochester and received his master's degree in music in 1932.[273] His master's thesis was a large piece entitled, *The Ordering of Moses*, for chorus and orchestra. For a few weeks in the fall of 1931, he was at the Normal School of North Carolina, due to a commitment he had made before his difficulties at Hampton.[274]

With a large black community, Rochester, New York, was generally a good place for black Americans to live. It had been one of the principal places of the Underground Railroad in the nineteenth century and many white families there took immense pride in the fact that their families had helped runaway slaves, many of whom settled in Rochester or moved on to Canada. The Eastman School of Music not only had black students, but also demonstrated a strong interest in black American music. The charismatic director of Eastman, Howard Hanson, whose tenure began in 1924, was a strong champion of American music and American composers and particularly interested in black and Native American music. Dett studied modern harmony with Hanson.[275]

Dett recognized that Perry needed basic music training, so he arranged for her to study theory with Mr. Johnson and with Bert Mathis, in addition to private piano lessons with him.[276] Perry remembered that "Mr. Johnson didn't believe that I could do anything. He was always telling me, 'I'm not going to put your name on the roll until you do this and that.' Then I'd have to pass a certain thing before he would put me on the roll." When asked if this was because of her age and gender or because of her race, she replied, "It could have been both. I finally convinced him when I was playing piano. I played 'The Place Where the Rainbow Ends' of R. Nathaniel Dett and I played it on a program there.[277] And Mr. Johnson said, 'Well, you can play piano, can't you?'" She did remember clearly that he was white and from the South.[278]

Perry's vivid memories of her studies with Dett provide an interesting picture of this important American musician and composer:

> He had a studio at the conservatory that had a place where they grow a lot of plants—an atrium. He used to go around watering the flowers while I was taking my lesson. There was a fireplace on either end of the room. This was a part of the school. I could never figure out how he knew. I could play a piece and he could tell me exactly which finger I was playing with and he'd be around there watering the plants. "Zenobia Powell, you didn't play that with your third finger. You played that with your fifth finger." He knew.[279]

Apparently, she studied his piano music with him, as well. She particularly liked his piece "Morning." "It sounds almost like a waterfall and it was the first one I ever saw which had four staves for two hands and that happens for six or seven pages. He was married and had two daughters. Josephine was the most musical and Helen was more like him in business. His wife played piano very well. They would always race when he wrote a piece to see who would play it first, whether she would play it first or he would play it first."[280]

At Eastman, Dett studied piano and composition with Max Landow, orchestration with Bernard Rogers (1893–1968), counterpoint with

CHAPTER 7

Edward Royce (1886–1963), and modern harmony with Howard Hanson. Rogers, who had a Guggenheim Fellowship in the 1920s, also studied with Boulanger in Paris.[281] Dett's stay at Eastman was extended through part of 1933. Reluctant to surrender his Hampton position that he had held for nineteen years, he did so in 1932. Afterward, his wife and daughters moved to Rochester and he continued teaching at his private studio at 154 East Avenue, Room 309 of the Davis Building.[282] It seems, however, that Dett was moving toward being a full-time composer and away from college teaching.[283]

According to Zenobia Perry,

> Nathaniel Dett was a very dynamic conductor. He went about his work with all the enthusiasm one could probably muster, and he took everybody along with him. I remember once that he was going to go to be in the Sesquicentennial to direct the chorus. I didn't realize it until we got there that there were seven hundred in the chorus and he was standing on top of a big drum. I have never seen anything like it. He just seemed to be able to enthuse people to do things. "Come on now, you can sing that bass!" And he was a little man—not much taller than I am! His friends called him "Nat" because he was so small.[284]

She credited Dett with inspiring her to consider composition:

> If I had not had Dett as a teacher, I don't think I ever would have been a composer. I was practicing on a Beethoven sonata and out of something to do, I changed the rhythm of it. I substituted something for the bass. He came in and says, "What are you doing?" And I said, "I'm practicing." And he says, "That wasn't Beethoven, was it?" And I said, "Yes." He said, "Well, you don't do another person's music like that. If you don't like what he wrote, why don't you write your own?" Well, I had never thought about that. I just stopped doing that. So the next time I went to my piano lesson, he said, "What have you written down?" I said, "Nothing." He said, "When you come next week, you have to write something down. If you don't, don't come." That scared me and that's how I got started.[285]

Aware of the conflicts Perry had with her father, Dett used to say to her, "You have to decide what you want; not what others want from and for you, but what you want. They only know one side of you, but you know the other. You decide." This was crucial support for Zenobia Perry, at this time in her life, because of her father's continued opposition to her pursuit of a professional career in music.[286] She knew that Dett was under pressure during those years, particularly related to his position as Hampton. Given that he had a large following and support outside of the Institute, she felt the true reason for his difficulties was professional jealousy on the part of his less talented and less well-known Hampton colleagues.[287]

R. Nathaniel Dett was a tremendous influence on Zenobia Perry. One way this is exhibited is in her life-long pursuit of education. Even after having received an honorary doctorate from Howard University in 1924 and from Oberlin College in 1926, Dett went to Eastman to complete a master's degree in composition (1932). Prior to that, he had studied at eight different universities and music conservatories. Zenobia knew him all those years, while he pursued his professional career and continued to study. She witnessed first-hand his commitment, perseverance, and hard work, even in the face of opposition. She pursued higher education throughout her life, while working professionally in music. Dett won awards and prizes for his composition and literary writings. Perry also wrote beautifully, both prose and poetry.

Zenobia Perry spent two semesters in Rochester. After Easter 1932, her mother called her to come home to play for a program, planned for May 29. School was not out until later in May, but her mother insisted that she come home immediately. So Zenobia took her exams early and went home. She was not able to return to Rochester in the fall. She believed her mother still thought she was too young to be out in the world and was worried, particularly given the racial strife in Oklahoma.[288]

About her stay in Rochester, Perry has written,

> Racism aside, I absorbed more nuances of white American culture during the months spent at Eastman than all of my previous years of existence. These cultural criteria added to my sense of respect for individual worth and incidental intellect. At this point in my life I keenly felt the distinction between white and black American life. However, the best of both was and is exhibited in art, dance and music. I also became aware that music courses taught in all schools in America were western Euro-centric in content. Composers most revered were German and the mathematical efficacy was more apparent than tunefulness to my young ears. Franz Schubert was the composer whose works I really liked and he was Austrian.[289]

Under Dett's tutelage, Perry made steady improvement in her piano technique and had made a start in music theory, but once again her music training was interrupted. The stock market crash of 1929 had plunged the country into the Great Depression, which would last until the outbreak of World War II in 1941. Like so many others, her parents were having difficulties in Oklahoma.

Her brief period of study with Nathaniel Dett changed Perry's life forever,[290] convincing her that she could be a serious musician. Dett provided a substantial role model, with his dynamic career as a pianist, composer, arranger, conductor, and advocate for black American music.

Zenobia would develop all these aspects of a professional career in her own life. Even though she was unable to continue her studies in music immediately, Dett's encouragement sustained her for years to come. A professional life in music, however, would not become a reality for her until the late 1940s.

Cortez Donald Reece, Langston University

Zenobia Powell studied for two semesters at Langston University in Oklahoma, before going to Tuskegee Institute in 1935. There she met Cortez Donald Reece, a recent graduate of Fisk University, who was a visiting professor and two years younger. A violinist, he was so tall that he often stood to play the piano.[291] Zenobia remembered that, at the time, she thought Cortez was from a "questionable" family. His mother lived in New Mexico; he was part Mexican and had gone to school in New Mexico and Arizona.

Because Reece was her music theory teacher, she played for him some of her piano pieces for children. He encouraged her to write more; he said there was a market for such teaching pieces and he knew other women had been successful in that area. This support was especially meaningful then, because she was pregnant with her first child and her marriage was dissolving. Her lessons with Reece helped solidify her conviction to seek additional training in music and to concentrate on composing. Although she had several difficult years following her studies with him, his words of support sustained her, and helped her hold on to her dream.

Cortez Donald Reece was born in 1910, in Guthrie, Oklahoma, and died July 30, 1974, in Los Angeles. He received his A.B. from Fisk University and his M.A. and Ph.D. from the University of Southern California. His 1953 Ph.D. dissertation on the music of West Virginia[292]—at more than one thousand pages—was the longest in the department's history. After teaching at Langston University,[293] he became chair of the Music Department and Division of Humanities at Bluefield State College, West Virginia.[294]

DETT, REECE, AND DAWSON

William L. Dawson and Tuskegee Institute

"William L. Dawson and Zenobia Powell Perry Embrace at Columbus, Ohio Concert," *from an unidentified newspaper.*

In 1935, Zenobia Powell went to Tuskegee Institute.[295] When she enrolled, the Registrar gave her the middle name "Jean," a practice at Tuskegee for students who enrolled with only a first and last name. Tuskegee Institute is a private, independent co-educational college. Founded in the one-room log cabin tradition, and originally called the Tuskegee Normal School for the Education of Colored Teachers, Booker T. Washington emphasized practical knowledge and job skills. Robert Russa Moton, formerly of the Hampton Institute, was president from 1915 to 1935, followed by Frederick D. Patterson, from 1935 until 1953.

Many distinguished teachers served on the Tuskegee faculty, among them Dr. George Washington Carver, whom Zenobia Perry remembered:

> Dr. Carver scared me the first day I was on campus at Tuskegee. I was going up Tomkin Hall. Now Tomkin Hall is built like the capital building in Washington,

D.C., and you go up these huge steps to get to the dining hall. I started up these huge steps, up one flight and started up the second, and this voice said, "Little girl! Little girl! Better go get your coat." I looked around and I didn't see a soul. I started up the steps. "Better go get your coat." That scared me.... I found this little man holding a net of some kind. He was catching some kind of bug. He had on a shirt that hadn't been ironed, [although] it was clean.... Same thing for his trousers and a cap with the bill broken. And I said, "Why would you ask me to go get my coat?" He says, "It's going to rain."...

He was a small man and he had a very high-pitched voice. Something had happened to him in his early childhood to make his voice like that.... To sit through one of his lectures you had to really listen intently to know what he was saying. He was quite a man.[296]

After World War I, many black American composers began to make inroads, including: Will Marion Cook (1869–1944), Clarence Cameron White (1880–1960), R. Nathaniel Dett, J. Rosamond Johnson (1873–1954), Harry Lawrence Freeman (1869–1954), William Grant Still, Florence B. Price, Edward H. Boatner (1898–1981), John Wesley Work, Jr. (1872–1925), and William Levi Dawson (1899–1990).

William Dawson, a native of Anniston, Alabama, ran away from home at the age of thirteen, to attend Tuskegee Institute, graduating in 1921. He played in the band and orchestra, was music librarian, and traveled with the Institute Singers for five years.[297] He continued his studies at Washburn College in Topeka, Kansas, then at the Horner Institute for Fine Arts in Kansas City, where he graduated with honors in composition after studies with the Danish-American composer and conductor Carl Busch. Dawson received his Bachelor of Music degree in 1925. He played trombone with the Chicago Civic Orchestra, while studying at the Chicago Musical College and the American Conservatory of Music, from which he received a master's degree in 1927. While in Chicago, he began composing his *Negro Folk Symphony*, which would be premiered by the Philadelphia Orchestra in 1934. Along with Florence Price and William Grant Still, Dawson was among the first African-American symphonists. By the early 1930s, he was internationally known as a composer and arranger of spirituals.

During Robert Russa Moton's tenure as Tuskegee's president, the School of Music was established in 1931 with Dawson as director, to coincide with the Institute's fiftieth anniversary celebration. Dawson established a four-year curriculum leading to a music degree, offering students a choice between a Bachelor of Music degree in performance or music composition and a Bachelor of Public School Music, concentrating on the General Supervisors Course or the Instrumental Supervisors Course. The degree in public school music was the most popular; only one student graduated from Tuskegee with a B.M. degree. The Institute offered opportunities to perform with the following ensembles: the Institute Choir, Senior Orchestra, Junior Orchestra, Institute Band, Girls' Glee Club, and Men's Glee Club. These ensembles performed for a variety of on-campus and off-campus functions, including evening dinners in the dining hall, chapel services, Founder's Day, commencement, graduation, special concerts, and tours. Because of a lack of financial support, the Music School folded in 1940, although the Institute continued to award diplomas in music to students who had earned Bachelor of Science degrees in other fields.[298]

Having been a student at Tuskegee at the end of Booker T. Washington's life and tenure as president, Dawson often quoted Washington as having said, "Every one of my students must know and sing the 'plantation melodies.'" Dawson's choir performed these songs during the Sunday morning and evening chapel services on the Tuskegee campus, as well as on tours throughout the Southeast and the Northeast, and on radio broadcasts for ABC, CBS, and NBC. The most famous broadcast—which put Tuskegee on the national map—was the choir's appearance at the opening of Radio City Music Hall in New York City, in 1932. The choir made subsequent trips to New York in 1946 and 1949, when they appeared on *The Edgar Bergen/Charlie McCarthy Show*.

In 1955, they made their final trip to New York, appearing on the television show *Frontiers of Faith*, and presenting a concert at the Metropolitan Opera House for the United Negro College Fund's Convocation Week. They also made a recording of Negro spirituals for the Westminster Record Company.

Among the prominent black musicians Dawson recruited to teach in the School of Music were pianists Hazel Harrison (1883–1969) and Lorenza Jordan Cole (1897–1994); sopranos Abbie Mitchell (1884–1960) and Florence Cole Talbert (1890–1961); and organist Orrin Suthern. Captain Frank L. Drye was the bandmaster and Andrew F. Rosmond[299] was the orchestra director. Abbie Mitchell began her career in musical comedy in 1898, singing in Will Marion Cook's *Clorindy*. She sang with Black Patti's Troubadours, the Walker and William companies, the Memphis Students, and Cook's Southern Syncopated Orchestra. She taught at Tuskegee from 1932 to 1934 and appeared as "Clara" in *Porgy and Bess* in 1935. Florence Cole Talbert made her New York début in 1918. She was a graduate of Chicago Musical College and toured throughout the United States and Europe in the 1920s.[300]

CHAPTER 7

Dawson's impact on students went well beyond their music education. The personal and professional discipline and perspective on life that he taught served them well throughout their careers in other fields. A stern taskmaster, he demanded the undivided attention of his students. For example, they could be dropped from the choir for daring to show up late for rehearsal.[301]

Under Dawson's leadership, the Tuskegee Institute Chorus became one of the finest college choirs in the country, particularly since Dett was no longer at the Hampton Institute. Dawson won awards for his choral works and arrangements of spirituals, including three Wanamaker Awards in 1930 and 1931. His Tuskegee Choir gave concerts throughout the United States and Europe until his retirement in 1955, generating a continuous flow of publicity about the Institute. There are several recordings of his choir. His *Negro Folk Symphony* was recorded by Stokowski and the American Symphony Orchestra, in a revised form which Dawson made after returning from a trip to West Africa in 1952. In addition, he also recorded *Out in the Fields*, and many other arrangements of spirituals. He was published by Kjos, Shawnee, and Warner.[302]

Zenobia accompanied the choir, playing piano solos every time the singers went off-stage to change costumes. Because Dawson loved Chopin, she often played Chopin during intermissions. She wrote:

> Being interested in all musical activities on campus, the choir held a special attraction as most of my school connections had been with choirs. I never thought of myself as a singer, nevertheless I passed the audition and joined the Tuskegee Institute Choir as a singer under the direction of the widely acclaimed William L. Dawson. Under his guidance the choir sang numerous concerts during Christmas holidays for many years at Radio City, New York City. On campus at times I accompanied the choir's rehearsals. All concerts were sung *a cappella* but frequently at intermissions for the program "Wagonwheels," broadcast from a radio station on Peachtree Street in Atlanta, Georgia, I was scheduled to play a piano solo.[303]

Perry described Dawson's style: "Mr. Dawson was very exacting but very cordial. He was a slender, tall man. And he wouldn't take anything at all that was wrong from the choir. If he saw that you were not listening, he'd say, 'While I'm directing, you look at me. I'm directing and I'll tell you what to do.' And sometimes people would look away and he'd throw his baton at them. And they wouldn't do that anymore."[304] She recalled that he "never just had one baton up there."[305] Having known many people who had sung these spirituals when they were children in the nineteenth century, "he used to tell us, 'There is no such word as I [pronounced "eye"] in a Negro Spiritual. It is 'Ahh': 'Ahh' went to so and so, 'Ahh' did so and so.'"[306]

Most members of the choir were not music majors, but were recruited from the general student body; a few later developed professional careers. The repertoire of the choir greatly influenced choral singing throughout the United States. Commenting on Dawson's national impact, Zenobia Perry said, "Most of the spirituals that all the choirs sang until about 1975 were by William L. Dawson of Tuskegee."[307]

Altogether Dawson arranged twenty-three Negro folk songs over a sixty-year period, from 1925 to 1967. The list includes "Ain't That Good News," "Behold The Star," "Ev'ry Time I Feel the Spirit," "Ezekiel Saw de Wheel," "Feed-a My Sheep," "Hail Mary," "I Couldn't Hear Nobody Pray," "I Wan' To Be Ready," "In His Care-o," "Jesus Walked This Lonesome Valley," "Lit'l Boy Child," "Mary Had A Baby," "My Lord What A Morning," "Oh, What a Beautiful City," "Soon Ah Will Be Done," "Steal Away," "Swing Low, Sweet Chariot," "Talk About A Child," "There's a Lit'l Wheel A-Turnin'," "There Is a Balm in Gilead," "You Got To Reap Just What You Sow," and "Zion's Walls."[308]

In the Institute's 1938 yearbook, the Tuskegee Choir was described as follows:

> Distinctive from the mission of any other campus organization is the mission of the choir. One cannot say that the choir has not claimed a favorable degree of attention, especially during this year. Under the able guidance of Mr. W. L. Dawson, the choir is in all possible ways improving the voices of its members and building an appreciation for good vocal music. Acting as a representative body of the Institute, this organization has enjoyed unusual success in its broadcasts with the National Broadcasting Company [NBC] and concert appearances, in the creation of a friendly and cooperative relationship between the world and the school. The school is greatly appreciative of the associations the choir has made possible. This organization is composed of three divisions: the Women's Glee Club, the Male Chorus and the Tuskegee Quintet. With the efficient aid of the choir's president, Earl Williams, each does its work in a manner which is hard to surpass. With a vision and a salvation for human life the choir is more than an interesting organization.[309]

Admitted to Tuskegee as a freshman in 1935, Perry finished in three years, taking courses day and night, sometimes as many as twenty-one units a semester. She described her schedule there:

> As a work student I was told by my advisor [Mr. Davis] that I was taking too many hours and if I earned only a "C" in any course I would be required to drop half of my class load. So my name was always on the honor roll. My daily schedule was so tight that there was no time for any unrequired [sic] activity any day of the week. I wanted to graduate as soon as possible in order to be home when Lemuel begins his formal schooling. Because I wrote for

CHAPTER 7

the *Campus Digest*—one of Tuskegee's two journals—I was allowed to have a key to the research entrance of the library. Piano practice at 7:00 a.m. began my day except on Sundays. Saturday from 8:30 to 11:00 am was scheduled for editing, arranging, or writing for the campus journals. Visitors especially enjoyed the Sunday morning parades to chapel by the uniformed student body.[310]

Also on the faculty of Tuskegee was world-renowned black American pianist Hazel Harrison (1883–1969), who had inspired Perry more than two decades earlier. She wrote:

> My most pleasurable teacher assignment was piano with Hazel Harrison. However, in a few weeks she left to head the piano division at Howard University in Washington, D.C., and I was reassigned to Miss Cole. Sometimes she invited Portia Washington—a relative [daughter] of Booker T. Washington—to hear my lessons. The music department was being dissolved. The Johnson brothers who taught violin and cello also left to go to Howard University. Those brasses, reeds and percussions [sic] necessary for band were left intact. Piano—essential to music education—and methods courses were not phased out. No incoming freshmen were accepted as music majors.[311]

Portia Washington Pittman had returned to Tuskegee in 1928 after the breakup of her marriage to Sidney Pittman. She taught music and conducted the choir until William Dawson arrived. While living in Berlin, she had been a friend to Abbie Mitchell; they had both lived at the same address in Berlin, but not at the same time. They spoke German together while at Tuskegee, in an effort to maintain their fluency in the language.[312]

Lorenza Jordan Cole was also on the Tuskegee faculty when Zenobia was there, from 1936 until 1939. Born August 6, 1897, in Los Angeles, she was a concert pianist and teacher. After graduating from the Juilliard School in 1930, she went to London to study with Tobias Matthay (who had been the teacher of Myra Hess, and the first accompanist of Roland Hayes). After a year in London, she went to Switzerland, where she began performing the works of black composers. In 1936, she was invited by Dawson to head the Tuskegee piano department, replacing Hazel Harrison. She said, "I was there for three years until they closed the music department because of a lack of money. I think there were three departments that were closed and, of course, music was one of them. They still taught music, but at the time I was there they were giving degrees in music and they had to cut out the college music department."[313] She returned to Los Angeles in 1939, graduating from UCLA with a Bachelor of Arts degree in music education. Subsequently, she became a public school music teacher, and made a tremendous impact on the development of several generations of black musicians in Los Angeles.³¹⁴

Also on the faculty in those days was Hazel Hooligan, a niece of Booker T. Washington, who taught piano. Zenobia Perry recalled, "We had all kinds of interesting musicians come and stay for five weeks. Hazel Harrison came. ... Marian Anderson came. Roland Hayes and Matthew Burt, who was quite a tenor [also visited]. We enjoyed having these people coming to teach a few weeks at the university."³¹⁵ R. Nathaniel Dett was often a visitor there, as well. Since the choir performed his works, he was invited to the campus either to conduct or to give his approval of their performances.

Zenobia recalled that it was at Tuskegee that she started to compose on her own. The first piece she wrote was *Childhood Capers*. "Some visitor, I think his name was Walter White, a violinist, there, said, 'That sounded like a piece I'd like to have my student play because it sounds very childish.' And he asked me if I would share it with him. So I wrote it on my theory notebook paper and gave it to him. He asked me if I had a copy and I said no. He said, 'Well, you need to keep a copy for yourself. You're a composer, did you know it?' That's how I got started. It is one of the pieces in *Piano Potpourri* ... the very first piece I wrote down and kept."³¹⁶

While at Tuskegee, Dawson encouraged Perry to compose. She remembered, "Sometimes Mr. Dawson would come in. I would get there before the choir got there and I wanted to see what they were going to practice that day. And sometimes I'd begin doodling [at the piano] and he'd say, 'What was that you were just playing?' I'd say, 'I don't know.' He said, 'Well, give it a name and write it down. I want to see it.'"

Zenobia Perry also worked on some arrangements for the choir. Occasionally she would criticize one of Dawson's arrangements: "'That doesn't sound like you right here. This ought to be so and so.' And he'd say, 'Don't tell me what it oughta be ...' and then he'd say, 'Now, what did you say that oughta be?' Sometimes there was a collaboration between us for certain phrases of the songs."³¹⁷

All three—R. Nathaniel Dett, Cortez Reece, and William L. Dawson—were important role models for Zenobia Perry; each encouraged her to pursue composition and to take herself seriously as a musician. Their interest and support were crucial to her musical development as she learned how to create a professional career in music in the black community of the 1930s.

LANGSTON UNIVERSITY DEPARTMENT OF MUSIC

Langston, Oklahoma

FINE ARTS RECITAL

Wednesday Evening, July 12, 1939 at 8:00 o'clock
in Page Auditorium

Program

Minute Waltz Op. 46 —————————————————— Chopin
    Edwina Morrison

Rondo Capriccioso, Op. 14 ————— F. Mendelssohn-Bartholdy
    Nerissa R. Williams

Scherzando ——————————————————— Carl M. Beecher
    Thelma Thompson

Viva ——————————————————————————— Bach
Ave Maria ————————————————— Bach-Gounod
O Divine Redeemer ——————————————— Gounod
    University Women's Choir

Novelette, Op. 46 ————————————————— MacDowell
    Henry L. Shegog

Hungarian Dance No. 5 ———————————————— Brahms
    Laura Paxton Cato

Ezekiel Saw de Wheel ————————————— arr. Burleigh
Walk Together Children ————————————— arr. Burleigh
There's a Meeting Here Toinght ———————————— arr. Dett
    University Women's Choir

Mammy, from Magnolia Suite ————————————— Dett
    Parthenia Jordan

Concerto in A minor, Op. 16 ———————————————— Grieg
Allegro Moderato
    Zenobia Powell
    Second piano will be played by H. Miller Yancy

THE PUBLIC IS CORDIALLY INVITED

Those desiring to leave before the termination of the program, will please do so between numbers.

Concert program from Langston University, July 12, 1939.

8. Zenobia Powell Perry
An "Ambiguous Woman"

Let happy throats be mute;
only the tortured reed is made a flute!
Only the broken heart can sing
and make of song a breathless and lovely thing!

—*Donald Jeffrey Hayes, from* Threnody[318]

This chapter examines the issues related to gender in the development of Zenobia Perry's career and personal life, and points to some of the crucial differences in the lives, circumstances, and opportunities of women and men composers in the United States in the twentieth century. Zenobia Perry discovered, after two attempts to conform to society's expectations of her to be a wife and mother, that she needed to be financially independent and single, in order to pursue composition and the career in music she envisioned for herself.

Her first marriage, in 1932 to a musician, was an attempt to free herself from her dependence on her father, who did not support her professional efforts in music. The plan backfired: she became even more dependent on her parents to care for the son resulting from this liaison. Her second marriage, into which she entered reluctantly, was an effort to regain parental authority over her son and to make a home for him, away from her parents.

CHAPTER 8

After these two attempts, she no longer tried to center her life around a husband, but accepted total responsibility for her life and financial needs. Only after the death of her father in 1942 did she come into her own, when she assumed the role as head of her family and breadwinner. At that point, she was completely responsible for the financial support and care of her own two children, as well as that of her elderly mother and her brother's three children.

Since 1970, biographies of prominent women from many fields have proliferated. Literary critic Carolyn G. Heilbrun's provocative essay, *Writing A Woman's Life*, addresses questions of how women's biographies are written and what issues need they cover, in light of recent feminist ideology. She explains that concepts of biography have profoundly changed in recent decades, especially biographies of women. In the introduction, she writes,

> But while biographers of men have been challenged on the "objectivity" of their interpretations, biographers of women have had not only to choose one interpretation over another but, far more difficult, actually to reinvent the lives their subjects led, discovering from what evidence they could find the processes and decisions, the choices and unique pain, that lay beyond the life stories of these women. The choices and pain of the women who did not make a man the center of their lives seemed unique, because there were no models of the lives they wanted to live, no exemplars, no stories. These choices, this pain, those stories, and how they may be more systematically faced, how, in short, one may find the courage to be an "ambiguous woman," are what I want to examine in this book.[319]

While Zenobia Perry was still alive, it was possible to ask her to describe her own choices, rather than to "reinvent" her life.[320] Yet this issue of Perry's being an "ambiguous woman" is provocative in the context of her life story. Although she married twice, her marriages were brief—each resulted in the birth of a child, but she only lived with each husband for a short time. She neither made a man the center of her personal life, nor did she have a woman composer mentor to help her develop a concept of how to make a professional career; her musical mentors were men.[321]

Heilbrun's "ambiguous woman" is a reference to the work of feminist theorist Deborah Cameron, who stated, "Men can be men only if women are unambiguously women."[322] Heilbrun explains that to be "unambiguously a woman" is to "put a man at the center of one's life and to allow to occur only what honors his prime position . . . one's own desires and quests are always secondary."[323] She continues, "When biographers come to write the life of a woman, they have had to struggle with the inevitable conflict between the destiny of being unambiguously a woman and the woman subject's palpable desire, or fate, to be something else."[324] This emerges as a clear issue in Perry's life, as it does with many women composers of her generation. From a young age, she had a palpable desire for a life in music, despite what others wanted for her.

Dr. Calvin Powell, Zenobia's father, was a formidable man. He dominated his wife and children, controlled their activities, and directed their futures. As the first of his four children, she put her father's wishes first. But what conflicts develop when the father opposes the life's work chosen by that daughter? Powell was certain his daughter should become a doctor or a nurse, following in his own footsteps. Zenobia, however, knew as a young girl that music was to be her life, and, although he supported her early musical studies, he balked when it came to professional training in music. "My father often said, 'I wouldn't give you a red dime to go anywhere to study music.' I don't know what a red dime is, but I know what he meant."[325]

Zenobia's parents had high expectations for their children, girls and boys equally. Uncommon among men of his generation, Dr. Powell sent both of his daughters to college. One wonders if this attitude came from his own mother, who had traveled from the United States to Africa to London with her three children. Where was she born? Was she educated? Was she married to a missionary or was she, herself, a missionary? Was she a teacher? Whatever the truth, Calvin Powell did not share it with his daughters. In any case, there may be a suggestion in the story he told his children that his mother had some special qualities, which led him to his progressive attitudes about women. Although there was no doubt that Zenobia would go to college, her field of study was always at issue. Only after his death did she feel free to act on her own decision to study composition.

Powell was not unique in his opposition to his child's pursuing a career in music. William Grant Still, born in 1895—thirteen years before Zenobia—faced intense family opposition to his choice of a career in music. The similarity in Still's and Perry's upbringing is striking:

> When I was along in my school years, my mother engaged a teacher to give me violin lessons, and encouraged me to study music. However, I didn't want to be a performer. I wanted to compose, and no sooner did I learn to read music than I wanted to write it. This was fine, as far as my mother was concerned, until she learned that I wanted to make music my life's work. Then she opposed me. This seemed strange to me at the time, because my mother was herself a person of more than ordinary artistic ability. She taught English in the secondary school, wrote and directed plays, painted, and played the piano a little. Her own goals were high. She constantly urged me to make something of myself, and not to follow the path of least resistance. However, a career in music was outside the bounds of consideration for her and, as she

persisted in her efforts to discourage me, I began to understand why. The Negro musicians of her day were not socially accepted into the better Negro homes. In fact, many Colored people considered them immoral. They disapproved of their drinking, and they certainly looked down on their earning capacity! My mother was very explicit on the latter count. She pictured me as wearing threadbare clothes, starving, and unable to provide the bare necessities of life. Her ridicule was fairly constant and unwavering. She wanted me to become a doctor so I could make enough money to live on.... You can understand that when I tell you that not until I got to Oberlin and reached my majority did I ever hear a symphony orchestra![326]

Dr. and Mrs. Powell shared these concerns. Many young middle-class blacks of this generation, particularly women, studied the piano, voice, and other instruments, but their parents had not intended for them to become professional musicians.[327]

Knowing that some musicians from Boley had gone to Oberlin Conservatory, at one time Perry had hoped to go there on scholarship, but her father opposed it. She also faced his ridicule, a tool used in some families to discipline stubborn children. Although she began to think about studying music elsewhere, she was financially dependent on her parents. Perry wrote,

> He sent me to Burrell Memorial Hospital in Roanoke, Virginia. At the close of the freshman year one decides on a career choice, specializing in a field in nursing or laboratory technology. While the many facets of health encompassed in operating a hospital were awe inspiring, the loss of all connections with music left me feeling incomplete. Of course uniform of dress is imperative in the medical field and helps one establish identification in the profession. I looked forward to the daily personal inspection taken every morning. Through the study of kinesiology the names and functions of all muscles is learned. Now I knew the name and functions of all muscles involved in playing the piano.
>
> Then it happened: the day I fell unconscious on the basketball court and was rushed to surgery. Appendicitis had troubled me previously but never had I lost consciousness before. Being seriously anemic, two weeks after the emergency appendectomy, I was sent home to recuperate. So ended my exposure to the medical field as a career choice.[328]

When she returned home, her father encouraged her to seek work in a local school, assisting the teachers. But she continued to plan how she would obtain professional music training, having had the best instruction available in Boley, far surpassing Mayme Jones's level of musicianship. When Zenobia Perry returned to Boley, after staying with her uncle Frank and his family, her parents finally agreed to send her to Hampton Institute, to study medicine or education. She chose Hampton, hoping to study with Nathaniel Dett there, and then followed him to Rochester.

During that year, 1931–32, Perry's parents had serious problems in Boley: they lost their life savings in a stock scam, and her father was injured in a racially motivated attack. In the spring of 1932, they demanded that Zenobia return to Oklahoma. When she arrived, she found they had moved to a modest house in Bartlesville and had reduced their living expenses. Dr. Powell, who had been in private practice for more than three decades, took a staff position at a black hospital in Tulsa.[329] She was disappointed not to be able to return to Rochester to continue her studies with Dett.

> I felt that I was dropping out of the bottom of the world in that summer of 1932 as I went to Frederick to teach a six-weeks term rural primary school. How does one teach basic educational processes to children who have little in the way of nourishing food, scant clothing, no bed to sleep in, or don't live in a house they can call home? They were of average size for their ages but shy and a bit taken aback by my size. I boarded with perhaps the best situated among them. A woman—who was field-hand overseer—a meticulously clean housekeeper and excellent country cook. She knew each child by name and his or her field work accomplishments. None of the children seemed to have a goal to which they were aspiring, apart from their fieldwork.
>
> When the six-week term was over and reports were in, I failed to sign up for the winter session but returned to Tulsa somewhat depressed. My thoughts were only for continuing my own formal education in music.[330]

Later that summer, she met jazz violinist "King" Earl Gaynor.[331] "He played better than anybody I had every heard. Every time I knew he was playing, I'd be there." He played concerts in the Tulsa area and was auditioning for larger jazz bands in northeastern Oklahoma. Trained in classical music and folk music, he played two of her favorites: "Berceuse" from *Jocelyn* by B. Godard and *Cavatina* (edited by Gruenburg) by Gustave Hollander, Opus 26.

> I gladly accompanied him, mainly just to hear him play. Complimenting me on my playing, he told me that any college I chose would welcome me as a gifted, hardworking music student. Having satisfied the Oklahoma State requirements for teaching, I found it easy to enroll in music at Langston University above the freshman level. Earl Gaynor helped me choose the courses I should take, select a room and roommate off campus, and settle all student fees for the first term. We were married on Thanksgiving Day.[332]

Zenobia's uncle Clem, her mother's brother, lived near Langston, where he farmed acres near her grandfather Thompson's farm and served as minister to a Baptist congregation in Coyle. Clem had three sons and a

CHAPTER 8

daughter of his own, but adored his niece and wanted to help her, despite the fact that his farm was not flourishing. Because of this, her parents were supportive of her decision to move to Langston to enroll in school. It is not clear whether they knew about Earl Gaynor, when they agreed to her plan.

She had high hopes for her relationship with Gaynor. He was an older, accomplished musician, working professionally, who appreciated her talents and encouraged her to do what her heart desired—to continue her education in music.

> I remember when I told Nathaniel Dett I was going to get married a few months before I did and he said, "Who ever heard told about an old maid like you getting married?" . . . My father used to say, "Nothing interests her but that piano. She'll come in and go to that piano. She practices on that piano. When she leaves that piano, her mother will tell her to do something. She'll do that and then go back to that piano. Every morning before she puts on her clothes, she goes to that piano." I was always at the piano. That's why they said I'd die an old maid.[333]

Not only did Earl Gaynor encourage Zenobia to go to college, but he also helped her financially. She recalled, "So finally he asked me to marry him and that's how Lemuel [their son] got here. My mother was so upset when I got married. He was going around playing and he wasn't taking me with him. I was alone and he was playing all over the country. So I went home and got a divorce. My father didn't want me to do it until after the baby, but I wanted to get it over."[334]

Had Perry thought that marriage would free her once and for all from her father's control? Had she thought that marriage to a musician, who seemingly understood her love of music and her deep desire to become a professional musician—perhaps even a composer—would help her follow the path she desired? It is easy to see how seductive Earl Gaynor's praise and encouragement had been. Although already in her twenties, Zenobia was still financially dependent on her parents, so this solution to her predicament had its appeal. Marrying a musician could perhaps mean a life in music, which her father would not help her develop. Neither Zenobia nor Earl thought about pregnancy as a possible stumbling block to their career plans.

Between the stress and break-up of her marriage, her pregnancy, and the deepening of the economic depression in Oklahoma, Zenobia Perry's stay in Langston was difficult. Her parents did not approve of her marriage and were upset about the pregnancy. However, her teacher Cortez Reece encouraged her to compose and to take her music more seriously. He was particularly interested in some children's teaching pieces she showed him. "Perhaps he felt it a safe and promising avenue in which to direct my energies, as he knew of other women in the field."[335]

> Spring [1933] found me pregnant and ill, unable to do most of the activities my husband and I had so carefully planned. He became less and less interested in me—a sick woman—a partner who could not function in her planned capacity. At the close of the school term I went to Tulsa and after a week or two found myself deserted. Going to Bartlesville where my parents were, I started a piano class and accompanied the summer school program at Douglass High School. August 21, 1933, my son, Lemuel, was born.
>
> His bassinet was made of a fruit basket and a pillow. It became a custom for me to place his bassinet on a chair near the piano as I practiced. He seemed to enjoy the piano music. Regardless of my many repetitions of spot passages, he lay quietly or slept. However, if my practice went badly, he would cry.

With the continued help of her parents, she became a first-grade teacher in the Douglass schools for the 1934–35 academic year. Having divorced Earl Gaynor, who refused to help with Lemuel's support, she taught piano to neighborhood children and played in the church.

Reluctant to send his daughter back to school, Dr. Powell had resigned himself to her teaching school while raising her infant son and living at home. He felt that her studies in Rochester had been a waste of time and money, because she received neither a diploma nor a certificate and could not make enough money as a musician to support herself and her son. However, Perry was restless and wanted to return to her studies. She convinced her father to allow her to go to Tuskegee Institute in September 1935, to complete her college education. Having saved some money from her work as a teacher, she was accepted at Tuskegee as a work-study student. By the time she entered Tuskegee, she was nearly twenty-seven years old, a single mother, and conscious of being an "older student." Her parents insisted on taking care of Lemuel while she was in Alabama.

Perry hoped to study music at Tuskegee, but to please her father, pursued a B.S. in education, with majors in mathematics and English. Her advisor at Tuskegee told her that, if she put down her true age on the enrollment documents, she would be denied financial assistance. After some soul searching, she subtracted six years and gave her birth date as 1914.[336]

In fact, Zenobia was fortunate to find a home, an education, and employment at Tuskegee in the mid-1930s. By 1933, more than one-fourth of all urban blacks were on relief; by 1934, 52 percent of blacks in northern and border states were on relief, compared to only 12 percent of whites. As a black student at Tuskegee, she found a friendlier and more supportive environment than she had in Rochester. "I felt much more comfortable when I was at Tuskegee because I was with black people."

These were also sad years for Zenobia Perry. She missed her son and her parents. "When I started to think about things at home, I went to the library and studied harder."[337] This time she would finish her degree and prepare for a career as a teacher, while studying music. She studied with William Dawson, sang in the Tuskegee Choir, performed the piano in concert, and learned to arrange, to conduct, and to accompany. She was afraid of disappointing her parents once again; their voices saying, "We told you so!" echoed in her head. She was determined to succeed.

During her last year at Tuskegee, Zenobia served as a student teacher. After graduation, she was hired as a lead teacher in the Tuskegee training school, sponsored by the federal government. She was befriended by Eleanor Roosevelt, who arranged for her to attend graduate school to obtain a master's degree in education. Although Perry had a full-time position, her parents would not let her take her son to Alabama, insisting that he remain with them in Oklahoma. They had usurped her parental authority and considered her ungrateful and impractical to suggest otherwise. She spent vacations with Lemuel and her parents in Bartlesville and kept in touch by phone and through correspondence. By this time, Lemuel had entered elementary school.[338]

In part to try to regain parental authority over her child, in 1941, Zenobia Powell married Jimmie Rodgers Perry (1916–2003), whom she had met in a math class at Tuskegee. He had joined the Navy before the outbreak of World War II, and like many young couples, they felt the pressure of pending separation. Zenobia Perry described the marriage:

> My special friend and classmate in mathematics at Tuskegee enlisted in the Navy. He made acquaintance with my father through letters and by telephone because he wanted to marry. And I kept putting the matter in the future. Papa called him my oceanic lover because he was stationed at Pearl Harbor. Jimmie Rodgers Perry sent me a telegram asking if I had a white dress. I thought the message was from Minnie, my ex-roommate, who lived in Needles, California, and the telegram was from California. She had said that she was going to come back to Tuskegee to get married in the chapel there and she wanted me to be in her wedding. I had no way of knowing that the message was from Jimmie. I went to the train station in Montgomery, Alabama, to meet Minnie, got on the train to help her off, passed right by Jimmie without seeing him. When I didn't see her and got off the train, there he stood. He asked, "Aren't you going to speak to me?" I said, "Hello. Did you see Minnie? I got this telegram from her, so I came to meet her." He said, "Let me see that telegram." He took it and said, "I sent that message after we left San Diego, California!"

AN "AMBIGUOUS WOMAN"

We were married in Booker T. Washington's Study in May 1941. At the end of May and the school year I went to Amite, Louisiana, to meet Jimmie's mother and brother, then home to Bartlesville, Oklahoma. Somehow my husband managed to get "a leave" and the three of us: Jimmie, Lemuel, and I spent some time together roaming through the West. Lemuel had to have a Navy outfit and wore it all the time.[339]

Jimmie Rodgers Perry.   Lemuel Powell Perry.

In September 1941, Zenobia went to Greeley, Colorado,[340] to enter graduate school and, to her chagrin, realized that, once again, she was moving away from her goal of becoming a professional musician. There was little time to practice; she had trouble even finding a piano to play. She tried to switch her major to music education, but that would have required an additional summer of coursework and there was no music training in the laboratory school that was sponsoring her graduate work.

On December 7, 1941, her husband, Jimmie, was on board ship at Pearl Harbor, when the Japanese bombed it. As a result of his wartime experiences, he suffered many emotional problems.[341] The following May, she resigned from Tuskegee, "because my musical life was wilting under the demands of administration at the Farm Security Administration. I spent the summer doing things around the home place my parents had not had the time to do. Lemuel's piano practice time was scheduled; he became acquainted with the violin. A neighborhood children's music class was started and I began to help with the church choirs."[342]

CHAPTER 8

Then her father died:

> In late August 1942 Papa and I were sitting in the porch swing talking when he asked me to get Mr. Grayson to trim the shade trees across the front lawn late this fall. To which I responded, "You are right here. Why can't you ask him yourself?" He replied, "O, I'm going to meet my Maker before the leaves are gone from the trees." Since he sometimes made predictions in the distant future, I didn't suspect that he was ill without him actually telling me so, and did not continue the health side of our conversation.
>
> Lemuel and I had gone to Tulsa for a week when Mamma phoned me to come home right away. She said, "Your papa is ill and won't pay any attention to what I tell him." I asked her to send him to the hospital and Lemuel and I would be home as soon as possible. That happened the first week of October and Papa died the next week, before the leaves were gone from the trees.[343]

She recalled that her mother, weary from sitting beside his hospital bed, needed a break and told Zenobia to sit with her father. "He told me to get the man to cut the trees. I told him, 'You're here. You can do it.' He answered, 'When the sun goes down, I'm going, too.' And he did. He knew he was going to die."[344]

When the first-grade teacher at a local school took a maternity leave for the school year 1942–43, Zenobia Perry was hired, enabling her to support her mother and Lemuel. Doctors advised her to have a child to shake her husband out of his depression. Janis was born in August 1943, in Tulsa, Oklahoma, while Jimmie Perry was overseas and Zenobia was alone. Her pregnancy was particularly difficult, requiring extensive bed rest during the summer of 1943; the whole extended family was asked to pray for her health and that of the baby. "When Janis was finally presented to grandfather Charlie Thompson, then 105 or 106 years old, he said, 'Is this what the big fuss was about?'"[345]

Perry remembered, "My husband's mother put first baby pictures of father and daughter side by side and announced that they were identical, except for the dress, and that was how she could tell the 'he' from the 'she.'"[346] Zenobia was desperately hoping to create a family of her own, which would provide financial and moral support and allow her to continue her music. Once her father had died, she felt more comfortable setting music as her priority. She had made him proud with her administrative work and her teaching, but she was not doing what she envisioned for herself. It was difficult to try to balance her own needs and desires with her family obligations. She had not anticipated that Jimmie would become too disabled to be the husband and father for her children that she needed.

In the fall of 1943, Zenobia was offered a job as Music Director of

AN "AMBIGUOUS WOMAN"

Community Services for the Tennessee Valley Authority. Her mother refused to go with her, however, so she declined the job and taught at a school in Pawnee, Oklahoma, during 1943–44. On October 2, 1943, R. Nathaniel Dett died of a heart attack, a day before Perry's thirty-fifth birthday. How difficult for her to lose her father and her mentor within the same year! The country was still at war, her husband was suffering from a nervous breakdown caused by his military service, and she was under-employed as a primary school teacher, still yearning to become a professional musician.

After Jimmie Perry's return from overseas, they tried to live together, but it did not work. When they eventually divorced, he stayed in Milwaukee.[347] About her husband, Zenobia Perry said, "We just couldn't agree on what should go into the upbringing of a child and I said rather than have her subjected to him, we'll just forget it and I'll take the girl and do what I wish. Now he's very appreciative of the fact that what I wanted to do turned out to be the better thing for her. He says she would not have reached the heights she has reached if she had stayed with him."[348]

Perry attended classes in the summer of 1944, as well as the spring and summer semesters of 1945. She received a Master's of Art degree in Elementary Education at the University of Northern Colorado in Greeley in August 1945.[349] That summer, she was a guest teacher at Lincoln University in Missouri. From 1945 until 1947, she worked for the Tennessee Valley Authority in Benton, Kentucky, on a special project in Arts Education. In March of 1946, her son, Lemuel, died from a ruptured appendix. A nurse she had known from Prairie Farms, Alabama, cared for Janis. Her mother lived with her, as did the children of her brother Douglass. He had divorced his wife, Margaret, and Zenobia and her mother took in his children, Patricia, Athenea Rea, and Douglass, Jr. According to Janis-Rozena Peri:

> That was a case of my mother really putting her foot down in the family, because Uncle Douglass, she didn't think, was being a fit father, so she literally went to Washington, D.C., and took the kids from him. She said, "You'll get your kids back when you clean up your act." She kept the kids for two or three years.[350]

Douglass, Sr., worked as a chef at the Pentagon in Washington, D.C., and sent some money to help support the children, but Zenobia was the primary financial support for the entire family. While living with Zenobia and grandmother Birdie, Douglass, Jr., died at age 7, also of a ruptured appendix.

In 1947, Zenobia Perry was offered a teaching post in West Memphis,

Arkansas. She wrote Mrs. Roosevelt and her supervisor Mrs. Deitz to ask permission to take the new position and they agreed, telling her that the Farm Security Administration program was being phased out. After teaching for the summer, she went to the campus of Arkansas Agricultural, Mechanical and Normal College in Pine Bluff, and stayed there nine years. When she arrived, the president of the university told her, "We don't know much about music, but we are willing to learn so I want you to help to build a music department." Finally, she had secured a full-time position in music, as an assistant professor of music, and eventually was promoted to associate dean of Arts and Sciences.

When Janis-Rozena Peri was in first grade, Patricia and Athenea went to live with their father and his new wife. Grandmother Birdie moved back to Oklahoma, freeing Zenobia to focus on her new job. Although she had many administrative duties, she managed to compose some pieces during those years. In the summers, Janis often stayed with her grandmother in Oklahoma, while her mother continued her education at the University of Wyoming. There she studied composition with Allan Willman and Darius Milhaud, graduating with a master's degree in composition in 1954. She wrote music while in Arkansas, but was not considered to be a composer there, even after she finished her composition degree. Writing pieces for students was simply a part of her regular teaching duties.

It was during her seventh year at Arkansas that she realized she was more a composer than a pianist. "I had been doing a lot of piano, along with others, then I realized that half of the time when I was playing music of somebody else, I really wished it had been done another way. And I said, 'Well, I'll have to forget this and move on and play my music and compose my music.'"

In 1955, Zenobia Perry made an extraordinary decision. She had been asked by Charles Wesley, president of Central State College, to come to Ohio to teach. She said she would, but only if she could teach theory and composition and not do administrative work. He agreed, naming her Composer-in-Residence. She resigned her position at Arkansas in the middle of the semester and moved, with her daughter, to Wilberforce, Ohio. She took a cut in pay, and a lower status academic position as faculty, having served as an administrator in Arkansas. But she was finally in a position where she could teach what she loved most, while pursuing composition, with the security of an academic post. She was fortified enough to make such a decision, because of the support and encouragement she had received from Willman and Milhaud, both of whom, without hesitation, considered her to be a composer and a colleague. She remained at Central State University from 1955 until her retirement in 1982, focusing on composition and performances of her own music.

Zenobia Perry's decision to take this job in mid-semester was influenced in part by a factor that reveals another facet of Perry's life at that time. According to her daughter, Janis-Rozena Peri, one of the reasons she wanted to leave Arkansas was that, in the fall of 1955, the civil rights movement was planning an action to force integration of the Arkansas schools.

> Mother was active in the NAACP in Arkansas and there was a meeting at our house about integrating the schools. I overheard them say, "We have chosen the nine in Little Rock and seven in Pine Bluff and Janis is one of the seven." I heard my mother say, "Oh, really?" After the meeting, there was a flurry of phone calls and letters and we moved to Ohio. The irony of this is that I was in the group that integrated the schools in Xenia, Ohio.

Although Zenobia supported the group's desire to integrate the school, she resisted the idea of her daughter being used in this manner, due in part to Perry's position at the university. She and Janis were on their own; it seemed too risky.

After two attempts to build a family life through marriage, Perry decided that being alone was preferable, because she could be free to pursue composition. At that time, wanting to compose represented "unwomanly ambition,"[351] particularly for a black woman at a black college. She needed an income and "a room of her own,"[352] that she could establish through her teaching. The only other black woman composer she knew teaching theory and composition in the entire country was Undine Smith Moore, at Virginia State College in Petersburg. To this day, there are very few black women teaching theory and composition on the university level, and still only a few theory and composition programs at the predominantly black colleges.[353]

In her book on writing women's biographies, Carolyn Heilbrun proposes that we "examine 'unwomanly' ambition [such as composing], marriage, friendship with women and love for women, aging, female childhood—[which] can be seen accurately only in the light of movements toward public power and control."[354] It is clear how Perry moved steadily toward a career of more public power and control: status in her community as a university administrator, performing artist, and teacher; and more control in her personal life, giving her the opportunity to study composition, even without family or institutional support. Finally, she was financially independent and could make her own decisions. Studying theory and composition was something she wanted to do for herself.

If Perry's marriages had been more successful, would she have had a more successful career as a composer? Many women stopped composing altogether after marriage and/or giving birth, including such luminaries as Clara Schumann (1819–1896) and Alma Mahler (1876–1964). One notable exception was the highly productive American composer Amy Beach (1867–1944), whose husband was adamant that she devote her energies to composing, rather than teaching, concertizing, or managing a household. On the other hand, the career path of Ruth Crawford (1901–1953) shifted dramatically after her marriage to Charles Seeger in the 1930s, from one of the most innovative composers of her generation to an arranger of American folk songs for children.

Being a single mother may have slowed down Perry's development as a musician, but it served to motivate her to become independent and self-supporting. Zenobia Powell Perry offers an extraordinary role model for women who hope to achieve success in their music careers, while being mothers and/or involved family members. Although her marriages did not succeed, at least not in the ways she intended, nevertheless, her experiences as a mother deeply enriched her life and her music. There were no female models for the life she wanted to live as a composer, but she mustered the courage and obtained the professional training to make her dream a reality, against substantial odds.

9. Professional Teaching Career and Graduate School

Although Zenobia Perry still wanted to become a professional musician and composer, she studied for a degree in education and a teaching credential at Tuskegee Institute. During the spring semester of her senior year, a student teaching assignment off-campus at the Mitchell's Mill School proved to be an experience that would change the direction of her life. The director of student teaching was ill, so Perry was put in charge until the director returned. She recalled,

> In a van designated for elementary education rural visitation, all visiting and practice teachers were driven to their assignments. Going by the County Superintendent's office for supplies, I was handed a Teacher's Rollbook and a small box of pencils. There were no textbooks, writing pads, slates or blackboards and chalk for Mitchell's Mill School. To my dismay I found a porch on which set an upright piano in very poor condition, subject to the weather. Inside was only a large empty room with a roll-top desk and high stool, and a potbelly wood stove in the middle of the room. This was Mitchell's Mill School.[355]
>
> Equipment was scarce. There were no books or materials found in the empty room. The children and I made seats from willow shoots and nail kegs given by the Mitchell Lumber Mill. Wrapping paper was given by the butcher where soup bones were purchased; heavy twine and crayons were bought from the "Five and Dime Store" in Tuskegee on the way to Mitchell's Mill the next

semester. These were used to make charts—in lieu of books to teach reading, spelling, writing, arithmetic, and music. Each child brought a vegetable, a spoon, and a tin emptied from products the family had purchased so that they could eat the lunch that they had prepared. All chores and activities were used to make stories for charts for teaching.

Practice teachers and observers in education were instructed to go on with routine work and pay no attention to visitors—who perhaps were making evaluations for the U.S. Department of Education or philanthropists of Tuskegee. Often these visitors asked children about their activities. The following is a typical conversation.

Visitor: Why are you two counting the words on these cards?

Pupil: Miss Powell told us there should be ten words on each line of this chart.

Visitor: Why are you making this chart?

Pupil: All of our lessons are on charts that we make and we make charts about everything we do.

Pupil: Yesterday we picked black walnuts.

Visitor: What did you do with the walnuts?

Pupil: We spread them out in the grass to dry. We will make some stain to finish the floor (with the hulls).

Pupil: The insides nuts are good to put in cookies and candy. To make the chart we have to spell the words and make a list, make-up and write the sentences, read them, then copy some of the chart.

Different groups of children were engaged in activities necessary to assemble the chart: measuring paper for pages of the chart; drawing lines for the text; selecting colors of crayolas for the text to make the chart attractive; selecting the wood for the pole and readying it for the axis of the chart and securing the string for hanging.

Among our visitors were Mrs. Eleanor Roosevelt, wife of President Franklin D. Roosevelt, and Mrs. Mary McLeod Bethune, Director of the Division of Negro Affairs for the National Youth Administration. Mrs. Roosevelt made many visits to my classroom. She had made three visits before I knew who she was.[356]

Zenobia Perry was surprised to discover the desperate conditions of the sharecropping farmers who were being served by this project:

During the period 1938–42 Tuskegee Institute was playing a vital role in the rehabilitation of black tenant and sharecropper farmers whose conditions were tantamount to slavery. In some instances, no attempt was made to

TEACHING CAREER AND GRADUATE SCHOOL

conceal plantations run just the way they were in slavery. At the beginning of my senior year, I chanced upon one such plantation. (Mrs. Roosevelt said I looked innocent and naive and could do on site investigation without being apprehended.) Families were relocated on Prairie Farms in Macon County, Alabama, by the Farm Administration. Aside from houses and farmland to accommodate family size, they had a school and clinic for the community. I was involved in the school and adult community arts and crafts.[357]

She also enjoyed a good relationship with Eleanor Roosevelt, who opened many doors for her, including graduate study. Perry once remarked, to Mrs. Roosevelt's surprise, that the cotton in the feed sacks at the school was a wonderful fabric for clothing. So Zenobia sewed Mrs. Roosevelt a suit from the cotton feed sacks, which the First Lady wore on several occasions, explaining to those who asked that it came from her visits to the training schools. Zenobia remembered warm words of support and encouragement from Mrs. Roosevelt over several years.[358]

Mrs. Roosevelt said about Zenobia Perry, "Miss Oklahoma has more know-how than the people are teaching. Her methods should be part of your curriculum." She made arrangements to pay Perry's salary for seven years, saying, "I'll help you be anything you want to be but President of the United States. That's my husband's job."[359]

To illustrate her efforts to put together the classroom and to teach, Zenobia told the following story:

> I asked one of the little boys, "Do you know how to go to the Mill?" He said, "Around the bend down there." "Does it take long?" "No, my mamma said, 'Be back before that [licked his finger and held it in the air].' So I took all the children down to the mill and I asked them if they had some empty nail kegs. Each child got a nail keg and I got two because Meldosia's brother wasn't big enough to carry one. And we brought those nail kegs back and we thought of a way to fasten them to the braided willows that we had and we had chairs.[360]

Her memories of those days and the poor conditions of the students remained vivid. At the time, she had little idea that she was playing a role in the Roosevelt Administration's plan to change the conditions for blacks in the South.[361]

After defeating Hoover in 1932, Franklin Delano Roosevelt's inaugural message was, "The only thing we have to fear is fear itself." He promised a "New Deal," which began with a succession of legislative acts within the first one hundred days of his term, including relief for those in desperate need; recovery assistance in the form of loans, subsidies, and other assistance to big business; and reform to prevent future depressions. The most important innovations were the Civilian Conservation Corps, the Federal Emergency

Relief Administration, and the Works Progress Administration. The Tennessee Valley Authority was established to construct dams and power plants, to provide electricity in seven states; the Social Security Act was established to provide financial security to the aged and unemployed; and the Securities and Exchange Commission was established to regulate stock exchanges and securities trading. The New Deal included some of the most important legislation in U.S. history, however it did not end the Depression. Unemployment remained above 10 percent until 1941, peaking at 23 percent.

Eleanor Roosevelt (1884–1962), who had a particular interest in education and improving the living conditions for black Americans, supervised some of the work herself. In *The Autobiography of Eleanor Roosevelt*,[362] she describes the work of the Tennessee Valley Authority. A dream of Senator George Norris, the project began during World War I and continued through the 1930s and '40s:

> Scarcely eight years later, after the housing and educational and agricultural experiments had had time to take effect, I went through the same area, and a more prosperous region would have been hard to find. I have always wished that those who oppose authorities to create similar benefits in the valleys of other great rivers could have seen the contrast as I saw it. I realize that such changes must come gradually, but I hate to see nothing done. I wish, as my husband always wished, that year by year we might be making a start on the Missouri River and the headwaters of the Mississippi. Such experiments, changing for the better the life of the people, would be a mighty bulwark against attacks on our democracy.[363]

Although FDR never spoke about black-white relations during his presidency, he had the widespread support of black Americans. He even refused to condemn lynching, out of fear that he would anger white Southern politicians. Eleanor, however, was the communications link between the black community and Washington officials. Her close friend Mary McLeod Bethune (1875–1955) was named Director of Negro Affairs in the National Youth Administration; the Secretary of the Interior was Harold Ickes, a former Chicago NAACP officer; and Harry Hopkins was a New Deal relief administrator. Several dozen government agencies hired black administrators in response to pressure from black leaders. After 1936, blacks generally registered and voted Democratic, leaving the party of Lincoln.

Perry wrote this account of her first meeting with Eleanor Roosevelt:

> About three weeks later, these people came in as visitors of Tuskegee. We were told before we left campus that there were going to be some people from

TEACHING CAREER AND GRADUATE SCHOOL

the State Department visiting Tuskegee. "Whenever they come into your classroom, regardless of what you are doing, don't stop. Keep doing what you are doing. And if you are to meet these people it will be after the class and not before." So these people came in. And one man came in and I will never forget him. He was the Secretary to the Secretary of State. He had the worst case of halitosis I had ever seen. So I called him "Halitosis."

The next day, "Halitosis" and this woman came in and I said, "They sure make a good pair because she doesn't look like a thing and he's got this terrible breath." And do you know who they were? Henry Wallace, the Secretary of Agriculture, and Mrs. Roosevelt. But I didn't know that. She started walking around, looking at what the children were doing and she saw one little boy who seemed to be more restless than the rest, so she asked him what his name was. He said, "My name is Robert Alexander." And she said, "Well, what are you doing?" And he said, "Miss Powell gave me these seeds. I got to go out here and plant these turnips. Everything we got to do, we got to write about it, we got to sing about it, we got to talk about it. I get so tired of doing everything." She said, "Do you mind if I go out with you?" He said, "You can come along."

So he and another little boy who helped him measure the string and Mrs. Roosevelt went out to plant the turnips. When they came back, I wanted him to tell what he had done and then I wrote what he had done on this chart. And then they were to read it. She looked at what we were doing and she came back a third day and I wondered what she was going to do. Anyway, at the end of the week, Mr. Love said to me, "When we go back to campus you got to report to Dr. Clark." And I said, "What did I do wrong?" He said, "I don't know. I'm just supposed to tell you what he said." So I went to the office and was wondering, "Did I take the kids off the campus? Was that illegal?" I wondered what I had done wrong. But when I got in the office, lo and behold here was that same little homely woman sitting in there and Dr. Clark said, "I want to congratulate you, Miss Powell. You have made quite a name for yourself. You helped to establish a school where there was no school. You have a curriculum that is helping children arise from nowhere to about a fifth-grade level. I want you to meet somebody," and that's when he introduced me to this woman.

In the course of the conversation, she said, "I would like to have this type of teaching done all over the South because it encourages participation and respect for themselves and the children have gone so far beyond what we do in a normal school. So I suggest that you become a member of the faculty of Tuskegee Institute. The problem here is your youth and that you have had no graduate training. I told them that I would be responsible for that." She committed to pay my salary and see that I get some graduate work done.[364]

How did Perry know what to do for those poor black children? "When we were in Boley, we were taught to take what you have and make what you need. Mamma didn't say that so much, but my grandmother and my uncle. Everybody was saying that. So we never complained about what we didn't have."[365] That was Tuskegee Institute's philosophy, too: to develop self-

CHAPTER 9

reliance and independence. This experience was quite instructive. Having grown up in Boley with excellent public schools and a strong commitment in the community to educating black youth, Zenobia was upset to see the difficulties faced by these poor blacks in Alabama. She improved her own teaching methods under these conditions, as she came to realize how difficult life was for blacks in Alabama and elsewhere in the South.

When Perry graduated from Tuskegee, she returned to Oklahoma: "I was surprised, you know. When I finished, I went home, all of my—there were 336 people in my class and when we finished we usually got not only our diplomas but also our contract for a job. 335 of them got contracts and I didn't get one. I was kind of disgusted to think that I had done just as much, I thought, as anybody else then, and I didn't have a contract."[366] She thought that her work with the Farm Security Administration had been her "undoing," that it had disqualified her for a real job contract. She graduated on May 22, 1938, with a bachelor's degree and was the only student to receive special commendations.

She wrote, "I wondered if my unusual student status was responsible. Nevertheless, I was glad to be going home. Home to Lemuel, my son, and of course, home to my parents." She rejoined her family and, on June 4, 1938, took a job at the country club near Bartlesville, Oklahoma, the home of Frank Phillips and Phillips 66 Oil Company. She had worked there briefly before she went to Tuskegee and remembered making biscuits for a special party hosted by Wiley Post (1899–1935).

> In those days, such notables as Frank Lloyd Wright (1899–1935), Frank Phillips of Phillips Petroleum, and Will Rogers, celebrated cowboy visited the club, and Mrs. H. V. Foster managed it. Mr. H. V. Foster at the time was said to be the richest man west of the Mississippi River. Mrs. Foster had made it known that she wanted a "colored college graduate" to be responsible for menus on days the club was open so I had no trouble getting on the Wednesday, Thursday pie staff and had the duty of arranging salads for other days the club was open—much to the dismay of veteran staff workers.[367]

Had she gone to Tuskegee and sacrificed those years from her infant son to become a baker at a white country club in Oklahoma? Zenobia Perry was very unhappy and felt she had once again failed. But on August 1, 1938, she received an urgent phone call from her father, telling her to come home immediately. He sent a taxi for her.

> When I arrived at home Dr. Frederick Patterson, President of Tuskegee, had come to Bartlesville to offer me the faculty job at Tuskegee and explained that I was not offered a contract upon graduation because the administrative staff was deliberating my ability to handle the situation of instructing former

classmates in rather unconventional classroom procedures that differed from methodology they had been taught, creating a disciplinary problem, plus the fact that I had no advanced training beyond what I had gotten at Tuskegee. However, recommendations from persons in the U.S. Department of Education and Mrs. Roosevelt tipped the scale in my favor. So I was on hand at the opening of school September 1938.[368]

She began teaching as a "Model" teacher in Off-Campus Laboratory Schools of the Department of Education, in affiliation with the U.S. Farm Security Administration Rehabilitation Program. "My father was beside himself with pride. He said, 'My, my, you are starting out in an administrative position. I know you aren't going to take Lemuel to be subjected to the rigors of a job that keeps you on the go from place to place when he is at home and happy here.' Although I went through an internal emotional struggle, my father won and Lemuel was left with my parents."[369]

On July 12, 1939, Zenobia Powell and H. Miller Yancy played the *Allegro Moderato* of the Grieg *Piano Concerto in A minor, Op. 16*, at a concert of the Langston University Department of Music, in a two-piano version. The "Fine Arts" concert was held in Page Auditorium and included, among others, the University Women's Choir. The program featured two pieces by Nathaniel Dett: "Mammy," from the *Magnolia Suite* and his arrangement of "There's a Meeting Here Tonight." The printed program does not indicate who organized the concert, but Zenobia recalled that Cortez Reece had something to do with her invitation to play the Grieg.[370]

During the later part of the summer of 1939, her job took her to southern Georgia, near Dixie.

> There I experienced living practices among farm workers and reported findings to the Farm Security Administration and Tuskegee Institute. The workday began at dawn and ended at sundown, with an hour's break at noon. There was always some chore needing collective attention. For instance: Making Molasses—cutting and hauling cane; running the stripper; then the press; straining the syrup and bottling while some syrup cooked more to the thick dark consistency of molasses in the large outdoor cooking vats. Usually one cook made taffy candy which children divided and pulled to make it right. Another group of adults were digging and baking sweet potatoes which children cleaned and sorted, while yet another young group was digging and threshing peanuts. For the first time in my life I tasted boiled fresh peanuts. During the height of activities of the seasons two men and two women cooked for the workers. A third young man, whose intelligence seemed slightly less than average, helped with serving the food. In the center of the kitchen cabin stood a large butcher's block table misshapen by use. Two huge black cast iron stoves with water boiler tanks framed one side of the room. A series of ovens and a fireplace were on a side wall. On hot days large iron pots were

secured over open fires for boiling while on cool days they hung over fire in the fireplace. Food was served from cooking vessels into individual bowls with wide rims and cups made of metal with a coat of porcelain.

The community latrine was covered with morning glory flowering vines but the smell of lime disinfect identified its presence. Families were housed in huts of two rooms. The inner room had an opening, which served, as a window without glass but a shutter that could be opened or closed at will. Straw mattresses for sleeping covered most of the inner room floor. All other activities took place in the front room. Here was a fireplace for cooking and heating in winter. Cooking utensils were an iron pot for boiling, a frying pan and a coffee pot. Furnishings included a table, one or two chairs, a stool or two and a chest for their scant clothing. Members of the family often made items that decorated their cabins and enhanced the quality of their lives. On a bench or stand near the outside door was a metal wash pan and water pitcher for tidying up.

Some huts had entrance doors, others had fabric like the cotton-picking durable "ducking" draped over the entrance. Health was fair throughout the community. Every household stocked Castor Oil, sulphur (powdered), Epsom Salts, turpentine, Golden Seal and dried peach tree leaves. A supply of Horehound candy was purchased for the children to ward off colds and coughs. A visit to a doctor was practically unheard of except as the very last resort in a life or death situation. Available doctors were white and blacks feared them.

Prenatal care was very unpopular in the community. In fact, the mention of it was taboo. One woman was quite miffed when I unknowingly asked her if she had experienced prenatal care from a nurse or a doctor. She very assertively told me, "No nurse or doctor helped me get this baby and I don't need 'em to help me have it." I never attended a marriage celebration but was told that two, three or four couples "jump the broom" at the same celebration, then each couple tried to be the first to have a baby and receive a "prize" from the landlord.[371]

By the second week of September of that year, she went to Macon County, Alabama, to work with the newly formed community of Prairie Farms, which had been set up to help destitute black farm families and relocated sharecroppers. Personnel from the Farms Security Administration and the Tuskegee Institute staffed the facilities, including an elementary school, a health center, and a commissary. Zenobia was assigned to the Prairie Farms Elementary School and evening adult classes. At one point, she was working on a steel houseboat, which floated up and down the Mississippi River to provide teacher training, books, and supplies to towns along the river.

Her work was so demanding during those years that she lost touch with her siblings. Her brother Calvin had become ill and was denied a scholarship, because of his race. Her younger brother, Douglass, was employed in food service at a Tulsa hotel, working on the side as a musician. Thelma was teaching in an elementary school in Virginia. "My parents were feeling as though the family was slipping away, establishing themselves away from Oklahoma, so they were holding to Lemuel for a semblance of a family."[372]

There was a need for teachers with advanced degrees to further the teaching certification of the program's trainees, so after two years at Prairie Farms, Perry was sent to spend two summer terms at Colorado State College of Education at Greeley. She described how Eleanor Roosevelt helped her with graduate school:

> Then she [Eleanor Roosevelt] wanted to know where I wanted to go to graduate school because I would have to go in the summer and I said Colorado. I wanted to be close to home. I didn't know of any graduate schools in Oklahoma which were reputable. There may have been some, but I didn't know. But I knew about those in Colorado. She said, "Why Colorado?" I said, "Because half of the books I had studied were from Colorado, either from teachers or from writers." She said, "Well, all right." And she said, "Which school?" and I said, "Greeley because I knew [Horace] Greeley [1811–72] had come through and made quite a name for himself because he had ridden a horse all the way from New York to Colorado and he was teaching philosophy and math at Greeley. So that's the reason why I chose Greeley.[373]

She got to graduate school; "where I had a mixed class, I never felt intimidated like other blacks in the class did. I never did. I still don't."[374] Perry described one incident of flagrant racism during her year in Colorado, related to a mathematical evaluation: she was told by the professor that the best grade she could expect to earn in his class would be a C, but a C would not count in the graduate program.[375]

Her work with the Farm Security Administration had a profound impact on her life. When she began, she was not at all aware of the deprived conditions in which many Southern blacks lived, given her own middle-class upbringing and her experiences at the well-endowed Tuskegee Institute. At first, she was shocked to be sent to a school for black children where there were no desks, chairs, books, or other teaching materials. The experience made her realize what a difference she could make as a teacher. It gave her confidence, as she developed leadership abilities and management skills that would serve her well in her future employment. She also completed a master's degree, which distinguished her among American blacks in education in the 1940s and opened the door for her to a university teaching and administrative position.

CHAPTER 9

Arkansas Professor

Zenobia Perry met Lawrence Arnett Davis, President of Arkansas A. M. & N., who told her they needed to expand and develop their music department. "He knew nothing at all about music but was willing to learn and I thought that was such a beautiful philosophy. He sent a man named Armstrong from Missouri who said, 'We want you to come and see the campus and see what you think of it first, before we make any commitments.' I went there and we talked. 'We'll try in West Memphis,' which had a summer school, because at that time Arkansas didn't have a summer school at Pine Bluff. So I went to West Memphis after I had finished summer school. They had a second session and I started teaching elementary school teachers. When the regular semester began I went to Pine Bluff."[376]

Davis became president in 1943, at the age of twenty-nine. According to a college bulletin, "Under his dynamic and forceful guidance, the College has developed phenomenally and is one of the fastest growing institutions of higher learning in the entire South."[377] The school was, at the time, Arkansas's only state-supported college dedicated to the higher education of its Negro citizens.[378] Enrollment in the college was 1,310, with another one thousand in other departments, including "sub-collegiate" classes for veterans. For the 1949–50 school year, its annual operating budget was more than a million dollars. The mission of the school was "to provide such environment for learning and to promote such activities which will develop students into healthy, well-balanced personalities, useful citizens, clear and accurate thinkers, and effective leaders in the communities which they will serve."[379]

Zenobia Perry first learned about the music program of Pine Bluff from Mr. Russell, an assistant dean of the college. Ariel Lovelace had been choral conductor at the school for many years, but when the university decided to create a music degree program, they recognized a need to have qualified professionals to guide them.

The brochure gave the following description of the Division of Arts and Sciences:

> The famous College choir, which will be enlarged to 125 voices for the school year 1949-1950, is one of the finest college choral groups in the nation. In the spring of 1949 the choir made a tour of Louisiana, Mississippi, Arkansas, and several points in the Middle West, including Milwaukee, Beloit, Chicago, Gary, Detroit and Evansville.

The Department of Music gives invaluable experience to students who are interested in other fields but find music a "source of pleasure and an important element in personal living," as well as "those talented students who intend to make music their profession or engage in some occupation which demands musical knowledge."[380]

The College also boasted a College Marching Band, and weekly radio broadcasts of the choir from the College auditorium.[381] With her master's degree in education, Perry was a valuable asset to the college.[382] It was historically a black college, founded in 1873 as a branch of the Arkansas Indus University, and originally known as Branch Normal College.

When Zenobia Perry was invited to Pine Bluff, it was as Assistant Dean of Arts and Sciences and as music faculty.[383] She was not named chair of the Music Department, so as not to insult Ariel Lovelace, who had served the university for so many years with such devotion and was a generation older than she was. He had become chair of the Music Department in 1946, the year that a music major was first offered. Perry and Lovelace had a good relationship, working well together in developing the new music department.

Lovelace was a choral conductor with a "natural ability," according to Grace D. Wiley. Under his direction the choir sang a variety of music, from opera excerpts and classical requiems and oratorios to spirituals and folk music. He initiated the annual *Messiah* sing-along in Pine Bluff that continued, under the direction of his student, S. J. McGee. He left Pine Bluff in 1959 to take a position at another black school, Tougaloo College, near Jackson, Mississippi, and Wiley became chair.[384]

Zenobia Perry quickly realized that, in building a music department, she would have to make her own decisions. Lovelace told her, "You know, I never thought I'd be making bargains with a woman. I thought I'd be making bargains with a man. But you're just as tough as any man." She had a clear idea of what she needed to do to make it work and she did it.

When asked about her memories of life in Arkansas, Janis-Rozena Peri said,

> I loved it. I was in what was called the A. M. & N. Training School until I was in third grade. Then I was thrown out because I was a discipline problem. Then she [Mother] put me in a Catholic school for a year and in the course of that year, they discovered I was bored. That's why I was a discipline problem. So they moved me ahead into the fourth grade. Then the next year I went to public school because Mother said I needed to feel what it was like with the larger segment of the public because when I was in the training school, and then the Catholic school, my friends were very select and she said, "Your life's not going to be like that. You need to meet a larger segment of people."

CHAPTER 9

Public schools were kind of a shock to me. I just didn't like it. It was Carver Elementary School and Merrill Junior High. When we moved to Ohio, I was in the eighth grade.[385]

In addition to her university duties in Pine Bluff, Zenobia served as organist and choir director at the St. Andrews Episcopal Church from 1950 to 1955. In 1954, she received a merit award from the State of Arkansas in the field of music.

Music educator Arthur Kelton Lawrence from Columbus, Ohio, was also a pianist on the faculty in Arkansas.[386] He received his B.S. degree from West Virginia State College and his M.A. from Ohio State University and, at Zenobia's suggestion, did post-graduate studies at the University of Wyoming.[387] He taught music history, public school music, and music appreciation. They met in 1947, at a teacher-training workshop in Missouri where they both were leading workshops on music education. Working with the Vronsky & Babin piano duo at Wyoming, Perry and Lawrence decided to start their own piano duo to recruit students for the music program at Pine Bluff.[388]

They performed in Oklahoma, Kansas, Nebraska, Arkansas, and the Texan Panhandle. In Arkansas, they usually traveled by bus, but for performances outside of the state, they traveled in Lawrence's automobile. Their repertoire included Mozart, Beethoven, Chopin, Milhaud's *Scaramouche*, transcriptions of Bach, and Zenobia's arrangements of Florence Price's *Dances in the Canebrakes*. Most of the concerts were in high schools and community centers, but a few were in churches. The Arcasonic Piano Company of St. Louis, a division of Baldwin, provided a pair of six-foot grand pianos for their performances. Only occasionally did they have to play on old pianos. They were usually reimbursed for their expenses, but any fees they received beyond expenses were turned over to the university.

Perry recalled: "Once we went to a place called Sweet Home, Arkansas, and we had to play on two upright pianos. I'll never forget Sweet Home! But mostly we had excellent instruments provided by the piano company." For the daytime concerts, they wore professional clothes, but occasionally they dressed in concert attire for special events, Kelton in tails and Perry in a concert gown made by her.

Zenobia Perry and Kelton Lawrence were very close friends for many years; he adored Janis, but "romance never came up." During those years, Zenobia's mother lived with Janis and her, and was available to watch Janis while Zenobia was out of town, giving concerts. Kelton died three years after Zenobia moved to Wilberforce, suffering a major heart attack on Thanksgiving Day. She said, "We were dependent on each other for many things and were very close friends. Janis and I were very sad to lose him."

Zenobia Powell Perry and Kelton Lawrence, Duo-Piano Team, Pine Bluff, Arkansas. Zenobia Perry made her own gown.

CHAPTER 9

Despite her many administrative duties, Perry managed to compose some pieces during those years, including *Arkansia*, for violin and piano, dedicated to a violinist named Barker, on faculty at the University of Wyoming. She rearranged the work for string orchestra, with a violin solo for the second movement.

Perry wrote several pieces for students in the department. "The things that were available for student performance to me sounded so stilted and they belonged in a certain period. I said, 'They have to have something else to play.' And I'd ask one of the students, 'How would you like it if I wrote something just for you?'" Her first composition was *Essay, for Piano*, written for Alma Edwards.

It was during her seventh year at Arkansas that Perry realized that she was a composer, more than a pianist.[389] Perry "reinvented" herself once again: she resigned her position as an administrator at the University of Arkansas and became an Assistant Professor of Theory and Composition at Central State University in Ohio, so she could focus on her work as a composer.[390]

This took courage and a commitment to creating the life she envisioned for herself. She had no safety net, only what she could provide for herself and her daughter by her own labor. She was twice divorced, her father was dead, and her mother was not able to help financially. Perry was forty-seven at the time, considered to be middle-aged for her generation. There were no guarantees for her in Ohio; she accepted the position based on her assessment of the sincerity of the CSU president, Dr. Charles H. Wesley. At Aspen, he could clearly see she was becoming a composer, despite the fact that her colleagues in Arkansas did not acknowledge this change. This demonstrates Wesley's wisdom as a college president, in that he knew to ask her what it would take to entice her to move to Wilberforce. She answered him directly and a deal was made—a deal that changed her life and the life of Central State. The story of how Milhaud and Willman became her mentors and helped prepare her to make this transition in her life is also a "distinctively American" story.

10. Becoming a Composer
Studies with Milhaud and Willman

"You could have bought me for a penny that day because Milhaud was interested in me taking composition classes with him."

—*Zenobia Powell Perry,* September 30, 2001

Zenobia Perry was forty-one years old when she decided to seek additional training in theory and composition. She was an assistant dean and faculty member at the University of Arkansas, teaching piano and giving concerts. She had heard that there were good theory teachers at the University of Wyoming, particularly a counterpoint teacher with whom she wanted to study. When she auditioned in the spring of 1949, she was introduced to Darius Milhaud, who invited her to study composition with him. Allan Willman suggested that she enroll in the master's program in composition, because, at that time, they were not offering a doctorate in composition.

CHAPTER 10
Allan Arthur Willman

Allan Willman, c.1947–48.
Courtesy of Jo Ann Haycraft.

Allan Arthur Willman (1909–1989) began teaching at the University of Wyoming in fall 1936 and became chair of the Music Department in 1945, a position he held until his retirement in 1974.[391] Born in Hinckley, Illinois, he grew up in Abingdon, Illinois, and received his B.M. degree from Knox College and his M.M. degree from the Chicago Musical College, where he studied with Maurice Aronson, Alexander Raab, and Lillian Powers. After hearing him perform an original composition, Frederick Stock presented him with a check to use as he wished. Willman submitted an orchestral work to the Paderewski Competition in Boston and won first prize, one thousand dollars, which he used to travel to Paris, for studies with Nadia Boulanger and Thomas de Hartmann. The Paderewski prize was awarded for his symphonic poem, *Solitude*, which was first performed by the Boston Symphony Orchestra, with Serge Koussevitzky conducting in 1936. He studied in Europe for a year, making many important contacts, including the French composer Darius Milhaud. Soon after returning to the United States in 1936, he began his academic career at the University of Wyoming in Laramie, and, in 1940, was in residence at the MacDowell Colony.

Willman was drafted into the U.S. Army in March 1943, where he became assistant director of a military band and wrote original music for the Army Air Corps radio program, as well as for a small orchestra. While stationed in Texas, he was given a leave to return to Laramie to play a concert with Darius Milhaud on May 6, 1945. The gala concert at the University auditorium featured the works of Milhaud, including his second cello concerto, with the Belgian Joseph Wetzel as soloist, and *Scaramouche* (1939) in a version for two pianos, performed by Willman and Milhaud.[392] It included the expanded University Symphony Orchestra, conducted by Robert Becker. The orchestra had been augmented with musicians from Cheyenne, Torrington, Wheatland, Douglas, Casper, and Sheridan, Wyoming, as well as Denver, Colorado. Also on the program were Milhaud's arrangement of an Overture and Allegro by Couperin, three of Milhaud's *Souvenirs from Brazil*,[393] the Suite from *Les Songes*, and Schubert's *Unfinished Symphony*.[394] The concert was a tremendous success; when it was over, Willman returned to military service.

Darius Milhaud mentions Willman in his autobiography, *Notes Without Music*,

> Throughout my illness, which lasted several months, I continued teaching, my pupils coming to me in my bedroom. I was suffering from such a great deficiency of calcium that the doctors thought I should never be able to walk again. I did not undertake any more journeys alone, except to Laramie, Wyoming. Allan Wilman [sic], who teaches music in the University of Wyoming, had organized a series of annual concerts of contemporary music, the first of which he had reserved for me. I was to conduct my *Cello Concerto*, played by Wetzel, a Belgian soloist. As there were not enough students to form an orchestra, many of them having been called up, Allan Wilman [sic] recruited his players from schools sometimes very remote from Laramie, had them over for several week-ends of rehearsals, and lodged them in the university for the week before the concert. Thus my orchestra consisted wholly of young people filled with an abundance of goodwill and enthusiasm. How it warmed one's heart to see them![395]

Willman resumed his duties as chair of the Music Department in 1948. He is credited widely for expanding the department from a little Music Hall to a Fine Arts Center and for his outstanding abilities as a musician, teacher, and administrator.[396]

In 1953, Willman toured Europe with violinist Rudolf Kolisch, appearing four times at the Darmstadt Summer Festival of Contemporary

Music. They played Roger Sessions's *Duo* (1942) and Arnold Schoenberg's *Phantasie,* Op. 47 (1949), to great critical acclaim.[397] They also performed works of Ernst Krenek, Edward Kilenyi, Beethoven, and Schubert. Kolisch was first violinist of the Pro Arte Quartet, which performed regularly at the University of Wyoming.

A brochure entitled "Music Study at the University of Wyoming," published in 1950 or 1951, describes the program offered there when Zenobia Perry was a student. It states that the following musicians had performed there: Isaac Stern, Gregor Piatigorsky, Dorothy Maynor, Grant Johannesen, Nelson Eddy, Roth String Quartet, Minneapolis and Denver Symphony Orchestras, Ballet Russe, and Burl Ives. Both Milhaud and American composer Roy Harris had conducted festival programs of their own music. It lists the faculty as Willman (piano and composition), George W. Gunn (voice), Robert R. Becker (violin, viola, and director of the University Orchestra), Hugh A. MacKinnon (organ and theory), Robert S. Vagner (woodwinds, director of the University Band), Helen H. Hylton (pianist, music literature), Bruce Rodgers (voice, theory, choral groups), Theodore P. Walstrum (piano, music literature), Marysue Barnes (cello, theory), and Edgar J. Lewis (brass instruments). Harry J. Carnine and Anola E. Radtke are listed as faculty for music education. Biographical sketches of the faculty members are included in the brochure.[398]

A splendid pianist, Willman's compositions include at least two large orchestral works, chamber music, piano pieces, and songs. Zenobia studied both composition and piano with him. He was the perfect mentor for her in many ways. Not only was he a fine musician, dedicated to performing works of contemporary composers, but he also was a talented composer with widespread contacts throughout the United States and Europe. He knew several successful women composers. He had studied with Nadia Boulanger and, while at the MacDowell Colony in 1940, he had made friends with Mabel Daniels and Jeanne Behrend, both accomplished East Coast composers. He had taught several women composition students, and his wife, Regina Hansen, was a composer. Needing no convincing that women could compose, he took women musicians seriously and treated them with respect.

At the University of Wyoming, Willman is also remembered for developing the music curriculum and the music collection in the libraries; establishing festivals and concert and lecture series; and overseeing the building of new facilities for the music program.[399] Because of his extensive network, he arranged for many distinguished artists to visit the University of Wyoming during his tenure there, significantly enhancing the university's public profile. For example, in 1947, Johanna and Roy Harris, whom he had met in Paris while a student of Nadia Boulanger, were guests at the University of Wyoming. Willman's own compositions were performed by the Chicago Civic Orchestra, the NBC Radio Orchestra, the Denver Symphony, and the Cleveland Quartet, among others.[400]

In 1949, Willman established the five-week summer Creative Arts Workshop at the University of Wyoming. He invited the Milhauds (Darius, Madeleine, and their son Daniel) to stay at the Willman home during the inaugural workshop. Milhaud was then Professor at the Conservatory of Paris, Professor of Music at Mills College, and Honorary Director of the Music Academy of the West in Santa Barbara.[401] At that festival, Milhaud premiered *L'Enfant Aimé* for piano, a suite of five pieces (July 1, 1949); he composed his *Fourth Piano Concerto* while staying with the Willmans.[402] The Creative Summer Arts Festival and Workshop continued annually from 1949 until 1952. Besides Milhaud, other composers featured at the workshop were Ernst Bacon (1898–1990), and Roger Sessions (1896–1985), as well as pianists Edward Kilenyi and Gunnar Johannsen, and the Pro Arte Quartet from the University of Wisconsin.[403] Ernst Bacon (1898–1990), a talented composer remembered particularly for his art songs, became a friend of Willman's. Gunnar Johannsen (1906–1991) was a Danish-American concert pianist and composer, who settled in U.S. after 1929, and was Artist-in-Residence at the University of Wisconsin from 1939 to 1976. Edward Kilenyi, Jr. (b.1910) was a pianist and teacher who was on the faculty of Florida State University in Tallahassee.[404]

The Vronsky & Babin piano duo was also at Wyoming and at Aspen during those years.[405] Vitya [Victoria] Vronsky was a Russian-American pianist, born in Evpatoria in the Crimea in 1909 (d.1992). She studied at the Kiev Conservatory, then with Petri and Schnabel in Berlin, and later with Cortot in Paris. She married the pianist Victor Babin in 1933, who was also Russian, born in Moscow in 1908 (d.1982). He studied at the Conservatory of Riga, Latvia, and, after graduating in 1927, went to Berlin, also to study with Artur Schnabel. He studied composition with Franz Schreker at the Berlin Hochschule für Musik. In 1937, the couple went to the United States, where they toured widely as the Vronsky & Babin piano duo. From 1943 to 1946, Babin served in the United States Army and became a naturalized American citizen in 1944. From 1951 to 1954, he taught at the Aspen Music School and, in 1961, was appointed director of the Cleveland Institute of Music, where he and his wife taught in the 1960s. He composed two concertos for two pianos and orchestra and several duo-piano pieces, which he and his wife performed often.[406]

CHAPTER 10

Zenobia remembered that the Vronsky & Babin duo played "Sheep may safely graze," a Bach chorale, which they had arranged for two pianos, Gershwin's *American in Paris,* and works by Chopin. Although she did not study piano with either of them, she did attend all their concerts in Wyoming and at Aspen. They had a tremendous impact on her performing career in Arkansas, particularly in terms of repertoire selection.

She began her studies at the University of Wyoming[407] in the summer of 1949, when Darius Milhaud (1892–1974) was in residence, and continued studying there in the summer of 1950.

Studies with Milhaud at Wyoming and Aspen

Darius Milhaud overheard Zenobia Perry improvising at a piano, while waiting for her formal audition with Willman.

> It was around the noon hour so none of the offices were open, so I sat down in the Student Union and some Wyoming dancers came in to practice. They had a large mirror that covered the entire wall, so they could look in the mirror and see what they were doing. So I sat down at the piano and started to improvise to their dancing. One was doing a two-four, so I'd start to do that. Someone else came in, doing a three-four, so I'd change to six-eight. Somebody else came in with four-four so I added that. Whatever they did, I tried to go along. This man was sitting in the corner and enjoying it and he started laughing out loud. Then the bell rang and everybody stopped and went upstairs. He was later introduced to me as the French composer Darius Milhaud. I'd never seen him before, although I had seen him in books. But he was fatter and more homelike than he was in these pictures I had seen. You could have bought me for a penny that day because Milhaud was interested in me taking composition classes with him.[408]

While sitting in the lounge, Milhaud heard her, but did not introduce himself. When they met later that day, during her audition for admission to the music department, he asked her if she would like to study composition with him, admitting that he had overheard her earlier in the day. She studied with him that first summer at the University of Wyoming,[409] then returned in the summer of 1950, but Milhaud did not.[410] In the summer of 1951, she was composer of the Creative Arts Workshop Leaders Committee, which included dancer Betty Thompson, artist Fred Conway, sculptor Hale Boyle, and dramatist William Saroyan. From the workshop, she went to Aspen to continue her studies with Milhaud.

This was the first year for the Aspen Summer School and Conference on Contemporary Music, organized by Mack Harrell at the request of Walter Paepcke. It was attended by students from thirty states, plus Alaska, Hawaii, Canada, and Norway. Victor Babin was the director from 1951 to 1954. The faculty included theorist and composer Charles Jones, bassist Stuart Sankey, pianist Rudolph Firkusny, flutist Albert Tipton, pianist Mary Morris, and cellist Claus Adam. College credit was granted through the Lamont School of Music at the University of Denver; tuition for the eight weeks was $280.[411] Milhaud mentions this summer in Aspen in his autobiography:

> The Aspen Festival, to which is now attached a summer music school where we both teach, made quite a long stop for us. We settled down in this tiny town, which had enjoyed the highest prosperity in 1890, and which now, thanks to the magic wand of Walter Paepcke, who has restored its position as a cultural center, was crowded with students, instrumentalists, singers, and composers. Some of them had already worked with us. The night of our arrival they serenaded us outside our apartment. The month of August, which we spent there, was marvelously exhilarating. Trips to the mountains alternated with concerts. We were surrounded with friends, including Claire Reis, Florence Heifetz and her children. Jo [Josefa] Heifetz had studied composition with me in Paris; she had spent the winter there, and had become a member of our small Paris circle.[412]

According to Charles Jones, Milhaud became a member of the Aspen faculty, because the director of the music department at Music Academy of the West, where Jones and Milhaud both taught, sold Walter Paepcke the Santa Barbara composition faculty "like a baseball team."[413] Having attended the festival in 1950 for the premiere of his eighteenth string quartet, Milhaud founded the Conference on Contemporary Music at Aspen the following year, attending for the next sixteen summers.[414] His wife, Madeleine, taught French diction and later opera production, and staged numerous operas at the festival. Charles Jones became co-director of the composition program.[415]

Milhaud was a splendid teacher for Zenobia Perry at that point in her development. The eminent French composer came to the United States in July 1940, at the outbreak of World War II, and taught at Mills College in Oakland, California. He immigrated because his name was on Germany's wanted list of prominent Jewish artists. In 1947, he returned to France to accept a position as a professor at the Paris Conservatory, returning annually to the United States. He retained his position at Mills College until 1971 and taught at Aspen during the summers. Perry remembered hearing him quip that he had left his household furniture on the boat in the Atlantic, because he could not decide whether to live in France or in the United States.[416]

Darius Milhaud with students at the University of Wyoming, 1949.
Zenobia Powell Perry is on the left,
Howard Brubeck and Henry Brubeck on the right.

Milhaud was very interested in black music. His own ballet, *La Création du monde* (1923), which portrays the Creation in terms of "Negro cosmology," is often cited as the earliest example of the use of blues and jazz in a symphonic score. Perry reported:

> I said to Darius Milhaud, "Sometimes I think we can take an idiom that is racial and develop it to one of the European standards." He said, "Like what?" And I said, "Did you ever hear tell of writing a sonata in jazz?" He said, "Oh, why don't you do that for me?" I was surprised that he took me up like that and then two days later, he asked me, "How are you coming with your work?" And he had everyone listen to it then.
>
> One of the students there then said, "I think I'll have to call my piece Opus One-Half because after hearing this, I've got to do something else with what I have done." So he wouldn't let me see what he had done until the next week.

BECOMING A COMPOSER

By then I knew what he had presented was his and not trying to imitate somebody else. We got to be pretty good friends. Howard and Henry Brubeck were in the class, Dave Brubeck's brothers. Howard, particularly, wrote quite a lot. But I don't know why we never hear anything of Dave's brothers. Perhaps Howard was there to give Henry a backing because Henry was very, very sensitive and very, very shy. And sometimes when he had things to do on the piano he would come in and nobody was playing the piano, he'd play until he got exhausted and then crawl up on the piano and go to sleep. I never saw anybody do that before.[417]

Howard Brubeck (1916–1993) studied with Milhaud at Mills College and received his M.A. in 1941. He was Milhaud's assistant from 1944 until 1950. Between 1950 and 1953, he taught at San Diego State College, where he later became chair of the music department and, in 1966, dean of humanities at Palomar College.[418]

As a part of her assistantship at the University of Wyoming, Zenobia took some musical dictation from Milhaud, when his arthritis was inflamed, and generally acted as his personal assistant while on campus.

Milhaud's style as a compositional teacher has been described as "characteristically undogmatic."[419] He said, "Teaching composition involves, I believe, allowing [students] to liberate themselves from all the conventional formulae helping them, by a sort of cleansing process, to realize their often sensitive and refined personalities, which many years of strict, but necessary exercises have prevented from flowering."[420]

Perry recalled,

> He would give us an idiom [a melodic idea] and perhaps a rhythm for a couple of measures and he says, "Now see what you'd like to do with that." You could change it if you wanted to. Then the class would perform them or someone would play them at the piano. We did a lot of sight-reading of everybody's music. He would ask the class to critique it first, then he would do it. I thought he was always very, very gentle. Like he would say about something I wrote, "That sounds almost like a sonata in jazz." Another student would say, "I don't see jazz in that." Milhaud would say, "What kind of rhythm would you call that?"[421]

He was always encouraging. "Instead of saying the piece was trite, he would say, 'This is a part of you that can be even unlimited if you'd go just a little farther and then the next piece you write will be beyond that. I'm sure it will be.' He said this most of the time. I was quite fascinated by the fact that he didn't try to make me write like he wrote. In fact, he didn't ask any of us to do that."[422]

Perry added, "He was very, very complimentary. He never seemed to discourage any student effort. If he thought that you perhaps could have made something more than what you were doing, he would make a suggestion, but he wanted you to write as you would write. For instance, I was doing a violin piece and he said, 'You know, that violin piece would sound fine if you could make a low E on the violin, but you can't. If you hear a string that has to make that E, perhaps you have to use another instrument. It would make a fine duet.' So without telling me I would have to write a duet, he told me that what I was doing was out of focus on my instrument. He did that sort of thing with all of his students."

Milhaud was kind and compassionate with his students. "I remember a student came up with a piece that had Opus One-Half on it and Milhaud said, 'What's the one-half for? You mean that half of you went through this motion or do you mean that this is half of what you were writing? Now, where did you put the other half?' The student had no suitable explanation. He said, 'Well, I think I wrote it kind of half-heartedly.' And Milhaud said, 'How do you write half-heartedly? You either have to write it or you don't write it, don't you?' Those are the sort of things that he would engage in."[423] With Milhaud, Perry not only learned how to compose, but she also learned ways of teaching composition.

Milhaud was loved for his keen sense of humor, but Perry remembered that, "occasionally his arthritis would get the better of him and he would listen to what we had written as he had suggested and then not say a word for the whole time. We could see this because his hands would be swollen."[424]

The Russian-born pianist, conductor, and composer, Alexander Tcherepnin, spent the summer of 1952 in Aspen, at the invitation of Milhaud. Tcherepnin (1899–1977) was born in St. Petersburg and had had his principal residence in Paris until 1949. Between 1934 and 1937 he made two visits to the Far East, performing in Japan and China, where numerous composers studied with him. He married Chinese pianist Lee Hsien-Ming. In 1949, he and his wife joined the faculty of De Paul University in Chicago, where he taught for fifteen years. His opera, *The Nymph and the Farmer*, had its premiere at Aspen on August 13, 1952. Zenobia Perry was impressed with them, recalling that "he was a very charming person. Tall and slender and he was married to a little Chinese woman who was about 4' 7". He'd always walk in front of her and she'd follow him."

In the summer of 1956 or 1957, Perry took her daughter Janis to Aspen: "Mrs. Milhaud was just fascinated with Janis. She would take her and keep her all day if I would let her. Janis would come back speaking French."[425] Janis-Rozena Peri recalls,

I thought he [Milhaud] was a fabulous human being. He was the most magical human being. He also had great candy.... He was so clever, so witty. I was not accustomed to European sophistication, wit. He would say things which days later I'd figure out were funny. That was new to me.

It was very interesting for me to see my mother in that position, as a student. I was used to seeing her as the boss, so to see her in a situation where she wasn't the boss was really unique for me. It was almost puzzling, strange.[426]

In Aspen, Perry also studied orchestration with Charles Jones (b.1910), a Canadian-born composer and teacher. He taught at Mills College from 1939 to 1944, before going to the Juilliard School and Mannes College of Music. He began teaching at Aspen in 1951, continuing until the 1980s.[427]

Charles Jones, Aspen Music School Faculty, at home in New York.
Photo by Jeannie Pool, 1994.

Perry graduated from the University of Wyoming on August 20, 1954, with an M.A. degree in music.[428] Her thesis was a piece for orchestra that was performed by the University Orchestra in Casper, Wyoming, with a second performance in Denver a few months later.

Willman, Milhaud, and Jones revealed an entirely new world of music to Zenobia Perry. Through them, she discovered many composers, particularly European, but also American, whose works she had never heard. They introduced her to the style of international contemporary music, which dominated the new music scene in America and Europe in the late 1940s and '50s. This included the music of Ernst Krenek, Roger

Sessions, Ernst Bacon, Roy Harris, Igor Stravinsky, Aaron Copland, Elliott Carter, Walter Piston, Virgil Thomson, Benjamin Britten, and Olivier Messiaen, among others. These composers were not performed on black college campuses during this time, nor did Perry have opportunities to hear them elsewhere. Her teachers opened her ears and her mind to new concepts in music and new approaches to composition. Through them, she also met many internationally known performers, writers, dancers, and other artists. To gain access to this international contemporary art world via Laramie, Wyoming, and Aspen, Colorado, was truly an amazing experience for this black Creek Indian woman from Oklahoma. Her life would never be the same.

The Move to Ohio

In the fall of 1955, Perry accepted a position at Central State College in Wilberforce, Ohio. Originally named the Ohio African University by the Methodist Episcopal Church, the school was founded in 1844. It was closed briefly in 1862, due to financial problems, and purchased by the AME Church as a site for a seminary. The name was changed in 1860 to Wilberforce University—not to be confused with Wilberforce College, which is another institution in the same town. By 1951, it began using the name of Central State College, and became a university in 1965.

The period 1951–1965 was one of exceptional growth and development for Central State College[429] and it was during this time that Perry was asked to come and teach. Before coming to Wilberforce University as its president in June 1942, Dr. Charles H. Wesley had spent twenty-eight years at Howard University. He held a Ph.D. from Harvard University, had also studied abroad, and held eight honorary degrees, including a Doctor of Divinity degree from Wilberforce University (1928).[430] There were many difficult issues during the first decade of his presidency, but by 1955, the college had stabilized. Between 1955 and 1965 the student population grew from 947 to 2,241. By 1965, the year it became a university, the faculty had 101 members.[431] The average salary for faculty in the 1959–60 academic year was $6,593—lower than other state colleges in Ohio and in the region. Intent on raising the quality of the education, Dr. Wesley increased the salaries and hired better-qualified teachers, including thirty-nine Ph.D.s by 1965. Dean Howard H. Long established a system of merit increases in

1954 and systematic evaluation of all teachers by 1960, which contributed to the educational quality of the school.[432]

Central State College had a reputation for helping its students, "drawn so heavily from rural and inner city poor families."[433] Wesley was well-known for being able to find sources for financial assistance, beyond traditional forms of financial aid, and an extensive work-study program. This caused some problems later in his administration, because he often let needy students continue at CSU without paying fees.[434] He knew that many of the students who matriculated at Central State between 1951 and 1965 were not well prepared for college life, compared to other college freshmen, but Central State was committed to raising them up, by providing remedial education and financial assistance.[435] He was clearly dedicated to helping black students "learn to achieve a new mental health for themselves."[436] His goal was to create a program to improve the students' chances for academic success. He retired in 1965, but his tenure at Central State was the most formidable of any president in the institution's history.[437]

Central State was promoted as an interracial, intercultural, and international institution.[438] The number of white students increased by almost 20 percent between 1951 and 1962. According to the student paper, *The Gold Torch*, two white Central State students were arrested in Jackson, Mississippi, for attempting to integrate a "white only" bus station lunch room in June 1961.[439] Central State also had a reputation for "its strong religious moral atmosphere. Just as it assumed a quasi-parental role in improving its students socially, culturally, and academically, so it was willing to maintain tough moral and ethical standards."[440] Students from twenty-seven different denominations attended in 1950–51, only eleven of 769 said they had no church affiliation.[441] Wesley was committed to fostering "a fully integrated personality and not merely a mind crammed with sufficient facts to pass the required examinations and accumulate the total units of credit. We expect our graduates to have personal integrity, character, human understanding and stable conduct. Here students of various religions may live in mutual respect and complete fellowship."[442] A deeply religious man, Dr. Wesley encouraged faculty to provide moral and spiritual models of behavior.[443] Central State College attracted more than half of the student body from outside Ohio, even though out-of-state students had to pay one and one-half times more in fees than in-state students.[444]

Zenobia Perry described her first meeting with Dr. Wesley, during the summer of 1955:

> Dr. Wesley was attending a conference at Aspen. The music at Aspen was held in a big tent. The various classes would meet in the morning and practice and

do all the things necessary to get ready for the afternoon concerts. You had to pass by this tent to get to a news conference. Dr. Wesley passed by. He saw this little black spot in the tent during a rehearsal and he wondered who it was and he came by and asked.

He said, "Have you ever thought about teaching?" I said, "Oh, yes, I teach in Arkansas in the regular term." He said, "We need you in Ohio." From that day, he wrote me, he called me, he sent me telegrams, asking me to come to Central State and he kept it up until I finally said yes. School was going on when I got here [in Ohio]. It was in November when I came. I saw him and I told him, "I just can't jump up and leave Arkansas. I have to get some replacement. I'll have to tender my resignation." [445]

Grace Wiley, a 1954 graduate of Arkansas A. M. & N. was given Perry's position at Arkansas, so she moved with her daughter, Janis, to Ohio in the middle of the semester. At Central State, she was named Composer-in-Residence and was made an assistant professor of music.[446] Her duties included teaching theory, composition, and counterpoint.

When she first arrived in Wilberforce, Zenobia and Janis stayed in the barracks on campus provided for faculty. As soon as they were financially able, many of the faculty members moved out of the barracks and purchased homes. Zenobia had trouble finding someone who would rent or sell her a house, because she was a black single parent, and an Episcopal, whereas Methodists dominated the economy of the area. Eventually she decided to build a home of her own. According to daughter Janis, "At that time, there were very few single mothers in Wilberforce. I think Mother might have been the only one. So there were lots of questions about why she was divorced. I think if Mother had just lied and said [her husband] had died, it would have been much easier for her."[447]

After months of searching, she found someone who would sell her a lot within walking distance of campus. She developed her own building plans, filed them with the appropriate county agency, and had them approved. She purchased an old frame house from nearby Wright Patterson Air Force Base and had it moved to the site. Having taken one course in construction at Tuskegee Institute, she felt she knew enough to build her own house. She sought a carpenter to work with her, but all of the local white carpenters refused. Finally, while visiting a hardware store in nearby Johnstown, she found a retired carpenter named Steiner, a white man, who agreed to help her. With his assistance, Zenobia Perry managed to build her house in 1956; she and Janis moved in. She continued to reside in that home— which survived the tornado in 1974—for the remainder of her life.

Zenobia Powell Perry in front of the house she built in Wilberforce, Ohio.
Photo by Jeannie Pool.

When Zenobia first arrived at Central State University, the chair of the music department was Anna Terry. She was from Cambridge, Massachusetts, and had trained at the Boston Conservatory in music education and piano performance. She welcomed Perry, for she had been wanting to expand the department to include composition as an area of specialization for music majors. Under Terry's leadership, the department had a positive spirit and worked closely, like a family, to create a program that would develop the talents of their students. Many of the students were preparing for careers in music education or church music, although there were some gifted performers. By the 1960s, however, the department began to attract a higher caliber of music students, including those who wanted to major in theory and composition.

Also on the faculty was Beatrice O'Rourke, who became one of Perry's closest friends and colleagues. She too was recruited by Dr. Wesley, who asked her to build a hundred-voice choir to represent the university. In the 1950s and early '60s, the college choir sang at the weekly Sunday morning church service on campus. They toured the United States and Europe, and participated in numerous competitions. O'Rourke proofread much of Perry's music and directed premieres of several of Perry's choral pieces. About Zenobia, she said, "She's just forever writing, forever writing. She writes so well and her scores are so neat."[448] O'Rourke retired in the early 1980s, after which she continued to teach part-time.

Faculty from that period in the school's history recalled digging into their own pockets both to help students travel to professional auditions and also to help clothe them appropriately. "The old pattern of faculty self-sacrifice was firmly rooted in CSU history."[449] Both Beatrice O'Rourke and Zenobia Perry recalled that Anna Terry once gave a student the shoes off her own feet, so the student would make a more favorable impression at an audition. Perry recalled buying tickets for her students to attend visiting orchestra performances in nearby cities, taking with her as many students as could pile into her car.[450] Although the faculty members were not highly paid, and had little money to buy teaching materials and extra items needed for the music curriculum, nevertheless they managed to be resourceful and find what they needed to provide good education for their students.

When Anna Terry retired in 1965, after thirty-one years at CSU, she returned to Massachusetts, to become active on the school board.[451] The new chair was not as supportive of the faculty and reassigned Perry to teach piano and other fundamentals. He caused so many political problems in the department, that he was eventually promoted to an administrative position in the university, and a new chair was appointed.

Like her mentor, Nathaniel Dett, Zenobia Perry continued her education throughout her life. She took additional music courses at Iowa State University (spring 1962 and summers 1963 and '64) and the State University of New York at Potsdam (summer 1964). From 1964 until 1970, she also hosted a radio show, *Musical Classics*, on WCSU, the campus radio station, heard Sunday evenings, from 6 to 8 p.m.

Wilberforce was an oasis of sorts, during this period, despite the racial tension in neighboring Dayton, Cincinnati, Springfield, and Columbus in the 1950s and '60s. Zenobia joined the Greene County Branch of the NAACP in 1962 and served that organization throughout her life.

When Janis was a sophomore in high school, Grandmother Birdie came to live with Janis and Zenobia. In the 1960s, Birdie had married a man named Jenkins whom she had known for nearly thirty years. After his death, she moved to Wilberforce, where she died in 1967. According to Janis Peri,

> Mr. Jenkins evidently always had a crush on my grandmother. The grandchildren were less nice about it than the children. The children tried

to be nice about it. Mr. Jenkins was a fine human being. He was a good person. The thing is that he just did not have much formal education and we were accustomed to our grandmother wanting to be with people with more education. My grandmother, herself, did not have much education. My mother told me once that maybe things were hard for Mama being around people who had so much more education than she had. Maybe she thought she'd like a husband she felt like she could talk to. She was very formal. My grandmother and grandfather had a great love match of all times, but nevertheless she was very much in awe of him.[452]

In 1974, 70 percent of CSU's facilities were destroyed by a tornado—thirteen of the fourteen main campus buildings were destroyed and four people killed. Afterwards, life at CSU was dominated by rebuilding the campus, a major economic recession, decline in enrollment, and significant cuts in funding from the State of Ohio. Now, the CSU Music Department is located in a new multi-million-dollar building called the Paul Robeson Cultural and Performing Arts Center, and the university takes pride in the internationally known guest artists who have performed there.

Another valued colleague at Central State University was Arthur Herndon, who performed some of Perry's works.

> Mr. Arthur Herndon, tenor, born in Cincinnati, Ohio, has received the Bachelor of Music Degree from the Cincinnati College Conservatory of Music where he studied voice under the late Robert Powell.
>
> Mr. Herndon was the recipient of the John Hay Whitney Fellowship Award, and the Fulbright Award.... Presently, Mr. Herndon is an Instructor in Voice at Central State University, Wilberforce, Ohio; he is also Director of the University's Concert Chorale, Chorus and Opera Workshop.[453]

Accomplished and handsome, Herndon was a substantial addition to the CSU music faculty. He sang many of Zenobia's songs and presented her choral works in performances by the CSU Concert Chorale, which he directed. He was very talented as a singer and conductor, but had only earned an undergraduate degree. Janis Peri said, "He was not treated very well by the CSU Administration and was told to go back to school to get a master's degree, so he did. While he was in Cincinnati earning his master's degree, CSU let him go,"[454] and Zenobia Perry lost a supportive colleague.

During the 1980–81 academic year, an investigative team of the Office of Civil Rights, U.S. Department of Education, visited six state-assisted institutions of higher education. The 1981 report stated: "Although the State of Ohio had made improvements in providing access to higher education for black students, it was nevertheless in violation of Title VI of the 1964 Civil Rights Act. The finding was based specifically on the state's action

CHAPTER 10

which 'dissuaded white students from choosing to attend Central State.'"[455] This was a terrible blow to CSU, which had always been underfunded, compared to other institutions in the state university system. This report and other actions in the 1980s led to yet another decade of instability for CSU.

In 1982, Perry retired from Central State University to compose full-time. One of her students, Lennard V. Moses, was later given her position at the University.[456] When asked why she did not stop composing when she retired, she said, "It's just a part of me. I feel so relieved and good. I used to tell my daughter that I feel as good as I did when she was born. It's a fulfillment."[457] She continued, "It is very rewarding because, while I was teaching, a number of times, I would put down things that I wanted to develop, and by the time I got ready to develop them, they had changed."[458] The twenty years following her retirement were very productive for her as a composer, with many new pieces, including some major commissions and premiere performances.[459]

Professor Emerita Zenobia Powell Perry, 1985.

Music in Community Living (1958)*

by Zenobia P. Perry

Wherever people are found, regardless of how remote or secluded they may be, there also will music be found. For one of the most estimable qualities of music is that it ministers to all our moods—soothing our sorrows; voicing our triumphs, and giving a sense of satisfaction to our hours of leisure. . . .

It is interesting to note how the rise of music has paralleled the rise of all nations throughout history. Unquestionably a nation's highest ideals are revealed in its music, for it is one of the most reliable tests of values in the life of any people. With its vocabulary changes and use of new idioms it is possible for music to express in its own peculiar way the times in which man lives. If we wish proof of the way imagination in a composer is stirred by the times in which he lives, we can find no more significant example than in our own day. For in listening to contemporary music in its many facets with an attempt to comprehend the meaning, we find trends of equal social significance with those of the past. However, the modern movement in music is a many-sided one influenced by new technical problems resulting from social changes, modern educational developments, international relations and wide communication. The wheels of industry, the grinding of cranks and shafts, moving in pulsating rhythms, have inspired much in contemporary music wherein the basic elements of life, the dynamics of motion and sound, are used subjectively for expression. . . .

The use of music among primitive people indicates a continuous movement between extreme points of action and rest, suggestive of a monotonous repetitious movement from a high and excited pitch of tone to a low and relaxed one within a limited range. Also primitive man may have found rhythm of body movement in work and dance suggestive of his tonal utterances. This lends much to the possibility that solo and choral singing were practiced side by side from the beginning. Combined singing of persons of different age levels and of both sexes must have produced a crude polyphony and unintentional yet satisfying ornamentation of their monotonous melodies. . . .

While every country has its own folk music, some races and nations have shown unusual vitality in preserving their traditional melodies and using them in their art music. There are many authentic American folk songs. Included among them are Indian songs of many tribes, their songs of religious rites and secular ceremonies and celebrations. Some are more primitive than others. . . . But among the imported folk music materials that have become definitely Americanized, greatest significance is given to the African. Negro spirituals represent an interpretation of the Bible and are strongly influenced by the conditions of Negro life in slavery. In addition there are Negro work songs, banjo-accompanied dance songs and lively singing games. All of the old minstrel shows grew out of the slaves' activities for entertaining their masters.

CHAPTER 10

Even our contemporary dance music is based upon rhythms borrowed from Negro folk music. For we have witnessed the thunderous two-way fusion of African and Cuban rhythms; and the number of successful blends are becoming more abundant. . . .

Today music of many distinct varieties serves as a background for our daily activities; and by means of musical communication, such as is afforded by radios and record players, America lessens the fatigue, pressures and tensions of her peoples' busy lives. Meanwhile, the idea of every person participating in making music is steadily growing and including more and more people of every age level in every community throughout the nation. Once again, as history repeats itself, festivals are gaining enormous popularity. But now industries are the patrons contributing to the support of these musical gatherings throughout the world. Many of the old world sovereigns have disappeared, but performances are still given in castles and halls which were built partially for this purpose. And again many more people are seeking and finding experiences in music through festival participation. Through the invention and wide distribution of radio, the fields are green again and music may be heard as cheaply as one obtains water. For the more we hear music the more we tend to find experiences in it. At present we are a well-informed people, by radio and the press, of musical offerings presented for entertainment around the world.

Besides the physical, psychological and socializing effects of music there is also the ability of certain types of music to elevate man emotionally, attune him to the infinite and make him more receptive to the communion of ideas. And being great and sensitive human beings, we know both doubt and joy, despair and exultation and seek to find these same qualities expressed in music. For, All the music that ever was still sounds; all the music that is to be still slumbers. Life and death are one, and in the truest sense, the whole universe is a song.

---

*From a special issue titled "Perennial Springs of Human Values," *Journal of Human Relations* 6/3 (Spring 1958), published at Central State College, Wilberforce, Ohio. The purpose of this issue was the hope that to "expand the nature, function and value of these perennial sources of human culture would stress remembrance of this rich cultural heritage in this our age when 'the world is too much with us'—a world that seeks peace through ballistic means. Through contemplation of these offerings may there come a measure of faith in man's humanity to man!" (xiv).

11. Analysis of Musical Style and Selected Works

Zenobia Powell Perry wrote music in many genres. She composed art songs; choral works, including a cantata; an opera; works for concert band and symphony orchestra; chamber music, including sonatas, suites, and string quartets; and works for solo piano. In addition, she arranged many spirituals for solo voice or choir with piano accompaniment. This chapter surveys her musical output and studies some of the general stylistic characteristics, as well as the details, of particular works. It considers the issue of whether or not arrangements of spirituals and other folk material should be considered "composition," rather than "arranging." It discusses several premiere performances and the reasons Perry wrote more often in some genres than in others. Some of the musical examples found in this chapter are in Perry's own hand. Her musical handwriting reveals much about her personality and character, and about the clarity and precision of her musical thought.[460]

Some general observations can be made about Zenobia Perry's musical style and harmonic language. Most of her writing was straightforward and conventional. Some pieces reveal a fondness for the rich harmonic language of ninth, eleventh, and thirteenth chords. Often she left the tonic out of the bass, producing a series of first-inversion chords. She alternated between major and minor. Her melodic lines were often modal or pentatonic and she sometimes used a flat third (or flat ninth) in the melody or in the chord accompanying the melodic line, against a major third in the bass. She also used half-diminished seventh and ninth chords. Often her *appoggiaturos* resolved upward. Many of her dissonances did not resolve. Some of her pieces seemingly start on dominant chords, not apparent until the key of the piece is established, often after lengthy introductory material. In some pieces, she worked with tritones and quartal harmony. She often used parallel voicing that increases the sensation of modal, rather than tonal, harmony. She also used word-painting in setting texts. Every note in her writing seems carefully thought out and placed. There are many lovely surprises in her choices of harmonies, revealing an individual and personal musical language. The influence of twentieth-century French composers can be observed in her work, particularly Debussy's use of parallel fourths and Milhaud's so-called jazz chords. Other elements in her music can only be described as being "distinctively American."

When asked if she composed at the piano, Perry replied, "No, I write before I go to the piano, and then I usually have to change it when I get to the piano. It's so strange. I can have something that I think, 'This is it!' and there is something about the piano that suggests that the time is not quite right or the rhythm is a little bit off. I always have to go to the piano to get my rhythms and times straight."[461] She described her daily habit of writing: "Most often I start in the morning and after the day is over, I start again. So I begin and end the day with music writing."[462]

Like many composers, Perry was never satisfied with her compositions. "I really am never quite 100 percent pleased with anything that I write. I write it and it's there, but it seems that it is a bit under what I'd really like it to be. And I say [to myself] that the next piece will be better. That's what I think and that's what happens."[463] After her death, there remained a large stack of pieces waiting for revision and correction. They are not listed here.[464]

Art Songs

Perry's art songs are the most widely performed of all her pieces. She set to music a variety of texts, including poetry by black and white poets, many by her contemporaries, but also her own texts, including poems and a libretto.[465] She wrote five major song cycles, and several individual songs. The earliest song cycle, composed between 1969 and 1972, is *Threnody*, for soprano and piano, which includes "Threnody," "Alien," "Benediction," "Poet," and "Pastourelle," based on poems by Donald Jeffrey Hayes. The second song cycle is *Life Cycle,* for baritone and piano (1971), which includes "O Whisper, O My Soul,"[466] set to poetry of Claude McKay;[467] "A Toast," to poetry of Frank Horne; and "Life," to poetry of Paul Laurence Dunbar.[468] The third group of songs is her *Cycle of Songs on Poems of Paul Laurence Dunbar*: "Sunset," "On a Clean Book," "Spring Song," "Life," and "Drizzle," composed between 1977 and 1983. The fourth cycle is *The Hidden Words of Bahá'u'lláh,* for soprano, flute, and piano, written in 1977 for her daughter, Janis-Rozena Peri, who was at that time a member of the Bahá'í Faith. Based on Arabic texts translated into English, it was premiered at Carnegie Recital Hall that same year. A fifth cycle is "Three Songs for Christmas," for soprano and piano, composed in 1989, including "Kid Stuff," setting a poem of Frank Horne; "Fulfillment," to Perry's own text; and "Mary Had A Baby," based on a traditional American folksong.[469]

Among the individual songs are: "Philosophy," for flute, cello, and voice, based on poetry by Paul Laurence Dunbar (1984); "To All of You," for soprano and piano, poetry by Frank Horne (1970); "Immortality," for medium voice and piano, on a poem by Frank Horne (1970); and "How Charming Is the Place," for soprano and organ (or piano), based on a poem by Samuel Stennett.[470]

Soprano Jo Ann Lanier has analyzed many of Perry's solo songs in her D.M.A. dissertation.[471] Although there is no need to duplicate Lanier's work, a few observations should be made about Perry's vocal music. Most of her songs were written at the request of specific individual singers, including her daughter,[472] students, and colleagues. Therefore, as she described it, the songs often came to her with "the voices attached"; in other words, as she was writing the songs, she heard in her head the specific voice of the person for whom she was writing. She knew the individual's vocal range, and strengths and weaknesses, and her goal was to write a custom-made song or song cycle for that person. "I don't know, but for some reason, when an idea comes, the voice that should sing it comes with it. And then I say, this is for Janis and this is for Sebronette [Barnes]. This is for Lennard [Moses]. This is for William. You know, it just fits their voices."[473]

Perry wrote beautifully for solo voice and piano, reflecting a well-developed sensitivity to the nuances of the texts and her own high level of skill as an accompanist. The accompaniments, ranging from relatively easy to moderately difficult, are composed to serve the vocalist and to support and enhance the vocal line. The elegant vocal writing ranges from the simple

CHAPTER 11

to the demanding, resting comfortably in the *tessitura* for the selected voice. It is clear that the talents and abilities of the individual performer who had requested the song often determined the level of difficulty. For example, the song cycle *Threnody*, with its virtuosic vocal lines, was written for Janis-Rozena Peri, who by that time was established as a professional opera singer and concert performer.

Janis-Rozena Peri, 2008.
Photograph by Sue Amos.

Consider, for instance, the opening song in *Threnody*, composed in 1969, with its wonderful dramatic flair and appeal. The range is D to high A. The opening chord in the piano accompaniment, a rolled B♭–F–G–D♭–A♭ chord, may be called a B♭^{7} chord with an added sixth (D♭). The key signature of four flats indicates A♭ major or F minor. In bar 3, we have an E♭^{9}, which continues through bar 11, with the E♭ functioning as a pedal; then the surprise of an F^7 augmented chord (spelled F–A♮–D♭–E♭–F; the D♭ may have been written as C#). One might expect an F^7 here. If we were to consider D♭ as the tonic of this chord, instead of a sharp V (spelled D♭–F–A♮–E♭–F–E♭); then we would still have an augmented chord (D♭

augmented ninth chord, without the 7th). So what key are we in: B♭ or F (major/minor)?

This ambiguity is the source of the drama and intense color of the song's opening; it is a technique Perry used often in her work. The text, by Donald Jeffrey Hayes, begins, "Let happy throats be mute; only the tortured reed is made a flute! Only the broken heart can sing and make of song a breathless and a lovely thing!" In bar 13 (to the text "lovely thing!"), we have again the opening chord from bar 1, a minor B♭^{7} chord, which could be considered a dominant seventh chord in both the keys of F major and F minor. The D♭^{9} chord in bar 15 is followed by a key change and a sudden move to D major. This is typical of Perry's harmonic idiom.

Although the voice part is always supported, it does not always get its pitch from the piano. For example, in bar 7, the soprano's F is not in the piano, so the singer has to think B♭–D♭–F♮ (a major triad) to find her pitch over the E♭ ninth chord in the piano. When the soprano sings an E♭ at the end of bar 11, the piano clearly gives that pitch, beginning with an E♭ in the left hand, followed by a group of seven sixteenth-notes on beat 2: E♭–D♭–E♭–A♭–D♭–E♭; then an E♭ in the right hand on beats 3 and 4.

POETS SET TO MUSIC
BY ZENOBIA POWELL PERRY
(in alphabetical order)

William Stanley Braithwaite (1878–1962)

Paul Laurence Dunbar (1872–1906)

R. H. Grenville (fl.1941–1958)

Thomas Hardy (1840–1928)

Donald Jeffrey Hayes (b.1904)

Frank Smith Horne (1899–1974)

Mildred N. Hoyer (fl.1960s)

James Weldon Johnson (1871–1938)

Martin Luther (1483–1546)

Claude McKay (1890–1948)

Zenobia Powell Perry (1908–2004)

Christina Georgina Rossetti (1830–1894)

Samuel Stennett (1727–1795)

Anonymous texts of spirituals; poetry in Arabic from the Bahá'í faith.

CHAPTER 11

Example 1. "Threnody," by Zenobia Powell Perry, page 1.

ANALYSIS OF MUSICAL STYLE

Example 2. "Benediction," by Zenobia Powell Perry, page 1.

CHAPTER 11

One of Perry's loveliest songs is "Benediction," from this same cycle, composed in 1972. The opening piano introduction, marked "Adagio, molto cantabile," is a B-minor ninth chord (without the seventh), spelled B–D–F#–C#. With a key signature of three sharps, it could be A major or F# minor. In F# minor, this opening chord could be a subdominant ninth chord. In bar 2, we have D–G–B–F#, which in F# minor is a II^7 with the fifth in the bass (6/4 chord); in B minor, it is a I chord, with an added sixth with the third in the bass. On beats 3 and 4 of the second bar, we have C#–A–D–F#–B, which is a B-minor ninth (this time with the seventh), but with the ninth in the bass, thus a I-6/4. But in bar 5, when the voice enters, we are clearly in F# minor, which turns out to be the key of the piece. This mysterious, dark opening is appropriate for the words, "Not with my hands, but in my heart, I bless you. . . . May peace forever dwell within your breast!" There is a peacefulness about the ostinato pattern in the piano's right hand, which alternates between dissonance and consonance. In bar 7, we have V^9 (in F# minor) with the G# and D in the piano's left hand (a 6/4 chord) which moves to a D-major chord, to which the soprano adds a C# in bar 8 (the seventh), moving up to E (the ninth)–B–then to C#, with A and C# in the piano part (A major), and so forth, as the ostinato figure returns in the right hand of the piano. This handling of musical material continues throughout this song.

"Arioso," the third song from *The Hidden Words* cycle, was composed in 1976 in A–B–A form. It opens with an A-minor chord and a grand gesture, a declaration by the soprano, "O Children of Men!" The constant meter changes from 3/4 to 4/4 and back again accommodates the jagged rhythm and phrasing in the text, an original translation of the original Arabic. The harmony in this song is based on an A-minor eleventh chord, A–C–E–G–B–D. When asked about her approach to these harmonies, Perry said she thought of them as two different chords played simultaneously: A minor plus G major, which she used melodically as well as harmonically. It sounds modal and adds an Arabic flavor. In some places in the song, she used these pitches as pentatonic melodic fragments.

This cycle is the only group of songs that was professionally copied, using a music typewriter although Janis-Rozena Peri is the only one to have sung them. Effective as a concert work, *The Hidden Words* cycle is hindered by ponderous words, which do not command the audience's attention. Perry did not choose these texts; she was commissioned to set them to music. In the *New York Times*, Peter G. Davis described them as "unpromising didactic texts," but conceded that "Perry has set them in a clean straightforward, and conservative style . . . making inventive and graceful use of this combination."[474]

An example of how she juxtaposed major and minor tonalities for its emotional impact is the song "The Cottage." Composed in 1964 and based on a poem by American transcendentalist poet Jones Very, it begins with a piano introduction, seemingly in D major. However, when the voice enters in bar 3, Perry has moved to a B-minor seventh chord with a flat fifth in first inversion (spelled D–B–F–A) with the third (D) in the bass. This would usually signal a return to the tonic, but instead the next three beats are in A minor, followed by a B-minor seventh chord, then back to A minor. The text begins, "The house of my earthly parent left, my heavenly parent still throws down. For 'tis of air." To emphasize "heavenly parent," the B minor seventh chord with a flat fifth, in first inversion (spelled D–F–A–B) is repeated, rolled in three octaves in the piano part, then resolving to A minor. The musical material from the piano introduction returns, marked "*a tempo*," but with these pitches: D–E♭–F–E♭. This use of color and a modal sound gives this song its "otherworldly" sensation and presents the audience its sacred message, the inner life of the poetry.

The song "Drizzle," composed in 1979, from the Dunbar song cycle, illustrates another facet of Perry as an art song composer. Through-composed, the song opens with a leisurely, yet steady pattern in the piano around a G# tonality, with a pentatonic melody: G#–B–C#–D–E. The song is composed in the style of a nineteenth-century black folksong or minstrel tune and the text is written in black dialect, for which Dunbar was well known in the 1890s. It tells how a damp, drizzling day reminds the poet of how some people talk incessantly and say nothing. The repeated piano ostinato captures and conveys not only the tediousness of incessant talking, but also the rain.

The text is syncopated throughout, against the steady rhythm of sixteenth notes in the piano part. At bar 13, the piano adds a countermelody to reinforce the vocal line. The perfect setting of the text clearly demonstrates Perry's adroitness with black dialect, while capturing the underlying meaning of the poem. In addition to this work, Perry wrote several other songs with texts in black dialect, and much of her opera, *Tawawa House*—for which she wrote the libretto—is in dialect.

CHAPTER 11

Example 3. "Arioso" by Zenobia Powell Perry, page 1.

ANALYSIS OF MUSICAL STYLE

Example 4. "The Cottage" by Zenobia Powell Perry, page 1.

CHAPTER 11

Example 5. "Drizzle" by Zenobia Powell Perry, page 1.

From these examples, it is clear how comfortably Perry wrote for voice and piano, displaying a keen sense of how to handle the particular demands of the text while honoring its integrity and beauty. Perry allowed the voice to soar on high notes with open vowel sounds and set consonant-intensive passages in the lower vocal range in a more declamatory style. She understood the challenges facing singers, regardless of the quality of their individual voices and gave them opportunities to display their talent and artistry.

Arrangements of Spirituals

Zenobia Powell Perry arranged many spirituals for voice and piano, and used melodies from the spirituals in her instrumental works.[475] The Center for Black Music Research in Chicago, the leading organization of its kind in the United States, does not document arrangements of spirituals by black American composers as part of its research; generally arrangements are not considered to be substantial enough to be counted as part of a composer's contribution. Unfortunately, this dismissal and marginalization of arrangements is damaging to the legacy of many composers, particularly black American composers.

Like most black composers of her generation working at black colleges and universities, Perry made arrangements of spirituals at the request of colleagues and students. In some cases, the only remnant of the spiritual with which the composer had to work was a solo melodic line and text. In other cases, she arranged spirituals from her memory of the songs, as sung when she was a child and young adult. Such examples include her settings of "Ah Got a Home in a Dat Rock"—dedicated to the memory of her grandfather, Charlie Thompson—"O de Angels Done Bowed Down," and "Oh, I Want Two Wings."

The reason for marginalization of spiritual arrangements is the attitude about the spirituals that has existed in some segments of the black community:[476] because the songs were born in slavery, they should be dropped by the contemporary black community, so that the living community can create a new musical culture as free men and women. William Grant Still explained this attitude in his article, "A Composer's Viewpoint":

CHAPTER 11

> Most of you are no doubt aware that there came a time in our musical history when American Negroes even looked down on spirituals, because they associated them with the days of slavery. Knowing this, you can well imagine the prejudice that existed against the blues which stemmed, supposedly, from the big city dives.... Fortunately, both spirituals and blues have emerged from the period of ill repute, and are now generally recognized as very important contributions of the Negro to our American life.[477]

On the other hand, James H. Cone and others argue that spirituals represent the key to black community survival into the future. Cone writes:

> Black music is a living reality. And to understand it, it is necessary to grasp the contradictions inherent in black experience. Who could possibly understand these paradoxical affirmations but the people who live them? "I love the blues, they hurt so nice," "I can't stand you, Baby, but I need you," "You're bad, but you're oh so good."

The spirituals embody this same paradoxical affirmation: they originated in slavery, but, as Cone writes, they tell "about the divine Spirit that moves the people toward unity and self-determination." He adds, "It is not possible to be black and encounter the Spirit of black emotion and not be moved." Indeed, it is not possible to be *human* and not be moved by the universal appeal of the spirituals. The purpose of Cone's study is to "uncover the theological presuppositions of black music as reflected in the spirituals and the blues," which he does in an inspiring way.[478] His book, published in 1972, is representative of other work in that decade which laid the groundwork for a revival of spirituals, which continues today.

Spirituals and blues have emerged from "the period of ill repute,"[479] and certain negative attitudes linger. Composers who have used folk music materials do not suffer from this prejudice; for example, Béla Bartók's use of Eastern European folk music materials. Many of the compositions of Zoltán Kodály, Antonín Dvořák, Franz Liszt, Georges Enescu, and even Aaron Copland are based on folk materials. Would anyone dare say this practice was not composition?

Many arrangements of spirituals enjoyed considerable popularity and were financially lucrative, particularly those by R. Nathaniel Dett, William L. Dawson, Hall Johnson, and Jester Hairston. Selling tens of thousands of copies is a rare occurrence in the careers of concert music composers. Such success may have contributed to the bias against such arrangements. Although the melodies of spirituals are considered folk melodies and held in the public domain, arrangements of them are copyrighted by the individual composers. This is not the case in arrangements of contemporary popular songs, where the arranger cannot usurp the copyright of the original songwriter/lyricist.

ANALYSIS OF MUSICAL STYLE

It is helpful to consider the differences between a musical paraphrase, arrangement, and composition. Paraphrases, which were quite popular in the nineteenth century, are defined in *The Harvard Dictionary* as "a free rendition or elaboration . . . a reworking and free arrangement of well-known melodies, such as Liszt's concert paraphrases of Wagnerian operas."[480] Arrangement is described as "the adaptation of a composition for a medium different from that for which it was originally written, so made that the musical substance remains essentially unchanged."[481] Composition is "the process of creating musical works. . . . Literally meaning 'putting together,' the term is particularly suitable for early polyphonic music in which various voice parts are indeed put together." The *Dictionary* points out, "Only with reference to a given period is it possible to indicate to some degree what elements enter into the creative process. Thus, a symphony by Beethoven may be said to result from the coordination of traditional ingredients, such as tonality, harmony, rhythm, orchestration, and form, with others of a highly original and personal character, notably the gifts of melodic invention and dramatic development."[482]

Determination of what piece is an arrangement and what is a composition using folk music material seems arbitrary. Does "the musical substance remain essentially unchanged" in an arrangement of a spiritual, particularly in the hands of skillful composers?

In the late nineteenth and early twentieth centuries, the discussion about originality in music composition intensified; emphasis shifted to a concern about composing music that was entirely novel and innovative. This obsession with newness, which had not been a concern of earlier composers, involved the systematic downgrading of any composition which involved the reworking of pre-existing materials, i.e., folk melodies, popular songs, and the like.[483] Arranging became common in the early twentieth century, primarily as the result of developing new markets for American popular music, particularly related to Broadway shows and the use of songs to accompany films. Most of those who first called themselves arrangers were trained as composers, but by mid-century, arranging became a profession in itself.[484] In the film and television music industry and in the recording industry, arrangers have separate contractual agreements; their work is clearly described, quantified, and remunerated accordingly. They are unionized, while composers are not.

Defining arrangement as "the adaptation of a composition . . . [where] the musical substance remains essentially unchanged," points out the subjectivity in determining whether a piece is an arrangement or a composition. Are the original melodies and words for spirituals to be considered "compositions"? For example, if the original is an *a cappella* song, would adding a piano accompaniment be considered a composition? Has "the musical substance remained essentially unchanged"? Without comparing individual works to the original source for the spiritual, settings of spirituals are routinely designated "arrangements" and not compositions. A necessary step in the process, involving careful musicological investigation, has been skipped. Some are clearly arrangements (perhaps even arrangements of another arrangement). Others involve enough change of the original spiritual that they must be considered new compositions. The tendency to lump together all pieces based on spirituals as "arrangements"—without doing the work needed to make this determination—diminishes the creative work of many black American composers. A comparison of different arrangements of the same spiritual by different composers shows how much of the process is actually composition and how much is arranging.

In settings of spirituals, it is important to recognize that many of the spirituals were not known by the general public until they had been arranged, published, and widely performed. Without these arrangements, the living tradition of singing the spirituals may not have survived to our own time. Arrangers of spirituals gave these songs new life, guaranteeing their survival. These arrangements belong in the concert music corpus as part of the sacred music tradition in this country. The secular emphasis of most studies in the humanities tends toward dismissing or marginalizing any artistic work of a sacred or religious nature. However, arrangements of spirituals should be considered *composition,* based on folk material and should be documented, studied, and analyzed as part of the American musical legacy.

Among the spirituals that Zenobia Perry arranged are: "Ah Got a Home in a Dat Rock," for soprano and piano; "Certainly Lord," for tenor and piano; "Couldn't Hear Nobody Pray," for baritone and piano; "Done Made My Vow to the Lord," for SATB *a cappella*; "Go Tell It on the Mountain," for SATB *a cappella*; "Hallelujah to the Lamb," for soprano and piano; "Great Gittin' Up Mornin'," for SATB and piano; "It's Me O Lord, Standing in the Need of Prayer," for baritone and piano; "I've Done, Done," for SATB and piano; "Kum ba yah," for SATB *a cappella* (also a version for children's choir and conga drum); "Mary Had a Baby" for soprano, cello, and piano; "Oh, I Want Two Wings" (from *Tawawa House*, Act I), for solo voice and piano; "Precious Lord," for SATB; "Ride, Ride, Ride King Jesus," for SATB *a cappella*; "Sinner Man So Hard, Believe!" for soprano and piano; "O de Angels Done Bowed Down," for soprano and piano (also a version for SSAA quartet); and "There's a Lit'l Wheel A-Turnin'," for SATB *a cappella*.

Perry's piano accompaniments for the spiritual arrangements are not elaborate, but provide in a straightforward manner the necessary support for the choir or individual vocalist. Many of her spirituals were arranged for student recitals. For example, "Ah Got a Home in a Dat Rock" (1969) in F major, with a simple I–V–I in the bass line, allows the focus to be on the syncopation in the vocal line.

CHAPTER 11

Example 6. "O de Angels Done Bowed Down," arranged by Zenobia Powell Perry, page 1.

However, in "O de Angels Done Bowed Down," the opening chordal progression immediately sets up the devastating emotional content of this spiritual: "Jesus a-hanging upon the cross, the angels kept quiet and God went off." In the key of B minor, Perry begins with a minor iv^7 (spelled E–G–B–F#). The bass line moves to F# (V) with a triplet figure in the right hand that characterizes the melodic line. The next harmony is a dominant eleventh chord (F#–E–G–A#–D) without the fifth (C#), a deliberate dissonance, with the appropriate emotional impact to depict Christ on the cross. This chord appears through the song; for example, in bar 10 on the word "My" in the phrase, "O yes My Lord," it emphasizes the personal nature of the contemplation of the Crucifix. Whenever this chord appears, it resolves to the tonic, B–D–F#.

Perry's setting of "Sinner Man So Hard, Believe!" is an example of word painting, a technique found in many of her works. To accompany the text, "Don't ring those chiming bells till I get there," there are "bells" in both hands of the piano part, in the upper octaves.

In *Echoes from the Journey,* for soprano and chamber orchestra (1990), Perry set the spirituals "Wade in the Water," "I Want to Die Easy," and "Swing Low, Sweet Chariot," and also used some field hollers. Spirituals were used in her instrumental works as well, for example, in *Four Mynyms for Three Players*, which she wrote on the occasion of Milhaud's returning to France. Her opera, *Tawawa House*, has several spirituals in it. These works will be discussed below.

It is important to note that Zenobia Perry grew up among former African slaves and heard some of these songs sung by them in a style that is rooted in the mid-nineteenth century. Her studies with two master arrangers of the spirituals—R. Nathaniel Dett and William L. Dawson—provided an additional link to the nineteenth-century spiritual tradition. Both men advocated the preservation of Negro folk materials, and practiced it in their own work. Perry's grandfather, Charlie Thompson, was a black Creek, who sang the spirituals to her. In the twenty-first century, Zenobia Perry's music can provide a precious link to this era, before the American Civil War.

CHAPTER 11

Example 7. "Ah Got a Home in a Dat Rock," arranged by Zenobia Powell Perry, page 1.

ANALYSIS OF MUSICAL STYLE

Choral Works

In addition to Perry's choral arrangements of spirituals, other choral works should be mentioned. Largest is a cantata for soprano, mezzo-soprano, baritone, narrator, SATB choir, flute, timpani, harp, and organ, entitled "Sing Unto the Lord a New Song." It received several performances by the Dunbar Choir in 1976, and merits additional performances. She set another Bahá'í prayer for SATB *a cappella*, "O Lord, Make Thy Beauty," and also wrote for women's chorus, most notably, *Suite for Women's Voices* and "Gifts of God." The former is based on three poems by Thomas Hardy: "At Tea," "By Her Aunt's Grave," and "Outside the Window."

Throughout her career, Perry was involved with children and adult choristers in churches, and she wrote several pieces for children's choir, including *Hallelujah* for unison children's chorus and women's choir. She arranged the traditional Irish song, "Love Came Down at Christmas," for children's chorus and strings (to words by C. Rossetti), and "Kum ba yah" for children's chorus and conga drum.

Her arrangement of *Lift Every Voice and Sing* for SATB and band was written for Central State University's dedication of the new music building in 1975. The melody was composed in 1900 by Rosamond Johnson to words by his brother James Weldon Johnson; it is known as the "Negro National Anthem." This piece was a favorite of Booker T. Washington and Tuskegee Institute; Zenobia Perry considered it a privilege to arrange it for such an important occasion in CSU's history.[485] She also wrote an arrangement of "A Mighty Fortress Is Our God" in 1975 for choir and concert band, performed at the dedication of two other new buildings at CSU.

Over the years, she arranged many Christmas songs for use by church choirs, including "The Twelve Days of Christmas." She wrote three choral pieces for Carol Longsworth and the Oberlin Community Chamber Singers: "Notes of Christmas," which includes "The Quiet of Christmas," based on a poem by Mildred N. Hoyer; "Christmas Is More," based on a poem by the Canadian poet, R. H. Grenville; and "Silently." They were first presented in 1993 as *Music from Ohio*.

Perry wrote two experimental choral pieces. The first, composed in 1974, is called *Choral Suite* no. 1 for tape sounds, percussion, piano, and 16-voice mixed chorus.[486] The Canada Council Arts Festival presented it in 1974 on a concert with works by George Crumb, Larry Trauz, György Ligeti, and Robert Suderburg, at the University of Victoria in British

Columbia. Perry was unable to attend the performance. In 1974, she attended a summer workshop on electronic music composition at the State University of New York at Potsdam. As a composer and educator, she felt that it was important for her to know more about electronic music, but she worked very little in this medium. She was unable to secure the resources to build an electronic music studio at Central State University or in her own home for her use and experimentation.

The second experimental choral piece is "Sound Patterns" for vocal ensemble (spoken) and B♭ clarinet, of which there are several versions. She encountered resistance from choirs to perform it, probably because of its nonsensical text.[487] She rewrote it several times, perhaps to accommodate the complaints. An excerpt is found below.

Perry's choral works show a masterful understanding of choral writing, learned through her association and work with Dett and Dawson. Her piano accompaniments are clearly the work of a composer with life-long experience in accompanying and directing choirs, reflecting the same sensitivity and deep appreciation of poetry found in her works for solo voice and piano.

GIFTS OF GOD (1984)*

by Zenobia Powell Perry

Do you find the springtime lovely?
Do you bask in summer sun?
Fall's gracious bounty;
Fall's vivid colors
herald the winter's cold
with snow covered hills
and mystical magic of whiteness.

Friends to share our smiles
and friends to share our misery
are priceless treasures.

All are gifts of God
sent from his wondrous store of love for us

Let us prove grateful,
always.

Zenobia Perry set this poem for SSA Chorus a cappella in 1984.

ANALYSIS OF MUSICAL STYLE

Example 8. "Sound Patterns," by Zenobia Powell Perry, page 1. *Composer's manuscript.*

CHAPTER 11

Larger Works for Orchestra and Concert Band

Unfortunately, both institutions where Zenobia Perry taught, Arkansas A. M. & N. and Central State University, had weak orchestral instrumental programs and only occasionally managed to put together an orchestra. From time to time, Arkansas A. M. & N. had a string orchestra. Central State University's 1965 attempt to establish a university orchestra with Shirley Strohm Mullins[488] conducting and Zenobia Perry playing in the violin section did not endure. Although Perry had high hopes of writing for orchestra, the opportunities to be performed were so limited that she wrote little until late in her life. For many black composers at black colleges and universities in the country, the emphasis is on band instruments, a marching and a concert band, if there is an instrumental music program at all.

Perry's *Symphonic Poem* for full symphony was composed as her master's thesis at the University of Wyoming, with the guidance of Willman, Milhaud, and Jones. It was performed by the University of Wyoming Orchestra, not in Laramie, but at concerts in Casper, Wyoming, and in Denver, Colorado, with other student works.[489] She was unable to attend the performance, since she was teaching full time in Arkansas, so she never knew if the piece was successful in performance. She later arranged it for concert band, so it could be performed in 1955 by the Arkansas A. M. & N. Concert Band for a Founder's Day program. In 1988, she revised the piece for narrator and chamber ensemble (piccolo, 2 flutes, alto saxophone, tenor saxophone, trumpet, timpani, tenor drum, conga drums, tambourines, gong, bass drum, and piano) with the addition of a text by Paul Laurence Dunbar, using the title, *Ships That Pass in the Night*. Here is the text to Dunbar's poem:

> Out in the sky the great dark clouds are massing:
> I look far out into the pregnant night,
> Where I can hear a solemn booming gun
> And catch the gleaming of a random light,
> That tells me that the ship I seek is passing, passing.
> My tearful eyes my soul's deep hurt are glassing;
> for I would hail and check that ship of ships.
> I stretch my hands imploring, cry aloud
> My voice falls dead a foot from mine own lips,
> And but its ghost doth reach that vessel, passing, passing.

ANALYSIS OF MUSICAL STYLE

O Earth, O Sky, O Ocean, both surpassing.
O heart of mine, O soul that dreads the dark!
Is there no hope for me? Is there no way
That I may sight and check that speeding bark
which out of sight and sound is passing, passing?

Zenobia Perry wrote about this text and her use of it in *Ships That Pass in the Night*:

> These words of fear and frustration should be cradled in music. Instead of setting these meaningful words to a melody, I chose to have the music free to set the imagery and mood and make comments on the narration. The piece displays my innate use of racial idioms in its melody, some dissonance, and outbursts of irregular rhythms. Percussion instruments were chosen to enhance imagery, provide pulse and progressive movement. Melodic instruments were chosen for their quality of emotional portrayal. None can wail better than the saxophone, or cry out of joy or outrage better than the piccolo. Simple factual statements are in the domain of the trumpet, and ethereal expressions can best be stated by the flute. Words of the poem expressed my feelings at that point in time of my creativity. When I compose, I feel the isolation associated with being a woman in a white male dominated field of music. Therefore, I am able to relate to the emotion expressed in Dunbar's poem, and elaborate musically on that emotion.[490]

Given the fact that the music was originally composed in the early 1950s for her dissertation at the University of Wyoming, it can be assumed that Perry felt frustration due to "the isolation associated with being a woman in a white male dominated field of music," as expressed in the Dunbar poem. She wanted to compose for orchestra, but had very little opportunity to do so. The only way to develop and improve as a composer is to write works, hear them in live performance, and then apply that experience to the next piece. Rarely are a composer's first few pieces for orchestra good. Orchestral composers develop from repeated opportunities to write and hear their works performed.[491] Few college music departments offer this opportunity to students and faculty, and practically none in black colleges and universities in the United States.[492] *Ships That Pass in the Night* was premiered in January 1989, at West Virginia University, with Lawrence Christiansen as narrator and James L. Tully conducting. It was performed a second time in January 1994, at Cleveland Heights High School in Ohio, with Dr. Frederick R. Mayer conducting and Philomena McClellan as narrator.

CHAPTER 11

Example 9. "Ships That Pass in the Night," for instrumental ensemble and narrator, by Zenobia Powell Perry, page 1.
Composer's manuscript.

ANALYSIS OF MUSICAL STYLE

Another piece for orchestra was *Arkansia Suite,* written in 1955 for violin and piano, then orchestrated for string orchestra and performed at the University of Arkansas at Pine Bluff. In 1986, Perry wrote another piece for orchestra, entitled *Pastels,* scored for flutes, oboes, clarinets, bass clarinet, bassoons, horns, trumpets, trombones, tuba, timpani, and strings. One movement was read in a workshop by the Detroit Symphony, conducted by Alan Freeman, as part of the annual Afro-American Composers Festival in Detroit. It was not performed again, nor did she get a tape of the rehearsal.

Perry did write several works for concert band, in addition to those mentioned above for concert band and choir. *Introduction, Prelude and Danse for band* (1968) was dedicated to the Central State University Band for performance on Charter Day in 1968. Originally, the piece had two movements; the *Prelude* was added at a later date. It is scored for 2 flutes, 3 clarinets, bass clarinet, 2 bassoons, 2 alto saxophones, 1 tenor saxophone, flugelhorn, 3 trumpets, 2 horns in F and 2 horns in E, 3 trombones, 3 basses, bass drum, and cymbal. The premiere was conducted by Ian Polster, whose "Holiday for Brass" was also on the program. Perry wrote about her piece: "It is an expression of re-alignment of various 'harmonious forces' felt in activities of our communities. The combined sound of two keys related equidistantly from a tonal center is used for the idea of this re-alignment."[493]

Using the poetry of R. H. Grenville, Perry wrote *Tempo* (1993), for soprano and concert band, for Janis-Rozena Peri, who premiered it in 1994 at West Virginia University. The single-movement work is scored for piccolo, oboe, clarinets, alto clarinet, bass clarinet, bassoon, alto saxophone, tenor saxophone, baritone saxophone, 3 trumpets, 4 horns, baritone horn, 3 trombones, basses, timpani, drums, and soprano. It is in a simple binary form, with a closing coda. Like others of Perry's works, the piece appears from the key signature to be in F major, but starts with a C in the bass; F major is not established until bar 10. Once again, we see the play between major and minor, with the flatting of the third (E♭), harmonically and melodically, and the movement from C to C# in the bass (bars 5 and 6). Unfortunately there are some difficult passages in this work, particularly in the horn parts, which may have precluded an acceptable premiere performance.

CHAPTER 11

Example 10. "Tempo" by Zenobia P. Perry, page 1. *Composer's Manuscript.*

ANALYSIS OF MUSICAL STYLE

Like most of Perry's works, the musical material is rich and intriguing. The voice is well supported throughout; however, one might desire more use of bass instruments generally throughout the piece. The tempo marked in the score (half-note=116) is clearly too fast. The problems of this composition—among other of Perry's pieces—could have been remedied, had the work been given subsequent performances. This is the problem facing most contemporary composers: first performances are relatively easy to get; subsequent performances not so easy. Yet it is only through those subsequent performances, and readjustments and improvements in the score, that a piece is truly allowed to develop. Perry's art songs have benefited from such repeat performances and rewrites.

In 1990, at the age of 81, Zenobia Perry was given the opportunity to write a piece for soprano and orchestra, *Echoes from the Journey*. Commissioned by the Cleveland Chamber Symphony, it was supported with funds from the Ohio Arts Council's New Works Program. Perry recalled, "When I was asked by Edwin London, director of the orchestra, and Jo Ann Lanyé to write something for Negro History Week, they said they wanted it to be representative of black music and so I said, 'So, you want something that is a composite or do you want something which assimilates all this?' Ed London said, 'We want both.'" The composition starts with a field holler, then a spiritual, then "an assimilation of African rhythms, jazz, blues, modern jazz, and I end up with a kind of reflection."[494]

CHAPTER 11

Example 11. *Echoes from the Journey*,
by Zenobia Powell Perry, page 1.

The program notes, written by Perry, reveal the main philosophical quest of her life in music:

> The continuing civil rights struggle of blacks in the United States plays a large part in my frame of reference. There is no way to live without pain. But then there is music. Music contributes to the animating principle of mankind and has the revolutionary power of healing, expanding, and revitalizing. All people are aware of inward explorations of black music only to the extent they comprehend the metaphysical urges that are part of every Afro-American.
>
> *Echoes from the Journey* is the resultant composition of conversation with Dr. J. Lanyé, soloist for this premiere. It begins with a simple tune that was sung by blacks during the years of reconstruction, that is phrased regularly and offered with an instrumental accompaniment made more interesting by a polyphonic duet announcement. In the next musical period the voice emerges with an independent melody and instruments are used only for rhythmic and harmonic punctuations. Words seem like disjunct outbursts spoken in irregular meter rather opposed to song. "Well, Well, Well So I Can Die Easy," a late nineteenth-century favorite, follows with its mood and rhythmic drive ushering in the twentieth-century blues with a jazzy use of instruments. Turbulence of the sixties and frustrations of the seventies and eighties are presented in an uneasy waltz setting of "Swing Low Sweet Chariot." The last "Echo" is created by a change of musical imagery similar to the beginning tune in simplicity heralding hope for future successes in the quest for freedom.[495]

At its performance, Perry was surprised to receive a standing ovation. The reviewer Robert Finn wrote in the *Cleveland Plain Dealer*:

> "Echoes from the Journey" is a curiosity. The mezzo-soprano soloist (in this case the rich-voiced Dr. Jo Lanyé) alternately sings and speaks a text about the black struggle, while the orchestra contributes fanfares, simple diatonic tunes, sustained chords, bits of blues rhythm and other more or less uncoordinated fragments. While the composer's sincerity is obvious, the piece seems simplistic, a kind of musical propaganda poster. Lanyé did the spoken sections effectively and sang beautifully—but only the words of the spoken portions came through.[496]

The term "musical propaganda" seems harsh, but the critic is right about the piece's lack of overall integration and development. *Echoes* received a second performance six or seven months later, with the same orchestra.[497]

CHAPTER 11

Solo Piano Music

Zenobia Perry's works for solo piano can be divided into two types: concert works and teaching pieces. The first category includes: *Essay, for piano* (1958), *Rhapsody* (1960); *Sonata* (1960); *Piano Sonatina* (1962); *Times Five* (1963?); *Fantasy, for piano* (1972, revised 1992); *Three Expressions* for piano (1973-74; lost in the tornado); *Pavanne* for piano (1975); *Promenade* (1988); and *Homage to William Levi Dawson on his 90th Birthday* (1990). Her teaching pieces are found in the collection, *Piano Potpourri* (1990), which consists of fifteen pieces written throughout her career, including her earliest piece, *Childhood Capers*, from her days at Langston University and at Tuskegee in the 1930s. *Homage to William Levi Dawson* is the only piece of Perry's to be published and performed regularly. Perry described it:

> One piano piece I have written is dedicated to William L. Dawson for his 90th birthday... *Homage to William L. Dawson*. It starts off with a Spiritual, "I've Been Buked and I've Been Scorned." It goes from there into a development section. I played it for him and since then it has became a part of the William L. Dawson Memorial. He died right after his 90th birthday.[498]

Perry premiered it in concert at the Tuskegee Institute Alumni Association national meeting in Indianapolis in 1990. Her piano music is well written for the instrument, as one would expect from a composer who is a pianist. Most of these works she herself premiered in concert, with the exception of the *Rhapsody* from 1960, composed for Janis-Rozena Peri, who premiered it on her senior recital at Otterbein College.

Perry also wrote pieces for organ solo, including *Festival* [Festive] *Overture* (c.1954); *Prelude* (1973); and *Prism* (1975). These have been performed by organists Mike Moss at Southern Connecticut State University and William Haller at West Virginia University. She also has made arrangements for two pianos to perform with her duo partner, Kelton Lawrence, at the University of Arkansas, Pine Bluff; one such arrangement was of *Dances in the Canebrakes* by Florence Price.

Chamber Music

Most of Perry's chamber music was composed in response to specific requests by students and colleagues. Given the fact that she studied and played the violin, it is not surprising that her first piece of chamber music, *Arkansia* (1955), was written for violin and piano. She later orchestrated this piece for string orchestra (6–4–2–6–3) and it was premiered by the String Choir of Forest City, Arkansas, with conductor Eugene Isom, Perry's colleague. *Excursions,* for violin, cello, and piano, was composed in 1989. She composed two string quartets, both in 1964. The first was premiered at Antioch College in Yellow Springs that same year. The second string quartet, called *Three Designs for Four Strings,* was read at the Conference/Workshop on 20th-Century String Quartets by Women Composers, in March 1980, in New York City.

Four Mynyms may have been written in 1968, on the occasion of Milhaud's return to France. The third movement uses the rhythm of "Swing Low, Sweet Chariot," possibly a reference to Milhaud's going home. The idea of this piece came from 1963, when her colleague Jim Field asked her to write a piece for Milhaud's birthday concert in San Francisco.

Perry wrote *Conversations for two flutes and piano* (1975), which has three movements, "Greetings," "Chit-Chat," and "Gossip." She composed several pieces for brass instruments: *Episodes I and II,* for horn and piano, written in 1983; *Elegy for Brass* (1989), originally composed for trumpet, 2 horns, trombone, and tuba, and later arranged for clarinet, 2 horns, and 2 bassoon; and some of the music of her opera first appeared in a piece for trumpet and piano, called *Tawawa Nights.*

Tawawa House: An Opera

In an interview, Zenobia Perry said, "A person should know something about the place where they live." When she arrived in Wilberforce, she tried to discover the origins of the town's name. No one knew much about it. After considerable research, she discovered the town was named after an Englishman, William Wilberforce (1759–1833), who tried to end the slave trade. During her query, she came across the story of Tawawa House, the largest hotel east of the Mississippi River. She wanted to share what she had learned with her neighbors, so she wrote a musical drama, detailing the history of Wilberforce and its 200-room hotel.[499]

In researching about William Wilberforce, Perry obtained ten volumes of writings from England about his life. He had never been in the town that bore his name. He was so committed to ending the slave trade between

CHAPTER 11

Africa and the New World that he spent his life trying to stop it. In 1833, he asked Parliament to outlaw slave shipment from Africa to America and then tried to end global slave trade (without success). Because people in Wilberforce, Ohio, did not know this story, Perry decided to write an opera to tell it.

In 1850, Elias Drake, lawyer and former speaker in the Ohio General Assembly, purchased property and named it "Tawawa" (from the Shawnee for clear, golden water). He developed a health resort hotel surrounded by summer cottages, valued for its mineral-rich springs, and hired former slaves to serve as hotel management and staff. However, because it was popular among Southern planters to bring slave entourages whenever they came—much to the consternation of nearby antislavery sentiment—the resort did not fare well. In October 1855, the Cincinnati Conference of the Methodist Episcopal Church began negotiations for its purchase, and bought Tawawa Springs—fifty-four acres and the hotel and cottages—to establish a university for African Americans, which they called "The Ohio African University." When the transaction was formalized in 1856, the university was renamed "Wilberforce University," after English abolitionist William Wilberforce, and was dedicated to the higher education of African Americans. Wilberforce University became an important station on the Underground Railroad during this time; a large number of African Americans who were freed slaves settled in Greene County. During the Civil War, declining enrollment caused the first university to fail in 1862.

The following year, Bishop Daniel A. Payne purchased the property, on behalf of the African Methodist Episcopal Church. Payne became the first president of the newly established Wilberforce University, making him the first African American to lead such an institution. The community was not entirely receptive: on April 14, 1865, a mob from Cincinnati burned down the main buildings, over resentment of having such a school in Ohio.

Zenobia Perry's opera is dedicated to her parents, Dr. and Mrs. C. B. Powell, who had faced similar hardships when they were forced to leave their beloved Boley, Oklahoma, in the late 1920s. It is in two acts, scored for a chamber orchestra and seventeen singers. Perry wrote the libretto, based on her research. She began the opera in 1974; its first performance was in 1987, sponsored by grants from the Ohio Arts Council, the Ohio Humanities Council, and the National Endowment of the Arts, with cooperation from the National Afro-American Museum and Cultural Center.

The opera opens with an orchestral overture, which previews the musical and dramatic shape and contents of the entire work. The harmonic idiom is consistent with Perry's style, including pentatonic melodic lines and harmonies based on seventh, ninth, and eleventh chords. The overture moves directly into an opening chorus, with the entire cast on stage, singing in four-part harmony:

> Let the knowing speak
> let those who were oppressed
> speak of their countless fears.

The choral writing is solid, traditional, and suitable for amateurs and semi-professional singers; in other words, perfect for students. In every detail, Perry addressed the potential challenges of a community/student production. She was always practical as a composer, realistic in her assessment of the potential of the performers at her disposal, and providing them with appropriate support.

TAWAWA HOUSE

To the Memory of My Parents, Dr. and Mrs. Calvin B. Powell

Synopsis of *Tawawa House*
by Zenobia Powell Perry

This musical drama is the unfolding history of the newly established hotel at the watering hole at Xenia Springs, Ohio. In its life span 1852 to 1865, it becomes first a fabulous resort—SPA, if you will—called Tawawa House, with prices of $2.00 per day and Cottage Holders discount prices of $5.00 per week in 1852. Rise of political unrest throughout the nation in both the Whig party and the Democrats in the mid 1850s made financing of the SPA less and less important. Dwindling support of the enterprise led to economic concern. Humanitarian concern of the Cincinnati Conference of the Methodist Episcopal Church for the many colored persons staffing and surrounding TAWAWA HOUSE led to the purchase of the place in 1856 for a school for colored youths.

Briefly it was the Ohio African University. Then the Cincinnati Con-ference engaged the help of the General Conference, which is national in scope, so the name was changed, in honor of the great English abolitionist William Wilberforce, to Wilberforce University. Church supporters were also financially involved in the growing struggle which led to the Civil War, and support of the school declined. In 1863 the property was purchased by Daniel Payne and committee for a school, to be run by the African Methodist Episcopal Church. Influence of the school led to naming the environs Wilberforce.

Growing resentment of such a school for colored people in Ohio peaked in 1865, culminating in burning to ashes the main building—formerly TAWAWA HOUSE, on April 14, 1865, by a mob of irate citizens of the

CHAPTER 11

surrounding area and Cincinnati. The drama is played out largely by the colored personnel.

ACT I
Scene 1. Near the back entrance to Tawawa House, 1852
Scene 2. A clearing on the far back lawn of Tawawa House, 1853
Scene 3. Same as Scene 2

ACT II
Scene 1. Front lawn-near entrance to Tawawa House, 1855
Scene 2. Conference Room of Methodist Church, 1855
Scene 3A. Near the entrance to Tawawa House, 1856
Scene 3B. Interior of University's Auditorium, 1856
Scene 4. Front lawn of Wilberforce University, 1862
Scene 5. Study in the University Auditorium, 1865
Scene 6. Outside Front Entrance, altered by fire

Soprano solo (from Act I): ***Oh, I Want Two Wings***

> Oh, I want two wings to veil my face
> Oh, I want two wings to fly away,
> Oh, I want two wings to veil my face
> Oh, I want two wings to fly, to fly away.
>
> O meet me Jesus; meet me Lord;
> Meet me in de middle of de air,
> An' if my two wings should fail me Lord
> I'll hitch on another pair.

Chorus (from Act I): ***Follow the Drinkin' Gourd***

> When the sun comes back and the first quail calls
> Follow the drinkin' gourd.
> Where the old man is a waiting for to carry you to freedom
> Follow the drinkin' gourd.
> Now the river ends between two hills
> There is another river running on the other side
> Where the little river meets with the great big one
> Follow the drinkin' gourd.
> There the sailor is a waiting for to carry you to freedom
> Follow the drinkin' gourd.

The question arises whether the material transcends its original purpose of a piece that teaches the Wilberforce community about its history. Is it opera? Many of the songs and instrumental numbers are beautifully written, emotionally charged, and well-crafted. But some of the story is told, rather than acted, and in some places recited, as in a lecture hall; it can be somewhat pedantic. An example is on page 105, where the libretto contains a long speech by the narrator. These long narrations should be acted and presented through dialogue; as recitations, they stop the momentum and hold the work back from being as dramatic as it could be. In some places, the dialogue is long-winded and tedious; for instance, on page 129, when each of four male characters has a long monologue. Such dramatic problems could have been solved during multiple rehearsals and public performances, and in collaboration with key figures in the production group, had that been available. New musicals and new operas are often in rehearsal for months before they are ready for public presentation; the collaboration of production crews, lighting designers, music directors, etc., all helps the composer work out the rough edges. *Tawawa House* is a laudable first stage in the process of developing a major opera; Perry did not have the financial resources available to see it through the entire process.

Tawawa House contains spirituals, folk dances, *recitativo*, and arias. It concludes with the chorus singing, "Oh, freedom, o, freedom, Hear the bells of freedom ringing, up over my head, up over my head," from the old spiritual, as well as an affirmation of faith: "I see freedom in the air, O Lord, I believe there's a God somewhere."

The Central State University Music, Drama, and English departments and Wilberforce University Student Activities Division presented the premiere performance. Guest artists were Janis-Rozena Peri, Benny Pritchett, and Corliss Taylor-Dunn. William Caldwell directed the CSU Concert Chorale, Lennard V. Moses directed the CSU Percussion Ensemble, and the Community Chamber Orchestra was conducted by Donald Carroll.

Zenobia Powell Perry had a remarkable output as a composer, considering that she only started to compose in her forties. She continued to write, well into her nineties. Like most American contemporary concert music composers, she would have benefited from more access to large performing ensembles, to experiment with and develop compositional techniques, particularly in terms of orchestration. She was most successful with her art songs, piano pieces, and choral works. There is no doubt, however, that Perry developed her own individual and distinct voice as a composer and that her body of work stands with the work of her contemporaries, men and women, black and white.

CHAPTER 11

Program, *Tawawa House* premiere, May 1987.

Underlying Conviction

The underlying conviction in Zenobia Perry's life was that, rather than dwell on disappointments and frustrations, she felt grateful and moved forward. From time to time, she was asked to speak on the injustices of discrimination against black American composers, particularly women, and she did this eloquently. But, rather than become an advocate, she demonstrated what she believed, by her daily practice of composing, which is the ultimate measure of success as a composer in our society. She knew what all musicians know: that the reward is found in the moment of writing. There was nothing that engaged all of her faculties simultaneously more than this and, like all composers, she lived for those moments. It was the process of composing which gave her a rich and gratifying life, a process she recommended, without reservation.

A. Chronology

1908 October 3	Zenobia Powell is born to Dr. Calvin Bethel Powell and Birdie Lee Thompson Powell in Boley, Okfuskgee County, Oklahoma.
1915 August 22	Zenobia meets Booker T. Washington, who is speaking at a city park in Boley. She sings the Tuskegee anthem for him; he declares her a future Tuskegegian.
1919	Zenobia wins piano competition, at age 11.
1925 May 22	Zenobia graduates from Boley High School.
1929 Summer	Zenobia studies at Cecil Berryman Conservatory in Omaha, Nebraska.
1931 Fall	Zenobia goes to Hampton Institute to study with R. Nathaniel Dett; follows him to Rochester, New York, and studies with him privately until May 1932.
1932 Thanksgiving	Zenobia marries violinist "King" Earl Gaynor.
1933 August 21	Son, Lemuel Powell, is born.
1933	Zenobia and "King" Earl Gaynor separate; they eventually divorce.
1935 September	Zenobia enters Tuskegee Institute as a freshman.
1938 May 26	Zenobia receives B.S. degree from Tuskegee Institute.
1939 July 12	Zenobia performs movement of Grieg's *Piano Concerto* at Langston University.
1941 May	Zenobia marries Jimmie Rodgers Perry (born August 13, 1915).
1941 September	Zenobia Perry begins degree program at Colorado State Teachers College in Greeley.
1942–43	Zenobia Perry teaches first grade.
1942 October	Father, Calvin Bethel Powell, M.D., dies at the age of 79.
1943 August 29	Daughter, Janis [Janis-Rozena Peri], is born in Tulsa, Oklahoma.
1943 October 2	R. Nathaniel Dett dies at the age of 61.
1943–44	Zenobia Perry works as teacher in Pawnee, Oklahoma, where she comes to the attention of First Lady Eleanor Roosevelt.

APPENDIX A

1945 August 31	Zenobia Perry graduates from Colorado State College of Education, with Master of Arts degree.
1946 March 15	Son, Lemuel, dies of ruptured appendix.
1947–1955	Zenobia Perry teaches at Arkansas A. M. & N. College in Pine Bluff.
1949 Spring	Zenobia Perry begins studies at University of Wyoming: piano and composition with Allan Willman, composition with Darius Milhaud. Attends Aspen Music Festival for special workshop with Milhaud.
1949–1955	Zenobia Perry tours in piano duo with Kelton Lawrence, to recruit students for Arkansas A. M. & N College.
1954 August 20	Zenobia Perry receives Master's of Music in composition from University of Wyoming.
1955 April 19	Performance of *Symphonic Poem* on Founder's Day program in Caldwell Hall Auditorium, Arkansas A. M. & N. College, by the College Band, Harold S. Strong, *conductor*.
1955 October	Zenobia Perry joins faculty of Central State University in Wilberforce, Ohio.
1957 Summer	Zenobia Perry participates in Aspen Conference on Contemporary Music.
1963 September 29	Zenobia Perry, along with Darius Milhaud and Dave Brubeck, is honored at San Francisco concert by Emme Kemp Trio and pianist William Hollis.
1967 August 15	Mother, Birdie Lee Thompson Powell Jenkins, dies at the age of 77.
1970 June 1	Premiere of *Heritage and Life, A Cycle of Songs*, at Library and Museum of the Performing Arts, Lincoln Center, New York, New York, by Janis-Rozena Peri, *soprano*, and Judith Gels, *piano*.
1974 October 25	Performance of *Choral Suite* no. 1, for tape sounds, percussion, piano, and mixed chorus, on Canada Council Arts Festival Concert at University of Victoria, British Columbia, Canada.
1977 May 22	Premiere of *The Hidden Words of Bahá'u'lláh* at Carnegie Recital Hall, Janis-Rozena Peri, *soprano*; favorable review in *New York Times*.
1980 March 8	*Three Designs for Four Strings* (1964) is read at Conference/Workshop on 20th-Century String Quartets by Women Composers, New York, New York.
1981 March 29	Zenobia Perry participates in First National Congress on Women in Music, at New York University, where Janis-Rozena Peri sings *Cycle of Songs on Poems by Paul Laurence Dunbar*.
1982	Zenobia Perry retires from Central State University.
1985	Zenobia Perry is appointed Faculty Emerita, Central State University.
1986 April	Zenobia Perry is Guest Composer at Dana New Music Festival at Youngstown State University in Ohio, Jo Ann Lanier, *conductor*.
1987 May	Premiere of opera *Tawawa House*, Central State University.
1987 October 17	Zenobia Perry is honored by Ohioana Library Association with Music Citation for distinguished service to Ohio in the field of music.

CHRONOLOGY

1987 February 20–21	Zenobia Perry works are performed at Symposium in Celebration of Black American Women in Music, at California State University, Northridge.
1988 March 19	Zenobia Perry is honored by Ohio National Organization of Women [NOW] at NOW Banquet in Columbus, as a part of second annual women's history celebration.
1988 May 15	*Four Mynyms for Three Players* is performed in concert of Music of Black American Composers at National Museum of American History at the Smithsonian Institution, Hall of Musical Instruments, Washington, D.C.
1989 January 31	Premiere of *Ships That Pass in the Night* at West Virginia University, on graduate recital of James L. Tully.
1989	Zenobia Perry is diagnosed with and treated for breast cancer.
1990	*Homage to William Dawson on his 90th Birthday* is published by Hildegard Publishing Company.
1991 February 17	Premiere of *Echoes from the Journey*, by Cleveland Chamber Symphony, Edwin London, *conductor*; Jo Ann Lanyé, *soprano*.
1991 September 28	Zenobia Perry is inducted into the Greene County [Ohio] Women's Hall of Fame.
1993 April 13	Concert at West Virginia State University includes *Tempo for Wind Ensemble and Soprano* and *Ships That Pass in the Night*, Don Wilcox *conductor*; Lawrence Christianson, *narrator*.
1993 May 12	Zenobia Perry is inducted into Ohio Senior Citizens Hall of Fame.
1996 Spring	Zenobia Perry endures surgery and health problems.
1998 May 30	Zenobia Perry is honored as Outstanding Alumni of University of Wyoming.
1998 November 18	*Dayton Daily News* names Zenobia Perry as one of Top Ten Women for 1998.
1999 March 14	*Echoes from the Journey* is performed by Afro-American Chamber Music Society Orchestra, Dwayne E. Smith, *conductor*; Leberta Clark, *mezzo-soprano*, at Holman United Methodist Church in Los Angeles, California.
1999 April 25	Zenobia Perry receives Woman of the Year Award at Paul Laurence Dunbar House State Memorial in Dayton, Ohio.
2000 May 20	Zenobia Perry is named 2000 Outstanding Senior Citizen of Green County, Ohio.
2002 January 18	Zenobia Perry is elected to membership in American Society of Composers, Authors and Publishers (ASCAP), as a composer.
2002 January 21	Zenobia Perry receives 2002 Cultural Arts Award for outstanding contributions in the field of Music Education, by National Afro-American Museum, Wilberforce, Ohio.
2003 October 1–5	95th Birthday Concert Tour features performances of Perry's music at colleges and other venues throughout Ohio.
2004 January 17	Zenobia Powell Perry dies in Xenia, Ohio, at the age of 95.

Zenobia Powell Perry on her 95th birthday, 2003.
Photo by Beverly Simmons.

B. List of Compositions

This list is in alphabetical order, by title. All selections ASCAP, and published by Jaygayle Music.

***Aftermath**—see **Narrative**.*

***Ah Got a Home in a Dat Rock**,* for soprano and piano (1969). "In memory of my grandfather Charlie Thompson." 6 pages. Based on a spiritual.

***Angels Done Bowed Down**—see **O de Angels Done Bowed Down**.*

Arkansia, Suite for violin and piano (1955). Contents: (1) "Landscape"; (2) "Folk Song"; (3) "A Bit of Fun." Originally composed for violin and piano, for Joseph. Orchestrated for string orchestra: 6-4-2-6-3. Premiered ["Folk Song" and "Divertissement" only] on January 10, 1955, at Arkansas A. M. & N. College by the String Choir of Forest City, Arkansas, Eugene Isom, conductor. Duration: 6:53.

***At Tea, suite**—see **Suite for Women's Voices**.*

***Atmosphere Cycle**—see **Threnody**.*

***Benediction**—see **Threnody**.*

***A Bit of Fun**—see **Arkansia**.*

***Cantata**—see **Sing Unto the Lord a New Song**.*

Capriccio, for solo piano (1961).

Capriccios, suite of ten pieces for piano (1972). Renamed and consolidated into **Piano Potpourri**.

Certainly Lord, for tenor and piano (1974). Based on a spiritual.

***Chit-Chat**—see **Conversations for two flutes and piano**.*

***Choral Suite* no. 1**, for tape sounds, percussion, piano, 16-voice choir (1963). Performed October 25, 1974.

***Christmas Is More**—see **Notes of Christmas**.*

Conversations for two flutes and piano (1975). Contents: (1) "Greetings"; (2) "Chit-Chat"; (3) "Gossip." Duration: 3:03.

APPENDIX B

The Cottage, for soprano and piano (1964). [Copyright 1965.] Text: Jones Very. Premiered by Joyce Mathis. 5 pages. Duration: 2:33.

Couldn't Hear Nobody Pray, for baritone and piano (1978). 3 pages. Based on a spiritual.

Cycle of Songs on Poems of Paul Laurence Dunbar, for voice and piano (1977–83). Contents: (1) "Sunset" (1977), 5 pages; (2) "On A Clean Book" (1979), 3 pages; (3) "Spring Song" (1979), 4 pages; (4) "Life" (1978), 4 pages; (5) "Drizzle" (1979), 4 pages. Duration: 15:13.

Done Made My Vow to the Lord, for SATB (1974). Duration: 3:04. Based on a spiritual.

Dreams—see ***Three Sketches.***

Drizzle—see ***Cycle of Songs on Poems of Paul Laurence Dunbar.***

Echoes from the Journey, for soprano and chamber orchestra (1990). Text: Zenobia Powell Perry. 32 pages. Duration: 14:03. Instrumentation: flute, oboe, B♭ clarinet, trumpet, two percussion players, strings, and piano. Contains "Field Hollers" with trumpet. Includes the spirituals "Wade in the Water," "I Want to Die Easy," and "Swing Low, Sweet Chariot." Premiered by Cleveland Chamber Symphony, Edwin London, *conductor*, at John Carroll University, Cleveland, Ohio, February 1991.

Elegy for Brass Quintet, for trumpet, 2 horns in F, trombone, and tuba/euphonium (1980, rev. 1989). 7 pages. Duration: 6. There is also a version for B♭ clarinet, 2 horns, and 2 bassoons.

Episodes I and II, for horn and piano (1983). Duration: 3:17. A third movement was added: ***Prelude*** (2000). 16 pages.

Essay, for piano (1958). Duration: 4:16.

Excursions, for piano trio (1989). 12 pages. Duration: 4:21.

Fantasy, for piano (1972, rev. 1992). Duration: 3:15.

Fantasy, for violin and piano (1968; rev. 1972). 9 pages. Duration: 3:15.

Festival overture, for organ. Duration: 3:04.

Florence Price's Dances in the Canebrakes, arrangement for two pianos.

Folk Song—see ***Arkansia.***

Four Mynyms for Three Players, for flute, oboe, and piano (1963; rev. 1968 and 1979). Contents: (1) "Pensive"; (2) "Jovial"; (3) "Melancholy"; (4) "Jubilant." Duration: 6:00.

Fulfillment—see ***Three Songs for Christmas.***

Gifts of God, for SSA and piano (1980). Text: Zenobia Powell Perry. Duration: 2:12.

Gloria in Excelsis, for soprano and piano (1991).

LIST OF COMPOSITIONS

Go Tell It on the Mountain, for SATB *a cappella* (1974). Duration: 3:02. Based on a spiritual.

Gossip—see *Conversations for two flutes and piano.*

Great Gittin' Up Mornin'—see *Tawawa House.*

Hallelujah, for unison children's chorus and SS chorus (1972). Duration: 1:22.

Hallelujah, for brass octet (1984). There is also a version for woodwind octet, performed in 1991.

Hallelujah to the Lamb, for soprano and piano (1969; rev. 1982). 7 pages. Based on a spiritual.

Heritage, for baritone and piano (1968). Text: Claude McKay, from the poem, "The White House." Duration: 2:40. There is also a version for soprano and piano; see *Heritage and Life.*

Heritage and Life: A Cycle of Songs, for soprano and piano. Text: Frank Horne. Contents: (1) "Heritage"; (2) "Rhapsody"; (3) "Immortality"; (4) "Kid Stuff"; (5) "A Toast"; (6) "To All of You."

[The] Hidden Words of Bahá'u'lláh, for soprano, flute, and piano (1977). Contents: (1) "O son of spirit"; (2) "O children of men"; (3) "O son of being"; (4) "O friends abandon not the everlasting beauty"; (5) "O companion of my throne"; (6) "O oppressors on earth withdraw." 23 pages. Duration: 14:08. Commissioned by Janis-Rozena Peri for New York début recital.

Homage to William Levi Dawson on his 90th Birthday (1990)—see *Piano Potpourri.*

How Charming Is This Place, for soprano and organ or piano (1994). Text: Samuel Stennett (1787). 2 pages. Written for Janis-Rozena Peri. Composed for the dedication of the redecorated nave and chancel of Christ Episcopal Church, Xenia, Ohio.

Humoreske—see *Three Sketches.*

Hymn for Brass Quartet (1963).

Impromptu, for solo piano (1957).

In the Great Gittin' Up Mornin', for SATB and piano.

Introduction, Prelude and Danse for band (1968). Orchestration: 2 flutes, 3 clarinets, B♭ bass clarinet, 2 bassoons, 2 alto saxophones, tenor saxophone, flugelhorn, 3 trumpets, 2 horns in F, 2 horns in E, 3 trombones, 3 basses, bass drum, and cymbal. Dedicated to Central State University Band for performance at Charter Day, 1968. Premiered by the CSU Band, Ian Polster, *conductor*. Duration: 4:22.

It's Me O Lord, Standing in the Need of Prayer, for baritone and piano (1974). 3 pages. Based on a spiritual.

Journey—see *Echoes from the Journey.*

APPENDIX B

Jovial—see ***Four Mynyms for Three Players.***

Jubilant—see ***Four Mynyms for Three Players.***

Kid Stuff—see ***Three Songs for Christmas.***

Kum Ba Yah, for SATB (1975). Based on a spiritual.

Kum Ba Yah, for children's chorus and conga drum. Based on a spiritual.

Lamb of God, for SSA (1958). Duration: 2:03.

Landlord's Ballad—see ***Three Sketches.***

Landscape—see ***Arkansia.***

Latino rhythms, for 2 trumpets and piano (1959). Duration: 4:02.

Life—see ***Cycle of Songs on Poems of Paul Laurence Dunbar.***

Life—see ***Life Cycle: Three Songs for Baritone and Piano.***

Life Cycle: Three Songs for Baritone and Piano (1971). Contents: (1) "O Whisper, O My Soul" (1969), text: William Stanley Braithwaite, duration: 3:10; (2) "A Toast" (1970), text: Frank Horne, duration: 2:09; (3) "Life" (1971), text: Paul Laurence Dunbar, duration: 1:42.

Lift Every Voice and Sing (J. Rosamond Johnson), for SATB and band (1975). Text: James Weldon Johnson. Orchestration: flutes, oboe, clarinets, saxophones, trumpets, trombones, basses, timpani, snare, cymbal, chimes. Premiered at opening of new music building at CSU, January 1975. 12 pages.

Love Came Down at Christmas, for unison children's chorus and strings (1972). Text: C. Rossetti. 6 pages. Duration: 1:41.

The Love of God, for SATB *a cappella* (1991). Text: Zenobia Powell Perry. Duration: 3:00.

Marche, for piano (1974). Duration: 2:48.

Mary Had a Baby—see ***Three Songs for Christmas.***

Mass in F# minor for soprano and bass soli, SATB, and piano or organ (1968). Contents: (1) Kyrie eleison; (2) Credo; (3) Sanctus; (4) Agnus Dei; (5) Gloria in excelsis.

Melancholy—see ***Four Mynyms for Three Players.***

A Mighty Fortress Is Our God (Martin Luther), arranged for instrumental ensemble and chorus (1975). "In Celebration of the opening of two new buildings at CSU." Translation: Frederick Henry Hedge. Instrumentation: piccolo, 2 flutes, 2 clarinets in B♭, 2 saxophones in E♭, 1 B♭ saxophone, 2 trumpets, 3 horns in F, 2 trombones, baritone horn, 2 basses, 3 percussionists, string bass, mixed chorus. 15 pages.

Moods, for mixed quartet of voices, marimba, and conga drum. Premiered on July 25, 1974, by North County New Music Performers, Zenobia Perry, conductor.

LIST OF COMPOSITIONS

Music from Ohio, for SATB and piano (1993). Includes "Silently" and "Christmas Is More." See also ***Notes of Christmas***.

Narrative, for flute, narrator/soprano, two percussionists, and piano (1975). Contents: (1) "Tornado" (2) "Aftermath." Text: Zenobia Powell Perry. Premiered July 25, 1974, by North Country New Music Performers, Zenobia Perry, *conductor*. 18 pages. Duration: 5:52. [A version of this was presented November 7, 1974, as ***Narrative, for speaker, flute, and piano***. Another version was presented April 2, 1975, as ***Narrative, for flute, narrator, and piano (after the tornado April 3, 1974)***: (1) "Prologue"; (2) "Narrative."]

Night in Tawawa, for trumpet and piano (1963).

Nocturne, for piano (1961).

Notes of Christmas, for SATB and piano (1991). Contents: (1) "The quiet of Christmas," for SATB *a cappella*, text: Mildred N. Hoyer, 5 pages; (2) "Christmas Is More," text: R. H. Grenville, duration: 5:32, 16 pages. Dedicated to the Oberlin Community Chamber Singers, Carol Longsworth, *director*. [At one point, this may have been called ***Music from Ohio*** (1993), and there was a movement called "Silently."]

Nova Sonos, electronic music on tape. Premiered at North Country Music Festival, Potsdam, New York.

O de Angels Done Bowed Down, for mezzo-soprano and piano (1973). There is a version from 1969, with the following inscription: "As sung by my grandfather, Charlie Thompson." There is also a version for soprano and piano (1973). There is another version for SSAA quartet (2000). Based on a spiritual.

O Lord, Make Thy Beauty, for SATB *a cappella* (1991). Text: prayer. Duration: 2:08.

O Peter, Go Ring Dem Bells, for SATB and piano. Based on a spiritual.

O the Angels Done Bowed—see ***O de Angels Done Bowed Down***.

O Whisper, O My Soul—see ***Life Cycle***.

Of Life and Love, for soprano and piano. Text: Paul Laurence Dunbar. Contents: (1) "Sunset"; (2) "On a Clean Book"; (3) "Spring Song"; (4) "Life"; (5) "Drizzle"; (6) "Philosophy." Duration: 15:13. See also ***Cycle of Songs on Poems by Paul Laurence Dunbar***, which is a version of some of these songs for baritone and piano.

On a Clean Book—see ***Cycle of Songs on Poems of Paul Laurence Dunbar***.

Pastels for orchestra (1986). Orchestration: 2 flutes, 2 oboes, 2 B♭ clarinets, bass clarinet in B♭, 2 bassoons, 4 horns in F, 2 trumpets in B♭, 3 trombones, tuba, timpani (28", 25", and 23"), and strings. 15 pages. Duration: 6:20. This was read by the Detroit Symphony Orchestra, but not publicly performed.

Pavanne, for piano (1975). Duration: 3:18.

Pensive—see ***Four Mynyms for Three Players***.

APPENDIX B

Philosophy, for flute, cello, and voice (1984). Text: Paul Laurence Dunbar. 8 pages.

Philosophy—see ***Of Life and Love.***

Piano Potpourri (1990)

1. ***Vignette no. 1*** (originally a teaching piece)
2. ***Orrin and echo***
3. ***Ties***
4. ***Flight***
5. ***A jazz trifle***
6. ***Blaize***
7. ***Promenade (1988)***
8. ***Times seven***
9. ***Soliloquy***
10. ***Homage to William Levi Dawson on his 90th Birthday*** (1990). Contents: (1) Smooth flowing; (2) Cantabile; (3) Moderate. Published in *Black Women Composers: A Century of Piano Music, 1893–1990*, ed. by Helen Walker-Hill (Bryn Mawr, Penn.: Hildegard Publishing, 1992). 3 pages.
11. ***Round and round***
12. ***Teeta***
13. ***Rhapsody***
14. ***Vignette no. 2***
15. ***Childhood Capers***

Piano Sonata no. 3 (1959–60). Premiered in 1960.

Piano Sonatina (1962).

Precious Lord, for SATB and piano (1976). Based on a spiritual.

Prelude, for horn and piano—see ***Episodes I and II.***

Prelude and aria, for clarinet (1969).

Prelude and danse, for band (1968)—see ***Introduction, Prelude and danse for band.***

Prelude for organ (1973). 2 pages.

Prism for organ (1975). 7 pages. Duration: 2:55. There is also a version for solo piano.

Quiet of Christmas—see ***Notes of Christmas.***

Redemption, for SATB (1963).

Rhapsody, for medium voice and piano (1968; copyright 1974). Text: William Braithwaite. 4 pages.

Rhapsody for piano (1960). Written for Janis-Rozena Peri.

Rhyme for saxophone and piano, for alto saxophone and piano (1968; rev. 1977). Duration: 2:46.

LIST OF COMPOSITIONS

Ride, Ride, Ride King Jesus, for SATB *a cappella* (1974). Duration: 3:14. Based on a spiritual.

Salon du Capriccii, for piano (1972). Contents: (1) "Kofi"; (2) "Trek"; (3) "Gettera"; (4) "Paen"; (5) "Mumura"; (6) "Nino"; (7) "Jangada"; (8) "Balzo"; (9) "Vele." Duration: 12:09.

Sanctus and Agnus Dei (1969).

Ships That Pass in the Night, for instrumental ensemble and narrator (1988). Text: Paul Laurence Dunbar. Orchestration: piccolo, flute, alto and tenor saxophones, 2 trumpets, timpani, bass and tenor drums, conga drums, tambourine, gong, piano, and speaking voice (narrator). Performed by Cleveland Chamber Symphony. [This is a revised version of her *Symphonic Poem.*] Duration: 8:16. 22 pages.

Sing Unto the Lord a New Song, a cantata, for soprano, mezzo-soprano, baritone, narrator, SATB, flute, timpani, harp, and organ (1976). Text: Zenobia P. Powell. Contents: (1) "Introduction," for organ; (2) "Petition," for soprano, mezzo-soprano, narrator, and timpani; (3) "For the Lord is a Great God," for narrator, SATB, flute, harp, and organ; (4) "Sing unto the Lord a new song," for SATB and organ; (5) Ensemble: "The Lord is High Above All Nations," for soprano, mezzo-soprano, flute, and organ; (6) "Thanksgiving, Hallelujah, How Good it is to Sing Praise," for narrator, SATB, and timpani; (7) "Laud, praise, and glory," for SATB, flute, and organ; (8) "Canzonet," for mezzo-soprano and organ; (9) Finale, Chorale, and Amen: "Laud, praise, and glory." Duration: 37:12.

Sinner Man So Hard, Believe! for soprano and piano (1967; rev. 1969). 4 pages. Based on a spiritual.

Sonata for clarinet and piano (1963). Contents: (1) Lively; (2) Moderate; (3) Three-quarter time; (4) Very fast. Duration: 7:43.

Sonata for piano (1960). Contents: (1) Andante; (2) Lento; (3) Allegro. Duration: 6:23.

Sonata for violin and piano. Contents: (1) Allegro non troppo; (2) Adagio; (3) Presto. Written for Dimistrios Cokinos. Score is lost.

Sonata no. 3 (1959–60). Duration: 6:23.

Sonatine for piano (1963). Contents: (1) Allegro; (2) Lively.

Songs for Nobody, for SATB. Texts: Zenobia Powell Perry. Premiere by the Jackson State College Choir, Ariel Lovelace, *director*, Jackson College, Mississippi, December 1961.

Sound Patterns, for narrator and clarinet (1978). Text: Zenobia P. Powell. 4 pages. Duration: 3:17. There is a version of this piece for Spoken Voice Ensemble and B♭ clarinet (1980).

Spring Song—see ***Cycle of Songs on Poems of Paul Laurence Dunbar.***

APPENDIX B

Standing in the Need of Prayer, for baritone and piano (1976).

Still, Still (1972). Arrangement of an Austrian Christmas carol.

String Quartet no. 1 (1964). Premiered at Antioch College in Yellow Springs, Ohio, March 14, 1964; Myron Kartman, *conductor*. Score has been lost.

String Quartet no. 2 (1964)—see *Three Designs for Four Strings.*

Suite for piano (1963). Contents: (1) Caprice; (2) Nocturne; (3) Times Five.

Suite for Women's Voices, for SSAA and piano (1963; rev. 1984). Contents: (1) "At Tea"; (2) "By Her Aunt's Grave"; (3) "Outside the Window." Text: Thomas Hardy. 21 pages. Duration: 6:12.

Sunset—see *Cycle of Songs on Poems of Paul Laurence Dunbar.*

Symphonic Poem, for orchestra (1954). Orchestration: 2 flutes, 2 clarinets, 2 oboes, 2 bassoons, 2 trumpets, 4 French horns, 2 trombones, 2 tubas, timpani, cymbal, and strings. This was Perry's University of Wyoming master's thesis project (later revised and presented under the name, *Ships That Pass in the Night* [1988]). Premiered on July 9, 1954, in Casper, Wyoming, and Denver, Colorado, with the University of Wyoming Orchestra, Saul Caston, *conductor*. Duration: 7:13. A version for band was performed on April 19, 1955.

Tawawa House, opera in 2 acts for SSSAATTBB (1985). Text: Zenobia Powell Perry. Orchestration: 2 flutes, 2 oboes, 2 B♭ clarinets, 2 bassoons, 2 French horns, 2 trumpets, 2 tenor trombones, bass trombone, tuba, timpani, bass drum, and strings. Solo voices: 3 sopranos, 2 mezzo-sopranos, 2 tenors, baritone, and bass-baritone. Premiered at the Paul Robeson Cultural and Performing Arts Center, Central State University, Ohio, in 1987. Duration: two hours with intermission.

Tempo for Wind Ensemble and Soprano (1993). Text: R. H. Grenville. Orchestration: piccolo, flute, oboe, 3 B♭ clarinets, alto clarinet, bass clarinet, bassoon, alto saxophone, tenor saxophone, baritone saxophone, 3 trumpets, 4 French horns, baritone horn, 3 trombones, basses, timpani, drums, and soprano solo. Written for and performed by Janis-Rozena Peri with the West Virginia University Wind Ensemble, Spring 1994. 17 pages.

There's a Lit'l Wheel A-Turnin', for SATB *a cappella* (1976). Duration: 2:58. Based on a spiritual.

Three Designs for Four Strings (String Quartet no. 2) (1964). Contents: Allegro moderato; Adagio; Allegro. Premiered by Antioch Quartet (Myron Kartman), 1966. 33 pages. Duration: 10:25. At one time, this was called *Three Designs for Four Players.*

Three Expressions for Piano (1973–74). Contents: (1) "Preface"; (2) "Merry-Go-Round"; (3) "Ballad." Score is lost.

Three Sketches, for piano (1960). Contents: (1) "Sketches"; (2) "Humoreske" (1955); (3) "Landlord's Ballad"; (4) "Dreams." Duration: 5:44.

LIST OF COMPOSITIONS

Three Songs for Baritone and Piano—see ***Life Cycle.***

Three Songs for Christmas, for soprano and piano (1989). Text: Zenobia Powell Perry. Contents: (1) "Kid Stuff" (1970), text: Frank Horne, duration 3:02; (2) "Fulfillment" (1989), duration 2:25; (3) "Mary had a baby," for soprano, violoncello, and piano (1980), duration: 2:32. [This is an arrangement of a folksong.] "Kid Stuff" was recorded by Sebronette Barnes, *soprano*, and Elise Auerbach, *piano*, on the compact disc, *You Can Tell the World: Songs by African-American Women Composers* (Senrab Records SRR988, 2000).

Threnody Song Cycle, for soprano and piano. Contents: (1) "Threnody" (1969); (2) "Alien" (1970); (3) "Benediction" (1972); (4) "Poet" (1969); (5) "Pastourelle" (1971). Text: Donald Jeffrey Hayes. Written for Janis-Rozena Peri. Duration: 12:57. At one time, this was called ***Atmosphere Cycle***; the first performance included "Threnody," "Poet," and "Pastourelle." There is also a version of "Benediction" for violin and piano.

Times Five, for solo piano. Performed in 1963 by William Hollis, San Francisco. See ***Suite for piano***. Score may have been lost.

To All of You, for soprano and piano. Text: Frank Horne. Premiered June 1, 1970, by Janis-Rozena Peri at New York Public Library at Lincoln Center.

A Toast, for baritone voice and piano (1970). Text: Frank Horne. 2 pages. See ***Life Cycle.***

Tornado—see ***Narrative.***

Tranquility and Commotion for orchestra. Orchestration: 2 flutes, 2 oboes, 2 clarinets, 2 bassoons, 4 horns, 2 trombones, tuba, timpani, and strings. Commissioned by the Columbus Symphony, premiered in November 1982. Duration: c.18:00.

The Twelve Days of Christmas, for SATB and piano [arrangement].

Two Letters for clarinet, violoncello, and piano (1975). Contents: (1) "Written in Spring" (2) "Written at Summer's End." Premiered at Dayton Chamber Music Society, September 28, 1975. 13 pages. Duration: 3:34. There is another version of "Written in Spring" for violin, cello, clarinet, and bassoon.

Up Over My Head, for soprano, oboe, and piano. Based on a spiritual.

Variations for Piano (1961).

Whisper, O My Soul, O—see ***O Whisper, O My Soul.***

You Hear the Constant Drumming, for baritone.

Zenobia Powell Perry, honored at the Centennial Convention of Mu Phi Epsilon International Fraternity, Cincinnati, Ohio, 2003.
Photo by Beverly Simmons.

C. Inventory of Documents Related to the Life and Career of Zenobia Powell Perry

1910 APRIL 26 **Thirteenth Census of the United States**: Population, Boley City, Okfuskee County, Oklahoma. Includes records of C. B. Powell, wife and daughter.

1915 JANUARY 23 **School Enrollment Record** for Zenobia Powell, Boley, Oklahoma.

1934 APRIL 27 **Souvenir Program**, R. Nathaniel Dett in Recital, Pine Bluff, Arkansas.

1938 MAY 26 **Diploma**, Tuskegee Institute. "By authority of the Board of Trustees and upon recommendation of the faculty, Tuskegee Institute hereby confers upon Zenobia Jean Powell the degree of Bachelor of Science in Education with all the rights, honors, and privileges appertaining thereto."

1939 JULY 12 **Concert Program**, Langston University, Fine Arts Recital. Concerto in A Minor by Grieg; Zenobia Perry, *piano*.

1943 AUGUST 29 **Notification of Birth Registration** for Janis Perry; filed in Oklahoma City, Oklahoma. States father as Jimmie Rodgers Perry, age 28; mother as Zenobia Powell, age 29.

1945 AUGUST 31 **Diploma**, Colorado State College of Education. "The Trustees of Colorado State College of Education, upon the recommendation of the Faculty and by virtue of the authority in them vested, have conferred upon Zenobia Powell Perry, who has satisfactory pursued the studies, passed the examinations, and complied with all the other requirements therefor, the degree of Master of Arts with all rights, privileges, and honors thereunto appertaining."

1947 JANUARY 26 **Concert Program**, Hazel Harrison, *piano*. Carver Junior High School Auditorium, Tulsa, Oklahoma.

[C.1951] **Brochure**, Arkansas State Agricultural, Mechanical, and Normal College, Pine Bluff. Includes photographs of Zenobia Perry and Kelton Lawrence.

[C.1952] **Brochure**, Music Study at the University of Wyoming.

APPENDIX C

1952 APRIL 24 — **Concert Program**, 79th Founder's Day Celebration, A.M. & N. College, Pine Bluff, Arkansas. Annual Band Concert, John Williams, *conductor*. Concerto in A Minor by Grieg; Zenobia Perry, *piano*.

1952 APRIL 24 — **Concert Program**, 80th Founder's Day Celebration, A.M. & N. College, Pine Bluff, Arkansas. *Arkansia*: Suite for Piano and Violin by Zenobia Perry; William Haithcock, *violin*, Zenobia Perry, *piano*.

1954 AUGUST 20 — **Diploma**, University of Wyoming. "The Graduate School Know all men by these presents, That Zenobia Jean Perry having completed the appropriate Course of Study prescribed by the Graduate Faculty and having fulfilled all other requirements, is therefore granted the degree of Master of Arts in Music."

1955 JANUARY 10 — **Concert Program**, Gamma Sigma and Pine Bluff Alumni Chapters of Kappa Alpha Psi Fraternity, 44th Founder's Day, A.M. & N. College. *Arkansia Suite* by Zenobia Perry; Bro. W. H. Haithcock, *violin*.

1955 APRIL 19 — **Concert Program**, 83rd Founder's Day Celebration, A.M. & N. College, Pine Bluff, Arkansas. *Symphonic Poem* by Zenobia Perry; The College Band, Harold S. Strong, *conductor*.

[1956] — **Faculty Newsletter**, Central State College, Wilberforce, Ohio. Includes brief biography of Zenobia Perry, "instructor in composition and piano."

1956 NOVEMBER 4 — **Concert Program**, Central State College, Wilberforce, Ohio. The College Women's Club presents Zenobia Powell Perry, pianist, in chamber recital. Includes works by Chopin, Bach, Schumann, Liszt, Dett, Carpenter, Griffes, and two pieces by Perry, "Prelude" and "Humoreske."

[1956?] — **Concert Program**, Music Department, Central State College, presents Zenobia Powell Perry, *piano*. Includes works by Bach, Handel, Mozart, Schumann, Debussy, de Falla, Griffes, Carpenter, and her own work, *Humoreske*: "One of four piano sketches composed during the Thanksgiving holidays 1955 on Central State College campus."

1957 SUMMER — **Copy of letter** from Charles H. Wesley, President of Central State College, to Dean Norman Singer, Music Associates of Aspen, Aspen Music School, recommending Zenobia Perry for Aspen Music School.

1957 SUMMER — **Concert Program**, Aspen Music Festival; Izler Solomon, *Festival Director* and *Conductor*.

1957 OCTOBER 15 — **Faculty Concert Program**, Department of Music, Central State College. Zenobia Perry played *Impromptu* no. 3 by Fauré, "Barcarolle" and "Juba" from *In the Bottoms* by R. Nathaniel Dett, and her own *Impromptu*.

1959 APRIL 19 — **Concert Program**, Senior Choir of Middle Run Baptist Church, Zenobia Perry, *piano*, and Janice Perry, *mezzo-soprano*. Includes *Chromatic Fantasy and Fugue* by Bach; "Mammy" by Dett; *Impromptu* no. 3 by Fauré; *Reflets dans l'eau* by Debussy; *Elegie* by Rachmaninoff; *Impromptu* and *Danza* by Carpenter.

1961 DECEMBER 17 — **Concert Program**, National Association for the Advancement of Native American Composers and Musicians, Art Institute, Dayton, Ohio. Zenobia Perry played her own "Capriccio," "Nocturne," and "Variations for Piano." Other composers on the program were Karol Fahnestock, Kathleen Bogan, and Garland Anderson.

1963 MARCH — **Concert Program**, "A Composer at Work," presenting compositions of Zenobia Powell Perry. Includes *Sonatine* for piano; Hymn for Brass

DOCUMENT INVENTORY

Quartet; two spirituals, "O de Angels Done Bowed Down" and "Redemption"; Sonata for Clarinet and Piano; Suite for piano; *Night in Tawawa* for trumpet and piano; *Choral Suite on Poems of Thomas Hardy*. Performers include Blaine Ellis, Zenobia Powell Perry, Janice Perry, Mrs. Gladys Neal, and Henry Garcia, *piano*; Howard Smith, Cecil Whiting, and Burrell Bowie, *trumpet*; Clarence Walls, *clarinet*; Barbara Smith, *soprano*; The Choral Ensemble, Mrs. Beatrice O'Rouke, *director*.

1963 MARCH 15 **Article**, *Xenia [Ohio] Gazette*, "Wilberforce News," by correspondent Mrs. Henry Garcia [Louise]. Report on Yellow Springs Branch of American Association of University Women concert of compositions by Zenobia Powell Perry.

1963 SEPTEMBER 29 **Concert Program**, An Evening with the San Francisco Quartet in Tribute to Darius Milhaud, Dave Brubeck, and Z. Perry, featuring Emme Kemp Trio. International Music Hall, San Francisco. Includes *Times Five* and Sonata by Perry; William Hollis, *piano*.

1965 MAY 6 **Concert Program**, Central State University School of Music and Art presents The Symphony Orchestra, Shirley Strohm Mullins, *conductor*. Perry performed in the violin section of the orchestra.

1967 MAY 25 **Concert Program**, Oberlin College Conservatory of Music, Kulas Recital Hall. Janis Peri, *soprano*; Terry Van Nelson, *piano*. Includes Perry's "The Cottage" and "Ah Got a Home in a Dat Rock."

1967 MAY 28 **Concert Program**, Miami University Alumni Association, New Artists of 1967; Janis Peri, *soprano*; Terry Van Nelson, *piano*. Includes Perry's "The Cottage" and "Ah Got a Home in a Dat Rock."

1968 MARCH 27 **Concert Program**, Central State University School of Music and Art presents The University Concert Band, Ian Polster, *conductor*. Inclues Perry's *Introduction and Danse* for concert band.

1968 MAY 5 **Concert Program**, Central State University School of Music and Art presents The University Concert Band, Ian Polster, *conductor*. Inclues Perry's *Introduction and Danse* for concert band.

1968 MAY 23 **Concert Program**, Central State University School of Music and Art, Senior Recital of Reginald L. Eberhart, *trombone*. Zenobia Perry was one of the accompanists.

1969 APRIL 13 **Award**, Akron Junior Chamber of Commerce. "Certificate of Award to Zenobia Perry for Outstanding Accomplishment in the Field of Music."

1969 JUNE 8 **Concert Program**, Central State University, The University Baccalaureate. Includes Perry's *Sanctus* and *Agnus Dei*; University Choir, Samuel J. Roberson, *director*.

1969 JUNE 11 **Concert Program**, Library and Museum of the Performing Arts, New York Public Library at Lincoln Center; Janis Peri, *soprano*; Zoran Jovanovic and Ronald Herder, *piano*. Includes Perry's arrangements of "O de Angels Done Bowed Down" and "Hallelujah to the Lamb."

1969 OCTOBER 29 **Concert Program**, Central State University School of Music and Art, Janis Peri, *soprano*; Judie Gels, *piano*. Includes Perry's *Heritage and Life, A Cycle of Songs* (premiere performance): "Heritage," "Rhapsody," "Immortality," "Kid Stuff," "A Toast," "To All of You."

APPENDIX C

1969 — **Concert Program**, Central State University, School of Music and Art presents Elsie Harriet Banks, *soprano*; Barbara Beittel, *accompanist*. Senior Vocal Recital. Includes Perry's *Cycle of Song*.

1970 MARCH 1 — **Concert Program**, Central State University, School of Music and Art presents The University Chamber Orchestra, Shirley Mullins, *conductor*. Perry performed in the violin section of the orchestra.

1970 JUNE 1 — **Concert Program**, Library and Museum of the Performing Arts, New York Public Library at Lincoln Center. Janis Peri, *soprano*; Judith Gels, *piano*. Includes Perry's *Heritage and Life, A Cycle of Songs* (New York premiere).

1971 MAY 2 — **Concert Program**, Central State University Department of Music, Senior Recital of Mable Lewis, *violin*; Zenobia Perry, *accompanist*.

1971 MAY 16 — **Concert Program**, Central State University Department of Music, Senior Recital of Corliss Taylor, *soprano*; Barbara Beittel, *accompanist*. Includes Perry's *Atmosphere Cycle*: "Threnody," "Alien," "Poet," and "Pastourelle;" and arrangements of "I Got a Home in a Dat Rock," "O de Angels Done Bowed Down," and "Sinner Man, So Hard, Believe."

1972 FEBRUARY 21 — **Concert Program**, Central State University Department of Music, Faculty Recital. Includes Perry's *Four Mynyms for Three Players*: Pensive, Jovial, Melancholy, and Jubilant. Alvin E. Amos, *clarinet*; Warren E. James, *flute*; Barbara Beittel, *piano*.

1972 — **Concert Program**, Central State University Department of Music presents Opera-in-the-Round, the University Opera Workshop, William de Valentine, *director*; Zenobia Perry and Paula Rockhold, *piano*.

1972 APRIL 23 — **Concert Program**, Central State University Department of Music presents Gioacchino Rossini's *Stabat Mater*; University Chorus, William de Valentine, *conductor*; Zenobia Perry and William Smith, *accompanists*.

1972 MAY 23 — **Concert Program**, Central State University Department of Music, The Concert Chorale; Clyde Battles, *conductor*; Zenobia Perry, *accompanist*.

1972 NOVEMBER 1 — **Calendar of Events**, Central State University Department of Music. Includes "Performance of Original Compositions by Students and Faculty," Zenobia Perry, *coordinator*.

1972 NOVEMBER 19 — **Concert Program**, Dayton Chamber Music Society, Donald Hageman Studio, 834 Riverview Terrace. Includes Perry's *Four Mynyms for Three Players*; Warren H. James, *flute*; Alvin E. Amos, *clarinet*; Barbara Beittel, *piano*.

1972 CHRISTMAS — **Concert Program**, Central State University Department of Music, A Feast of Carols Concert; The Concert Chorale, Arthur Herndon, *director*; Zenobia Perry, *accompanist*; Henry Garcia, *organist*; with The Children's Choir of Christ Episcopal Church; University Brass Ensemble, Julian Northington, *conductor*; Zenobia Perry, *director*. Includes Perry's arrangements of "Love Came Down at Christmas" and "Still, Still."

1973 MARCH — **Press Release**, Hampton Institute. Announces March 8 concert. Roberson described as "assistant professor of voice at Hampton Institute and director of the opera theater at the college, . . . a graduate of the Cleveland Institute of Music and the University of Michigan."

1973 MARCH 4 — **Concert Program**, Central State University Department of Music Senior Recital; David Leston, *trombone*; William Smith, *piano*; LeRoy Trotman, *trombone*; Zenobia Perry, *piano*.

DOCUMENT INVENTORY

1973 MARCH 8   **Concert Program**, The Hampton Institute Department of Music, Faculty Recital, Samuel Roberson, *baritone*; Norman Voelcker, *piano*. Includes Perry's *Life Cycle*: "A Toast," "Whisper, O My Soul," and "Life."

1973 MARCH 12   **Letter** from Samuel Roberson to Zenobia Perry, on Hampton Institute, Department of Music, letterhead: "Your cycle was a great success. Everyone spoke highly of it; especially those involved in composition. Again I want to thank you for the privilege of performing your compositions. I was not able to program the spirituals, but I will do them very soon."

1973 MAY 4   **Concert Program**, Bolinga Black Cultural Resources Center and Department of Music, Wright State University, present Janis Peri, *soprano*; Jerome Stanley, *piano*. Includes Perry's *Threnody*, Opus 12, *A Cycle of songs to poetry by Jeffrey Hayes*. [N.B. This is the only mention ever made of opus numbers with regard to Perry's compositions.]

1973 MAY 20   **Concert Program**, Central State University Department of Senior Recital, Levon Small, *mezzo-soprano*; Zenobia Perry, *accompanist*. Includes Perry's arrangement of "O de Angels Done Bowed Down."

1974 MAY 22   **Concert Program**, Central State University Department of Music, University Opera Workshop, William de Valentine, *director*; Zenobia Perry, *accompanist*. *The Impresario*, by Wolfgang Amadeus Mozart.

1974 JULY   **Letter** from Odean Long, Research Assistant, Department of English, University of Victoria, British Columbia, Canada. "Dear Professor Perry, I extend our sincere thanks for the information which you forwarded in response to my letter of 2 July 1974, and for both the time and the consideration you have taken on our behalf. We would be most grateful if at your convenience you would let us know your date of birth, since we hope to include such information in the composers' section of our Catalogue."

1974 OCTOBER 2   **Concert Program**, Central State University Department of Music, Faculty Concert. Includes Perry's *Three Expressions for Piano*, with the composer at the piano. Perry also accompanied Arthur Herndon, *tenor*, in a group of songs by Handel, Strauss, and Puccini.

1974 OCTOBER 25   **Concert Program**, Canada Council Arts Festival, Ninth Program, University of Victoria, British Columbia, Canada, University Chamber Singers, Cortland Hultberg, *director*. Includes Perry's *Choral Suite* no. 1 for tape sounds, percussion, piano, 16-voice mixed chorus. Other works on the program by George Crumb, Larry Trauz, György Ligeti, and Robert Suderburg.

1974 NOVEMBER 7   **Concert Program**, American Association of University Women, Dayton, Ohio, Branch, Prelude to Winter, "Women in Music." Includes Perry's *Narrative,* for speaker, flute, and piano; Deborah Bowman, *voice*; Alverdeen Huggins, *flute*; Zenobia Perry, *piano*. Also *Atmosphere—A Song Cycle*, Arthur L. Herndon, *tenor*; Zenobia Perry, *piano*.

1975 FEBRUARY 2   **Concert Program**, Mu Phi Epsilon Sorority, Gamma Eta Chapter presents "A Program of Black Music," featuring works of Zenobia Perry, residence of Mrs. Alverda Sinks Fitzgerald, Dayton, Ohio. Includes Perry's *Conversations for two flutes*, Alverdean Huggins and Mattie Burch, *flute*; *Life*, Valerie Hamm, *mezzo-soprano*; *Narrative,* for speaker, flute, and piano, Deborah Bowman, *voice*; Alverdean Huggins, *flute*; *Heritage*, June Boddie, *soprano*; June Boddie and Zenobia Perry, *accompanists*.

APPENDIX C

1975 FEBRUARY 14–23   **Concert Program**, Uhuru presents 1975 Annual Black Culture Week, Muskingum College, New Concord, Ohio. Includes Perry's arrangements of "Kum Ba Yah" and "Precious Lord," Central State University Concert Chorale, Arthur Herndon, *director*; Henry Garcia, *accompanist*; William T. Smith, *assistant director and accompanist*. "The Central State University Concert Chorale is one of the ensemble groups sponsored by the Department of Music. This much traveled group presents programs to varied types of audiences throughout the state. These programs embrace a wide range of Music literature. They perform traditional music as well as music by such black composers as Nathaniel Dett, Undine Moore, John Work, Samuel Coleridge-Taylor, and arrangements by William Dawson, Hall Johnson, Jester Hairston, etc. The Chorale has performed many times with the Dayton Philharmonic and with the Springfield Symphony. They recently sang at the Ohio Educators' Association Convention in Columbus, Ohio. They have been invited this year to sing in the Cincinnati May Festival with the Cincinnati Symphony Orchestra."

1975 FEBRUARY 25   **Concert Program**, The Dayton Music Club, Honoring Ohio Composers, Engineers Club Auditorium. Includes Perry's "O de Angels Done Bowed Down," Rosalie Hoffman, *contralto*; Louise Whyte, *piano*. "Zenobia Perry has a Masters Degree in Composition from Wyoming University where she began nine years of study with the French composer, Darius Milhaud. She has studied with Charles Jones of Juilliard. Mrs. Perry is Assistant Professor of Music and Resident Composer at Central State University. Her works include string quartets, chamber and solo works—both vocal and instrumental."

1975 APRIL 2   **Concert Program**, Central State University Department of Music Presents Anniversary Faculty Concert of Remembrance and Thanksgiving. Includes Perry's *Narrative*, for flute, narrator, and piano (After the Tornado, April 3, 1974: Prologue and Narrative), Warren James, *flute*; Harold Nadel, *narrator*; Zenobia Perry, *piano*.

1975 JULY 17   **Concert Program**, MMCP Composers, Potsdam, New York, Zenobia Perry, *conductor*. Includes Perry's *music concrète*, *Narrative*, and *Moods*. Other composers on the program were Peter Townsend, Pat Blandenberg, Rachel Salzano, Steven Myers, Selig Koch, Morton Feldman, Demar Gielenden, Ellen Wisorwild, Patricia Tolliver, John Specht, Paula Canivan, and Lui Ichiyanagi.

1975 SEPTEMBER 28   **Concert Program**, Dayton Chamber Music Society, Don Hageman Studio, 834 Riverview Terrace, David and Sharon Nichols, *chairmen*. Includes Perry's *Conversation for Two Woodwinds*, Warren James, *flute*; Alvin Amos, *clarinet*; and *Two Letters*, Alvin Amos, *clarinet*; Freida Denson, *cello*; Zenobia Perry, *accompanist*.

1975 OCTOBER 21   **CSU News**, Information Services, Central State University, Wilberforce, Ohio. "Faculty-Staff News and Notes": "Several compositions by Zenobia Perry, assistant professor of music, have been heard in public performance at the fall concerts of the Dayton Chamber Music Society and The Dayton Women's Club. The works performed include *Two Letters* for Clarinet, Cello and Piano and *Conversations for two flutes*. Ms. Perry also has been invited to discuss 'The Manhattanville Curriculum in Music' at the November meeting of the Ohio Theory and Composition Teachers at Ohio State University."

1975 NOVEMBER 6   **Concert Program**, Ohio Theory/Composition Teachers Association Conference, Ohio State University. Includes Perry's *Narrative*, for speaker, flute, and piano, performed by Harold Nadel, *narrator*; Warren James, *flute*; Zenobia Perry, *piano*.

DOCUMENT INVENTORY

1976 JANUARY 18   **Concert Program**, The Paul Laurence Dunbar Afro-American Cultural Arts Center Black Music Heritage Concert Series, The Dunbar Choir performs music by Zenobia Powell Perry. Special Guest Carolyn Brown Mitchell, *soprano*, Michael Frazier, *director*. St. Philip's Episcopal Church [Dayton, Ohio]. Includes Perry's *Sing Unto the Lord a New Song*, Leonard Happer, Sr., *narrator*; Lois Shegog, *alto*; Otis Jones, Sr., *baritone*; Mary Daniels, *flute*; Joyce Robinson, *piano*; Barbara Goodrich, *organ*; *Three Designs for Four Players*, Lois Shegog and Leslie Schwartz, *violin*; Vicky Sinclair, *viola*; Laura Handler, *cello*; "Ah Got a Home in a Dat Rock" and "Hallelujah to the Lamb," Carolyn Brown Mitchell, *soprano*; "Done Made My Vow to the Lord," "Precious Lord," "Ride, Ride King Jesus" [presumably performed by the entire choir].

1976 APRIL 3   **Article**. "Choir to perform," *Xenia [Ohio] Daily Gazette*, announces The Dunbar Choir of Columbus concert on April 4, 1976.

1976 APRIL 4   **Concert Program**, Central State University Lecture-Artist Series presents The Dunbar Choir performing music by Zenobia Powell Perry, Carolyn Brown Mitchell, *soprano*; Michael Frazier, *director*. [Same program as January 18, 1976, above.]

1976 APRIL   **Parish Newsletter** [Christ Episcopal Church, Xenia]: Zenobia Perry "has been selected for listing in *'Contemporary American Composers: A Biographical Dictionary'* [by E. Ruth Anderson]. This book provides biographical information on contemporary American composers. Zenobia's compositions have been performed in many areas of the United States and Canada. The Dunbar Choir of Columbus presented a recital featuring music by Zenobia at 3 p.m. Sunday, April 4, on Central State University campus. The choir is sponsored by the Paul Laurence Dunbar Afro-American Cultural Center."

1976 APRIL 15–17   **Announcement and Program**, College of the Scriptures of Louisville, Kentucky, Emphasis on Christian Youth, Education, and Music, featuring Zenobia Powell Perry's "A Workshop in Music for Christian Youth."

1976 MAY 1   **Concert Program**, Inter-Denominational Ministers' Wives Alliance presents Arthur Herndon, *tenor*; Mary Fahrenbruck, *accompanist*, at Mt. Zion Baptist Church, Springfield, Ohio. Includes Perry's "Sinner Man, So Hard, Believe."

1977 MAY 6   **Award**. "Iota Eta Chapter of Phi Mu Alpha Sinfonia Fraternity at Central State University Presents the Fraternity's Orpheus Award to Zenobia Powell Perry for significant and lasting contributions to the cause of Music in America."

1977 MAY 22   **Concert Program**, *The Hidden Words of Bahá'u'lláh*, the complete text, printed with permission of the Bahá'í Publishing Trust, U.S.A. "Zenobia Powell Perry, a native of Oklahoma, is a graduate of Tuskegee Institute, Alabama, where she began the study of music composition with William Dawson. Having earned the M.A. in Music Composition at Wyoming University, studying with Allan Willman, she continued study with Darius Milhaud in California and Aspen, Colorado, for several seasons. Her choral and chamber works, piano and vocal solos have been performed in many areas of the United States and Canada. She is a member of the Diocesan Music Commission of the Episcopal Church in Southern Ohio and composer-in-residence and faculty member at Central State University, Wilberforce, Ohio."

1977 MAY 22   **Review**. "Music in Review: Janis-Rozena Peri Sings Demanding Recital Well," by Peter G. Davis, *New York Times*. Describing premiere of *The Hidden Words of Bahá'u'lláh*, "The rather unpromising didactic texts are taken from a book written in 1858 by the prophet and founder of the Bahá'í Faith. Mrs. Perry

APPENDIX C

has set them in a clean, straightforward, and conservative style for soprano, flute and piano, making inventive and graceful use of this combination."

1977 MAY 26 **Letter to the Editor** by Ruth Colvin, Thursday, *Xenia [Ohio] Daily Gazette*: "Congratulations are in order for Zenobia Perry, CSU music professor for the premiere performance of her setting of *From the Hidden Words of Bahá'u'lláh*, and for being the mother of Janis-Rozena Peri, who made her recital debut at Carnegie Recital Hall on May 15. I believe Miss Perry's setting enhanced the majesty of the words of the Prophet Founder of the Bahá'í Faith. It was indeed a magical weekend. The weather was perfect and the temperature was moderate. The people were friendly and helpful. Everything went according to our plans and we had a lovely time. My only regret is that I slept for a few hours Saturday night and thereby missed something, no doubt, because New York is a very exciting place and they never close."

1978 FEBRUARY 10 **Concert Program**, Lyceum Committee of The University of Arkansas at Pine Bluff, Janis-Rozena Peri, *soprano*; Wayne Sanders, *piano*. Includes Perry's *The Hidden Words of Bahá'u'lláh*, Paul Orton (Pine Bluff faculty), *clarinet*; and Perry's arrangement of "O de Angels Done Bowed Down."

1978 MARCH 11 **Article**. "Perry 'Black Music' Guest Sunday," *The Call and Post* [Ohio]. Announces Perry will be featured on *Profiles in Black Music*, March 12, on WCMH-TV [produced and broadcast on a Columbus television station]. Reports that Perry appeared with the Tulsa Civic Orchestra and Omaha Symphony Orchestra, and that she serves as commentator of *Musical Classics*, on the university station WCSU-FM.

1978 APRIL 13 **Article**. *The Gold Torch* [CSU student newspaper], "CSU Teacher is Featured." Perry "was recently featured on the television series *Profiles in Black Music*, produced and broadcast by a Columbus, Ohio, television station."

1978 MAY 17 **Concert Program**, Dedicatory Banquet, Central State University, Mercer Hall. Perry played Dett's "Barcarolle" and "Juba."

1978 JUNE 3 **Article**. *Dayton [Ohio] Journal Herald*, by Richard Schwarze, on Zenobia Perry and Janis-Rozena Peri, in the "Accent on the Arts" section.

1978 JUNE 3 **Copy of personal thank-you note** from Zenobia Perry to Richard Schwarze for the article in *Dayton Journal Herald*, "My gratitude for the excellent display you gave to my daughter, Janis-Rozena Peri, and me in the June 3 *Journal Herald* issue on 'Accent on the Arts,' can hardly be contained in such ordinary words as 'Thank You.' Yet I know no other way to express my sincere and humble appreciation but to say, 'Thank you' a thousand times."

1978 JUNE 3 **Article**. *Xenia [Ohio] Daily Gazette*, "Janis-Rozena Peri to speak in Xenia." Peri would speak on "One World: Challenge and Rewards of Diversity," at the Xenia Library, mentioning that she is the daughter of Zenobia Powell Perry, composer and music professor at Central State University.

1978 AUGUST 25 **Copy of letter** from Zenobia Perry to Harold Ober Associates, New York City, requesting permission to set three poems of Langston Hughes.

1978 OCTOBER 10 **Letter** from Allan Willman, University of Wyoming Department of Music, to Janis-Rozena Peri, which includes his biography and photograph.

1978 DECEMBER 1 **Concert Program**, Central State University Choir and Central State University Madrigal Ensemble, Arthur Herndon, *director*; Zenobia Perry, *accompanist*. Includes Perry's arrangement of "The Twelve Days of Christmas."

DOCUMENT INVENTORY

1978 DECEMBER 3   **Concert Program**, Central State University Department of Music presents Central State University Concert Band, Danny Davis, *director*, and Central State University Choir, Arthur Herndon, *director*, in Annual Christmas Concert. Includes Perry's arrangement of "The Twelve Days of Christmas," performed by the CSU Madrigal Singers.

1979 FEBRUARY 1   **Letter** from Meet the Composer, New York, New York, to Janis-Rozena Peri: "Meet the Composer is pleased to support your Undine Smith Moore and Zenobia Powell Perry composer program June 30, 1979, with a grant of $150 to be used for composer's fee."

1979 JUNE 30   **Concert Program**, Concert at Theodore Roosevelt Birthplace [28 East 20th Street, New York City], Women and Music: Music and Women, Janis Rozena-Peri, *soprano*; Kelly Wyatt, *piano*; assisted by Norman Dee, *flute*. Includes Perry's *Five Songs to Texts by Paul Laurence Dunbar* (premiere performance). Concert repeated July 8, 1979, at Federal Hall National Memorial, 26 Wall Street, New York.

1979 JULY 14   **Review Article**. "Reading the Score: Janis-Rozena Peri and two composers," by Raoul Abdul, in *New York Amsterdam News*. "Both composers [Undine Smith Moore and Zenobia Powell Perry] were fortunate to have Miss Peri as an interpreter. Besides possessing a large voice capable of producing a variety of tonal colors, she has musical intelligence and dramatic sense of high order."

1980 MARCH 8   **Concert Program**, Conference/Workshop on Twentieth Century String Quartets by Women Composers, Trinity School, New York, jointly sponsored by International League of Women Composers and First National Congress on Women in Music, Jeannie G. Pool, *director*. Includes Perry's *Three Designs for Four Strings* in a sight-reading session, coached by Evan Paris.

1980 JUNE 18   **Concert Program**, Old Dominion University presents Janis-Rozena Peri, *soprano*, assisted by Norman Dee, *flute*; Frederick Wise, *cello*; Mimi Stern-Wolfe, *piano*; Robin Bushman, *violin*; Marilyn Reynolds, *violin*; Jennie Hansen, *viola*; Loretta O'Sullivan, *cello*; Carnegie Recital Hall. Includes Perry's "Benediction" and "Drizzle."

1980 OCTOBER 10   **Concert Program**, Old Dominion University, Department of Music presents Janis-Rozena Peri, *soprano*, and Harold Protzman, *piano*, assisted by Robert Kriner, *French horn*; Karen Paluzzi, *flute*; William Bartolotta, *trumpet*; John Lindberg, *snare drum*; Dennis Zeisler, *clarinet*; Janet Kriner, *violoncello*; Technology Theatre. Includes three sections from Perry's *The Hidden Words of Bahá'u'lláh*.

1981 MARCH 29   **Concert Program**, First National Congress on Women in Music, sponsored by Department of Music and Music Education, New York University; Jeannie G. Pool, *national coordinator*. Perry was a discussant in a session on Black Women in American Music, chaired by Raoul Abdul, music critic for *New York Amsterdam News*. Janis-Rozena Peri sang *Five Songs to Texts of Paul Laurence Dunbar* on a recital, accompanied by Mimi Stern-Wolfe.

1981 JUNE 4   **Review Article**. "Janis-Rozena Peri Sings Rachmaninoff and Bizet," by Edward Rothstein, *New York Times*. "There was the feeling that for this soprano, the use of her voice is no mere vocation. One was always conscious of both the pleasure she took in singing and her earnestness." Includes performance of Perry's *Threnody*, described in the review as "having a well-sustained air of leisurely melancholy."

1981 JUNE 23   **Concert Program**, National Association of Teachers of Singing presents Music of Black Composers, Janis-Rozena-Peri, *soprano*, Harold

APPENDIX C

Protzman, *piano*. Old Dominion University, Department of Music. Includes Perry's *Threnody*.

1982 MAY 29–30   **Boley Rodeo Program**, includes history and photographs of early Boley, Oklahoma.

1983–84   **Concert Program**, Aces Winterfest 3, Festival of the Arts, presented by the Arts Council of the Eastern Shore, "Hopes, Dreams and Fears: The Black Experience in Song." Janis-Rozena Peri, *soprano*; Jane Gallatin, *piano*. Includes Perry's "Kid Stuff." Gallatin was music librarian and part-time faculty at Old Dominion University.

1983 APRIL 24   **Concert Program**, Calvary United Methodist Church, Anna Howard Matthews Choir presents Arthur Herndon, *tenor*. Includes Perry's arrangements of "O de Angels Done Bowed Down" and "Sinner Man So Hard, Believe!"

1983 JUNE 1   **Concert Program**, Central State University Department of Music, Senior Recital, Ivan George Taylor, *horn*; Mary Fahrenbruck and Zenobia Perry, *piano*. Includes Perry's *Episode* for horn and piano.

1984 FEBRUARY 12   **Concert Program**, 14th Annual ACHE [Alabama Center for Higher Education] Arts Festival, "Montage of Black Culture," "Lift Every Voice," A Choral Festival, Montgomery Civic Center, Alabama State University. Includes Perry's "Done Made My Vow to the Lord," Karen Carter, *soprano*, with the Talladega College Choir, Arthur Herndon, *conductor*; Ronald Braithwaite, *accompanist*.

1984 APRIL 11   **Certificate, Oral History**, Central State University, Wilberforce, Ohio, "In recognition of the excellent services you provided in support of the indispensable skills programs, awarded to Ms. Zenobia Perry."

1984 APRIL 13   **Concert Program**, Norfolk [Virginia] State University, Expressions '84, A Festival of the Arts, Janis-Rozena Peri, *soprano*; Mimi Stern-Wolfe, *piano*; assisted by Norman Dee, *flute*, and Joycelyn Jolley, *cello*. Includes two songs from Perry's *The Hidden Words of Bahá'u'lláh*.

1985 FEBRUARY 10   **Concert Program**, Old Dominion University, Department of Music, Virginia Women Composers Faculty Recital, Janis-Rozena Peri, *soprano*, and Robert Brown, *piano*, Technology Theater. Includes *Philosophy* (premiere performance) by Perry.

1985 JUNE   ***Working Papers on Women in Music no. 1***, Department of Music, California State University, Northridge, published by the International Institute for the Study of Women in Music, mentions Perry's *Three Designs for Four Players* and her participation in the Conference/Workshop on Twentieth Century String Quartets by Women Composers.

1986 JANUARY 5   **Concert Program**, Expression in Black Song, a Musical Presentation by Jo Ann Lanier, D.M.A., Dayton Art Institute. [It is likely that she sang Perry's songs at this "informance."]

1986 APRIL 24–25   **Concert Program**, Dana [School of Music, Youngstown State University] New Music Festival II, with Elliott Schwartz, New Music Society Scholar-in-Residence, and Zenobia Perry, Guest Composer, with guest performers Richard Hobson, *flute*; Susan Jennings, *clarinet*; Maura Teague, *piano*; Dinos Constantinides, *violin*; Steven Brown, *piano*. Includes Perry's *Gifts of God*. Perry also was a panelist in the discussion, "Multi-Media Composition Resources," on April 24, as part of the festival. Other panelists included composers Peter Ware (Toronto), Richard Hobson, (Hamilton, Ohio), Daniel Godfrey (Syracuse University), and Dinu Ghezzo (New York

DOCUMENT INVENTORY

University). Moderator was Edward J. Largent (Youngstown State University Music Department).

1986 APRIL   **Poem** by Patrick Wallace, "Zenobia Sweet."

1987 FEBRUARY 20–21   **Concert Program**, International Institute for the Study of Women in Music, California State University, Northridge: A Symposium and Celebration of Black American Women in Music, Jeannie Pool, *coordinator*. Includes Perry's *Hallelujah, for Brass Octet*, members of the CSUN Wind Ensemble; *Conversations for two flutes* ("Chit-Chat," "Gossip"), Martin Glicklich and Margaret Chiang, *flute*; *Episodes I and II* for French Horn and Piano, Louise MacGillivray, *horn*; Deon Nielsen Price, *piano*.

1987 FEBRUARY 20–21   **Poster**, International Institute for the Study of Women in Music, CSUN: A Symposium and Celebration of Black American Women in Music.

1987 APRIL 4   **Award**, Omega Psi Phi Fraternity, Mu Chi Chapter, Certificate of Achievement presented to Mrs. Zenobia Perri [sic] for judging at the Annual Talent Hunt Program.

1987 MAY   **Concert Program**, Central State University Music Department, Central State University Drama and English Department and Wilberforce University Student Activities Division present Zenobia Powell Perry's *Tawawa House* (premiere), Central State Concert Chorale; Central State Percussion Ensemble, Lennard V. Moses, *director*; Community Chamber Orchestra, Donald Carroll, *conductor*; Jackie O. Carr, *piano*; Corliss Taylor-Dunn, *choreography*; Lois McGuire and Cheryl Welch, *stage directors*; Donald McBride, *set design*; special guest artists Janis-Rozena Peri, Benny Pritchett, and Corliss Taylor-Dunn.

1987 SEPTEMBER 8   **Concert Program**, West Virginia University, College of Creative Arts, Division of Music, Faculty Recital, Janis-Rozena Peri, *soprano*; John Crotty, *piano*. Includes Perry's "Benediction."

1987 OCTOBER 11   **Article** "Ohio Artists, writers win awards," *Columbus Dispatch*. Article and photograph of the 13 Ohioans honored by the Ohioana Library Association, October 17, 1987. Includes Perry's picture and biography.

1987 OCTOBER 17   **Award**, Ohioana Music Citation, 1987: "For distinguished service to Ohio in the field of Music ... for your outstanding ability as a performing artist, for your lifelong dedication to teaching; for your widely creative body of composition, The Ohioana Library Association proudly presents this Ohioana Music Citation, 1987."

1987 OCTOBER 23–24   **Concert Program**, Women & Music: Turning the Page, College of Creative Arts, Division of Music, West Virginia University, Morgantown. Zenobia Perry was a panelist; Janis-Rozena Peri was a performer and co-chair of the event.

1987 OCTOBER 27   **Article** "Area Briefs ... Zenobia Perry receives honor," *Xenia [Ohio] Daily Gazette*. Announcement of above-described Ohioana Music Citation.

1987   **Article**, "Zenobia Perry's Works Heard," *The Triangle of Mu Phi Epsilon*, Vol. 81:3. Describes Perry's recent activities at CSU, Northridge, and commission for *Tawawa House* from Ohio Arts Council/Ohio Humanities Council Joint Program in the Arts and Humanities.

1987 DECEMBER 2   **Letter** from Zenobia Perry to Mable Haddock of National Black Programming Consortium of Columbus, Ohio, granting permission for use of the videotapes sent to them from the performances of *Tawawa House*.

APPENDIX C

1988 MARCH 19 — **Concert Program**, Ohio NOW's 2nd Annual Women's History Event, Ramada Inn North, Columbus, Ohio. Includes "A Recognition of Zenobia Powell Perry, Ohio Musician, Composer and Teacher, Former Faculty Member of Central State for Her Achievements in the World of Music." She was presented the 1988 Women's History Award.

1988 MARCH 25 — **Article**, "Zenobia Perry Honored by NOW," *Xenia [Ohio] Daily Gazette*. Brief notice of NOW award.

1988 APRIL 28 — **Letter** to Zenobia Perry from Bernice Johnson Reagon, National Museum of American History, Washington, D.C., The Smithsonian Institution, inviting Perry to attend fourth annual "Music of the Black American Composer" concert, May 15, 1988.

1988 MAY 15 — **Announcement**, Program of Events, Music of the Black American Composer, National Museum of American History, Smithsonian Institute, Washington, D.C. Includes Perry's *Four Mynyms for Three Players*, Ada Saunders, *oboe*; Janese Sampson, *flute*; Constance Hobson, *piano*. Presented by Program in Black American Culture, Bernice Johnson Reagon, *director*.

1988 MAY 15 — **Concert Program**, Music of the Black American Composer, National Museum of American History, Smithsonian Institute, Washington, D.C., Hall of Musical Instruments. Includes biography of Perry.

1988 MAY 24 — **Article**, "Zenobia Perry Honored," *Xenia [Ohio] Daily Gazette*. Announcement of Perry's music played at the National Museum of American History, Smithsonian Institution.

1988 AUGUST 1 — **Letter** from William Haller, Morgantown, West Virginia, thanking Perry for sending a piece for his October recital.

1988 OCTOBER 12 — **Concert Program**, West Virginia University College of Creative Arts/Division of Music, Faculty Recital, William Haller, *organ*. Includes Perry's *Prism* (1975) for solo organ.

1989 JANUARY 31 — **Concert Program**, An Evening of Music, Graduate Conducting Recital of James L. Tully, Opera Theatre, College of Creative Arts, West Virginia University. Includes Perry's *Ships That Pass in the Night*, Lawrence Christianson, *narrator*. Noted as premiere performance.

1989 FEBRUARY 2 — **Concert Program**, Thursday Music Club, St. James Evangelical Lutheran Church, Wheeling, West Virginia, Janis-Rozena Peri, *soprano*; John Crotty, *piano*. "Women of Music (And a Few Men)"; includes Perry's "Benediction."

1989 JUNE — **Article**, "Composer of the month: Zenobia Powell Perry," by Mollie O'Meara, *The Phoenix* (publication of the Central Ohio Composers Alliance).

1989 AUGUST 24–26 — **Concert Program**, Summer Chautauqua. Sponsored by Yellow Springs Historical Society. Includes excerpts from Perry's *Tawawa House* performed on August 26, followed by an "Open Discussion on Greater Yellow Springs."

1989 AUGUST 30 — **Article**, "Chautauqua," *Yellow Springs [Ohio] News*. Photo of Zenobia Perry, dressed in costume. "Chautauqua, presented here last week by the Yellow Springs Historical Society, was a popular event. Among its features was *Tawawa House*, a musical drama written about area history by Xenobia [sic], professor emeritus of music at Central State University."

DOCUMENT INVENTORY

1989 NOVEMBER 11   **Concert Program**, 1989 Mankato [Minnesota] State University American Music Festival, Women of Class Trio. Includes Perry's *Four Mynyms for Three Players*, Geneva Handy Southall, *piano*; Faye Blakely, *flute*; Diana E. Washington, *oboe*.

1990 MARCH 6   **Concert Program**, Charter Day Convocation, Paul Robeson Cultural & Performing Arts Center, Central State University, Wilberforce, Ohio. Perry was a speaker.

1990 APRIL 26   **Concert Program**, Solo Songs of Six African American Women Composers, Miami University School of Fine Arts, Department of Music, Oxford, Ohio. Sebronette Barnes, *soprano*; Jerome Stanley, *piano*. Includes Perry's songs, "Drizzle," "Kid Stuff," and "Hallelujah to the Lamb." [Perry accompanied her own songs.]

1990 APRIL 29   **Concert Program** and announcement of concert: "Solo Songs of Six African American Women Composers," National Afro-American Museum and Cultural Center, Wilberforce, Ohio, Sebronette Barnes, *soprano*; Jerome Stanley, *piano*. Includes Perry's songs, "Drizzle," "Kid Stuff," and "Hallelujah to the Lamb."

1990 JUNE 23   **Concert Program**, NWSA 1990, University of Akron presents Janis-Rozena Peri, *soprano*; Christine Kefferstan, *piano*. Includes Perry's *Threnody*.

1990 SEPTEMBER 23   **Concert Program**, 40th Anniversary of Service and Appreciation, Wilberforce Multiplex Center, presented by The Links, Inc. Perry was a speaker: "Happiness is to be practiced like a violin."

1991 JANUARY 24   **News Release**, "Central State Profs Collaborate for Cleveland Symphony," Central State University, Communications. Announced Perry's symphony, *Echoes from the Journey*, to be performed at John Carroll University, Cleveland, by the Cleveland Chamber Symphony, Edwin London, *conductor*; J. Lanyé, *soprano*.

1991 JANUARY 27   **Concert Program**, Accord Associates 1990-91 Debut Series presents "An Evening of Music by Black Composers." Kulas Hall, Cleveland Institute of Music. Includes Perry's "Gloria in Excelsis," J. Lanyé, *soprano*; Patricia Connors-Mosley, *piano*; Accord Concert Choir; Forest Hills String Quartet.

1991 JANUARY 27   **Article Review** by Robert Finn, "Singers shine light on black composers," *Cleveland Plain Dealer*. "Also worth hearing was Zenobia Perry's stately and assertive 'Gloria in Excelsis.'"

1990–91   **Brochure**, Cleveland Chamber Symphony, announcing Perry premiere.

1991 FEBRUARY 14   **Article** by Steven F. Zabak, "CCS to present music by African-American composers," *The Cauldron* (student paper of John Carroll University). Announces performance of Perry's *Echoes from the Journey* by the Cleveland Chamber Symphony, on February 17, 1991.

1991 FEBRUARY 15   **Article**, "Local composer writes symphony," *Xenia [Ohio] Daily Gazette*, in the "Living" section. Announces performance of Perry's *Echoes from the Journey* by the Cleveland Chamber Symphony, on February 17, 1991.

1991 FEBRUARY 17   **Concert Program**, Cleveland Chamber Symphony, Kulas Auditorium, John Carroll University, Cleveland, Ohio. Includes Perry's *Echoes from the Journey*.

APPENDIX C

1991 FEBRUARY 17   **Review**, "Orchestra stylishly handles new black compositions," by Robert Finn, *Cleveland Plain Dealer*. Describes Perry's work as "overtly concerned with the black civil rights struggle.... *Echoes from the Journey* is a curiosity. The mezzo-soprano soloist (in this case the rich-voiced Dr. Jo Lanyé) alternately sings and speaks a text about the black struggle, while the orchestra contributes fanfares, simple diatonic tunes, sustained chords, bits of blues rhythm and other more or less uncoordinated fragments. While the composer's sincerity is obvious, the piece seems simplistic, a kind of musical propaganda poster. Lanyé did the spoken sections effectively and sang beautifully—but only the words of the spoken portions came through."

1991 MAY 5   **Concert Program**, Dayton Chamber Music Society. Includes Perry's *Hallelujah, for woodwind octet*, Central State Woodwind Ensemble, Karl Huff, director; *Conversations for two flutes*, Central State Flute Ensemble, William Denza, director; *Homage to William Levi Dawson on his 90th Birthday,* Zenobia Perry, *piano.*

[1991?] JUNE 7   **Concert Program**, Antioch College Presents Sebronette Barnes, *soprano*, Paul Rogers, *piano*. Zenobia Powell Perry, *piano*, Guest Composer, in a lecture-recital, The Solo Songs of African-American Women Composers, Horace Mann Hall. Concert includes Perry's "Kid Stuff," "Drizzle," and "Hallelujah to the Lamb."

1991 JUNE 27   **Article**, "New Jazz Hall of Famers given royal treatment," by Thomas J. Hale III, *The Oklahoma Eagle*. Mentions that Zenobia Perry and Janis Peri were special guests at a ceremony for the 1991 inductees to the Oklahoma Jazz Hall of Fame. Perry's former student, Cecil McBee, was inducted into the Oklahoma Jazz Hall of Fame at that event.

1991 JUNE   **Article**, "Inducted into the Jazz Hall of Fame," *[The Oklahoma Eagle]*. Regarding Cecil McBee, a Central State University graduate.

1991 SEPTEMBER 9   **Proclamation**, Congress of the United States House of Representatives, Washington, D.C. "Whereas, Zenobia Powell Perry is being honored by being inducted into the Greene County Women's Hall of Fame; and Whereas, she has promoted awareness by using the art of music; she has presented 'Xenia, Ohio, a Drama of the Underground Railroad' to elementary and high schools throughout Greene County, thereby offering an alternative form of education to students; and Whereas, Zenobia contributed her talents to young aspiring composers and musicians by directing choirs and sponsoring productions; and Whereas, her original compositions have been featured by the Music of the Black American Composer and the Public Broadcasting System as well as by the Ohio Composers Award, Central Ohio Composers Alliance, and Phi Mu Alpha; and Whereas, Zenobia has been recognized in the field of Women's History by the National Organization of Women; and Whereas, her enduring contributions to Greene County are commendable and her service to the community unique and inspiring; therefore be it Resolved that Congressman David L. Hobson congratulates Zenobia Powell Perry on her induction in the Greene County Women's Hall of Fame."

1991 SEPTEMBER 12   **Concert Program**, West Virginia University College of Creative Arts/Division of Music, Faculty Recital, Janis-Rozena Peri, *soprano*; Jack Crotty, *piano*; William Skidmore, *cello*. Includes Perry's *Threnody*.

1991 SEPTEMBER 28   **Concert Program**, Greene County Women's Hall of Fame Recognition Day, Wright State University Faculty Dining Room, Dayton, Ohio. Perry was inducted at this event; her biography appears in the program.

DOCUMENT INVENTORY

[1991 SEPTEMBER?]   **Photograph** by Beth Kerber/Gazette photo, in *Xenia [Ohio] Daily Gazette*, above caption, "Hall of Famers." "This year's inductees into the Greene County Women's Hall of fame stand with a plaque that will hang in the Greene County building. Pictured from left to right are: Kay Donges of Xenia, Zenobia Perry of Wilberforce, Sara Jane Lowe of Fairborn and Betty Lawless of Spring Valley. Not pictured was Cleo L. 'Jinx' Riley of Spring Valley."

1992 JANUARY 12   **Lecture Recital Program**, Monongalia Arts Center, Janis-Rozena Peri, *soprano*; Joyce Catalfano, *flute*; William Haller, *piano*. Includes Perry's "Benediction," "Poet," and "Pastourelle."

1992 JANUARY 26   **Concert Program**, "Remembering Dr. Martin Luther King, Jr.," Historic First United Presbyterian Church, East Cleveland, with Accord Chamber Choir, Dr. J. Lanyé, *conductor*; Patricia Conners-Mosley, *accompanist*; and guest artists Eliesha Nelson, *violin*; Elizabeth DeMio, *accompanist*; David A. Usis, *organ*. Includes Perry's *Done Made My Vow to the Lord*.

1992 MAY 3   **Concert Program**, Otterbein College, Integrative Studies Festival presents Janis-Rozena Peri, *soprano*; John Crotty, *piano*; Phyllis Hester, *flute*.

1992 NOVEMBER–DECEMBER **Article**, by Melinda Rickelman, "The Classics: A Family Tradition," in *Crisis*. About Janis-Rozena Peri and Zenobia Perry.

1993 JANUARY 18   **Concert Program**, Annual Martin Luther King Day Celebration, National Afro-American Museum and Cultural Center, Wilberforce, Ohio, Janice-Rozena [sic] Peri, *soprano*; John [Jack] Crotty, *piano*.

1993 MARCH 22   **Letter**, from Mike Payne of Ohio Department of Aging, Columbus, congratulating her on her induction into the Ohio Senior Citizens Hall of Fame.

1993 APRIL 13   **Concert Program**, West Virginia University, College of Creative Arts, Division of Music, WVU Wind Symphony and Concert Band, Don Wilcox, *conductor*; Janis-Rozena Peri, *soprano*. Includes Perry's *Tempo for Wind Ensemble and Soprano*.

1993 APRIL 27   **Press Release**, Office of the Governor, George V. Voinovich, "Ohio's Senior Citizens Hall of Fame Induction at Governor's Conference." Announces 11 inductees for 1993 including Zenobia Perry. Ceremony to take place May 12 in the Rhodes Building on the Ohio State Fairgrounds, Columbus.

1993 APRIL 29   **Certificate** of Recognition presented to Zenobia Perry, "In appreciation of your volunteer service to the Golden Age Center."

1993 MAY 14   **Article**, "Perry writes her way into fame," by Melissa Kossler, *Xenia [Ohio] Daily Gazette*. Article about Perry's induction into the Ohio Senior Citizens Hall of Fame, including an interview.

1993 JUNE 16   **Concert Program**, A Celebration of Women's Voices, Antioch College, Yellow Springs, Ohio. Vocal performance by Suzanne Raymond, accompanist Shirley Helm. Includes Perry's *Tempo* [arranged for voice and piano]. "*Tempo*'s text is from a poem by R. H. Grenville and was written for her daughter, Janis-Rozena Peri, an accomplished vocalist herself. She performed it with West Virginia's band."

1993 MAY/JUNE   Article, *SCI* [Society of Composers, Inc.] *Newsletter* indicates that Zenobia Perry gave a paper at the 27th Annual Conference of SCI, Cleveland State University, April 1993.

APPENDIX C

1993 — **Award**, Ohio Senior Citizens Hall of Fame: "Zenobia Perry, musician and community activist, is saving her best work for last. Like herself, her songs are sweetening and strengthening with age . . ."

1993 — **Certificate.** "The General Assembly of The State of Ohio, Ohio Senate, Congratulating Zenobia Perry on being inducted into the Ohio Senior Citizens Hall of Fame."

1993 — **Award** to Zenobia Perry, "In appreciation for your services rendered and contributions to the Greene County NAACP for the year 1994."

1993 DECEMBER 7 — **Concert Program**, Christmas Concert, Oberlin Community Chamber Singers, Carol Longsworth, *music director*; Jennifer Novak, *piano*. Premiere of Perry's *Music from Ohio*: "Silently" and "Christmas is More," for choir and piano.

1994 FEBRUARY 11 — **Concert Program**, Cleveland Heights High School Instrumental Music Department presents its Orchestras in Concert, Dr. Frederick R. Mayer, *director*, featuring Concert Orchestra Heights High Symphony with the Heights Brass Choir, Brian Appleby-Weinberg, *director*; Zenobia Perry and Senior Soloist Leonid Goldberg. Includes Perry's *Ships That Pass in the Night*, Philomena McClellan, *narrator*.

1994 MAY 11 — **Concert Program**, Unity Feast, hosted by Bahá'í Community of Yellow Springs, Friends Care Center. Includes Perry's song, "Teeta," Nacim McIlhargey, *voice*.

1994 SEPTEMBER 14 — **Letter** from Rev. Richard Watson, Christ Church of Xenia, Ohio, to Zenobia Perry and Janis-Rozena Peri: "Little did I know when I met Zenobia a few months ago what an impact you and your music would have on our little church. Without exaggeration, there were at least a half-dozen folks who told me that anthem moment ["How Charming is the Place!"] was not only a wonderful surprise but also one of the most powerful in their entire church memories. To say your combined work was beautiful is an understatement—it was truly awe-inspiring."

1995 MAY 25 — "**Certificate** of Appreciation Awarded to Mrs. Zenobia Perry for participation in History 101 as a guest speaker."

1995 JUNE 27 — **Letter** from Joseph D. Lewis, Central State University, to Zenobia Perry: "We are very grateful for your presentation on May 25, 1995. It was very good of you to share your wisdom and your knowledge with the students. It is unselfishness like yours that helps our young people every day to become better citizens and leaders for tomorrow. Again we thank you."

1995–96 WINTER — **Article** by Mike Payne, "Muse Visits Musician Early: Composer heard life's calling in sweet chords long ago," *Ohio's Heritage*, Winter 1995–96. Based on interview with Perry.

1997 MARCH 5 — **Concert Program**, Lincoln University Lectures and Recitals Committee presents Women's History Month Program, Sebronette Barnes, *soprano*; May Phang, *piano*. Includes Perry's "Kid Stuff" and "Spring Song."

1997 MARCH 12 — **Concert Program**, Ohio State University, College of the Arts, Graduate Student Recital Series, Lea Pearson, *flute*. Includes Perry's *Four Mynyms for Three Players*, Lea Pearson, *flute*; Yu-Chia Liao, *oboe*; Robert Brooks, *piano*. "*Four Mynyms* was written in 1968 for the occasion of Darius Milhaud's return to his native France. His students each wrote a piece in his honor to be played at a farewell concert. These short pieces offer a mixture of joy and sadness, a characteristic of much African

DOCUMENT INVENTORY

American music. The third movement uses the rhythm of the spiritual 'Swing Low Sweet Chariot,' possibly a reference to Milhaud's going home."

1997 MAY — **Concert Program**, International Congress on Women in Music, California Institute of the Arts, sponsored by the International Alliance for Women in Music; Jeannie Pool, *coordinator*. Darryl Taylor, *tenor*, and Deon Nielsen Price, *piano*, performed Perry song.

1997 OCTOBER 23–26 — **Concert Program** (partial), Women in Music: A Celebration of the Last One Hundred Years, Ohio University, Athens. Delores White, Assistant Professor of Music, Cuyahoga Community College, gave presentation, "A Comparison Analysis of the Piano Music of Several Ohio African American Women Composers," and includes Zenobia Perry's piano music.

1998 MARCH 30 — **Concert Program**, Georgian Court College presents Solo Songs by African-American Women Composers, Sebronette Barnes, *soprano*; May Phang, *piano*. Includes Perry's "Kid Stuff."

1998 — **Award** from College of Arts and Sciences, 1998 Outstanding Alumni Award from the University of Wyoming presented to Zenobia Perry "in recognition of her leadership in public education, contribution to the field of music, and her strong commitment to the liberal arts and sciences."

1998 APRIL 3 — **Article**, "Perry named outstanding UW alum," *Xenia [Ohio] Daily Gazette*. Announces awards dinner to be held May 30, 1998, in Wyoming.

1998 MAY 30 — **Concert Program**, College of Arts and Sciences 1998 Awards Banquet, honoring outstanding former faculty and outstanding alumni. Perry was honoree, her "Homage" from *Piano Potpourri* performed by Karla Tull.

1998 SPRING — **Article**, "1998 Outstanding Alumni and Former Faculty," A & S Report College of Arts and Sciences [University of Wyoming, Laramie], Spring 1998. Photo and biography of Perry.

1998 NOVEMBER 18 — **Article**, "Ten Top Women 1998," announces Zenobia Powell Perry named by *Dayton Daily News* as one of ten top women for 1998. Awards luncheon to take place at Sinclair Community College.

1998 NOVEMBER 18 — **Letter** from Vicki D. Pegg, Montgomery County Commissioner, Dayton, Ohio, to Zenobia Perry, congratulating her on being named one of Ten Top Women for 1998.

1998 DECEMBER 1 — **Letter** from Idotha Bootsie Neal, City Commissioner, City of Dayton, Ohio, to Zenobia Perry, congratulating her on being named one of Ten Top Women for 1998.

1999 FEBRUARY 15–17 — **Concert Program**, Second Symposium of Black Women Composers, Department of Music, Hampton University, Virginia. Lea Pearson, *flute*, performed; Helen Walker-Hill spoke.

1999 MARCH 4 — **Article**, "Zenobia Perry—A lifetime of musical note," *Yellow Springs [Ohio] News*. Describes Perry's life story.

1999 MARCH 6 — **Announcement**, A Community Forum: "Why We Live Here," National Afro-American Museum & Cultural Center, Wilberforce, Ohio. Zenobia Perry is one of four panelists.

1999 MARCH 14 — **Announcement** of concert, "In Celebration of Distinguished Black Women Composers," Afro-American Chamber Music Society Orchestra,

APPENDIX C

Holman United Methodist Church, Los Angeles. Includes Perry's *Echoes from the Journey,* Leberta Clark, *mezzo-soprano*; Dwayne E. Smith, *conductor.*

1999 MARCH 19 **Announcement, Concert Program**, Women in Music panel discussion, National Afro-American Museum and Cultural Center, Wilberforce, Ohio. Zenobia Perry is one of five speakers; Carol Sampson, *mistress of ceremonies.*

1999 **Certificate** of Recognition "for your volunteer efforts at Golden Age Senior Center, presented to Zenobia Perry. Thank you for your gift of time!"

1999 APRIL 16 **Letter** from David L. Hobson, Member of Congress, Washington, D.C., addressed to Zenobia Perry, congratulating her on "recognition as the Golden Age Senior Citizen's Center Honoree for National Volunteer Recognition Week."

1999 APRIL 25 **Award**, Woman of the Year 1999. "To Zenobia Powell Perry, for your outstanding service to the community and your support for the programs and activities of the Paul Laurence Dunbar House State Memorial."

1999 **Certificate**, The Ohio House of Representatives, Representative Steve Austria, House District #76. "On behalf of the members of the House of Representatives of the 123rd General Assembly of Ohio, we are pleased to extend special recognition to Zenobia Perry on being named Volunteer of the Year at the Golden Age Senior Citizens Center."

1999 SEPTEMBER 17–19 **Award**. "This certificate of appreciation is awarded to Zenobia Perry for outstanding participation in the William Dawson Centennial Celebration: Focus on African American Music, University of Dayton."

1999 SEPTEMBER 17–19 **Concert Program**, William Dawson Centennial Celebration: Focus on African American Music, University of Dayton. [Perry's name is not on the printed program.]

1999 OCTOBER **Article**, by Elizabeth Studebaker, *Xenia [Ohio] Daily Gazette*, "Perry named top Golden Age volunteer," with photograph of Perry driving a small drag racer in the parking lot of the Golden Age Senior Center. "She has spent many hours with students from Arrowwood Elementary School, teaching them various aspects of Native American history."

1999 OCTOBER 6 **Concert Program**, "Solo Songs of Six African-American Women Composers," Denison University, Department of Music, Sebronette Barnes, *soprano*; Elise Auerbach, *piano*. Includes Perry's "Kid Stuff."

2000 FEBRUARY 7 **Concert Program**, "Solo Songs by Six African-American Women Composers," Ball State University, Muncie, Indiana; Sebronette Barnes, *soprano*; Liz Seidel, *piano*. Performances at Ball State University School of Music/ Monday Recital Hour; Conversation with Students, Music Lounge, Pittenger Student Center; and Muncie Community Performance, Community Civic Center. Includes Perry's "How Charming Is This Place" and "Kid Stuff."

2000 FEBRUARY 23 **Concert Program**, "Solo Songs of Six African-American Women Composers," Delaware Technical & Community College, Stanton/Wilmington Campus, African-American History Celebration, Sebronette Barnes, *soprano*; Elise Auerbach, *piano*. Includes Perry's "How Charming Is This Place" and "Kid Stuff."

2000 FEBRUARY 24 **Concert Program**, "Solo Songs of Six African-American Women Composers," Community Room at Penn State York, "Glorious," featuring

DOCUMENT INVENTORY

Sebronette Barnes, *soprano*; Elise Auerbach, *piano*. Includes Perry's "How Charming Is This Place" and "Kid Stuff."

2000 MARCH 25   **Certificate**, "Omega Psi Phi Fraternity, Mu Chi Chapter, Certificate of Achievement presented to Mrs. Zenobia Perri *[sic]* for participating as a Judge in Mu Chi Chapter's Talent Hunt Program."

2000 MAY 11   "**Certificate** of Achievement, Awarded to Zenobia Perry, for academic leadership in the higher education community for your work in the Geritech Project, presented by College of Arts & Sciences, Central State University, Wilberforce, Ohio."

2000 MAY   **Certificate** of Appreciation Awarded to Zenobia Perry. "For your 'gift of time' to Golden Age Senior Citizens, Inc., in the year 2000. Thank you!"

2000 MAY 16   **Certificate**, "2000 Outstanding Senior Citizen Award Zenobia Powell Perry, Green County."

2000 MAY 17   **Article** by Elizabeth Studebaker, "Perry named Outstanding Senior," *Xenia [Ohio] Daily Gazette*. With photograph taken by Studebaker.

2000 MAY 19   **Letter** from David L. Hobson, Member of U.S. Congress, Washington, D.C., to Zenobia Perry, congratulating her for receiving "Outstanding Senior Award on the 2000 Senior Citizens Day."

2000 MAY 22   **Article** by Elizabeth Studebaker, "Piano has taken Perry coast to coast," *Xenia [Ohio] Daily Gazette*. "[Perry's] compositions have been sanctioned by the Vatican for the year 2000 activities and will be performed during the Rome Jubilee Celebration by Eleanor McClellan, a soprano living in Rome. McClellan's contribution will be a concert of sacred music by Black American Women Composers."

2000 SEPTEMBER 28   **Concert Program**, Rust College Lyceum Series, Morehouse Auditorium, Doxey Center, presents Sebronette Barnes, *soprano*, and Ms. Elise Auerbach, *piano*. Includes Perry's "Drizzle" and "Kid Stuff."

2001 MARCH 6   **Concert Program**, Albright College, "You Can Tell the World: Songs by African-American Women Composers," Sebronette Barnes, *soprano*; Elise Auerbach, *piano*. Includes Perry's "Drizzle."

2001 APRIL 5   **Concert Program**, West Virginia University College of Creative Arts, Division of Music, A Faculty Recital, Joyce Catalfano, *flute*. Includes Perry's *The Hidden Words of Bahá'u'lláh*, Janis-Rozena Peri, *soprano*; Joyce Catalfano, *flute*; Jack Crotty, *piano*.

2001 APRIL 10   **Concert Program**, Kutztown University, Pennsylvania, College of Visual and Performing Arts, "Her-Story/His-Story: Songs by African-American Composers," Sebronette Barnes, *soprano*; Nancy Hampton, *piano*. Includes Perry's "Drizzle."

2001 NOVEMBER 16   **Letter** to Jeannie Pool from Division of Vital Records, Oklahoma State Department of Health, confirming that a birth certificate for Zenobia Powell Perry could not be located.

2002 JANUARY 21   **Announcement**, The Rev. Dr. Martin Luther King, Jr., 2002 Cultural Arts Awards Celebration. Perry among honorees.

2002 JANUARY 21   **Award**, National Afro-American Museum and Cultural Center, "The Rev. Dr. Martin Luther King, Jr., 2002 Cultural Arts Award presented to Mrs. Zenobia Perry for outstanding contributions in the field of Music Education."

APPENDIX C

2002 JANUARY 21   **Concert Program**, The Rev. Dr. Martin Luther King, Jr., 2002 Cultural Arts Awards Celebration. Includes Perry's "Kid's Stuff," Melody Kelly, *soprano*, former Perry student and Xenia educator; "Homage," Matthew Jackson, *piano*; "Benediction," Oweka Eguaroje, *violin*; Zenobia Perry, *piano*.

2002 JANUARY 22   **Article** by Mary Jo Milillo, "Speakers Say volunteering 'something to celebrate,'" *Xenia [Ohio] Daily Gazette*. Describes Martin Luther King, Jr. 2002 Cultural Arts Award presented to Perry.

NOT DATED   **Miscellaneous** packet of concert reviews related to Janis-Rozena Peri's career as a soprano (not related to performances of her mother's music).

*The Zenobia Powell Perry Collection has been donated to the Center for Black Music Research at Columbia College in Chicago.

POETRY
by Zenobia Powell Perry

A WISH

I want to be as sturdy as the tree
That stands through all the storms, though fierce they be
So sweeping passions cannot alter me.

I want to be as warming as the sun
Whose face brings light and hope and work and fun,
That I may lend a smile to everyone.

I want to be as lovely as the flower,
That grows lovely despite the ills of now,
To lend the world more beauty every hour.

THE SEA WAVES

I'd like to sit again beside the sea
And watch the waves come racing in with glee
They are such jovial company
And they can lend a picture of all life to me.

I'd like to see them as they reach the shore,
And hear their loud complaints made o'er and o'er,
For as they reach the goal they yearned before,
They miss the jovial laughter they once bore,
And all of life is fashioned just like this,
Loads of cares must follow bits of bliss,
And as our goals we reach, our stars we kiss,
[words missing] toils and struggles we *[words missing]*

Published in a newspaper, no date. The bottom of the clipping is torn.

Notes

INTRODUCTION

[1] Jeannie Gayle Pool, "The Life and Music of Zenobia Powell Perry: An American Composer," Ph.D. diss. (Claremont Graduate University, 2002).

[2] I hosted a two-hour weekly program from 1981 until 1997. Archival air-check recordings, including interviews and live concert broadcasts, are available from the Cambria Archives, P. O. Box 374, Lomita, CA 90717.

[3] See Beth Michaels, "Xenia to Honor Zenobia Perry Today," *Dayton Daily News,* July 11, 2002.

[4] See www.zenobiapowellperry.org.

[5] *Music of Zenobia Powell Perry, Volume I, Art Songs and Piano Music* (Cambria CD-1138, 2002). Zenobia Perry's music was also featured at the Southern California Chapter of the International Alliance for Women in Music, April 26–27, 2003, at the Church of the Lighted Window, La Canada, California.

[6] Deon Nielsen Price (D.M.A., University of Southern California) is a prize-winning pianist, commissioned composer, recording artist, and author. She has presented workshops at Mu Phi Epsilon conventions (and elsewhere) using her books, *Accompanying Skills for Pianists* and *SightPlay with Skillful Eyes* (Culver Crest). The Price Duo can be heard on compact disc: *America Themes, Clariphonia,* and *SunRays II: City Views* (Cambria Master Recordings). A catalog of her music, books, and recordings can be found at www.culvercrest.com.

[7] Berkeley Price (D.M.A., Eastman School of Music) is widely known in North America, Europe, and Asia for his live and recorded solo and chamber performances on many instruments of the clarinet family. For the past ten years, he has toured internationally with the mother/son Price Duo. He returned to California after serving as assistant professor at West Virginia College, and currently teaches at Antelope Valley College in Lancaster, California.

[8] Darryl Taylor (D.M.A., University of Michigan) is a vocal artist whose performances in opera, oratorio, recital, and on recordings have been highly acclaimed. As founder of the African American Art Song Alliance, he has debuted numerous works, including Deon Nielsen Price's "To the Children of War" (poem by Maya Angelou). Drs. Price and Taylor have collaborated on several international tours. His recordings, *Love Rejoices: Songs of H. Leslie Adams* (Albany Records Troy 428, 2001) and *Dreamer: A Portrait of Langston Hughes* (Naxos 8.559136, 2002) have received widespread praise. He is currently on the music faculty at the University of California, Irvine.

[9] For more details, visit the Mu Phi Epsilon web site at http://home.muphiepsilon.org/.

NOTES

[10] This tour was the first public admission of Zenobia's actual age. Many of her friends and neighbors were surprised to learn that she was celebrating her 95th birthday and not her 89th.

[11] John Crotty (D.M.A., Eastman School of Music) has been on the West Virginia University faculty since 1986; he is currently an associate professor of music.

[12] Donald Rosenberg, "A Woman of Note," *Cleveland Plain Dealer*, September 30, 2003: E.1.

[13] Beverly Simmons and I wrote a report on the concert tour, "Royal Celebration of Zenobia Perry's 95th Birthday," *IAWM Journal* 10, no. 1 (2004): 16–17. Because the article was published after her death, it became her obituary. Several of the tour events were videotaped; there are plans to make a documentary on her life and music.

[14] Published obituaries included: Alicia Herbstreit, "Legacy Will Live On: Beloved Zenobia Perry Will Be Remembered," *Xenia Daily Gazette,* January 21, 2004: 1, 2A; Jeannie Pool, "Zenobia Powell Perry," *Triangle of Mu Phi Epsilon* (Winter 2003): 26; "In Memoriam," *CBMR Digest* 17, no. 1 (Spring 2004): 11; Jeannie Pool, "Zenobia Powell Perry," *Composer USA* (Winter 2003–04): 11.

CHAPTER 1: Zenobia Powell Perry: Articulate Link to American Culture

[15] This date of birth has been confirmed by 1910 U.S. Census data, at P400 at 047 0136,0226 for Okfuskee County, Oklahoma: C. B. Powell, age 39, born Tennessee; Berdia, age 21 from Arkansas; Zenobia Perry, age 1½, born in Oklahoma. However, this could not be confirmed by the Oklahoma State Department of Health, Division of Vital Records, which had no record of her birth. Many sources incorrectly give 1914 as her date of birth. Her father, born in 1863, was actually 47 in 1910.

[16] Confirmed via phone by Treva Rogers, Central State University (December 18, 2001).

[17] Among the vocalists who have sung her songs in concert are Janis-Rozena Peri, Sebronette Barnes, and Jo Ann Lanier [Lanyé].

[18] The fact that many composition prizes and awards are only available to young composers represents age discrimination in the field of composition.

[19] Nicolas Slonimsky told me on several occasions that he added new contemporary composers to *Baker's Biographical Dictionary of Musicians,* 8th ed. (New York: Schirmer Books, 1992) only after the composer's music received three reviews during a single concert season in New York, Los Angeles, Boston, or San Francisco. This methodology excluded many women and minority composers, as well as composers in the Midwest and South.

[20] Peri, an associate professor of voice at West Virginia University in Morgantown until retiring in 2008, has been her mother's most ardent supporter and promoter.

[21] Helen Walker-Hill included Zenobia Perry's "Homage to William Dawson on his 90th Birthday" in the anthology *Black Women Composers: A Century of Piano Music, 1893–1990* (Bryn Mawr, Penn.: Hildegard Publishing, 1990).

[22] Zenobia Perry, taped interview (September 30, 2001), Morgantown, W.Va.

[23] This is discussed in greater detail in chapter 10.

[24] Jo Ann Lanier (who later changed her name to Lanyé) wrote a D.M.A. dissertation, "The Concert Songs of Zenobia Powell Perry," at the American Conservatory of Music in Chicago in 1988, available through UMI Press. Unfortunately, her dissertation contains misinformation, some of which was provided by Perry herself.

NOTES

[25] Although Zenobia Perry is not mentioned in any of musicologist Eileen Southern's books, I remember introducing them to each other at the First National Congress on Women in Music in March 1981, at New York University. Other black women composers and musicians present at that session included Undine Smith Moore, Ora Williams (who performed music of Camille Nickerson, Florence B. Price, Lillian Evanti, Margaret Bonds, Dorothy Rudd Moore, and Azalia Hackley, accompanied by her sisters Dottie Stallworth, Barbara Williams, and Thelma Williams), Jacqueline Thompson, Dorothy Rudd Moore, and Jeraldine Herbison. Zenobia Perry was asked to speak, as well. Barbara Garvey Jackson, of the University of Arkansas (Fayetteville), also spoke about her important early research on Florence B. Price. Janis-Rozena Peri sang a song by Dorothy Rudd Moore. The session was chaired by writer and historian Raoul Abdul.

[26] Helen Walker-Hill, *From Spirituals to Symphonies: African American Women Composers and Their Music* (Urbana: University of Illinois Press, 2007), discusses Undine Smith Moore, Julia Perry, Margaret Bonds, Irene Britton Smith, Dorothy Rudd Moore, Valerie Capers, Mary Watkins, and Regina Harris Baiocchi, among others.

[27] (White Plains, N.Y.: Kraus International Publications, 1987), ix.

[28] Ibid., xvi.

[29] Anne K. Simpson, *Hard Trials: The Life and Music of Harry T. Burleigh* (Metuchen, N.J.: Scarecrow Press, 1990).

[30] (Chicago: Fitzroy Dearborn Publishers, 1999), 2 vols. I was asked to write an entry on Zenobia Powell Perry, but I was unable to complete it because I had not yet resolved the many discrepancies in her chronology. Therefore, she is not included in the dictionary.

[31] It was announced as "forthcoming," in the Florence B. Price biographical entry, authored by Rae Linda Brown, in Floyd, *International Dictionary*, 496. The original dissertation was entitled "Selected Orchestral Music of Florence B. Price (1888–1953) in the Context of Her Life and Work" (Ph.D. diss., Yale University, 1987).

[32] *In One Lifetime* (Fayetteville: University of Arkansas Press, 1984).

[33] Judith Anne Still, ed., *William Grant Still and the Fusion of Cultures in American Music* (Flagstaff, Ariz.: The Master-Player Library, 1972; reprinted 1995) and Catherine Parsons Smith, ed., *William Grant Still: A Study in Contradictions, with Essays by Gayle Marchison and Willard Gatewood and Contemporary Sources from the 1930s* (Berkeley and Los Angeles: University of California Press, 2000).

[34] Judith Tick, *Ruth Crawford Seeger: A Composer's Search for American Music* (New York: Oxford University Press, 1997).

[35] Adrienne Fried Block, *Amy Beach, Passionate Victorian: The Life and Work of an American Composer, 1867–1944* (New York: Oxford University Press, 1998).

[36] Catherine Parsons Smith and Cynthia S. Richardson, *Mary Carr Moore, American Composer* (Ann Arbor: University of Michigan Press, 1987).

[37] Virginia Bortin, *Elinor Remick Warren: Her Life and Music*, Composers of North American 5 (Metuchen, N.J.: Scarecrow Press, 1987); by the same author, *Elinor Remick Warren: A Bio-bibliography* (Westport, Conn.: Greenwood Press, 1993).

[38] Martina Helmig, *Ruth Schonthal: Ein Kompositorischer Werdegung* (Hildesheim: Olms, 1994). English translation published as *Ruth Schonthal: A Composer's Musical Development in Exile* (Lewiston, N.Y.: Edwin Mellen, 2006).

[39] Crystal Britten, phone interview (October 2001). This black French horn player told me that she was not allowed to include Perry's *Episodes I and II* for horn and piano (1983)

NOTES

in her D.M.A. recital. The fact that there was so little published material available on Zenobia Perry caused Britten's committee to question Perry's importance as a composer. Thus the cycle continues: lack of published materials on black American women composers discourages performances of their music, which are needed to encourage published materials on their lives and music.

[40] (New York: Penguin Books), 1992.

[41] Bateson, 1. Bateson is the daughter of anthropologists Margaret Mead and Gregory Bateson.

[42] Ibid., 3.

[43] Zenobia Perry was reluctant to talk to me about her years teaching elementary school children, because she felt it had little to do with her later career as a college music teacher. However, there is no doubt that the patience and methodologies she learned while teaching young children helped her become an excellent college-level pedagogue, especially with previously untrained music students who were in need of remedial work.

[44] Bateson, 4. This patchwork quilt analogy is particularly satisfying when applied to Zenobia Perry's life story, because she herself was a master quilter and taught quilting at the local senior citizen home for women aged 64 to 95.

[45] Ibid., 5.

[46] For example, how seriously is arranging considered as a kind of composition? Most black American composers have arranged spirituals and, in so doing, have kept the tradition alive. In their hands, this has been composition, not simple transcription or transposition.

[47] Bateson, 5.

[48] Ibid., 6.

[49] Ibid., 9.

[50] Ibid., 13; emphasis added.

[51] Ibid., 14.

[52] Ibid., 15.

[53] Zenobia Perry spoke of her mother's deep desires that her children be educated and "uplifted" and how, throughout their childhood, she steered them to every available opportunity to learn and improve themselves. This characterizes black middle-class life in the twentieth century; accounts of composers Florence Price's and William Grant Still's upbringing reveal the same family focus.

[54] Undine Smith Moore (1904–1989), "My Life in Music," *IAWM Journal* 3, no. 1 (February 1997): 9–15, edited and with an introduction by Jeannie Pool.

[55] See Jeannie Pool, "A Critical Approach to the History of Women in Music," *Heresies* 10 (Fall 1980): 2–5. Carol Neuls-Bates, *Women in Music: An Anthology of Source Readings from the Middle Ages to the Present*, rev. ed. (Boston: Northeastern University Press, 1996) includes many such examples from all periods in music history.

[56] The long list of women composers whose daughters contributed to their careers includes Clara Schumann, Pauline Viardot-Garcia, Elisabeth Lutyens, and Gloria Coates.

[57] Peter G. Davis, "Janis-Rozena Peri Sings Demanding Recital Well," *New York Times* (May 22, 1977). In the 1970s, I was a student at Hunter College of the City University of New York, where Louise Talma (1906–1996) had served on the music faculty for more than five decades (1928–1979). I talked to her many times about issues related to women

NOTES

composers and she insisted that gender was irrelevant and I should not waste my time researching women composers. After she was asked to retire due to her advancing age, she told me she finally understood the difference for women composers: her male colleagues were enjoying their retirement years with their children and grandchildren, while she had felt she must sacrifice motherhood to be a composer. Herein lies the source of the injustice. A case could be made that many composers without children or surviving spouses drift into undeserved obscurity soon after death, sometimes upon retirement.

[58] Bateson, 17.

[59] Ibid., 240–41. Thanks to Mary Catherine Bateson for this understanding and insight.

CHAPTER 2: Song and Verse in Boley: A Lifetime of Inspiration for an American Composer

[60] Published in *The Boley Progress* (October 16, 1905), 3, and well known to Boley residents.

[61] Both of these works are discussed in chapter 11.

[62] A copy of this song is found on page 15. Thanks to Henrietta Hicks for providing it.

[63] Perry's setting of this poem is one of her most popular songs, in a cycle of songs with poetry by black American Paul Laurence Dunbar, whose tragic death as a young man was widely mourned throughout the country, among both blacks and whites. See Gayle Addison's biography, *Oak and Ivy, A Biography of Paul Laurence Dunbar* (Garden City, N.Y.: Doubleday, 1971) and Charles M. Austin, *Paul Laurence Dunbar's Roots and Much More: A Scrapbook of His Life and Legacy*, ed. James B. George (Dayton, Ohio: A Sense of Roots Publications, 1989).

[64] Langston became the site of Langston University, a major black college in Oklahoma.

[65] *The Boley Progress* (May 5, 1905), as quoted in Velma Dolphin-Ashley, "A History of Boley, Oklahoma" (master's thesis, Kansas State Teachers College [now Pittsburg State University], 1940), 19. *The Boley Progress* was the city's main promotional instrument, distributed throughout the Southern and Midwestern states. According to Dolphin-Ashley (1910–1998), "These tracks were taken up, the station and the cross ties were sold. To many of the old settlers of the town the removal of the station was a very sad affair. Many of them stood on street corners and recalled the days when the Fort Smith and Western Railroad was first laid and when its officials gave encouragement to the early settlers of the town" (19). From the Oklahoma Historical Society, I have acquired a microfilm of *The Boley Progress* and other Boley newspapers from the period, which give a clear idea of the goals and aspirations of the community and of the Boley promoters. Velma Ashley was Zenobia Perry's sister Cleolla's closest childhood friend. After becoming Velma's friend, Cleolla changed her name to Thelma. Zenobia Perry and Janis-Rozena Peri, taped interview (February 2, 2002), Wilberforce, Ohio.

[66] She is identified as a Creek Freedman in Dolphin-Ashley, 10.

[67] Dolphin-Ashley, 10. She cites *The Boley Progress* (May 5, 1905), 4 col. 3 as her source.

[68] *The Boley Progress* (September 17, 1915), as quoted in Dolphin-Ashley, 12.

[69] Kenneth Marvin Hamilton, *Black Towns and Profit: The Promotion and Development in the Trans-Appalachian West, 1877–1915* (Urbana and Chicago: University of Illinois Press, 1991), 121. Chapter 4 is devoted to Boley's early history. A document sent to me by Mrs. Henrietta Hicks, President of the Boley Museum, identifies Mr. T. M. Haynes as the founder of Boley. He was born near Detroit, Red River County, Texas, and moved to Boley in 1899. His first attempt was to create a black town called Oxford, where Rusk Community is now,

NOTES

but it failed "on account of complications of Indian land" (1). Mr. Haynes organized the first day of school and the first Sunday School in Boley; the formal opening of the Town of Boley was held on September 22, 1904. On March 30, 1905, T. M. Haynes, H. C. Cavil, and Hillard Taylor presented to the Western District of the Federal Court at Sapulpa, Oklahoma, a petition for incorporation signed by 200 Boley citizens. The petition was heard and granted on May 10. "By means of massive advertising, T. M. Haynes publicly announced the purpose of the town and invited Blacks to come and settle. Boley was portrayed as a haven from oppression and a place where Blacks could govern themselves." By 1909 the town had a population of 7,000, with 25,000 in the surrounding communities of Rusk, Sandcreek, Ixl, Chilesville, Georgie Line, and Flat Rock.

[70] Enacted on February 8, 1887, and named after its sponsor, U.S. Senator Henry L. Dawes of Massachusetts, the Dawes Act (also known as the Dawes Severalty Act) authorized the president of the United States to have Native American tribal lands surveyed and divided into allotments for individual Native American families. Amended in 1891 and again in 1906 by the Burke Act, it remained in effect until 1934.

[71] Hamilton, 121. This arrangement led to legal problems later, due to Abigail's young age.

[72] Ibid., 122–23.

[73] In the 1880s in Nashville, Dr. Powell had witnessed the "Exodusters"—some 60,000 people who left for Kansas, precipitated by the federal withdrawal of troops from the South and the collapse of Reconstruction. The Exodusters hoped to find new lives in a free state. This was the first new movement of blacks after the Civil War. It was not until the twentieth century that millions of blacks left the South for the West, Midwest, and North.

[74] I/4, 5, under first column headed "Locals."

[75] I/4, 3. However, a "Professional Directory," which appeared regularly in *The Boley Progress*, did not list him.

[76] Quintin Jones, archivist at Meharry Medical College, phone interview (January 9, 2002). The records, called "The Matriculation Record Book" at Meharry, give his birthplace as Tennessee and his father's name as Calvin Powell. Attempts to find a birth certificate or a death certificate have been unsuccessful. According to Zenobia Perry, "He said, 'We just say I was born on the fourth of July.' I think that was just because he owed a certain amount of patriotism to this country because he was here." Zenobia Perry, taped interview (July 28, 1993), Yellow Springs, Ohio.

[77] In Mike Payne, "Muse Visits Musician Early: Composer heard life's calling in sweet chords long ago," *Ohio's Heritage* (Winter 1995–96): 6–7, Zenobia Perry describes her father as "the child of Somalian missionaries."

[78] Perry, interview (July 28, 1993). Zenobia Perry recalled that her father told her, "English missionaries came in and started a school. When he walked up to the school, he didn't know what to think about it. He said he was tired of eating rabbits—he called them hares—and he came up to this place where they were serving something else. He wanted to work to get a different kind of food from the hares he had been eating [for food]. From there, he went back home, then he came back again. The third time he came, he decided to stay with them if they would give him something to do." If this story is accurate, then Zenobia Perry's father was not a descendant of slaves. Later, Perry said in a phone interview (January 1, 2002) that his mother had been brought with her three children to London, England, then to Mound City, Ill.

[79] Perry had said "in the meantime his mother had died in childbirth and so he said he wanted to be a doctor to see what he could do that would help women having babies." It is not clear whether his mother died in childbirth in Illinois. Perry, interview (July 28, 1993).

NOTES

[80] Perry, interview (January 1, 2002). "Awareness of a family structure beyond my immediate parents and maternal grandparents came after my sister's birth. Returning from a visit with my grandparents, I noticed that the children across the street from our house had two sets of grandparents visiting them. I asked my father where his parents were and why they didn't come to visit us. He told me they were dead. 'But where is their house?' I asked. He replied, 'They had a house in Mound City, Illinois, a long way from here but your grandfather called Somaliland—the eastern horn of the way-a-way land of African near the big Indian Ocean—home." (Zenobia Powell Perry, unpublished autobiographical essay, May 1997, 3-4.)

[81] Not to be confused with Roger Williams University in Rhode Island founded in the twentieth century.

[82] The name was changed in 1883 to Roger Williams University and began to attract students from across the U.S. It had an all-white administration and about 250 students. Between the years of 1877 and 1899, it produced 76 college graduates, many of whom became founders and teachers of schools throughout the South.

[83] From their web site: www.mmc.edu. Meharry is listed among African American Historic Sites of the Metropolitan Historical Commission and Nashville Convention & Visitors Bureau. Walden University had an African Missionary Training School that trained Methodist missionaries who were sent to Africa. Calvin Powell attended Meharry Medical Department of Central Tennessee College, graduating in 1894.

Meharry Medical College, founded in 1876 near Nashville, claims to be the first medical education program established for African Americans in the United States. It is currently the largest private institution for the training of black health care professionals.

The founder and president of Meharry Medical College was George W. Hubbard (1841-1924), a white missionary dedicated to the education of blacks. In 1900, the name was changed to Meharry Medical College of Walden University; in 1915, it was granted a separate charter by the State of Tennessee.

[84] Perry, interview (July 28, 1993).

[85] (Fayetteville: University of Arkansas Press, 1999), xiv.

[86] Lovett, xiv.

[87] Ibid., 106.

[88] Archivist Quintin Jones confirmed Powell's graduation date as 1894.

[89] Perry, interview (July 28, 1993). Perry did not know any more about the circumstances of her father's mother's death or his first wife's death. It seems probable that C. B. Powell's parents were missionaries.

[90] It appears in William Loren Katz's *The Black West: A Documentary and Pictorial History*, rev. ed. (Garden City, N.Y.: Doubleday Anchor Book, 1973), 150, with the caption, "Boley Town Council ruled one of some twenty-five to twenty-seven all-black settlements built in Oklahoma from 1890 to 1910." This same photograph appears in Kenneth Marvin Hamilton, *Black Towns and Profit* (Urbana: University of Illinois Press, 1991), 125, with the caption: "The town council of Boley, Oklahoma, circa 1908-1910. Courtesy of the Archives and Manuscripts Division, Oklahoma Historical Society." In a phone interview (November 1, 2001), Mrs. Henrietta Hicks of the Boley Museum identified the men in the photograph: (left to right, bottom row) W. H. Wallace, T. B. Armstrong, D. J. Turner, T. M. Haynes, H. C. Cavil, M. J. Jones; (top row) Wash. Williams, Dr. C. B. Powell, C. C. Chambers, T. R. Ringo, and W. A. Kennedy. Of this group, Ringo, Powell, Paxton, Turner, and Kennedy each served at one time as Mayor of Boley (see Dolphin-Ashley, "Appendix A," 78. "Mayors of Boley

NOTES

Since 1905," listing the mayors who served between 1905 and 1937, taken from the *Minutes of the City Council*).

[91] He was elected on May 5, 1913, and served until May 3, 1915 (Dolphin-Ashley, 78).

[92] Perry, autobiographical essay, 1. This was the Masonic Temple, which was completed in 1912 and served as the town's meeting place and civic auditorium. O. H. Bradley was publisher of *The Boley Progress* from 1905 until 1910; it continued under the management of William M. Jones and E. M. Watson (Dolphin-Ashley, "History of Boley," 45).

[93] Zenobia Perry's father was a Mason, as were most men in Boley. The women participated in the auxiliary called The Eastern Star. *The Boley Progress* published lists of contributors to the building during the capital campaign, listing C. B. Powell's contribution of $5.00 in 1910. In 1914 the National Negro Business League held its national convention in Boley because of its black elected officials, its self-government, its $150,000 high school, some 82 businesses, an electric light plant, waterworks, a telephone system, and a Masonic Temple.

[94] Payne, 7.

[95] Perry, interview (July 28, 1993).

[96] Zenobia's sister, Thelma Felton, told Janis-Rozena Peri that she thought they were married in 1906; however, the 1910 census indicated that they had been married for only two years. The other bride was a close friend of Birdie's; no wedding pictures survive.

[97] Zenobia Perry set this poem in 1976 for baritone and piano; it has been a very popular song.

[98] Zenobia Perry confirmed this spelling (interview, November 7, 2001). In the 1910 U.S. Census, it is spelled "Luticia"; Calvin Powell's age is given as 39; Birdie as 21. It indicated that both could read and write.

[99] Booker T. Washington remarked in his famous 1908 article on his visit to Boley, "Indians have either receded—'gone back,' as the saying in that region is—on the advance of the white race, or they have intermarried with, and become absorbed with it. Indeed, so rapidly has this intermarriage of the two races gone on, and so great has been the demand for Indian wives, that in some of the Nations, I was informed, the price of marriage licenses has gone as high as $1,000." Washington's article from *The Outlook* (January 4, 1908), as reprinted in William Katz, *The Black West* (New York: Touchstone, 1996), 328–29.

[100] Perry, interview (November 7, 2001). He died in 1946 or 1947, at the age of 108. Luticia had died before Janis-Rozena was born in 1943, but the exact date has not been confirmed. Examination of several books, including Indian-commissioned census on Creeks in Eastern Oklahoma around 1900, show the surname "Thompson" as a common Creek family name. Birdie Powell did bookkeeping for Dr. Paxton and her husband one or two days per week when Zenobia was growing up (Zenobia Perry, phone interview, January 6, 2002). *The WPA Oklahoma Slave Narratives*, ed. T. Lindsay Baker and Julie P. Baker (Norman: University of Oklahoma Press, 1996) includes a narrative by Johnson Thompson of Fort Gibson, Oklahoma, who was born in 1853 in Bellview, Rusk County, Texas. The interview, which took place in the early winter of 1937–38, was conducted by WPA field worker Ethel Wolfe Garrison. Johnson Thompson's parents were slaves to W. P. Thompson, a mixed-blood Cherokee Indian. Johnson Thompson had six children, the oldest of whom was named Charley. "Master Thompson brought us from Texas [to Oklahoma] when I was too little to remember about it, and I don't know how long it was before we were all sold to John Harnage . . . [who] took us back to Texas, right down near where I was born at Bellview" (420). Could this be a relative of Zenobia Perry's grandfather Charlie Thompson? In any case, it describes the comings and goings of black slaves with Indian masters between Texas and Oklahoma, similar to her grandfather's story. Johnson Thompson's surname

NOTES

comes from the family who originally owned his parents. The same may be true for Perry's grandfather.

[101] A photograph of the school is reprinted in Katz, *The Black West*. In her history of Boley (52–53), Dolphin-Ashley writes, "The second private high school located at Boley carried a misnomer. It was called The Creek Seminole College." Founded in 1905 by William Leftwich, it was always underfunded. It closed in 1910 when it burned and "several children burned with it." It is not clear if Birdie attended the college before or after her marriage to Dr. Powell.

[102] I located Uncle Clem in the 1910 U.S. Census at T512: "Clem Thompson, age 27; Sarlie, age 26; Olibe, age 2, C. C. NR"; it stated that Clem was born in Arkansas and Sarlie in Texas. "Mamma's brother, Uncle 'Mudd' [Merridy Thompson] lived in Texas, near Dallas and he had all kinds of instruments from the Dallas Symphony. He was the caretaker or something for the symphony. Mudd Thompson was his name." Perry, interview (September 30, 2001).

[103] Perry, interview (September 30, 2001). I found the Charlie Thompson family in the 1910 Census, as well: "Chas Thompson, Husband, Male, Mulatto, age 57, born in Texas, father and mother born in Texas, farmer." It lists his wife as Luticia, age 51, with birthplace in Arkansas; daughters Artee, age 18, Nora, age 16, and Niva (Neva), age 14; all are listed as MU (mulatto). The three daughters all list their birthplace as Texas; Birdie Thompson reported to the same census under Dr. Calvin Powell's household as his wife and states her birthplace as Arkansas. No sons are listed at home in 1910 Census. The Goldthread-Thompson Family Reunion (including descendants of Charlie Thompson) was held in Chicago in July 2002, with more than 300 people in attendance. A drawing of this home hung in Perry's home in Wilberforce.

[104] Zenobia Perry's birthdate has been confirmed as 1908; Calvin, Jr.'s birthdate is confirmed in the Social Security Death Index [he died in May 1993]; however, the other birthdates have not yet been confirmed. In the 1920 U.S. Census, page 15 of the Boley section, 148/155, Calvin B. Powell is listed as 46; Berdia L. as 30; Zenobia Perry, 11; Thelma, 9; Calvin B. Jr., 7; Douglass [no age given]; father is listed as black and the mother and children as MU. Douglass and his second wife, Gladys, died in the 1970s in a car accident in the Washington, D.C., area. He was a chef at the Pentagon. Thelma lived in Virginia. Zenobia Perry recalled that, before her fourth birthday, the family moved to 116 Oak Street, on the east side of town.

[105] Perry, interview (July 28, 1993).

[106] Perry, autobiographical essay, 4.

[107] Ibid.

[108] Ibid.

[109] Ibid.

[110] Zenobia Perry, taped interview (July 21, 1993), Yellow Springs, Ohio. The poet for "The Organ" was not identified.

[111] Perry, interview (July 28, 1993).

CHAPTER 3: "Lift Every Voice and Sing": Booker T. Washington; Boley, Oklahoma; and the Political Reality for Blacks

[112] This poem, first published in 1899, is often referred to as "The Negro National Anthem." It was arranged by Zenobia Perry for SATB choir and band, to celebrate the

NOTES

opening of a new building at Central State University in 1975. The new building replaced one destroyed by the devastating 1974 tornado in Wilberforce and Xenia, Ohio.

[113] Perry, interview (July 21, 1993).

[114] Zenobia Perry, as a result of her experiences at Tuskegee with William Dawson, made numerous arrangements of spirituals throughout her composing career.

[115] Vol. 88 (January 4, 1908): 28–31. The entire text of his 1905 speech was reprinted in *The Boley Progress* on November 30, 1905. It mentions his speech in Guthrie on November 18, 1905, but there is no mention of an appearance in Boley. It was reported that the Langston (Oklahoma) Orchestra played at Booker T. Washington's speech.

[116] Norman L. Crockett, "Witness to History: Booker T. Washington Visits Boley," *Chronicles of Oklahoma* 67 (Winter 1989–90): 383. This is discussed in more detail in the next chapter.

[117] Ibid., 398.

[118] Ibid., 390.

[119] Katz, *The Black West*, 251–52.

[120] Perry, interview (July 28, 1993).

[121] Dolphin-Ashley, iii.

[122] Kenneth Hamilton, 133. Hamilton does not address the issue of blacks and Indians in his description of Boley. He focuses on Boley as an all-black town or as "the largest predominantly black town in the entire Midwest and Great Plains" (121). He mentions the complication of Indian land deals requiring approval of the Department of Interior. William Katz, on the other hand, emphasizes that it was a black-Indian town. According to materials sent to me by Henrietta Hicks, Boley, Oklahoma, was approved as an historical landmark district in May 1975 by the United States Department of the Interior, National Park Service, in Washington, D.C. Boley today has about one thousand people; in the 1970s the city hosted the oldest Black Rodeo in America during Memorial Day weekend, promoted as The Boley Rodeo & Bar-b-Q Festival, with some 40,000 people attending annually, including many celebrity guests.

[123] Part of Boley's problems had to do with century-old problems between Indians and the U.S. government and the complexity of the history of black Indians, discussed in chapter 5.

[124] Henrietta Hicks, in a phone conversation (November 11, 2001), said that this also had been her experience growing up in Boley.

[125] Perry, interview (July 28, 1993).

[126] Perry, autobiographical essay, 9.

[127] Perry, interview (July 28, 1993). When asked about Marcus Garvey, Zenobia Perry said, "My father knew him and they had some conversations. He [my father] used to say he'd like to sell out and go back to Africa with Marcus Garvey and she'd say, 'Well, you're not going to think about that.' He'd say, 'It's just an idea,' and [Mother would say,] 'That's an idea you can forget.' I never ever heard about it again and my mother when she disagreed with you, she said very few words, but you knew what she said. You never crossed her when you knew she had made up her mind."

[128] Jonathan Earle, *The Routledge Atlas of African American History* (New York: Routledge, 2000), 104–5. See also David E. Cronen, *Black Moses: The Story of Marcus Garvey and the*

NOTES

Universal Negro Improvement Association, 2nd ed. (Madison: University of Wisconsin Press, 1981).

[129] William E. Bittle and Gilbert Geis, *The Longest Way Home: Chief Alfred C. Sam's Back-to-Africa Movement*, with research assistance of Donald F. Parker (Detroit: Wayne State University Press, 1964), 7. This book was researched by examining *The Boley Progress* and *African Pioneer* newspapers and from interviews with people still living in the 1960s, who had witnessed the movement, including family members and descendants of some who made the voyage.

[130] Ibid., 2.

[131] Her source was her interview in 1940 with O. H. Bradley, who had been a close personal friend of the Powells.

[132] Bittle and Geis, 14.

[133] See Charles H. Wesley, "Lincoln's Plan for Colonizing the Emancipated Negro," *Journal of Negro History* IV (1919): 7–21.

[134] Bittle and Geis, 26.

[135] Ibid., 67.

[136] Ibid.

CHAPTER 4: Distinctively American: Race and Music

[137] As quoted and translated by Philip V. Bohlman in "Ethnomusicology's Challenge to the Canon; the Canon's Challenge to Ethnomusicology," *Disciplining Music: Musicology and Its Canons*, ed. Katherine Bergeson and Philip V. Bohlman (Chicago: University of Chicago Press, 1992), 116. Dutch ethnomusicologist Jaap Kunst quoted these eight lines from Johann Wolfgang Goethe as an epigraph in his work *Musicologica*, published in 1959.

[138] At conference sessions involving the black music research centers, there have been many remarks about "the party line" in that community, and mention of the fact that certain issues are not safe to bring up in public forums about black music.

[139] On the other hand, if she had emphasized her Native American roots, whites might become more interested in her work, perceiving her as more "exotic."

[140] Concert, Art Institute, Dayton, Ohio (December 17, 1961). It could not be determined if this organization still exists or when it folded.

[141] It may even deafen us to some intriguing aspects of American music, often identified as African elements, which do not trace back easily to Africa of the sixteenth and seventeenth centuries. Given the recent scholarship, perhaps black American music traditions should be re-examined for elements that have come from Native American musical traditions, as distinguished from those that came from Africa. Alternatively, we should drop these categories and speak of American music. The one ingredient of some African music that is agreed upon as influential in Afro-American music is additive rhythm; however, the little use of this in Zenobia Perry's music was the result of her own study of African music in the 1970s, while a professor of music at Central State University.

[142] Eileen Southern, "Afro-American Music," in *The New Grove Dictionary of American Music*, ed. H. Wiley Hitchcock and Stanley Sadie (New York: Grove's Dictionaries of Music, 1986), I:13.

[143] Ibid., 19.

[144] Ibid., 13.

NOTES

[145] See, for example, Travis A. Jackson, "Jazz Performance as Ritual: The Blues Aesthetic and the African Diaspora," and Ingrid Monson, "Art Blakey's African Diaspora," in *The African Diaspora: A Musical Perspective*, ed. Ingrid Monson (New York: Garland Publishing, 2000); also John Storm Roberts, *Black Music of Two Worlds: African, Caribbean, Latin and African-American Traditions* (New York: Schirmer Books, 1998); Gerhard Kubik's *Africa and the Blues* (Jackson: University Press of Mississippi, 1999); Carol Lems-Dvorkin, *Africa in Scott Joplin's Music* (Evanston, Ill.: C. Lems-Dvorkin, 1991); Frederick Kaufman and John P. Guckin, *The African Roots of Jazz* (Sherman Oaks, Calif.: Alfred Publishing, 1979); Samuel A. Floyd, Jr., *The Power of Black Music: Interpreting Its History from Africa to the United States* (New York: Oxford University Press, 1995); Ashenafi Kebede, *Roots of Black Music: The Vocal, Instrumental, and Dance Heritage of Africa and Black America* (Englewood Cliffs, N.J.: Prentice-Hall, 1982); Christopher Small, *Music of the Common Tongue: Survival and Celebration of Afro-American Music* (London: Jon Calder Riverrun Press, 1987).

[146] Monson, 3.

[147] Ibid., 2.

[148] Paul Gilroy, *The Black Atlantic: Modernity and Double Consciousness* (Cambridge: Harvard University Press, 1993), 102.

[149] "Overview" by Charlotte Heth on Native American music in "The United States and Canada," *The Garland Encyclopedia of World Music*, edited by Ellen Koskoff (New York: Garland Publishing, 2001), III:367–68. For more about Native American music, see Frank G. Speck, Leonard Broom, and Will West Long, *Cherokee Dance and Drama* (Berkeley: University of California Press, 1951; repr. Norman: University of Oklahoma Press, 1983); R. D. Theisz and Ben Black Bear, *Songs and Dances of the Lakota* (Rosebud, S.Dak.: Sinte Gleska College, 1976; repr. Aberdeen, S.Dak.: North Plains Press, 1984); Thomas Vennum, Jr., *The Ojibwa Dance Drum: Its History and Construction* (Washington, D.C.: Smithsonian Institution Press, 1982); Jill Drayson Sweet, *Dances of the Tewa Pueblo Indians: Expressions of New Life* (Santa Fe, N.Mex.: School of American Research Press, 1985); George P. Horse Capture, *Powwow* (Cody, Wyo.: Buffalo Bill Historical Center, 1989); Willie Smyth, ed., *Songs of Indian Territory: Native American Music Traditions of Oklahoma* (Oklahoma City: Center of the American Indian, 1989); William K. Powers, *War Dance: Plains Indian Musical Performance* (Tucson: University of Arizona Press, 1990); Charlotte Heth, editor, *Native American Dance: Ceremonies and Social Traditions* (Washington, D.C.: National Museum of the American Indian, Smithsonian Institution with Starwood Publishing, 1992); Bruno Nettl, *North American Indian Musical Styles* (Philadelphia: American Folklore Society, 1954).

[150] Would it not be possible to find additive drumming techniques among Native Americans in the sacred music traditions? I have asked many Native American musicians about this and the casual answer has always been, "It is possible."

[151] Gilroy. See, for example, A. Herle's "Dancing Community: Powwow and Pan-Indianism in North America," in *Cambridge Anthropology* xvii, no. 2 (1994), a special issue entitled, "Living Traditions: Continuity and Change, Past and Present," or Jeannie Pool's four-part radio documentary, *American Indian Arts: Sharing the Heritage*, broadcast originally on KPFK-Pacifica Radio, Los Angeles, in 1984. This radio series was produced from recordings made at the UCLA American Indian Studies Conference of the same title, coordinated by Charlotte Heth.

[152] Monson.

[153] Verna Arvey, "With His Roots in the Soil," in Still, 17.

[154] Perry, autobiographical essay, 25.

NOTES

[155] Los Angeles veteran record producer and black composer Ed Bland describes it as "black Europeanized religious music, usually liked by middle- and upper-class blacks and whites." Ed Bland, phone interview, February 27, 2002.

[156] See Jeannie Pool, "A Conversation with Pianist Althea Waites: Sexism, Racism, and Music," *IAWM Journal* (October 1994): 8–14.

[157] Richard Schwarze, "Zenobia Perry and Janis-Rozena Peri," *Dayton Journal Herald* (June 3, 1978), 27. Emphasis added.

[158] Ed Bland speaks eloquently on this aspect of American commercial music history.

[159] Quincy Jones and Benny Carter are the only black composers who have written a body of work for film and television; other black composers have written a few scores each during their careers.

[160] See William Kearns, "Overview of Music in the United States," in *The Garland Encyclopedia of World Music*, 539. This idea that the use of folk sources is the basis of a distinctively original high art culture comes from the eighteenth-century German philosopher Johann Gottfried Herder.

[161] There must be ways to write about and promote classical music and contemporary concert music that demonstrate its diversity and, therefore, its appeal.

[162] Still, i.

[163] Ibid., v–vi. Emphasis added.

[164] To confine a composer to musical material of his or her particular ethnic background is also indefensible.

[165] Ed Bland, phone interview (February 26, 2002). This is discussed on page 51.

[166] "Race, Ethnicity, and Nationhood," in *The Garland Encyclopedia of World Music*, III: 72.

[167] Monson, ibid.

[168] Small. It is a serious misconception to think that Afro-American music has nothing to do with "the great European classical tradition." Biographies of black American musicians, particularly from the Civil War until World War II, indicate that a high percentage of them studied, knew, and performed "great European classical" music and were quite familiar with Protestant hymns and other sacred music.

[169] Ibid., 5. Emphasis added.

[170] Thanks to Ed Bland for insights for the development of this idea.

[171] When I enrolled in a beginning composition class in the 1970s, the first class assignment was to write twelve bars for full symphony orchestra. The instructor was kind enough to give each student a blank piece of orchestral score paper for that purpose. I dropped out immediately, as did twenty-four of the thirty students; the six remaining were white men. Years later, when I asked the professor why he had done this, he admitted it was his way of getting rid of everyone but the "real composers"—those who as freshmen in college were not intimidated by such an assignment.

[172] Fats Waller's story is a clear example of this kind of exploitation. In some cases, the arrangers were black.

[173] This is probably an exaggeration, but the situation is well known. Many trained composers, arrangers, and orchestrators in Los Angeles work for famous black performers/songwriters, helping them write down their music, "charts," and "lead sheets." Composer

NOTES

Ed Bland said that, when he was asked to teach music to black youth at a community center in Los Angeles, the students told him they did not need to learn about music, because they could "sample" whatever music they needed. Ed Bland, phone interview (March 4, 2002).

[174] Many very fine, creative musicians—especially talented improvisers—did not become "composers," because they had not learned to write down their own music. Zenobia Perry said that she had encountered much resistance to learning music notation among her students at Central State. They would complain that, in the time it took them to write something down, they could have played a hundred pieces. Perry, interview (February 25, 2002).

[175] See William Zinsser, *Writing to Learn* (New York: Harper & Row Publishers, 1989).

[176] Composer and orchestrator Mauro Bruno, who has worked in Hollywood for fifty years, told me that after World War II, the music schools were flooded with G.I.'s from the music ensembles in the Armed Services. Faculty weeded them out by testing their skills in writing down music. Many talented, creative musicians were dismissed, although they played their instruments expertly, because they had never learned musical notation, and the music faculties in the late 1940s were unable and/or unwilling to train them.

[177] Perry, phone interview (February 25, 2002).

CHAPTER 5: The Hidden History: Blacks and Native Americans' Cultural Implications

[178] There is a current movement for reparations for descendants of African slaves.

[179] See Kim Dramer, *Native Americans and Black Americans* (Philadelphia: Chelsea House Publishers, 1997), 8.

[180] See the photograph of Zenobia Perry on page 54. Susan Straight, "The Content and Character of the Census: The Government's Latest Pigeonholes Amuse and Annoy These Kids" (*Los Angeles Times Magazine*, May 7, 2000), points out that children today seem to have much more common sense on these issues than their parents or grandparents: "Our nation's complexion has changed, and not in ways that can be easily measured. My daughters never knew the old color scheme, didn't understand the concept in kindergarten and don't understand it now." The 2000 U.S. Census allowed the option of marking "one or more races to indicate what this person considers himself/herself to be."

[181] See William Loren Katz, *Black Indians: A Hidden Heritage*, repr. (New York: Touchstone, 1996), 2.

[182] Dramer, 18–19.

[183] See Gloria Jahoda, *The Trail of Tears: The Story of the American Indian Removals, 1813–1855* (New York: Wings Books, 1975; reprinted 1995.)

[184] Katz, *Black Indians*, 137–38.

[185] Ibid.

[186] Ibid., 140. The evidence for this seems scant and romanticized. One family story about Zenobia Perry's grandfather Charlie Thompson may support this claim that the bondage was "milder." Charlie was a slave in Arkansas, helped in his getaway by the slave owners' daughter, so he could make a new start in Oklahoma. "One day the girl's father said to her that she should beat Charlie because he had done something, that she needed to whip him, but she didn't want to do that. So she took him behind the barn and said to him, 'I'm going to hit the barn so Daddy will think I'm mean, because I don't want to hit you.' So that's what she did." Janis-Rozena Peri, taped interview (May 8, 2001), Morgantown, W.Va.

NOTES

[187] Katz, *Black Indians*, 144.

[188] Ibid., 145. It is not clear that this is true: slavery is slavery. Oral histories with black Indian former slaves reveal a "wide range of relations between the groups" (see *The WPA Oklahoma Slave Narratives*, 5). One would be motivated to embrace this idea of Indian masters as being more humane and less brutal than white slave holders if one is trying to put in claim for the benefits of Indian heritage as defined by U.S. government policies and reparations. The brutality of slavery is precisely the reason why many black Indians separated themselves from their Native American roots. Blacks who have written favorably about the whites who held their ancestors as slaves have been reviled and ridiculed. Our society continues to seek grounds for reconciliation, but cover-up is not the answer. Katz's chapter, "Slavery in the West," in *The Black West*, raises more questions than it answers. *The WPA Oklahoma Slave Narratives* perhaps gives a more accurate picture of the behavior of Indian slave holders.

[189] *The WPA Oklahoma Slave Narratives*, 5–6. The authors offer a list of additional sources on this subject.

[190] According to Charles Eastman, "The attempted arrest of Sitting Bull in his cabin by Indian Police led to his death and the stampeding of his people. Several of the stampeded bands came down to Pine Ridge, where they were met by United States Troops, disarmed and shot down after one man had resisted disarmament by firing off his weapon. This was the massacre of Wounded Knee, where about 300 Indians, two-thirds of them women and children, were mown down with machine guns within a few minutes." See Charles Alexander Eastman, *The Indian To-day* (Garden City, N.Y.: Doubleday, Page, 1915), 33. Eastman was the medical doctor stationed at the Pine Ridge Agency by the BIA; he treated the Indian wounded, following the massacre.

[191] One wonders how many of this number were black Indians.

[192] By statehood, in 1907, blacks outnumbered both Indians and first- and second-generation Europeans in the Oklahoma population. First- and second-generation Europeans numbered 130,430 in 1907; Negroes totaled 137,612; and Indians 74,825. This is truly astounding, because, if the blacks and Indians had joined together at statehood, they could have blocked the segregationists. But they did not and the conflict between them in Oklahoma continues today. See Douglas Hale, "European Immigrants in Oklahoma," *Chronicles of Oklahoma* 52 (1975): 179. Douglas Hale donated his collected papers from 1910–1992 to the Oklahoma State University Libraries, Collection no. 93–036.

[193] Ibid., 151.

[194] This is described in more detail in chapter 3.

[195] Zenobia Perry and Beatrice O'Rourke, taped interview (August 12, 1994), Wilberforce, Ohio.

[196] Dramer, 48.

[197] Ibid., 49–52.

[198] The fact that Charlie Thompson had an eighty-acre plot, which he owned and farmed, may be additional proof of his mixed heritage. It is not known if he received this as a black Indian, as an adopted freedman, or in the land distribution of 1889 to new settlers of many racial and ethnic backgrounds.

[199] Ibid., 56. In the 1910 U.S. Census, Zenobia Perry's mother and the entire Charlie Thompson family were identified as MU (mulatto).

[200] Ibid., 74.

NOTES

[201] Ibid., 74–75.

[202] Ibid., 75.

[203] Washington's article from *The Outlook* (January 4, 1908), as reprinted in Katz, *The Black West*, 328–29.

[204] The Adept New American Museum for the Art of the Southwest—which addresses issues about mixed heritage—was founded in the 1970s in Mount Vernon, New York. Many of the sons and daughters of Native Americans who stayed in eastern Oklahoma to fight for their land rights were not educated and did not make economic advances as did many of the black families who "made it" into the middle class between 1920 and 1950.

[205] William Loren Katz, *Black Indians: A Hidden Heritage* (New York: Aladdin Paperbacks (imprint of Simon & Schuster), 1997), 18. This book was originally published in 1986 by Ethrac Publications, Inc. It is also available in an Atheneum Books for Young Readers edition.

[206] Perry, interview (July 21, 1993).

[207] Janis-Rozena Peri, taped interview (May 8, 2001), Morgantown, W.Va.

[208] When contacted for rights to record music of Florence Price, some of her relatives told the record company, through their lawyer, to do whatever we wished with the music, but not to mention their names as being relatives. We were told that they were "passing as white" and did not want anyone to know of their connection to their distinguished grandmother, who was black and Native American. These recordings of her piano music and art songs, which I produced on the Cambria label, contributed greatly to the revival of interest in Price's music in the 1980s and '90s.

[209] Several interviews and conversations over the years.

[210] Perry, interview (July 21, 1993).

[211] Peri, interview (May 8, 2001).

CHAPTER 6: Mentors, Allies, and Supporters: Crucial for Musical Development

[212] Perry knew about Florence Price's career in Chicago in the 1940s, but had never heard of another woman composer.

[213] Perry, autobiographical essay, 5.

[214] Perry, interview (July 21, 1993).

[215] Perry and O'Rourke, interview (August 12, 1994). In one interview, Perry said this concert took place when she was four, which would have been in 1912, perhaps a little early in Harrison's career for a concert tour performance in Boley. I did not find any mention of Harrison's concert in the few Boley newspapers I was able to examine. But the town had a rich concert life with regular performances in the Masonic Temple theater, at the high school, and in local churches, particularly the A. M. E. Church. For more details on Harrison's career, see Jeane E. Cazort and Constance Tibbs Hobson, *Born to Play: The Life and Career of Hazel Harrison,* Contributions to The Study of Music and Dance 3 (Westport, Conn.: Greenwood Press, 1983). This book includes photographs, appendixes, bibliography, and index, but not a list of her performances. In Europe from 1911 through 1914, Harrison did nevertheless concertize throughout the United States, beginning in 1914, and particularly in the 1920s. There are, however, no references to concerts in Oklahoma.

[216] See Cazort and Hobson.

NOTES

[217] The "27th Annual Catalogue of Lincoln Institute, 1897–1989, Jefferson City, Missouri," lists two girls with the first name "Mayme": Mayme L. Hunter (Elementary Division) and Mayme Clemens (Normal Division). Could one of these be Mayme Jones, the piano teacher in Boley?

[218] Perry, autobiographical essay, 6.

[219] Perry, interview (July 21, 1993).

[220] Perry, autobiographical essay, 6.

[221] Zenobia Perry, letter to Jeannie Pool (Fall 1993). In her interview with Mike Payne, Perry said her great-nephew Elwood Tomlin still had that old piano in his house in Boley.

[222] Dett was at Lincoln Institute in Jefferson City, Missouri, between 1911 and 1913; if she studied with him there, it had to be during those years. Lincoln Institute, which in 1921 became Lincoln University of Missouri, was established with funding from the 62nd and 63rd Colored Infantry members from the Civil War, to provide a basic education to black Americans. It was a Normal College (i.e., for teacher training) before becoming a university. (Thanks to Lincoln University archivist Mary Heady for her assistance.) Dolphin-Ashley recounts this story of how Mrs. Jones came to Boley: The founder of the Creek-Seminole College, William Leftwich, invited Mr. and Mrs. F. B. Jones to Boley in 1908 to run the school, a private high school. Mr. Jones was hired as President and Mrs. Jones was appointed head of the music department. "They found nothing with which to work except children. Leftwich explained to F. B. Jones that he could be paid if he raised the money. F. B. Jones resigned as did Mrs. Jones" (Dolphin-Ashley, 53).

[223] Ibid., 72.

[224] Perry, interview (July 28, 1993). There is no mention of Boley in Simpson's biography of Dett. I found nothing in the few available Boley newspapers about Dett's performances or visits in Boley.

[225] Perry, interview (July 28, 1993).

[226] Mrs. Henrietta Hicks, president of the Boley Museum, also studied with Mrs. Jones. According to Dolphin-Ashley, Mayme Jones moved to Boley in August of 1909 and taught piano from that time. When Zenobia Perry later moved to Rochester, she realized that music of black composers was not performed. She decided to memorize a great deal of music by black composers and gained a reputation for always playing music by black composers at the piano (Perry, interview, July 28, 1993).

[227] See Melissa Fuell, *Blind Boone: His Early Life and His Achievements* (Kansas City: Burton, 1915). There are at least four piano rolls from 1912, documenting his skills as a pianist.

[228] Perry, autobiographical essay, 8.

[229] Perry, interview (July 28, 1993).

[230] Ibid. Henrietta Hicks sent me a photocopy from *The Chronicles of Oklahoma* with a list of "Oklahoma-Born Jazz Artists," and a note that Claude Jones (b.1901) was a jazz trombonist and vocalist from Boley, who played with Duke Ellington. The attitude of the Powell parents was typical among middle-class black families, during these years.

[231] Perry, interview (July 28, 1993). This may have been an opera performance broadcast out of Chicago; the Metropolitan Opera was not nationally broadcast until 1931.

[232] Ibid.

[233] Perry, interview (February 2, 2002).

NOTES

[234] This would have been a terrible year to be a theater musician in Omaha, as it marked the distribution of "talkies" to movie theaters nationwide. Omaha had some twenty-five silent movie theaters, each with a pit orchestra of eleven or thirty-three players. Most of these musicians lost their jobs in 1929. The Louis B. Schnauber Collection at UCLA Music Library is a collection of silent film music used in Omaha during this period. Schnauber was a music director in Omaha, who was put out of business in 1929. He stored his collection of approximately 2,400 complete scores in the basement of his hardware business. There they remained until the 1990s, when they were given to the Film Music Society by his son. The author of this dissertation catalogued this collection and wrote a couple of articles for the Film Music Society publications on Schnauber and 1929 in Omaha. The inventory is available online at www.ucla.edu.

[235] Perry and O'Rourke, interview (August 12, 1994). Edvard Grieg (1843–1907), *Piano Concerto in A minor*, Op. 16 (1868).

[236] Sara Mull Baldwin, ed., *Nebraskana: Biographical Sketches of Nebraska Men and Women of Achievement Who Have Been Awarded Life Membership in the Nebraskana Society* (Hebron, Nebr.: Baldwin Company, 1932), 118.

[237] Bateson, 16–17. Bateson makes a case for changing educational institutions so they can prepare young people for real life. "The American version of liberal-arts education, since it is not closely career oriented, provides a good base for life-long learning and for retraining when that becomes necessary, but the institutions themselves often exemplify the opposite. Grassy campuses across the country beckon graciously to children leaving home for the first time; although they are no more than way stations for their graduates, they still suggest the old norm of lifetime commitment and security. For those who work in them, they represent it even more clearly than a monastery would, or a family farm. In effect, the best of our young men and women are educated by faculties deeply committed to continuity. Most of them have spent their entire lives in a single institution, often surrounded by the apparent tranquility of a small town, and may no longer be intellectually flexible or open to change."

[238] Bateson, 17.

[239] Perry, interview (July 28, 1993).

[240] Perry, interview (July 21, 1993). Pictures of these dugouts can be found in books on early Oklahoma history. Zenobia had a drawing of her grandparents' home in Flat Rock hanging in her house in Wilberforce, Ohio. The Powells enjoyed a comfortably middle-class lifestyle on a doctor's income.

[241] Perry, interview (July 28, 1993). Later in life, Zenobia became interested in dressmaking and designed several gowns.

[242] The school enrollment form, provided by the Okfuskee County Clerk, shows that Zenobia was enrolled by her father at the same time as he enrolled the housekeeper's daughter.

[243] Correspondence received from Henrietta Hicks, December 13, 2001.

[244] Perry, autobiographical essay, 4–5.

[245] Perry, interview (July 28, 1993).

[246] When C. B. Powell enrolled at Meharry Medical College, his record noted that he was Baptist.

[247] Dolphin-Ashley, 60–61.

NOTES

[248] Perry, interview (December 1, 2001). There is a photograph of the Antioch Missionary Baptist Church in Dolphin-Ashley, 59.

[249] Ibid.

[250] Perry, interview (July 28, 1993).

[251] Perry, autobiographical essay, 7.

[252] Perry, interview (July 28, 1993).

[253] Perry, interview (February 2, 2002).

[254] Peri, interview (May 8, 2001).

[255] Ibid.

[256] Perry, interview (July 28, 1993).

CHAPTER 7: Dett, Reece, and Dawson: Role Models for Careers in Black Music

[257] Bateson, 16.

[258] The family planned to send her sister, Thelma, to join Zenobia the next year. Her brother Calvin, Jr., started his college career at Tuskegee, then transferred to Hampton Institute, where he studied agriculture and chemistry.

[259] "A Composer's Viewpoint," by William Grant Still, in Still, *William Grant Still and the Fusion of Cultures in American Music*, 66.

[260] Perry, interview (December 1, 2001).

[261] Zenobia Perry, interview (September 30, 2001), Morgantown, W.Va.

[262] Ibid. Although her father did have a phone, long-distance service was expensive and difficult, so communication by telegram was preferred. Program notes for Cleveland Chamber Symphony state that she was fourteen years old when she went to Eastman; however, she had just turned 23. Her sister, Thelma, recalled that Zenobia went to Hampton in 1928, when she would have been nineteen or twenty years old. On September 30, 2001, daughter Janis asked her mother how long she had been at Hampton and Zenobia confirmed, "It had not even been a quarter."

[263] Thelma had a similar problem when she was sent to Walden University; upon arrival she decided she would not attend and went to Hampton Institute, instead.

[264] Perry, interview (July 28, 1993).

[265] In another interview (September 30, 2001), Perry gave her name as Miss Boggman.

[266] Perry, interview (July 28, 1993). A letter to the author dated July 12, 1994, from Vincent A. Lenti, Director, Community Education Division of Eastman School of Music, University of Rochester, states, "I can find no record of a student by the name of Zenobia Powell [Perry]. The lack of a record does not necessarily preclude the possibility that she studied in the Preparatory Department, since there was a period of time when the security of student records was somewhat lax. However, from the vantage point of having served as Director for almost 25 years now, I have serious doubts if such a record ever existed. The possible loss of student records, as far as I have been able to ascertain, involved portions of both the beginning (A–E) and end (W–Z) of the alphabetized record-cards. If this determination is correct, as I believe it is, this would indicate that a card would exist for Zenobia Powell [Perry] if she had been enrolled as a student."

[267] Perry, interview (July 28, 1993).

NOTES

[268] Perry, interview (September 30, 2001). She assumed her father took care of the requisite payments to Dett. She did not realize until she went to Tuskegee that she had not been enrolled at Eastman. She figured it out when there was no transcript and she was enrolled at Tuskegee as a freshman.

[269] Zenobia Perry would later study with Allan Willman, another student of Nadia Boulanger.

[270] See Eileen Southern's article on Dett in *The New Grove Dictionary of American Music*, I:610–11.

[271] For more information on the choir's history, see Marilyn Thompson, "The Hampton University Choir: Singing and Building a Priceless Tradition," *The Western Journal of Black Studies* 12, no. 4 (1988): 215–19, with photographs.

[272] Simpson, 210.

[273] According to Eileen Southern, *Biographical Dictionary of Afro-American and African Musicians* (Westport, Conn.: Greenwood Press, 1982), Dett taught at Hampton until 1932. However, his biographer Anne Simpson states that he stopped teaching at Hampton in the fall of 1931, but did not officially resign his position until 1932.

[274] Simpson, 211.

[275] Ibid. William Grant Still's symphonic poem, *Darker America*, was performed by the Rochester Symphony in 1927.

[276] Perry, interview (July 28, 1993). No other information is available on Bert Mathis or Mr. Johnson.

[277] This is the last piece in a suite entitled *Magnolia* (1912).

[278] Perry, interview (July 28, 1993). Originally she said his full name was J. J. Johnson. There was no Johnson on the Eastman faculty at that time. I have not found any information on Bert Mathis. Zenobia recalled that Mr. Mathis was a singer and had some connections in Boley. Her memory of her theory teacher Mr. Johnson was vague. In one interview, she said he told her that he could not put her name on the roll until he saw what she could do, although it was not clear to what roll she referred. So she had to play a solo on at least ten different instruments to prove that she knew what the instruments were. Then she had to write something for the instruments. Then he put her name on the roll, after she had been there for "a whole half year." A letter to the author dated July 12, 1994, from Vincent A. Lenti, director of the Community Education Division of Eastman School of Music, University of Rochester, states, "Concerning Mr. Johnson, I can find no information about any such person. . . . My understanding of theory teaching in the Preparatory Department during those early years is that all such teaching was done my [by] regular faculty who were members of the piano faculty. . . . Prior to writing, I called the only surviving members of the teaching staff from the late 1920s, Gladys Metcalf Leventon [who] joined the faculty in the late 1920s and taught piano and preparatory theory until the early 1970s. She recalls no one by the name 'Johnson.'" In any case, "Mr. Johnson" in Rochester should not be confused with Gunnar Johannsen, whom Zenobia Perry met in the late 1940s or early '50s at the University of Wyoming, where he was a visiting artist. See chapter 10. Mr. Johnson may have been a student colleague of Mr. Dett's.

[279] Perry, interview (July 28, 1993).

[280] Ibid.

[281] Ibid., 300.

NOTES

[282] Ibid., 217. His home address was 577 Plymouth Avenue. When I asked Zenobia Perry if the address of the Davis Building reminded her of anything, she said that, yes, she remembered that it was next to the post office. The wife of the postmaster was the one who provided her a room while she studied with Mr. Dett (Perry, interview, November 7, 2001).

[283] Ibid., 213-16.

[284] Perry and O'Rourke, interview (August 12, 1994).

[285] Ibid. On page 10 of her unpublished autobiographical essay, Perry quotes Dett as saying, "Young lady, don't you change a composer's music. If you don't like it, you write your own. Perhaps I should tear up your score."

[286] Perry, interview (November 7, 2001).

[287] Ibid.

[288] Perry, interview (July 28, 1993).

[289] Perry, autobiographical essay, 10. Vincent Lenti states in his letter of July 1994, "Finally I can offer you no real commentary concerning whether Eastman was a 'friendly environment' for black students. There are so few faculty members still around from those early years. The Preparatory Department had enrollments ranging from 600 to 1500 students per year, the lower numbers being during the earlier years of the Great Depression. I would personally think it strange if none of these were minority students, although I would imagine that they would have been few in number. Concurrent with the establishment of the Eastman School was the opening of the David Hochstein Memorial School, which was a 'settlement school.' Although I have no specific information, my guess is that the Hochstein School served a greater number of minority students, in the same sense that they served greater numbers of children from Russian and Polish immigrant families . . . and Italian kids too."

[290] Perry's biography, printed in a Central State College recital program (November 4, 1956) states: "She received a diploma in Piano from R. N. Dett Conservatory and was the first Negro student in music composition with Darius Milhaud at Wyoming University."

[291] Perry, interview (February 2, 2002).

[292] According to USC music librarian Rodney Rolfe.

[293] Archivist Betty R. Black at Langston University wrote in an email (January 24, 2002): "After extensive research I found only one reference to your inquiry. In *The Bulletin, Colored Agricultural and Normal University*, Vol. 35 no. 4, July 1, 1932, Catalogue Edition 1932-33, listed under broad heading 'Faculty' and further under 'Instructors' was 'Cortez Donald Reece, Fine Arts, Piano & Theory, A. B. Fisk University 1931, Music Major.' He was not in any other bulletins. I take this to mean that he only taught that one academic year. We do not have a yearbook for that period. There were no photographs." Zenobia Perry believed he was still connected to Langston in 1939.

[294] Suzanne Flandreau of the Center for Black Music Research in Chicago wrote (letter, November 16, 1994) that she had found Reece in Madison Carter, *An Annotated Catalog of Composers of African Ancestry* (New York: Vantage Press, 1986). He wrote pieces for piano and "unknown instruments." He also appears in Aaron Horne's bibliography of *Keyboard Music of Black Composers* (Westport, Conn.: Greenwood Press, 1992), which gives the above biographical information. His papers have been deposited at the West Virginia University Library, ironically the same university where Zenobia Perry's daughter Janis-Rozena Peri taught. Pat Connor at the WVU English Department is doing research on Reece.

NOTES

[295] The details of her marriage and the birth of her son, which took place during her studies at Langston University, are discussed in chapter 8.

[296] Perry interview (July 28, 1993).

[297] Southern, *Biographical Dictionary of Afro-American and African Musicians*, 98–100.

[298] David Lee Johnson, *The Contributions of William L. Dawson to the School of Music at Tuskegee Institute and to Choral Music* (Ann Arbor, Mich.: UMI Dissertation Services, 1987). This was Johnson's dissertation at the University of Illinois at Urbana-Champaign.

[299] Cazort and Hobson, 97, give his name as Andrew Rosemond, and mention that Catherine Moton Patterson, daughter of Tuskegee president Patterson, also taught there. She was an Oberlin Conservatory graduate.

[300] Eileen Southern, *The Music of Black Americans*, 3rd ed. (New York: W. W. Norton, 1997), 417–18.

[301] For another source on Dawson, see Mark Hugh Malone, "William Levi Dawson: American Music Educator" (Ph.D. diss., Florida State University, 1981).

[302] Eileen Southern, *The New Grove Dictionary of American Music*, I:590.

[303] Perry, autobiographical essay, 14.

[304] Perry, interview (July 28, 1993).

[305] Perry, interview (February 2, 2002).

[306] Perry, interview (July 28, 1993).

[307] Perry, interview (July 21, 1993).

[308] Of these, Zenobia Perry arranged "Mary Had a Baby," "There's a Lit'l Wheel A-Turnin'," and "Couldn't Hear Nobody Pray."

[309] *Tuskegee Institute 1938 Yearbook*, 22.

[310] Perry, autobiographical essay, 14.

[311] Ibid. For more about Harrison's years at Tuskegee, see Cazort and Hobson, 96–102. Zenobia Perry heard Harrison in concert on January 26, 1947, at Carver Junior High School Auditorium in Tulsa, Oklahoma. The program included Bach-Busoni, Liszt, Slonimsky, Rachmaninoff, Medther, Jelobinsky, and Scriabin.

[312] Cazort and Hobson, 97.

[313] Bette Yarborough Cox's interviews of May 5, 1978, and March 23, 1983, are transcribed and published in *Central Avenue—Its Rise and Fall (1890–c.1955) including the Musical Renaissance of Black Los Angeles* (Los Angeles: BEEM Publications, 1993, 1996), 157.

[314] In April 1982, she was honored at the Second International Congress on Women in Music at the University of Southern California, which I coordinated, at a special ceremony. She was one of the first black music teachers to teach in secondary schools in the Los Angeles Unified School District. She died in 1994.

[315] Perry, interview (July 21, 1993). The flamboyant choir director and storyteller Eva Jessye also visited Tuskegee during those years. Zenobia remembered that she was very vibrant on stage, but when she left the stage, she seemed to collapse.

[316] Ibid.

[317] Perry, interview (July 21, 1993). Payne quotes Perry as saying, "I went on to earn a diploma in Piano Performance at the Berryman School of Music in Omaha, Nebraska.

NOTES

Then I went to Tuskegee Institute in Alabama and studied under the great black composer Nathaniel Dett. At Tuskegee, I had to major in math and education instead of just music to keep my father happy. But not too long after I graduated from Tuskegee and came back to Boley, I got to play "Grieg's Concerto" with the Oklahoma Symphony. I was 21" (7). This chronology is entirely confused. This interview suggests that she studied with Dett at Tuskegee, not in Rochester. When she returned to Oklahoma from Tuskegee, her parents no longer lived in Boley, but in Bartlesville, just outside of Tulsa.

CHAPTER 8: Zenobia Powell Perry: An "Ambiguous Woman"

[318] Perry set the poetry of Donald Jeffrey Hayes in a cycle of songs called *Threnody*, one of her most popular song cycles.

[319] *Writing A Woman's Life* (New York: Ballantine Books, 1988), 31.

[320] Biographies of deceased black American women composers are much more difficult.

[321] Her mentor-teachers Dett, Reece, and Dawson are discussed in chapter 7; mentor-teachers Willman and Milhaud are discussed in chapter 10.

[322] In *Feminist and Linguistic Theory* (London: Macmillan, 1985), 155–56.

[323] Heilbrun, 20–21.

[324] Ibid., 21.

[325] Perry, interview (February 2, 2002).

[326] "A Composer's Viewpoint," by William Grant Still, in Still, *William Grant Still and the Fusion of Cultures in American Music*, 64–65. There are remarkable similarities in William Grant Still's and Zenobia Powell Perry's upbringing. He was raised in Little Rock, Arkansas, by parents who "wanted us above all else to be good Americans and to get a substantial education, so that we could compete on an equal basis with all other Americans" (63). This summarized the Powell family values, as well.

[327] See D. Antoinette Handy, *Black Women in American Bands and Orchestras* (Metuchen, N.J.: Scarecrow Press, 1981).

[328] Perry, autobiographical essay, 10–11. Apparently appendicitis is common in her family. Her son and nephew both died of appendicitis, and her daughter, Janis, also had it. Perry told the story of her studies at Burrell Memorial Hospital after the story of her studies with R. Nathaniel Dett, so there is some confusion about which took place first.

[329] Zenobia Perry wrote about this period, "Political unrest was rampant and tearing the staunch fibers of Boley apart. The town was armed to meet aggression within its borders. My father's medical practice took him well beyond the town's perimeter. He was seriously injured near the town of Sand Creek which was in the same county as Boley but about seven miles southeast. The injuries were to his head and left leg and foot. Initially, he went to Kansas for treatment. When he was able to ambulate, the family moved to Altus, to Bartlesville, Pawhuska, and then to Tulsa where I became accompanist to choirs in one of the large black churches in the city."

[330] Perry, autobiographical essay, 12.

[331] Ibid.

[332] Ibid. Perry discussed her marriage in detail in another interview (September 30, 2001).

[333] Perry, interview (September 30, 2001).

NOTES

334 Ibid.

335 Perry, autobiographical essay, 13. Cortez Reece is discussed in more detail in chapter 7.

336 Perry, interview (February 2, 2002). Until my dissertation, Zenobia Perry listed her birth date as 1914 on all documents, program notes, and biographies.

337 Ibid.

338 Ibid.

339 Perry, autobiographical essay, 21.

340 Ibid. "I had spent two summer terms at Colorado State College of Education at Greeley, so I applied for and received a permit for leave of absence to complete the terminal degree during the whole of the next school year. I planned to take the summer off to spend with my family. My son, Lemuel, was now commendably advancing through primary school in Bartlesville, Oklahoma. We kept in touch by letters and occasional phone conversations. And I looked forward to vacations with my parents and him."

341 According to Janis-Rozena Peri, during World War II, her father had been on two ships that were bombed, and it deeply affected him his entire life. When he was a child, his mother sent him to a boarding school, which she thought was a private school for black boys; but it turned out instead to be a school for delinquent boys. He and his brother, ages 8 and 10, had to find their way back home, some one hundred miles, by foot (Peri, interview, May 8, 2001).

342 Perry, autobiographical essay, 21.

343 Ibid., 22.

344 Perry, interview (November 7, 2001).

345 Peri, interview (February 2, 2002).

346 Perry, autobiographical essay, 22.

347 He remarried, but had no other children. The divorce was not final until 1950 or 1951, when Janis was seven years old and Zenobia had moved to Arkansas.

348 Perry, interview (July 28, 1993).

349 The Registrar of the University of Northern Colorado in Greeley confirmed by phone (November 7, 2001) that Zenobia Perry received this degree on August 9, 1945. Mary Linscome at UNC Archives confirmed by phone (January 28, 2002) that the commencement was not held until June 5, 1946, and Zenobia Powell Perry's name is found in the commencement program.

350 Peri, interview (May 8, 2001).

351 Heilbrun.

352 The feminist author Virginia Woolf said this was crucial for any woman who desired to do creative work, in her groundbreaking collection of essays, *A Room of One's Own*, published originally in 1929 (San Diego: Harcourt, 1989).

353 Tania León, who teaches theory and composition at Brooklyn College in New York, is another rare example.

354 Heilbrun, 17–18.

NOTES

CHAPTER 9: Professional Teaching Career and Graduate School

[355] In another letter, Perry described her experiences of teaching at Mitchell's Mill: "I guess I've been naive all my life. I didn't know that even though I had been in school for two years already, it hadn't occurred to me that there would be no books, desks or anything for black kids. Mr. Love, the driver, let me off and told me he'd pick me up after three. There was a long hall and two rooms and a fireplace back-to-back in each room and a large desk and a stool in front of the desk. There was a [tree] stump that someone had brought in. No seats or anything. And I was supposed to teach students. The woman [Robby] who was supposed to be my master teacher wasn't there and I waited. School was supposed to start at 9 o'clock and at 9 there was no Robby, so I tried to find a bell and I found one, rang it and the children came in. I said, 'We don't have any seats but I think we can do something about that if you don't mind.' One girl said, 'My name is Maldothia Jackson and my mother said you better not put your hands on me.' She had her little brother—she was carrying him on her hip. I said, 'Maldothia, that's such a pretty name,' and it completely disarmed her. She put the kid down and I said, 'My name is Miss Powell. We're going down and cut some willows and we are going to learn to braid some rows and learn to make things out of rows.'"

[356] Perry, autobiographical essay, 15–16. Perry's own words about this black teacher training project are practically the only available description by a teacher about the program and its goals. This program had a tremendous impact on education for black youth in the South in the 1930s, '40s, and '50s.

[357] Ibid.

[358] Perry, interview (February 26, 2002).

[359] Elizabeth Studebaker, "Piano has taken Perry coast to coast," *Xenia Daily Gazette*, May 22, 2000. She quotes Zenobia Perry in this article, who recalled her conversations with Mrs. Roosevelt.

[360] Letter to Jeannie Pool, September 1993.

[361] See Perry, autobiographical essay, for more details on her work with this program.

[362] Originally published by Harper & Brothers (New York, 1961; reprint Da Capo Press, 1992), 182–83.

[363] Ibid., 183.

[364] In a letter, Zenobia Perry also described how she met Eleanor Roosevelt: "Mrs. Roosevelt was one of the visitors who came to Mitchell's Mill School. When she appeared I did not know who she was. She walked among the children, talking to them about what they were doing. After the 2nd day of her visit I was introduced to her when I reported on campus on the day's activities to the education department. She expressed her excitement and pleasure in what I was doing and recommended that I become a model teacher in education. Subsequently, she was my friend and I became a faculty member for three years."

[365] Perry, interview (July 21, 1993).

[366] Ibid.

[367] Zenobia Perry, letter to Jeannie Pool (September 1993).

[368] Ibid. Also Perry, interview (July 21, 1993).

[369] Perry, autobiographical essay, 17.

[370] Reece was not officially on the faculty of Langston University in 1939.

NOTES

[371] Perry, autobiographical essay, 18.

[372] Ibid., 19.

[373] Perry, interview (July 28, 1993).

[374] Ibid.

[375] Ibid.

[376] Perry and O'Rourke, interview (August 12, 1994).

[377] His and this statement are on the first inside page of the brochure, published c.1950.

[378] Brochure, under section entitled, "Founder's Day, 1949."

[379] Ibid., 2.

[380] Ibid.

[381] Ibid.

[382] The UAPB Home Page gives a brief history of the university, including a complicated summary of the campus's name changes through the years.

[383] A note to the author (September 27, 1994) from V. Davis, at the University of Arkansas, Pine Bluff, said Zenobia Perry was an assistant professor of music from 1949 until 1954.

[384] Grace D. Wiley, phone interview (September 10, 1994). Also on the faculty at that time were Gussie Dickey, who later moved to Detroit, and William Haithcock, a violinist, who later went to Morgan State in Baltimore. Wiley remembered that Kelton Lawrence also taught dance and maybe played the violin. Wiley had never studied with Zenobia Perry, although she had been a student at Pine Bluff.

[385] Peri, interview (May 8, 2001). It is clear from the college brochure that this training school was for student teachers and faculty and staff children, supervised by the college's Division of Education.

[386] Miss Davis at the Pine Bluff library told me by phone that Lawrence came in 1949.

[387] John L. Fuller, of West Virginia State College, confirmed in a letter (November 17, 1994) that Lawrence attended that school from 1939 to 1943 and that he had gone to East High School in Columbus, Ohio.

[388] The college brochure pictures the duo at two nine-foot concert grand pianos.

[389] Perry, interview (July 21, 1993).

[390] Bateson calls this "lives of multiple beginnings . . . and reinventions" (Bateson, 17).

CHAPTER 10: Becoming a Composer: Studies with Milhaud and Willman

[391] Many thanks to Jo Ann Haycraft, who gave me a copy of her Ph.D. dissertation, "Allan Arthur Willman, Pianist and Composer, 1909–1989" (Claremont Graduate University, 2001). She had studied piano and piano pedagogy with Willman in the 1950s.

[392] Haycraft, 73–74.

[393] Perhaps this refers to *Saudades do Brasil*, twelve numbers in two books from 1921?

[394] James C. Stratton, "Milhaud Concert Proves Highlight of Season at UW," *Laramie Republican Boomerang* (May 7, 1945). Haycraft's dissertation includes copies of the program announcements and the press reviews for this performance.

[395] Milhaud, 295. Willman's name is misspelled.

NOTES

[396] Maria Madigan, "A conversation with Allan Willman," *The Laramie Sunday Boomerang* (November 20, 1988), 12, a copy of which was generously provided by Frederick Gersten, former chair of the Department of Music, University of Wyoming.

[397] Haycraft, 52.

[398] Two photographs of Zenobia Perry at the University of Wyoming are also printed in this brochure. One is reprinted on page 130.

[399] According to Haycraft, "Willman taught composition, performed frequently and chose a few piano student but his main duties were administrative" (80).

[400] Haycraft, 2. He died on May 7, 1989, after a long illness, just before his eightieth birthday.

[401] Haycraft, 42–43.

[402] Haycraft's dissertation contains a rare photograph of Milhaud sitting at a table in the Willman home, working on this concerto.

[403] Ibid., 80.

[404] Slonimksy, 914.

[405] Ibid., 73. He mentions that Babin taught at the Aspen Music School from 1951 until 1954, but he does not mention the University of Wyoming.

[406] After hearing the Vronsky-Babin duo, Zenobia Perry decided it would be a good idea to have a piano duo at Arkansas to do recruiting; hence the duo with Kelton Lawrence: "It would attract students. If we had an interesting program, one which would appeal to the public, of two pianos, people would come to see this unusual thing, then send their kids to Arkansas."

[407] Janis Peri received the following letter from Allan Willman in 1978: "Dear Miss Peri, Your good letter gave me much pleasure. I have never forgotten the terms, some twenty or more years ago, when your mother and I worked together—and I have always hoped to hear of her activities since then. Please give her my warm regards. Mrs. Willman and I admired her dignity, her talent, her refinement. I do remember meeting you, too, at that time. What joy your fine career must certainly give your mother.... Please tell your mother that I have retired as chairman of the music department—and that we have a magnificent new building, one of the finest to be found anywhere. Every good wish. Do send word of yourself and your mother when time permits. Sincerely, Allan Willman."

[408] Perry, interview (September 30, 2001).

[409] A photograph of her class with Milhaud is found on page 130.

[410] It is not clear which summers Perry was at Aspen. On February 2, 2002, she told me that she was there in 1953, but she believed that Milhaud was not there that summer because of health problems. She also was there in 1954 and 1956; in 1956, she took Janis with her. On another occasion, she recalled that her last summer there was 1957.

[411] Bruce Berger, *A Tent in the Meadow: An Intimate Historical Perspective: Celebrating 50 Years of the Aspen Music Festival and School, 1949–1999* (Aspen, Colo.: Sojourner Publications, 1999), 20–21.

[412] Milhaud, 319. This was his description of the summer of 1951. Note that the autobiography was finished in Paris, March 1952, so any subsequent trips to Aspen would not be mentioned here.

[413] Berger, 31.

NOTES

[414] Although many of his students taught at Aspen, Allan Willman did not; he continued his friendship with Milhaud during those years.

[415] Ibid.

[416] Milhaud's life in the U.S. is not well documented and, in fact, the major works on his life and music were: Georges Beck, *Darius Milhaud Etude suivie du catalogue chronologigue complet de son oeuvre* (Paris: Heugel, 1949) and Milhaud's autobiography, *Notes Sans Musique* (Paris: 1949), later revised as *Ma Vie Heureuse* (*My Happy Life*), trans. by Donald Evans and Christopher Palmer (London: M. Boyars, 1994). His impact on American music, particularly on composition in California, needs further exploration. The Darius Milhaud Society can be reached in care of Dr. Katherine Warne, President, 15715 Chadbourne Road, Cleveland, OH 44120; 216-921-4548.

[417] Perry, interview (July 21, 1993). George Moore, assistant to Dave Brubeck, said that Howard and Henry are not in the photograph of Milhaud from the University of Wyoming, although Zenobia believed they were.

[418] Slonimsky, *Baker's Biographical Dictionary of 20th Century Classical Musicians,* ed. Laura Kuhn (New York: Schirmer Books, 1997), 176.

[419] Jeremy Drake, "Darius Milhaud," in *Groves 2000* 2nd ed. (London: Macmillan Publishing, 2001) 16:677.

[420] Ibid.

[421] Perry and O'Rourke, interview (August 12, 1994).

[422] Ibid.

[423] Ibid.

[424] Ibid.

[425] Mrs. Milhaud wrote to me (September 28, 1994) that she did not remember Zenobia Perry from Aspen. She urged me to contact Charles Jones in New York. She wrote, "Nobody is actually writing about Milhaud's activities in the States." Charles Jones also did not remember meeting Zenobia Perry at Aspen, but remembered black American composer Julia Perry (taped interview, October 1994, New York City).

[426] Peri, interview (May 8, 2001).

[427] Charles Jones had interesting stories to tell about the Milhauds and the Aspen Festival. His affiliation with Juilliard gave that school a prominent connection to the Aspen Festival, which previously had been primarily a West Coast project. In later years, it was often called "Juilliard West." A photograph of Charles Jones is found on page 133.

[428] Confirmed by a letter from Chairman Frederick Gersten from the University of Wyoming, Music Department (October 12, 1993). Even after Zenobia Perry moved to Ohio, she continued to correspond with Milhaud. When he was a visiting lecturer in Cleveland, she traveled there by bus, to have lessons with him and show him her scores.

[429] Lathardus Goggins, *Central State University: The First One Hundred Years, 1887–1987* (Wilberforce, Ohio: Central State University, 1987), 32. Goggins graduated from CSU in 1954 with a B.A. and taught geography at the University of Akron. He was a history scholar.

[430] Ibid., 20.

[431] Ibid., 33–35.

[432] Ibid., 35.

NOTES

[433] Ibid., 38.

[434] Ibid.

[435] Ibid., 53.

[436] Ibid.

[437] Dr. Lewis A. Jackson was president for a year. In 1965, Dr. Harry E. Groves became president; Dr. Herman R. Branson became president in 1968; Lewis Jackson again assumed the presidency; Dr. Lionel Hodge Newman became president in 1972; Dr. Arthur E. Thomas became president in 1985.

[438] Goggins, 57.

[439] Ibid.

[440] Ibid.

[441] Ibid.

[442] From a report to the Board of Trustees for 1950–51, quoted by Goggins, 51. This is modeled after Booker T. Washington's philosophy and practice at Tuskegee.

[443] Ibid., 5.

[444] Ibid., 58.

[445] Perry, interview (July 28, 1993). Dr. Wesley had one daughter who was an opera singer and another who was an accomplished pianist; he himself loved music and also sang.

[446] Eventually she was promoted to associate professor. Her tenure began October 5, 1955, two days after her 47th birthday.

[447] Peri, interview (May 8, 2001).

[448] O'Rourke.

[449] Goggins, 127.

[450] Perry and O'Rourke, interview (August 12, 1994). Beatrice O'Rourke retired in 1983, after thirty-seven years of service at CSU, and she died in 2004.

[451] Ibid.

[452] Peri, interview (May 8, 2001).

[453] Concert presented by the Inter-Denominational Ministers' Wives Alliance, at The Mt. Zion Baptist Church, Springfield, Ohio (May 1, 1977). He sang Perry's "Sinner Man So Hard, Believe!"

[454] Perry, interview (February 21, 2002).

[455] Goggins, 113.

[456] Many of her former students performed Perry's compositions and maintained a friendship over the years, including Jo Ann Lanier, Joyce Mathis, Roberta Alexander, Gwendolyn Walters, and Barbara Boyd. One of her former students is jazz bassist Cecil McBee, who teaches at New York University. When he was enrolled in the Oklahoma Jazz Hall of Fame in 1991, Perry was there. James Brady is also teaching at New York University. A native of Trinidad, Lennard Moses had given a command performance for the Queen of England at age 14. At CSU, where he was a percussion major in the 1970s, he had built steel drums. After attending Northern Illinois University, he returned to Central State to take Perry's position. It was very gratifying for her to pass the torch and to know that her own teaching benefited not only the students she taught, but the next generation, as well.

NOTES

[457] Melissa Kossler, "Perry writes her way into fame," *Xenia Daily Gazette* (May 14, 1993), 6.

[458] Perry, interview (July 21, 1993).

[459] These are discussed in chapter 11.

CHAPTER 11: Analysis of Musical Style and Selected Works

[460] See Emanuel Winternitz, *Musical Autographs: From Monteverdi to Hindemith*, 2 vols. (Princeton: Princeton University Press, 1955); an enlarged and corrected edition (published by Dover in 1965) contains an excellent introduction to the collection, explaining approaches to examining the facsimiles and what they reveal about a composer. Unfortunately, only one piece of Perry's is published and "engraved." Most performances of her pieces have been prepared from photocopies of her original manuscripts, which are in need of editing, particularly related to dynamics and articulations. There is no doubt that she would be more widely performed if her music were readily available in published format.

[461] Perry, interview (July 21, 1993).

[462] Ibid.

[463] Perry and O'Rourke, interview (August 12, 1994).

[464] See the list of works in appendix B.

[465] See pages 178 and 214 for some of Perry's own poetry. Two books of poetry were most important to Zenobia: *The Book of American Negro Poetry*, chosen and edited with an essay on "The Negro's Creative Genius" by James Weldon Johnson (New York: Harcourt, Brace, 1922), 1031; and *American Negro Poetry: An Anthology*, ed. Arna Bontemps (New York: Hill and Wang, 1974; originally published in 1963). Perry said she started to write her own lyrics, "because when I got the idea I didn't have time to wait to get somebody else's okay on using their poetry, so I just made my own." Perry, interview (July 21, 1993).

[466] This song is also used in the opera, *Tawawa House*.

[467] Claude McKay (1891–1948) was first published in his native Jamaica, British West Indies. In his early twenties, he went to Tuskegee Institute to study agriculture and then to Kansas State University. After two years, he moved to New York City, where he became involved in the literary life. He went to London in 1919 and published there a volume called *Spring in New Hampshire* (1920). When he returned to the United States in 1920, he became editor of *The Liberator*.

[468] Florence Price set at least nineteen poems by Paul Laurence Dunbar between 1932 and 1945, including "Sympathy," one of her best-known songs.

[469] "Kid Stuff" and "Drizzle" were recorded by Sebronette Barnes on the compact disc *You Can Tell the World* (Senrab Records). There is some confusion about the organization of the song cycles, because individual songs from these cycles have been performed separately and often were transposed for different vocal ranges. Some of the names of the song cycles have changed over the years and/or were incorrectly listed on concert programs.

[470] There are additional songs, but Perry would not make them available because she felt they needed revision.

[471] Lanyé [formerly Lanier], a native of Youngstown, Ohio, taught at John Carroll University and was resident conductor of the Accord Concert Choir. A graduate of the Cleveland Institute of Music, New England Conservatory, and Pacific Western University, she holds two Doctor of Musical Arts degrees in voice, the latter from the American Conservatory of Music in Chicago. She received fellowships to the Aspen Music Festival, Tanglewood/Berkshire Music Center, American Institute of Music Studies in Graz,

NOTES

Austria, and Lake George Opera Theatre. She has held music faculty positions at Central State University, Karamu Theatre in Cleveland, Coe College in Iowa, Knoxville College in Tennessee, and Berea College in Kentucky (from program notes from January 5, 1986, appearance at Dayton Art Institute, "Expressions in Black Song").

[472] Janis Peri began piano lessons at age four, and was an honor student throughout her school years in Xenia, Ohio. When she enrolled at Otterbein College—on full academic scholarship—Zenobia insisted that she enroll as a piano major, because she wanted Janis to be a musician first and a singer second, since, in her opinion, so many singers never became real musicians. Janis continued her vocal studies in graduate school at Miami University in Oxford, Ohio, where she performed with the Opera Theatre and appeared frequently as soloist with orchestra. Special study with Richard Miller at Oberlin College Conservatory of Music led to her winning the Kate Neal Kinley Award, which brought her to New York. While in graduate school, she changed her name to Janis-Rozena Peri. She continued her studies at the Manhattan School of Music, studying privately with Olga Ryss, Camilla Williams, and Minna Cravi-Bozza, and was coached by Pierre Boulez, Otta Guth, and Caroline Segrera. She has specialized in singing modern black music—works of contemporary composers. In the 1970s, Janis married Glover Parham, who was a member of the Broadway cast of *Porgy and Bess*, and sang the role of Jim and the Night Club singer in the American Theater Productions' road tour of *Bubbling Brown Sugar*. They were both active members of the New York Bahá'í Faith Community and they lived in Harlem. They later divorced. Janis was appointed assistant professor of music at Old Dominion University in August 1979. She made her Carnegie Hall debut in April 1971, singing the role of the "Mater Floriosa" in Mahler's *Eighth Symphony* with the Hartford Symphony, conducted by Arthur Winograd. She recorded for EAV Records, and toured throughout Europe in 1973–74 as "Frankie" in *Carmen Jones*, with the Schwitzer Tournee Theatre Productions. She appeared as soprano soloist in the distinguished CBS-TV two-part *Camera Three* program, *Gustave Mahler in New York*, with James Levine and Pierre Boulez. Zenobia Perry always made her daughter's concert gowns.

[473] Perry, interview (July 28, 1993).

[474] Peter G. Davis, "Music in Review: Janis-Rozena Peri Sings Demanding Recital Well," *New York Times*, May 22, 1977.

[475] See Jon Cruz, *Culture on the Margins: The Black Spiritual and the Rise of American Cultural Interpretation* (Princeton: Princeton University Press, 1999) for a fascinating analysis of the history of spirituals and the impact on the development of cultural studies in American intellectual development.

[476] James H. Cone, *The Spirituals and the Blues: An Interpretation* (New York: Seabury Press, 1972) describes the power of song in the struggle for black survival and offers a socio-historical and theological interpretation. He writes, "I affirmed the reality of the spirituals and blues as authentic expression of my humanity, responding to them in the rhythms of dance. I, therefore, write about the spirituals and the blues, *because I am the blues* and *my life is a spiritual*. Without them, I cannot be" (7).

[477] Still, 65.

[478] Cone, 6.

[479] Perry, along with other black Americans, was very concerned about what was replacing the music she knew and loved in the black community and in America, particularly some "black" popular music that glorified drug use, violence, and sexual exploitation and degradation.

NOTES

[480] Willi Apel, *Harvard Dictionary of Music*, 2nd ed. (Cambridge: Harvard University Press, 1974), 642.

[481] Ibid., 56.

[482] Ibid., 189.

[483] The neoclassicists of the period between the two world wars in Europe challenged this attitude, most notably Igor Stravinsky.

[484] The American Society of Music Arrangers and Composers [ASMAC] was founded in the 1940s by Arthur Lange, to fight for better contractual agreements and compensation for commercial arrangers.

[485] This song, sung in a gospel style, was very popular in the 1950s and '60s. Through her arrangement, Perry was able to remind the CSU community of the history of the anthem.

[486] The program gives the date of the piece as 1963, but it more likely was 1973.

[487] Zenobia Perry encountered resistance by performers and performing ensembles at Central State University to the use of experimental techniques in her works. They complained, "By the time we learn one of these works, we could have learned 100 other pieces." This kind of opposition to experimentation and new music is not unusual at universities, but, because she was female and the only composer on campus, Perry lacked the clout to have much impact on this situation. In retrospect, her most significant effect was by serving as a living and working composer in that university community.

[488] Mullins still has a community symphony based in Yellow Springs, Ohio.

[489] Programs for these performances have not been found.

[490] Letter from Zenobia Perry to Jo Ann Lanyé (January 19, 1988), as quoted in Lanier, 88–89.

[491] This is precisely the reason why many American composers have worked in film and television music: it is the only industry in this country that offers composers regular access to professional orchestral musicians. One writes a piece, then hears it, and then moves on to the next project, developing technique along the way.

[492] While writing this biography, the author has asked many black composers if they know of any orchestra at a black college or university and the answer is always "no."

[493] Program notes, Central State University, The University Concert Band (March 5, 1968). It was performed a second time by the same band on March 27, 1968, at the CSU University Ballroom.

[494] Perry, interview (July 28, 1993).

[495] Concert program, Cleveland Chamber Symphony (February 17, 1991).

[496] Robert Finn, "Orchestra Stylishly Handles New Black Compositions," *Cleveland Plain Dealer*, February 18 or 19, 1991.

[497] Perry had two non-professional recordings of this work.

[498] Perry, interview (July 21, 1993).

[499] Kossler, 6.

Bibliography

Addison, Gayle. *Oak and Ivy, A Biography of Paul Laurence Dunbar*. Garden City, N.Y.: Doubleday, 1971.

Anderson, E. Ruth. *Contemporary American Composers: A Biographical Dictionary*. Boston: G. K. Hall, 1976.

Apel, Willi. *Harvard Dictionary of Music*, 2nd ed. Cambridge: Harvard University Press, 1974.

Arvey, Verna. *In One Lifetime*. Fayetteville: University of Arkansas Press, 1984.

Austin, Charles M. *Paul Laurence Dunbar's Roots and Much More: A Scrapbook of His Life and Legacy*. Edited by James B. George. Dayton, Ohio: A Sense of Roots Publications, 1989.

Baker, T. Lindsay, and Julie P. Baker, eds. *The WPA Oklahoma Slave Narratives*. Norman: University of Oklahoma Press, 1996.

Baldwin, Sara Mull, ed. *Nebraskana: Biographical Sketches of Nebraska Men and Women of Achievement Who Have Been Awarded Life Membership in the Nebraskana Society*. Hebron, Nebr.: Baldwin Company, 1932.

Bate, Charles James. *"It's Been a Long Time" and We've Come a Long Way: A History of the Oklahoma Black Medical Providers (The Black Healers)*. Muskogee, Okla.: Hoffman Printing Company, 1986.

Bateson, Mary Catherine. *Composing a Life: Life As a Work in Progress*. New York: Penguin Books, 1990.

Beck, Georges. *Darius Milhaud Etude suivie du catalogue chronologique complet de son oeuvre*. Paris: Heugel, 1949.

Berger, Bruce. *A Tent in the Meadow: An Intimate Historical Perspective: Celebrating 50 Years of the Aspen Music Festival and School, 1949–1999*. Aspen, Colo.: Sojourner Publications, 1999.

Bergeron, Katherine, and Philip V. Bohlman, eds. *Disciplining Music: Musicology and Its Canons*. Chicago: University of Chicago Press, 1992.

Berry, Faith. *Before and Beyond Harlem: A Biography of Langston Hughes*. New York: Wings Books, 1983.

Bittle, William Elmer, and Gilbert Geis, with research assistance of Donald F. Parker. *The Longest Way Home: Chief Alfred C. Sam's Back-to-Africa Movement*. Detroit: Wayne State University Press, 1964.

BIBLIOGRAPHY

Block, Adrienne Fried. *Amy Beach, Passionate Victorian: The Life and Work of an American Composer, 1867–1944.* New York: Oxford University Press, 1998.

Bontemps, Arna, ed. *American Negro Poetry: An Anthology.* New York: Hill and Wang, 1974 (originally published in 1963).

Borroff, Edith. *Three American Composers.* Lanham, Md.: University Press of America, 1986.

Bortin, Virginia. *Elinor Remick Warren: A Bio-bibliography.* Westport, Conn.: Greenwood Press, 1993.

———. *Elinor Remick Warren: Her Life and Music.* Composers of North America 5. Metuchen, N.J.: Scarecrow Press, 1987.

Bowman, Wayne D. *Philosophical Perspectives on Music.* New York: Oxford University Press, 1998.

Brooks, Christopher. "R. Nathaniel Dett." *The New Grove Dictionary of Music and Musicians.* Edited by Stanley Sadie and John Tyrrell. 2nd ed. New York: Oxford University Press, 2001, 17:259.

Brown, R[ae] L[inda]. "William Grant Still, Florence Price, and William Dawson: Echoes of the Harlem Renaissance." In *Black Music of the Harlem Renaissance.* Edited by S. Floyd, Jr., and J. Wright. Westport, Conn.: Greenwood Press, 1990, 71–86.

———. "Selected Orchestral Music of Florence B. Price (1888–1953) in the Context of Her Life and Work." Ph.D. diss., Yale University, 1987.

Capture, George P. Horse. *Powwow.* Cody, Wyo.: Buffalo Bill Historical Center, 1989.

Cazort, Jeane E., and Constance Tibbs Hobson. *Born to Play: The Life and Career of Hazel Harrison.* Contributions to the Study of Music and Dance 3. Westport, Conn.: Greenwood Press, 1983.

Citron, Marcia. "Feminist Approaches to Musicology." In *Cecilia Reclaimed: Feminist Perspectives on Gender and Music.* Edited by Susan C. Cook and Judy S. Tsou. Urbana: University of Illinois Press, 1994.

———. "Gender, Professionalism and the Musical Canon." *Journal of Musicology* 8 (1991): 533–43.

Cohen, Aaron I. *International Encyclopedia of Women Composers*, 1st ed. New York: R. R. Bowker, 1981.

Cone, James H. *The Spirituals and the Blues: An Interpretation.* New York: Seabury Press, 1972.

Cook, Nicholas, and Mark Everist, eds. *Rethinking Music.* Oxford: Oxford University Press, 1999.

Cotterill, R. S. *The Southern Indians: The Story of the Civilized Tribes Before Removal.* Norman: University of Oklahoma Press, 1954.

Cox, Bette Yarbrough. *Central Avenue—Its Rise and Fall (1890–c.1955) including the Musical Renaissance of Black Los Angeles.* Los Angeles: BEEM Publications, 1993, 1996.

BIBLIOGRAPHY

Crockett, Norman L. "Witness to History: Booker T. Washington Visits Boley." *Chronicles of Oklahoma* 67 (Winter 1989–90): 382–91.

Cronen, David E. *Black Moses: The Story of Marcus Garvey and the Universal Negro Improvement Association*, 2nd ed. Madison: University of Wisconsin Press, 1981.

Cruz, Jon. *Culture on the Margins: The Black Spiritual and the Rise of American Cultural Interpretation*. Princeton, N.J.: Princeton University Press, 1999.

Dalton, Ulysses Grant. "The Music Department of the University of Arkansas at Pinebluff: Its Development and Role in Music Education in the State of Arkansas, 1873–1973." Ph.D. diss., University of Arkansas, Pine Bluff, 1981.

Dinnerstein, Leonard, Roger L. Nichols, and David M. Reimers. *Natives and Strangers: Ethnic Groups and the Building of America*. Oxford: Oxford University Press, 1979.

Dolphin-Ashley, Velma. "A History of Boley, Oklahoma." Master's thesis, Kansas State Teachers College [now Pittsburg State University], 1940.

Drake, Jeremy. "Darius Milhaud." *The New Grove Dictionary of Music and Musicians*. Edited by Stanley Sadie and John Tyrrell. 2nd ed. New York: Oxford University Press, 2001, 16:674–83.

Dramer, Kim. *Native Americans and Black Americans*. Philadelphia: Chelsea House Publishers, 1997.

Earle, Jonathan. *The Routledge Atlas of African American History*. New York: Routledge, 2000.

Eastman, Charles Alexander. *The Indian To-day*. Garden City, N.Y.: Doubleday, Page, 1915.

Floyd, Samuel A., Jr. *Black Music in the United States: An Annotated Bibliography*. White Plains, N.Y.: Kraus International Publications, 1983.

———, ed. *International Dictionary of Black Composers*. 2 vols. Chicago: Fitzroy Dearborn Publishers, 1999.

———. *The Power of Black Music: Interpreting Its History from Africa to the United States*. New York: Oxford University Press, 1995.

Floyd, Samuel A., Jr., and Marsha J. Reisser. *Black Music Biography: An Annotated Bibliography*. White Plains, N.Y.: Kraus International Publications, 1987.

Forbes, Jack D. *Africans and Native Americans: The Language of Race and the Evolution of Red-Black Peoples*. Urbana: University of Illinois Press, 1993.

Fuell, Melissa. *Blind Boone: His Early Life and His Achievements*. Kansas City: Burton, 1915.

Gaster, Adrian, ed. *International Who's Who in Music and Musicians' Directory*, 9th ed. Cambridge: International Who's Who in Music, 1980.

Gilroy, Paul. *The Black Atlantic: Modernity and Double Consciousness*. Cambridge: Harvard University Press, 1993.

Goggins, Lathardus. *Central State University: The First One Hundred Years, 1887–1987*. Wilberforce, Ohio: Central State University, 1987.

Green, Michael D. *The Creeks: A Critical Bibliography*. Bloomington: Indiana University Press, 1979.

Green, Mildred Denby. *Black Women Composers: A Genesis*. Boston: G. K. Hall, 1983.

Hale, Douglas. "European Immigrants in Oklahoma." *Chronicles of Oklahoma* 52 (1975).

Hamilton, Kenneth Marvin. *Black Towns and Profit: Promotion and Development in the Trans-Appalachian West, 1877–1915*. Urbana: University of Illinois Press, 1991.

Handy, D. Antoinette. *Black Music: Opinions & Reviews*. Ettrick, Va.: BM&M, 1974.

———. *Black Women in American Bands and Orchestras*. Metuchen, N.J.: Scarecrow Press, 1981.

Hardy, Debby. *Wyoming University: The First 100 Years*. Laramie: University of Wyoming, 1999.

Haskins, James. *Black Music in America: A History Through Its People*. New York: T. Y. Crowell, 1987.

Haycraft, Jo Ann. "Allan Arthur Willman, Pianist and Composer, 1909–1989." Ph.D. diss., Claremont Graduate University, 2001.

Heilbrun, Carolyn G. *Writing a Woman's Life*. New York: Ballantine Books, 1988.

Helmig, Martina. *Ruth Schonthal: Ein Kompositorischer Werdegung*. Hildesheim: Olms, 1994.

Herle, A. "Dancing Community: Powwow and Pan-Indianism in North America." In *Cambridge Anthropology* XVII, no. 2 (1994). Special issue, "Living Traditions: Continuity and Change, Past and Present."

Heth, Charlotte. "Overview" on Native American music in "The United States and Canada." *The Garland Encyclopedia of World Music*. Edited by Ellen Koskoff. New York: Garland Publishing, 2001, 3:367–68.

———, ed. *Native American Dance: Ceremonies and Social Traditions*. Washington, D.C.: National Museum of the American Indian, Smithsonian Institution with Starwood Publishing, 1992.

———, prod. Various recordings of Creek Indian Music for Smithsonian Museum.

Hill, Mozell C. "The All-Negro Communities of Oklahoma: The Natural History of a Social Movement: Part I." *Journal of Negro History* 31, no. 3 (July 1946): 254–68.

Holly, Ellistine Perkins. *Biographies of Black Composers and Song Writers*. Dubuque, Iowa: William C. Brown, 1990.

Horne, Aaron, comp. *Keyboard Music of Black Composers: A Bibliography*. Music Reference Collection 37. Westport, Conn.: Greenwood Press, 1992.

———. *String Music of Black Composers*. Music Reference Collection 33. New York: Greenwood Press, 1991.

"In Memoriam." *CBMR Digest* 17, no. 1 (Spring 2004): 11.

BIBLIOGRAPHY

Jahoda, Gloria. *The Trail of Tears: The Story of the American Indian Removals, 1813–1855.* New York: Wings Books, 1975; repr. 1995.

Jenkins, Everett, Jr. *Pan-African Chronology III: A Comprehensive Reference to the Black Quest for Freedom in African, the Americas, Europe and Asia, 1914–1929.* Jefferson, N.C.: McFarland & Company, 2001.

Johnson, David Lee. "The Contributions of William L. Dawson to the School of Music at Tuskegee Institute and to Choral Music." Ph.D. diss., University of Illinois at Urbana-Champaign, 1987.

Johnson, James Weldon, ed. *The Book of American Negro Poetry.* New York: Harcourt, Brace, 1922.

Katz, William Loren. *Black Indians: A Hidden Heritage.* New York: Atheneum, 1986.

———. *Black People Who Made the Old West.* Trenton, N.J.: Africa World Press, 1992.

———. *The Black West: A Documentary and Pictorial History,* rev. ed. Garden City, N.Y.: Doubleday Anchor Book, 1973. Repr. New York: Touchstone, 1996.

Katz, William, and Paula A. Franklin. *Proudly Red and Black.* New York: Atheneum, 1993.

Kaufman, Frederick, and John P. Guckin. *The African Roots of Jazz.* Sherman Oaks, Calif.: Alfred Publishing, 1979.

Kebede, Ashenafi. *Roots of Black Music: The Vocal, Instrumental, and Dance Heritage of Africa and Black America.* Englewood Cliffs, N.J.: Prentice-Hall, 1982.

Koskoff, Ellen, ed. *The Garland Encyclopedia of World Music.* New York: Garland Publishing, 2001.

———. *Women and Music in Cross-Cultural Perspective.* Urbana: University of Illinois Press, 1989.

Kubik, Gerhard. *Africa and the Blues.* Jackson: University Press of Mississippi, 1999.

Lanier, Jo Ann. "The Concert Songs of Zenobia Powell Perry." D.M.A. paper, American Conservatory of Music, 1988.

Lems-Dvorkin, Carol. *Africa in Scott Joplin's Music.* Evanston, Ill.: C. Lems-Dvorkin, 1991.

Lewis, Edgar, Jr. *A History of the Department of Music, University of Wyoming.* Laramie: University of Wyoming, 1998.

Lovell, John, Jr. *Black Song: The Forge and the Flame.* New York: Macmillan, 1972.

Lovett, Bobby L. *The African-American History of Nashville, Tennessee, 1780–1930: Elites and Dilemmas.* Fayetteville: University of Arkansas Press, 1999.

Low, W. A., and Virgil A. Clift. *Encyclopedia of Black America.* New York: McGraw-Hill, 1981.

Malone, Mark Hugh. "William Levi Dawson: American Music Educator." Ph.D. diss., Florida State University, 1981.

BIBLIOGRAPHY

McBrier, Vivian Flagg. *R. Nathaniel Dett: His Life and Works (1882–1943)*. Sigma Pi Phi Series. Washington, D.C.: Associated Publishers, 1977.

McLoughlin, William G. "Red Indians, Black Slavery and White Racism: America's Slaveholding Indians." *American Quarterly* 26, no. 4 (October 1974): 367–85.

Milhaud, Darius. *Notes Without Music: The Autobiography of Darius Milhaud*. New York: Alfred A. Knopf, 1952.

Monson, Ingrid, ed. *The African Diaspora: A Musical Perspective*. New York: Garland Publishing, 2000.

Moore, Undine Smith. "My Life in Music." *IAWM Journal* 3, no. 1 (February 1997): 9–15.

Nash, Gary B. *Red, White, and Black: The Peoples of Early America*. Englewood Cliffs, N.J.: Prentice-Hall, 1974.

Nettl, Bruno. *North American Indian Musical Styles*. Philadelphia: American Folklore Society, 1954.

Neuls-Bates, Carol. *Women in Music: An Anthology of Source Readings from the Middle Ages to the Present*, rev. ed. Boston: Northeastern University Press, 1996.

Payne, Mike. "Muse Visits Musician Early: Composer Heard Life's Calling in Sweet Chords Long Ago." *Ohio's Heritage* (Winter 1995–96): 6–7.

Perry, Zenobia Powell. Untitled autobiographical essay. May 1977.

Pool, Jeannie. "A Conversation with Pianist Althea Waites: Sexism, Racism, and Music." *IAWM Journal* (October 1994): 8–14.

———. "A Critical Approach to the History of Women in Music." *Heresies* 10 (Fall 1980): 2–5.

———. "Interview with Zenobia Powell Perry." *Music of the Americas*, KPFK-Radio Los Angeles, October 1993. Also broadcast on WYSO, Yellow Springs, Ohio, October 1993.

———. "The Life and Music of Zenobia Powell Perry: An American Composer." Ph.D. diss., Claremont Graduate University, 2002.

———. "Twentieth Century String Quartets by Women Composers." *Working Papers on Women in Music*. Northridge, Calif.: Institute for the Study of Women in Music, 1985.

———. "Zenobia Powell Perry." *Triangle of Mu Phi Epsilon* (Winter 2003): 26.

———. "Zenobia Powell Perry." *Composer USA* (Winter 2003–04): 11.

Pool, Jeannie, and Beverly Simmons. "Royal Celebration of Zenobia Perry's 95th Birthday." *IAWM Journal* 10, no. 1 (2004): 16–17.

Powers, William K. *War Dance: Plains Indian Musical Performance*. Tucson: University of Arizona Press, 1990.

Redkey, Edwin S. *Black Exodus*. New Haven, Conn.: Yale University Press, 1969.

Rehrig, William H. *The Heritage Encyclopedia of Band Music: Composers and Their Music*. Edited by Paul E. Bierley. 3 vols. Westerville, Ohio: Integrity Press, 1991.

BIBLIOGRAPHY

Roach, Hildred. *Black American Music: Past and Present*. Boston: Crescendo Publishing Co., 1973.

Roberts, John Storm. *Black Music of Two Worlds: African, Caribbean, Latin, and African-American Traditions*. New York: Schirmer Books, 1998.

Sameth, Sigmund. "Creek Negroes: A Study of Race Relations." Master's thesis, University of Oklahoma, 1940.

Sartwell, Crispin. *Act Like You Know: African-American Autobiography and White Identity*. Chicago: University of Chicago Press, 1998.

Simpson, Anne Key. *Follow Me: The Life and Music of R. Nathaniel Dett*. Metuchen, N.J.: Scarecrow Press, 1993.

———. *Hard Trials: The Life and Music of Harry T. Burleigh*. Metuchen, N.J.: Scarecrow Press, 1990.

Slonimsky, Nicolas, ed. *Baker's Biographical Dictionary of Musicians*, 8th ed. New York: Schirmer Books, 1992.

Small, Christopher. *Music of the Common Tongue: Survival and Celebration of Afro-American Music*. London: John Calder Riverrun Press, 1987.

Smith, Catherine Parsons, ed. *William Grant Still: A Study in Contradictions, with Essays by Gayle Marchison and Willard Gatewood and Contemporary Sources from the 1930s*. Berkeley and Los Angeles: University of California Press, 2000.

Smith, Catherine Parsons, and Cynthia S. Richardson. *Mary Carr Moore, American Composer*. Ann Arbor: University of Michigan Press, 1987.

Smith, Eric Ledell. *Blacks in Opera*. Jefferson, N.C.: McFarland, 1995.

Smith, Hale. "Africa-American Music: The Hidden Tradition." *Chicago Symphony Orchestra Stagebill*, Spring 1995.

Smyth, Willie, ed. *Songs of Indian Territory: Native American Music Traditions of Oklahoma*. Oklahoma City: Center of the American Indian, 1989.

Southern, Eileen. "Afro-American Music." *The New Grove Dictionary of American Music*. Edited by H. Wiley Hitchcock and Stanley Sadie. New York: Grove's Dictionaries of Music, 1986, I:13.

———. *Biographical Dictionary of Afro-American and African Musicians*. Westport, Conn.: Greenwood Press, 1982.

———. *The Music of Black Americans: A History*, 3rd ed. New York: W. W. Norton, 1997.

———. *Readings in Black American Music*. New York: W. W. Norton, 1971.

Spady, J. G. *William L. Dawson: A Umum Tribute and a Marvelous Journey*. Philadelphia: Creative Artists' Workshop, 1981.

Speck, Frank, Leonard Broom, and Will West Long. *Cherokee Dance and Drama*. Berkeley and Los Angeles: University of California Press, 1951. Reprinted Norman: University of Oklahoma Press, 1983.

Spencer, Jon Michael. *The New Negroes and Their Music: The Success of the Harlem Renaissance*. Knoxville: University of Tennessee Press, 1997.

Stewart-Green, Miriam. *Women Composers: A Checklist of Works for the Solo Voice.* Boston: G. K. Hall, 1980.

Still, Judith Anne, ed. *William Grant Still and the Fusion of Cultures in American Music.* Flagstaff, Ariz.: Master-Player Library, 1972.

Strong, Willie. "Dawson, William Levi." *The New Grove Dictionary of Music and Musicians.* Edited by Stanley Sadie and John Tyrrell. 2nd ed. New York: Oxford University Press, 2001, 7:85.

Sweet, Jill Drayson. *Dances of the Tewa Pueblo Indians: Expressions of New Life.* Santa Fe, N.Mex.: School of American Research Press, 1985.

Theisz, R. D., and Ben Black Bear. *Songs and Dances of the Lakota.* Rosebud, S.Dak.: Sinte Gleska College, 1976. Reprinted Aberdeen, S.Dak.: North Plains Press, 1984.

Thompson, Marilyn. "The Hampton University Choir: Singing and Building a Priceless Tradition." *The Western Journal of Black Studies* 12, no. 4 (1988): 215–19.

Tick, Judith. *Ruth Crawford Seeger: A Composer's Search for American Music.* New York: Oxford University Press, 1997.

Vennum, Thomas, Jr. *The Ojibwa Dance Drum: Its History and Construction.* Washington, D.C.: Smithsonian Institution Press, 1982.

Walker-Hill, Helen. *Black Women Composers: A Century of Piano Music, 1893–1990.* Bryn Mawr, Penn.: Hildegard Publishing Co., 1992.

———. *From Spirituals to Symphonies: African American Women Composers and Their Music.* Urbana: University of Illinois Press, 2007.

———. *Piano Music by Black Women Composers: A Catalog of Solo and Ensemble Works.* Music Reference Collection 35. New York: Greenwood Press, 1992.

Washington, Booker T. "Boley: A Negro Town in the West." *The Outlook* 88 (January 4, 1908): 28–31.

Wesley, Charles H. "Lincoln's Plan for Colonizing the Emancipated Negro." *Journal of Negro History* IV (1919): 7–21.

Wickett, Murray R. *Contested Territory: Whites, Native Americans, and African Americans in Oklahoma, 1865–1907.* Baton Rouge: Louisiana State University Press, 2000.

Wiggins, Lida Keck. *The Life and Works of Paul Laurence Dunbar.* Naperville, Ill.: J. L. Nichols, c.1907.

Winternitz, Emanuel. *Musical Autographs: From Monteverdi to Hindemith.* 2 vols. Princeton: Princeton University Press, 1955.

Woolf, Virginia. *A Room of One's Own.* San Diego, Calif.: Harcourt, 1989.

Zaimont, Judith Lang, "String Quartets by Women: Report on Two Conferences." *The Musical Woman: An International Perspective, Vol. II, 1984–1985.* Edited by Judith Lang Zaimont, Catherine Overhauser, and Jane Gottlieb. New York: Greenwood Press, 1987.

"Zenobia Perry's Works Heard." *Mu Phi Epsilon Triangle* 81, no. 3 (1987): 17.

Zinsser, William. *Writing to Learn.* New York: Harper & Row Publishers, 1989.

BIBLIOGRAPHY

Zuberi, Tukufu. *Thicker Than Blood: How Racial Statistics Lie*. Minneapolis: University of Minnesota Press, 2001.

Newspapers

Boley Beacon
Boley Progress
Cleveland Plain Dealer
Dayton Daily News
Dayton Journal Herald
Laramie Republican Boomerang
Los Angeles Times
New York Amsterdam News
New York Times
Oklahoma Eagle
Xenia [Ohio] Daily Gazette

Web Sites

Center for Black Music Research. Columbia College, Chicago, Ill. www.colum.edu/cbmr.
Culver Crest Publications. www.culvercrest.com.
Paul Laurence Dunbar House State Memorial. Dayton, Ohio. http://ohsweb.ohiohistory.org/places/sw03/index.shtml.
International Alliance for Women in Music. www.iawm.org.
Meharry Medical College. Nashville, Tenn. www.mmc.edu.
Mu Phi Epsilon International Music Fraternity. http://home.muphiepsilon.org.
National Afro-American Museum & Cultural Center. Wilberforce, Ohio. http://ohsweb.ohiohistory.org/places/sw13/index.shtml.
Perry, Zenobia Powell. www.zenobiapowellperry.org.
Pool, Jeannie Gayle. www.jeanniepool.org.
University of California, Los Angeles. www.ucla.edu.
William Grant Still Music. Flagstaff, Ariz. www.williamgrantstill.com.

Index

ABC [American Broadcasting Company], 89
Abdul, Raoul, xvii, 203, 217
"Accent on the Arts," 202
Accompanying Skills for Pianists and *Sight Play with Skillful Eyes*, 215
Accord Concert [Chamber] Choir, 207, 209, 244
ACHE [Alabama Center for Higher Education], 204
Adam, Claus, 129
Adams, H. Leslie, xix, 215
Addison, Gayle, 219
Adept New American Museum for the Art of the Southwest, Mount Vernon, N.Y., 230
adoption of freedmen, 61
Africa, 44, 56, 97
African American Art Song Alliance, 215
African-American History of Nashville, Tennessee, The, 20
African diaspora, 226
African Diaspora: A Musical Perspective, 42, 226
African Methodist Episcopal Church [AME], 176
African Methodist Episcopal Church, Boley, Okla., 77, 84, 106, 117, 120, 229, 230
African Pioneer, 225
African slaves, viii, 4, 141, 161, 176, 214, 216, 222, 223
Afro-American Chamber Music Society [Orchestra], 183, 212
Afro-American Composers Festival, Detroit, Mich., 169
"Agnus Dei," 188, 197; see also *Mass in F# minor*

*"Aftermath"—See *Narrative*
*"Ah Got a Home in a Dat Rock," 155, 158, 159, 162, 185, 197, 198, 201
"Ain't That Good News," 91
Akron Junior Chamber of Commerce, 197
Alabama, 1, 102, 114
Alabama Center for Higher Education [ACHE], 204
Alabama State University, 69
Albany Records, 215
Albright College, 213
Alexander, Roberta, 243
American Association of University Women, 191, 197, 199
American Conservatory of Music, Chicago, 82, 88, 216, 244
American in Paris (George Gershwin), 128
American Society of Composers, Authors and Publishers [ASCAP], xiii, 10, 183, 185, 246
American Society of Music Arrangers and Composers, 246, 258
American Symphony Orchestra, 90
Amite, La., 103
Amos, Alvin E., 192, 198, 200
Anderson, Garland, 196
Anderson, Marian, 35, 93
Anderson, Thomas Jefferson (T. J.), 6
*"Angels Done Bowed Down, The"—See "O de Angels Done Bowed Down"
Anna Howard Matthews Choir, 204
Anniston, Ala., 88
Antelope Valley College, 215
Antioch College, Yellow Springs, Ohio, 175, 192, 208, 209
Antioch Missionary Baptist Church, 76, 77, 233
Antioch [String] Quartet, 192

257

INDEX

Apel, Willi, 246
Appleby-Weinberg, Brian, 204, 210
Arabic language, 150
Arcasonic Piano Company, St. Louis, 120
Archbishop of Canterbury, 76
Ardmore, Okla., 35
*"Arioso," 150, 152; see also *The Hidden Words*
Arizona, 86
Arkansas, 1, 57, 106, 107, 119, 120, 128, 136, 196, 216, 241
Arkansas Agricultural, Mechanical and Normal College [A. A. M. & N.], 1, 29, 106, 118, 119, 120, 136, 166, 182, 185, 195
Arkansia, 122, 169, 175, 185, 196
Armstrong, Louis, 33
Armstrong, T. B., 222
Army Air Corps, 125
Aronson, Maurice, 124
arrangement (musical), 157–58
Arrowwood Elementary School, Xenia, Ohio, 212
Art Institute, Dayton, Ohio, 196, 225
Arvey, Verna, 7, 227
ASCAP—See American Society of Composers, Authors, and Publishers
Aspen Conference on Contemporary Music, 1, 122, 182
Aspen Music Festival, x, 79, 129, 136, 182, 196, 244
Aspen Music School [Aspen Summer School and Conference], x, 79, 127, 129, 196, 241, 242
Atlanta Exposition, 30
Atmosphere Cycle, 193, 198; see also *Threnody*
Auerbach, Elise, 193, 212, 213
Austin, Charles M., 219
Austria, Steve, 212

Bahá'í faith, 145, 147, 201, 202, 210, 245
Babin, Victor, 120, 127, 128, 129, 241
Bach, Carl Philipp Emanuel, 71
Bach, Johann Sebastian, 71, 120, 128, 196
Bach [J. S.]-Busoni [Ferruccio], 236
Back-to-Africa movement, 33
Bacon, Ernst, 127, 134
Baiocchi, Regina Harris, 6, 217
Baker, Josephine, 33
Baker, Julie P., 222
Baker, T. Lindsay, 222

Baker's Biographical Dictionary of Musicians, 216
Baldwin, Sara Mull, 232
Ball State University, 212
Ballet Russe, 126
Banks, Elsie Harriet, 198
"Barcarolle" (R. Nathaniel Dett), 196, 202
Barnes, Marysue, 126
Barnes, Sebronette, 145, 193, 207, 208, 210, 211, 212, 213, 216, 244
Barnett, Abigail, 17, 18, 220
Barnett, James, 18
Barron, Alice, 76
Bartlesville, Okla., 99, 101, 102, 103, 114, 238
Bartók, Béla, 156
Bartolotta, William, 203
Bate, Charles James, ix
Bateson, Gregory, 218
Bateson, Mary Catherine, 8, 9, 11, 74, 79, 218, 219, 232, 240
Battle Creek, Mich., 82
Battles, Clyde, 198
Beach, Amy, 7, 11, 108, 217
bebop, 44
Beck, Georges, 242
Becker, Robert, 125, 126
Beethoven, Ludwig van, 11, 84, 126, 157
"Behold the Star," 91
Behrend, Jeanne, 126
Beittel, Barbara, 198
Bellview, Rusk County, Tex., 222
*"Benediction," 149–50, 203, 205, 206, 209; see also *Threnody*
Benton, Ky., 105
"Berceuse" from *Jocelyn* (Benjamin Godard), 99
Berea College, Ky., 245
Bergen, Edgar, 89
Berger, Bruce, 241
Berlin Hochschule für Musik, 127
Bernstein, Leonard, 11
Berryman, Cecil Wells and Alice Virginia, 72, 73, 237
Bethune, Mary McLeod, 110, 112
biographical writing, 6, 7, 8, 9, 10, 11, 95, 107
*"Bit of Fun, A"—See *Arkansia*
Bittle, William E., 225
Bizet, Georges, 204
Black, Betty R., x, 235
Black Atlantic, The, 42

258

INDEX

Black Bear, Ben, 226
Black History Month, 44
black Indians, vii, 16, 52, 56, 57, 58, 59, 60, 61, 63, 224, 228, 229
black medical care providers, 34
Black Patti, 89
Blakely, Art, 226
Blakely, Faye, 207
Bland, Ed, 48, 51, 227, 228
Blandenberg, Pat, 200
Blind Boone, 71, 231
Block, Adrienne Fried, 7, 217
Blossom, Tex., 23
Blue Feather, 63
Bluefield State College, W.Va., 86
blues, 41, 45, 49, 71, 130, 171
Boatner, Edward H., 88
Boddie, June, 200
Bogan, Kathleen, 196
Boggman, Miss, 233
Bohlman, Philip V., 225
Boley, "Captain" William, 18
Boley, J. B., 18
Boley, Okla., ix, 2, 12, 13, 14, 16, 17, 25, 26, 27, 31, 32, 34, 62, 63, 67, 68, 70, 71, 72, 73, 74, 75, 76, 77, 78, 99, 113, 181, 195, 219, 224, 230, 231, 234, 237
Boley Beacon, The, 19
Boley High School, 181
"Boley March, The," 14
Boley Museum, The, ix, 34, 220, 231
Boley Music Publishing Company, 14
Boley Progress, 19, 22, 219, 222, 224, 225
Boley Public School System, 75
Boley Rodeo & Bar-b-Q Festival, 224
Boley Town Council, 16, 221
Bolinga Black Cultural Resources Center, 199
Bonds, Margaret, xvii, 6, 8, 217
Bontemps, Arna, 244
Bortin, Virginia, 7, 217
Boston, Mass., 216
Boston Conservatory of Music, 137
Boston Symphony Orchestra, 124
Boston University, 216
Boulanger, Nadia, 4, 82, 84, 124, 126, 127, 234
Boulez, Pierre, 245
Bowie, Burrell, 197
Bowling, Lance, ix
Bowman, Deborah, 199
Boyd, Barbara, 243

Boyle, Hale, 128
Bradley, O. H., 35, 222, 225
Brady, James, 243
Braithwaite, Ronald, 204
Braithwaite, William Stanley, 147, 188
Brandt, Louis, 82
Branson, Herman R., 243
British Columbia, Canada, 163-64, 199
Britten, Benjamin, 134
Britten, Crystal, 218
Brockman, Mrs., 81
Brooks, Joanne, ix
Brooks, Robert, 210
Broom, Leonard, 226
Brown, Rae Linda, 7, 217
Brown, Robert, 204
Brown, Steven, 205
Brownbag Concerts, xvii
Brubeck, Dave, 131, 182, 197, 242
Brubeck, Henry, 130, 131, 242
Brubeck, Howard, 130, 131, 242
Bruno, Mauro, 228
Bryn Mawr, Penn., 216
Bubbling Brown Sugar, 245
Burch, Mattie, 199
Bureau of Indian Affairs [BIA], 59, 63
Burge, Louise, 69
Burke Act, 18, 220
Burleigh, Harry T., 7, 69, 94, 217
Burrell Memorial Hospital, 98, 237
Burt, Matthew, 93
Busch, Carl, 88
Bushman, Robin, 203
Busoni, Ferruccio, 69

Caldwell, William, 179
California Institute of the Arts, 211
California State University, Northridge [CSUN], 204, 205
Callaghan, Mr., 70
Calvary United Methodist Church, 204
Cambria Archives, 215, 230
Cambria Master Recordings, 215
Cambridge, Mass., 137, 216
Cameron, Deborah, 96
Canada Council Arts Festival, 163, 182, 199
Canivan, Paula, 200
Cantata—See *Sing Unto the Lord a New Song*
Capers, Valerie, 217
Capriccio, for solo piano, 185, 196
Capriccios, 185

INDEX

Capture, George P. Horse, 226
Carmen Jones (Georges Bizet), 245
Carnegie, Andrew, 29
Carnegie Recital Hall, 145, 182, 201
Carnine, Harry J., 126
Carpenter, John, 196
Carr, Jackie O., 205
Carroll, Donald, 179, 205
Carter, Benny, 227
Carter, Elliott, 134
Carter, Karen, 204
Carver, George Washington, 29, 87
Carver Elementary School, 120
Carver Junior High School Auditorium, 195, 236
Casper, Wyo., 125, 133, 166, 192
Castle, Okla., 18
Caston, Saul, 192
Catalfano, Joyce, 209, 213
Cauldron, The (John Carroll University), 207
Cavatina, op. 26 (Gustave Hollander), 99
Cavil, H. C., 220, 222
Cazort, Jeane E., 230, 236
CBMR Digest (Center for Black Music Research), 216
CBS [Columbia Broadcasting System], 89
Cecil Berryman Conservatory (Studio), Omaha, 72–73, 181
Centennial Convention, Mu Phi Epsilon International Fraternity, xviii
Center for Black Music Research, ix, xxi, 155, 216, 235
Central Avenue, Los Angeles, 236
Central City, Nebr., 72
Central Ohio Composers Alliance, 206, 208
Central State [College] University [CSU], Wilberforce, Ohio, ix, 2, 29, 106, 122, 134, 135, 136, 137, 139, 140, 163, 164, 166, 169, 178, 179, 182, 188, 192, 196, 197, 198, 199, 200, 201, 202, 203, 204, 205, 207, 208, 210, 213, 216, 224, 225, 227, 242, 243, 245, 246
Central Tennessee College, 20, 21, 221
*"Certainly Lord," 158, 185
Chambers, C. C., 222
Chautauqua, Yellow Springs, Ohio, 207
Cherokees, 57, 58, 59, 223, 226
Chiang, Margaret, 205
Chicago, Ill., xxi, 16, 69, 70,132, 155, 216–17, 223, 232, 245

Chicago Civic Orchestra, 88
Chicago Musical College, 88, 89, 124
Chicago University of Music, 69
Chickasaws, 57, 58, 59
Childhood Capers, 93, 174
Children's Star Light Band, Antioch Baptist Church, 77
Chilesville, Okla., 220
China, 132
Chisolm, Emmett, ix
*"Chit-Chat"—See *Conversations for two flutes and piano*
Choctaw Indians, 17, 18, 57, 58, 59
Chopin, Frédéric, 90, 120, 128, 196
Choral Suite no. 1, 163, 182, 185
Church of the Lighted Window, 215
Christ Episcopal Church, Xenia, Ohio, xix, xx, 198
Christianson, Lawrence "Larry," 167, 183, 206
*"Christmas is More," 210; see also *Notes of Christmas*
Chromatic Fantasy and Fugue (J. S. Bach), 196
Church of England, 76
Church of God in Christ, Boley, Okla., 77
Cincinnati, Ohio, xix, 16, 78, 138, 139, 176
Cincinnati May Festival, 200
Cincinnati Symphony Orchestra, 200
Civil Rights Movement, 3
Civil War (American), 56, 58, 161, 176, 220, 227
Civilian Conservation Corps, 111
Claremont Graduate University, x, 215, 278
Clark, [Dr.], 113
Clark, Leberta, 183, 212
Clark County, Springfield, Ohio, x
classical music, 45
Cleveland, Ohio, xix, 186, 208, 242
Cleveland Chamber Symphony, 2, 171, 186, 191, 207, 208, 233, 246
Cleveland Heights High School, Ohio, 167, 210
Cleveland Institute of Music, 127, 199, 207, 244
Cleveland Plain Dealer, viii, xx, 173, 207, 208, 216, 246
Cleveland State University, 210
Clorindy (Will Marion Cook), 89
Coates, Gloria, 218
Coe College, 245
Cole, Lorenza Jordan, 89, 92

INDEX

Coleridge-Taylor, Samuel, 200
College Women's Club (CSU), 196
Colorado, 1, 103, 105, 117, 125, 134, 166, 181, 182, 192, 195, 202, 238
Colorado State College of Education, Greeley, 117, 181, 182, 195, 238
Columbia College, Chicago, xxi
Columbia University, New York, N.Y., 82
Columbus, Ohio, 120, 138, 205, 206, 209, 240
Columbus [Ohio] Dispatch, 205
Colvin, Ruth, 201
Composer U.S.A. (National Association of Composers, U.S.A.), 216
Composing a Life: Life as a Work in Progress, 8, 74
Cone, James H., 156, 245
Confederacy, 58–59
Conference/Workshop on 20th-Century String Quartets by Women Composers, xvii, 175, 182, 203, 204
Congregational Methodist Episcopal Church, Boley, Okla., 77
Congress of the United States House of Representatives, 213
Connor, Pat, 236
Connors-Mosley, Patricia, 207, 209
Constantinides, Dinos, 204
Contemporary American Composers: A Bio-graphical Dictionary, 201
*Conversations for two flutes and piano, 175, 185, 199, 200, 205, 208
Conway, Fred, 128
Cook, Will Marion, 88, 89
Cook's Southern Syncopated Orchestra, 89
Copland, Aaron, 134, 156
Cottage, The, 151, 153, 186, 197
"Couldn't Hear Nobody Pray," 158, 186, 236
Couperin, François, 125
Cox, Bette Yarborough, 236
Cravi-Bozza, Minna, 245
Création du monde, La (Darius Milhaud), 130
Creative Summer Arts Festival and Workshop, 127, 128
*"Credo," 188
Creek Indians, vii, 1, 14, 23, 24, 30, 52, 55, 57, 58, 59, 63, 222
Creek-Seminole Business College and Agricultural Institute, 22, 23, 223, 231
Crockett, Norman L., 30, 224

Crotty, John "Jack," ix, xix, 205, 206, 208, 209, 213, 216
Crumb, George, 163, 199
Cruz, Jon, 245
CSUN—See California State University, Northridge
Culver Crest Publications, xix, 215
Cunningham, Arthur, 6
Cuyahoga Community College, 211
*Cycle of Songs on Poems of Paul Laurence Dunbar, xix, 15, 145, 151, 182, 186, 189, 198, 219

Dallas, Tex., 223
Dallas Symphony, 223
Dana New Music Festival, 182
*Dances in the Canebrakes (Florence B. Price)—See *Florence Price's Dances in the Canebrakes*
Daniels, Mabel, 126
Daniels, Mary, 201
Darker America (William Grant Still), 234
Darmstadt Summer Festival of Contemporary Music, 125
Davis, Danny, 203
Davis, Lawrence Arnett, 118
Davis, Miss, ix, 240
Davis, Peter G., 150, 201, 219, 245
Davis, Sister Lowena, 77
Dawes, Senator Henry L., 220
Dawes Act, 18, 59, 60, 61, 220
Dawes Commission, 61
Dawson, William Levi, 1, 4, 12, 14, 29, 69, 79, 88, 89, 90, 91, 92, 93, 102, 156, 161, 164, 200, 212, 216, 224, 233, 236, 237
Dayton, Ohio, 138, 200, 202, 208, 211, 219, 225
Dayton Art Institute, Ohio, 196, 245
Dayton Chamber Music Society, The, 193, 198, 200, 208
Dayton Daily News, 183, 211, 215
Dayton Journal Herald, 202
Dayton Music Club, 200
Debussy, Claude, 144, 196
Dee, Norman, 203, 204
de Hartmann, Thomas, 124
Deitz, Mrs., 106
Delaware Technical & Community College, 212
Delaware Indians, 58
de Lerma, Dominique René, ix
DeMio, Elizabeth, 209

INDEX

Democrats, 31, 60
Denison, Tex., 18
Denison University, 212
Denson, Freida, 200
Denver, Colo., 125, 166
Denver Symphony Orchestra, 126
Denza, William, 208
De Paul University, 132
Detroit, Mich., 220, 240
Detroit Symphony Orchestra, 169, 189
Dett, Helen, 73, 83
Dett, Josephine, 73, 82, 83
Dett, R. Nathaniel, 1, 2, 3, 4, 7, 8, 12, 70, 71, 73, 79–86, 88, 93, 94, 99, 100, 105, 115, 138, 156, 161, 164, 181, 195, 196, 200, 231, 233, 234, 235, 237
Dickey, Gussie, 240
Dilly Hunter, 63
Diocesan Music Commission, 202
*"Divertissement," 185; see also *Arkansia*
Djibouti, 20
DNA testing, 64
doo-wop (music), 45
Dolphin-Ashley, Velma, ix, 32, 76, 77, 219, 222, 223, 224, 231, 233
*"Done Made My Vow to the Lord," 158, 186, 201, 204, 209
Douglass, Enid, x
Douglass High School, 101
Doxey Center, 213
Drake, Elias, 176
Drake, Jeremy, 242
Dramer, Kim, 61, 228, 229
Dream—See *Three Sketches*
*"Drizzle," 151, 203, 207, 208, 213, 244; see also *Cycle of Songs on Poems of Paul Laurence Dunbar*
Drummondsville, Ontario, Canada, 82
Drye, Frank L., 89
Du Bois, William E. B., 29
Duke, Miss M. T., 75
Dunbar, Paul Laurence, xix, xx, 6, 15, 145, 147, 151, 166, 167, 182, 186, 188, 189, 190, 191, 192, 201, 203, 212, 219, 244
Dunbar Choir, The, 163, 201
Duncan, Todd, 69
Dvořák, Antonín, 156

Earle, Jonathan, 225
Eastern Star, The, 222
Eastman, Charles, 229
Eastman School of Music, ix, 3, 81, 82, 83, 84, 85, 215, 216, 233, 234, 235

EAV Records, 245
Eberhart, Reginald L., 197
Echoes from the Journey, 14, 161, 171, 172, 173, 183, 186, 207, 208, 212
Eddy, Nelson, 126
Edwards, Alma, 122
Eguaroje, Oweka, 214
Eighth Symphony (Gustav Mahler), 245
Eine kleine Nachtmusik (W. A. Mozart), 70
Elegie (Sergei Rachmaninoff), 196
Elegy for Brass Quintet, 175, 186
Ellington, Duke, 33, 231
Ellis, Blaine, 197
Emancipation Proclamation, 17
Emme Kemp Trio, 182, 197
Enescu, Georges, 156
Engineers Club Auditorium, 200
Episodes I and II, 175, 186, 204, 205, 218
Essay for piano, 122, 174, 186
Ethiopia, 20
ethnomusicology, 42, 56, 225
Etude (magazine), 72
Europe, 215
Evans, Donald, 242
Evans, Mr., 70
Evanti, Lillian, 217
"Ev'ry Time I Feel the Spirit," 91
Excursions for piano trio, 175, 186
Exodusters, 220
"Ezekiel Saw de Wheel," 91

Fahnestock, Karol, 196
Fahrenbruck, Mary, 201, 204
Fairfax, Virginia, 9
Falla, Manuel de, 196
Fantasy, for piano, 174, 186
Fantasy, for violin and piano, 186
Farm Security Administration, 103, 106, 111, 114, 115, 116, 117
Fauré, Gabriel, 196
Federal Hall National Memorial, 203
"Feed-a My Sheep," 91
Feldman, Mortimer, 200
Felton, Thelma—See Powell, Thelma
Festival Overture, 174, 186
Field, Jim, 175
Film Music Society, 232
Finn, Robert, 173, 207, 208, 246
Firkusny, Rudolph, 129
First National Congress on Women in Music, xvii, 182, 203, 217
Fisk University, 86, 235
Fitzgerald, Alverda Sinks, 199

INDEX

Five Civilized Tribes (Nations), 57, 58
Flandreau, Suzanne, ix, 235
Flat Rock, Okla., 23, 220, 232
Florence Price's Dances in the Canebrakes, 120, 174
Florida A&M University, 216
Florida State University, 127
Floyd, Samuel A., Jr., 6, 7, 226
*"Folksong"—See *Arkansia*
Foote, Arthur, 82
Forest City, Ark., 185
Forest Hills String Quartet, 207
Fort Gibson, Okla., 222
Fort Smith and Western Railroad Company, 17, 18, 219
Foster, Mr. and Mrs. H. V., 114
Founder's Day, 166, 182, 196, 240
Four Mynyms for Three Players, 161, 175, 183, 186, 198, 206, 207, 210
France, 82, 129
Frazier, Michael, 201
Freeman, Alan, 169
Freeman, Harry Lawrence, 88
Frizzell, John, ix
Frontiers of Faith, 89
Fuell, Melissa, 231
Fulbright Award, 139
"Fulfillment"—See *Three Songs for Christmas*
Fuller, John L., 240
funk (music), 44
Furth, Betsy, x
Fry, Stephen M., ix

Gallante, Jane, ix
Gallatin, Jane, 204
Gamma Sigma, 196
Ganz, Rudolph, 73
Garcia, Henry, 197, 198, 200
Garcia, Mrs. Henry [Louise], 197
Garrison, Ethel Wolfe, 222
Garvey, Marcus, 33, 35, 63, 224, 225
Gatewood, Willard, 217
Gaynor, "King" Earl, 99, 100, 101, 181
Geis, Gilbert, 225
Gels, Judie [Judith], 182, 197, 198
General Allotment Act, 60
Georgian Court College, 211
George, James B., 219
George Mason University, 9
Georgie Line, Okla., 220
Geritech Project, 213

Gershwin, George, 11
Gersten, Frederick, 241, 242
Ghezzo, Dinu, 205
Gielenden, Demar, 200
Gifts of God, 163, 164, 186, 204
Gilroy, Paul, 42, 226
Glicklich, Martin, 205
Gloria in Excelsis, 186, 188, 207
"Go Tell It on the Mountain," 158, 187
Godard, B., 99
Godfrey, Daniel, 205
Goethe, Johann Wolfgang von, 39, 225
Goggins, Lathardus, 242, 243
Gold Torch, The (CSU), 135, 202
Goldberg, Leonid, 210
Golden Age Senior Center, xviii, 209, 212, 213
Goldthread-Thompson Family Reunion, 223
Goodrich, Barbara, 201
gospel (music), 41, 44, 45
*"Gossip"—See *Conversations for two flutes and piano*
Grayson, Mr., 104
Great Depression, The, 85, 235
"Great Gittin' Up Mornin'"—See *Tawawa House*
Greeley, Colo., 103, 105, 117, 238
Greeley, Horace, 117
Greene County, Ohio, 176, 183, 210
Greene County Women's Hall of Fame, 5, 183, 208, 209
Greenwood Press, 217, 230, 234, 235
*"Greetings"—See *Conversations for two flutes and piano*
Grenville, R. H., 6, 147, 169, 189, 192, 209
Grieg, Edvard, 196, 232
Griffes, Charles Tomlinson, 196
Grigsby, Beverly, ix
Groves, Harry E., 243
Guckin, John P., 226
Guggenheim Fellowship, 84
Gunn, George W., 126
Guth, Otta, 245
Guthrie, Okla., 17, 33, 60, 86, 224
Guthrie Opera House, 30

Haas, Robert Bartlett, 46
Hackley, Azalia, 217
Haddock, Mable, 206
Hagedorn, Katherine, x
Hageman, Donald, 198, 200

INDEX

"Hail Mary," 91
Hairston, Jester, 156, 200
Haithcock, William H., 196, 240
Hale, Douglas, 229
Hale, Thomas J., III, 208
Hall, Frederick, 69
*Hallelujah, for brass octet, 187, 205
*Hallelujah, for unison children's chorus, 163, 187
*Hallelujah, for woodwind octet, 208
"Hallelujah, How Good It Is to Sing Praise"—See *Sing Unto the Lord a New Song*
*"Hallelujah to the Lamb," 158, 187, 197, 201, 207, 208
Haller, William, 174, 206, 209
Hamilton, Kenneth Marvin, 219, 221, 224
Hamilton, Ohio, 205
Hamm, Valerie, 199
Hampton, Nancy, 213
Hampton Institute [University], 3, 29, 73, 80, 81, 82, 84, 87, 90, 98, 99, 181, 198, 199, 211, 233
Handel, Georg Frideric, 70, 71, 196, 199
Handler, Laura, 201
Handy, D. Antoinette, 237
Handy, W. C., 80
Hansen, Jennie, 203
Hansen, Regina, 126
Hanson, Howard, 46, 83, 84
Happer, Leonard, Sr., 201
Hardy, Thomas, 6, 147, 163, 197
Harlem Renaissance, The, 33
Harmonious Blacksmith (G. F. Handel), 71
Harnage, John, 223
Hartford Symphony, 245
Harrell, Mack, 129
Harris, Johanna, 127
Harris, Roy, 126, 127, 134
Harrison, Hazel, 68, 69, 89, 92, 93, 195, 230
Hartmann, Thomas de, 124
Harvard University, 82, 134
Haycraft, Jo Ann, ix, 240, 241
Hayes, Donald Jeffrey, 6, 95, 145, 147, 199, 237
Hayes, Roland, 92, 93
Haynes, T. M. [Thomas M.], 18, 220, 222
Heady, Mary, x, 231
Hedge, Frederick Henry, 188
Heifetz, Florence (Vidor), 129
Heifetz, Josefa "Jo," 129

Heilbrun, Carolyn G., 96, 107, 238
Heinze, Victor, 69
Helm, Shirley, 209
Helmig, Martina, 217
Herbison, Jeraldine, 6, 217
Herder, Johann Gottfried, 227
Herder, Ronald, 197
Heresies, 218
"Heritage," 182, 187, 197, 198, 199
Heritage and Life: A Cycle of Songs, 182, 187, 197, 198
Herle, A., 226
Herndon, Arthur, 139, 198, 199, 200, 203
Hess, Myra, 92
Heth, Charlotte, 42, 226, 227
Hicks, Henrietta, ix, 34, 75, 219, 220, 222, 224, 231, 232
Hidden Words of Bahá'u'lláh, The, 145, 150, 182, 187, 201, 202, 203, 204, 213
Hildegard Publishing Co., 183, 216
Hill, Chauncy, 25
hip-hop (music), 44
Historic First United Presbyterian Church of East Cleveland, 209
Hobson, Congressman David L., 208, 212, 213
Hobson, Constance Tibbs, 206, 230, 236
Hobson, Richard, 204, 205
Hochstein Memorial School, David, 235
Hoffman, Rosalie, 200
Holiday for Brass, 169
Hollander, Gustave, 99
Hollis, William, 182, 197
Holman United Methodist Church, Los Angeles, 183, 212
Homage to William Levi Dawson on his 90th Birthday, 174, 183, 187, 190, 208, 216
Hope, Ark., 23
Hopkins, Harry, 112
Hooligan, Hazel, 28, 93
Horace Mann Hall (Antioch College), 208
Horne, Aaron, 235
Horne, Frank, 6, 22, 145, 147, 188, 193
Horner Institute for Fine Arts, 88
Houston, Tex., 18
*"How Charming Is This Place," 187, 210, 212, 213
Howard University, 69, 92, 134
Hoyer, Mildred N., 147, 189
Hsien-Ming, Lee, 132
Hubbard, George W., 221
Huff, Karl, 208

INDEX

Huggins, Alverdean, 199, 200
Hughes, Langston, 25, 202
Hultberg, Cortland, 199
Hungarian Rhapsodie (Franz Liszt), 70
*"Humoreske," 196; see also *Three Sketches*
Hylton, Helen H., 126
Hymn for Brass Quartet, 187, 196–97

"I Couldn't Hear Nobody Pray," 91
"I Wan' To Be Ready," 91
*"I Want to Die Easy," 161, 186—see also *Echoes from the Journey*
IAWM Journal (International Alliance for Women in Music), 7, 216, 227
Ichiyanagi, Lui, 200
Ickes, Harold, 112
Illinois, 20, 124, 217, 219, 221, 236, 243
*"Immortality," 197
Impressario, The (W. A. Mozart), 199
Impromptu no. 3 (Gabriel Fauré), 196
*"Impromptu," 196
Impromptu and *Danza* (John Alden Carpenter), 196
"In His Care-o," 91
In One Lifetime, 217
In the Bottoms (R. N. Dett), 196
In the Great Gittin' Up Mornin', 158, 187; see also *Tawawa House*
Indian Removal Act of 1830, 57
Indian Territory, 59, 61
Inter-Denominational Ministers' Wives Alliance, 201, 243
International Alliance for Women in Music, 7, 211, 215
International Congress on Women in Music, xvii, 211, 236, 278
International Institute for the Study of Women in Music, 205
International League of Women Composers, 203
International Music Hall, 197
Introduction, Prelude and Danse for band, 169, 187, 197
Iowa State University, 138
Isom, Eugene, 175, 185
*"It's Me O Lord, Standing in the Need of Prayer," 158, 187
*"I've Done, Done," 158
Ives, Burl, 126
Ixl, Okla., 220

Jackson, Barbara Garvey, 217

Jackson, Lewis A., 243
Jackson, Maldothia, 239
Jackson, Matthew, 214
Jackson, Minneola, 70
Jackson, Miss., 1
Jackson, Travis A., 226
Jackson, Veola, 70
Jahoda, Gloria, 228
James, Warren, 198, 200, 201
Japan, 132
Jaygayle Music, xiii, xix, 185, 244
jazz, 44, 45, 49, 51, 71, 130, 131, 171
Jazz Era, The, 33
Jefferson City, Mo., 231
Jenkins, Mr., 138, 139
Jennings, Susan, 204
Jessye, Eva, 6, 236
"Jesus Walked This Lonesome Valley," 91
Jewish artists, 129
Jew's harp, 70
"Jim Crow" laws, 2, 29, 31, 40, 60, 62, 80
Jocelyn (B. Godard), 99
Johannesen, Grant, 126
Johannsen, Gunnar, 127, 234
John Carroll University, 186, 207, 208, 244
John Hay Whitney Fellowship Award, 139
Johnson, Mr., 83, 234
Johnson, David Lee, 236
Johnson, Edith, 28
Johnson, J. Rosamond, 88, 163, 188
Johnson, James P., 7
Johnson, James Weldon, 27, 147, 163, 244
Johnson, Hall, 156, 200
Jolley, Joycelyn, 204
Jones, Charles, 1, 129, 133, 200, 242
Jones, Claude, 231
Jones, F. B., 231
Jones, M. J., 222
Jones, Mayme, 1, 69, 70, 71, 98, 231
Jones, Otis, Sr., 201
Jones, Quincy, 227
Jones, Quintin, ix, 220
Jones, William M., 222
Joplin, Scott, 70, 226
Journal of Human Relations, 142
Journey—See *Echoes from the Journey*
Jovanovic, Zoran, 197
*"Jovial," 198; see also *Four Mynyms for Three Players*
Juba Dance (R. N. Dett), 70, 196, 202
*"Jubilant," 198; see also *Four Mynyms for Three Players*

INDEX

Juilliard School, The, 133, 200, 242
Junior Pianists State Contest, 70

Kansas, 120, 220, 237
Kansas City, 16, 18
Kansas State Teachers College [Pittsburg State University], 219, 244
Kappa Alpha Psi Fraternity, 196
Karamu Theatre (Cleveland, Ohio), 245
Kartman, Myron, 192
Katz, William Loren, 31, 56, 57, 58, 63, 221, 222, 223, 224, 228, 229, 230
Kaufman, Frederick, 226
Kay, Ulysses, 6
Kearns, William, 227
Kebede, Ashenafi, 226
Kefferstan, Christine, 207
Kelly, Melody, 214
Kelly Hall (Antioch College), xvii
Kennedy, W. A., 222
Kerber, Beth, 209
*"Kid Stuff," 145, 187, 188, 193, 197, 204, 207, 208, 210, 211, 212, 213, 214; see also *Three Songs for Christmas*
Kiev Conservatory, 127
Kilbourne, Michael, ix
Kilenyi, Edward, 126, 127
King, Betty Jackson, 6
King, Rev. Martin Luther, Jr., 209, 213
Knox College, 124
Knoxville College, 245
Koch, Selig, 200
Kodály, Zoltán, 156
Kolisch, Rudolf, 125, 126
Koskoff, Ellen, 226
Kossler, Melissa, 209, 244, 246
Koussevitzky, Serge, 124
KPFK-FM, Los Angeles, xviii, 226
Krenek, Ernst, 126, 133
Kriner, Janet, 203
Kriner, Robert, 203
Kubik, Gerhard, 226
Kulas Hall (Cleveland Institute of Music), 207
Kulas Recital Hall (Oberlin College), 197
Kum Ba Yah, 158, 163, 188, 200
Kunst, Jaap, 225
Kutztown University, Pa., 213
*"Kyrie," 188

Lake George Opera Theatre, 245
Lakota, 226

Lamb of God, 188
Lamont School of Music, University of Denver, 129
Landow, Max, 83
*"Landscape"—See *Arkansia*
Langrum, Mr., 70
Langston, Okla., 18, 86, 99, 100, 219, 224
Langston [Okla.] Orchestra, 224
Langston University, x, 1, 86, 99, 115, 174, 181, 195, 219, 235, 236, 239
Lanier, Jo Ann (*aka* Lanyé), 145, 171, 182, 204, 207, 208, 209, 216, 243, 244, 246
Laporte, Ind., 69
Laramie, Wyo., 125, 134, 166, 211, 240, 241
Largent, Edward J., 205
Latino rhythms, 188
Lawless, Betty, 209
Lawrence, Arthur Kelton, 120–21, 174, 182, 195, 240, 241
Lawton, Okla., 35
Leftwich, William, 223, 231
Lems-Dvorkin, Carol, 226
L'Enfant Aimé (D. Milhaud), 127
Lenti, Vincent A., ix, 233, 234, 235
Léon, Tania, 6, 238
Leston, David, 199
Leventon, Gladys Metcalf, 234
Levine, James, 245
Lewis, Edgar J., 126
Lewis, Joseph D., 210
Lewis, Mable, 198
Liao, Yu-Chia, 210
Liberator, The, 244
"Life," 145, 198
Life Cycle, 145, 188, 198
Lift Every Voice and Sing, 163, 188
Ligeti, György, 163, 199
Lincoln, Abraham, 60
Lincoln Center, New York, N.Y., 182
Lincoln [Institute] University of Missouri, x, 105, 210
Lindberg, John, 203
Links, Inc., The, 207
Linscome, Mary, x, 238
Liston, F. M., 14
Liszt, Franz, 70, 156, 157, 196, 236
"Lit'l Boy Child," 91
Little Rock, Ark., 107, 237
Lock, E. Azalia, 69
London, Edwin, 171, 183, 186, 207
London, England, 19, 92, 97, 220
Long, Howard H., 134

INDEX

Long, Odean, 199
Long, Will West, 226
Longsworth, Carol, 163, 189, 210
Longy School of Music, 216
Los Angeles, Calif., 51, 64, 86, 92–93, 216, 227–28
Los Angeles Music Library, x
Los Angeles Times Magazine, 228
Los Angeles Unified School District, 236
Love, Mr., 113, 239
Love Came Down at Christmas, 163, 188, 198
"Love of God, The," 188
Lovelace, Ariel, 118, 119, 191
Lowe, Sara Jane, 209
Luther, Martin, 147, 188
Lutyens, Elisabeth, 218
Lytle, Gwendolyn, x

MacDowell Colony, 125, 126
MacGillivray, Louise, 205
MacKinnon, Hugh A., 126
Macon County, Ala., 111, 116
Madigan, Maria, 241
Magnolia Suite (R. N. Dett), 115, 234
Mahler, Alma, 108
Mahler, Gustave, 245
Mallory, William, Sr., xix
Mallory Center for Community Development, xix
"Mammy" (R. N. Dett), 196
Manhattan School of Music, 245
Manhattanville Curriculum in Music, 200
Mankato State University, Minn., 207
Mannes College of Music, viii, 133
Maple Leaf Rag (Scott Joplin), 70
Marche, for piano, 188
Marchison, Gayle, 217
*"Mary Had a Baby," 91, 236; see also *Three Songs for Christmas*
Masonic Temple [State Masonic Temple for Negroes], Boley, Okla., 15, 22, 68, 222, 230
Mass in F# minor, 188
Matthews, Anna Howard (choir), 204
Mathis, Bert, 83, 234
Mathis, Joyce, 186, 243
Mathonican, Mr., 70
Matthay, Tobias, 92
Mayer, Frederick R., 167, 210
Maynor, Dorothy, 126
McBee, Cecil, 208, 243

McBride, Donald, 205
McCabe, Edwin P., 17
McClellan, Eleanor, 213
McClellan, Philomena, 167, 210
McGuire, Lois, 205
McIlhargey, Nacim, 210
McKay, Claude, 6, 145, 147, 244
Mead, Margaret, 218
Meet the Composer, 203
Meharry Medical College, ix, 19, 20, 21, 220, 221, 232
Melancholy, 198; see also *Four Mynyms for Three Players*
Mendelssohn, Felix, 71
Menuet in G (Ignace Jan Paderewski), 71
Messiaen, Olivier, 134
Messiah (G. F. Handel), 70
Metropolitan Opera, 89, 231
Miami University (Oxford, Ohio), 197, 207, 245
Michaels, Beth, 215
Middle Run Baptist Church, 196
Mighty Fortress Is Our God, A, 163, 188
Milhaud, Darius, viii, ix, 1, 4, 12, 50, 52, 79, 106, 107, 120, 122, 123, 125, 126, 127, 128, 129, 130, 132, 133, 144, 161, 175, 182, 197, 200, 202, 210, 235, 237, 240, 241, 242
Milhaud, Madeleine, 127, 129, 132, 242
Mililo, Mary Jo, 214
Miller, F. Eugene Foundation, x
Miller, Richard, 245
Mills College, 127, 129, 131, 133,
Milwaukee, Wisc., 105, 118
Minneapolis Symphony Orchestra, 126
Mississippi River, 112, 114, 116, 175
Missouri River, 112
Mitchell, Abbie, 69, 89
Mitchell, Carolyn Brown, 201
Mitchell Lumber Mill, 109
Mitchell's Mill School, 109, 239
MMCP Composers, 200
Mongonalia Arts Center, 209
Monson, Ingrid, 42, 43, 226, 227
Montgomery, Ala., 102
Moods, 189, 200
Moore, Dorothy Rudd, 6, 217
Moore, George, 242
Moore, Lake, 18
Moore, Mary Carr, 7, 217
Moore, Undine Smith, 6, 8, 11, 107, 200, 203, 217, 218

INDEX

Morehouse Auditorium, 213
Morgantown, W.Va., 216, 228, 230, 233
Morning (R. N. Dett), 83
Morris, Mary, 129
Moses, Lennard V., 140, 145, 179, 205, 243
Moss, Mike, 174
Moton, Robert Russa, 87, 88
Motown (music), 44
Mound City, Ill., 20, 21, 221
Mount Auburn Presbyterian Church, xix
Mount Bayou, Miss., 17
Mount Vernon, N.Y., 230
Mozart, Wolfgang Amadeus, 11, 70, 120, 196, 199
Mt. Zion Baptist Church, Springfield, Ohio, 201, 243
Mu Chi Chapter, Omega Psi Phi Fraternity, 205, 213
Mu Phi Epsilon, xviii, xix, 199, 205, 215
Mullins, Shirley Strohm, 166, 197, 198
Muncie Community Performance, Ind., 212
Music Academy of the West (Santa Barbara), 127
*Music from Ohio, for SATB and piano, 189, 210
Music of the Americas, KPFK, xviii
music theory, 50, 86, 108
Musical Classics, WCSU, 138, 202
Musical Observer, 72
musicology, 225
Muskingum College, New Concord, Ohio, 200
Muskogee, Okla., 30, 31
"My Lord What A Morning," 91
Myers, Steven, 200

Nadel, Harold, 200, 201
*Narrative, for flute, narrator/soprano, two percussionists, and piano, 189, 199, 200
Nashville, Tenn., 221
Nashville Normal and Theological Institute, 20
National Afro-American Museum and Cultural Center, Wilberforce, Ohio, xix, xx, 176, 183, 207, 209, 211, 212
National Archives, ix
National Association for the Advancement of Colored People [NAACP], 3, 5, 29, 63, 107, 112, 138, 210
National Association for the Advancement of Native American Composers and Musicians, 40, 196

National Association of Negro Musicians [NANM], 82
National Association of Teachers of Singing [NATS], 204
National Black Programming Consortium, 206
National Endowment for the Arts [NEA], 176
National Museum of American History, Washington, D.C., 183, 206
National Negro Business League, 30, 222
National Organization for Women [NOW], 183, 206, 208
National Park Service, 224
Native Americans, 4, 12, 29, 30, 40, 42, 43, 44, 45, 46, 49, 52, 53, 55, 56, 57, 58, 59, 60, 61, 62, 63, 64, 65, 83, 196, 212, 220, 225, 226, 228, 229, 230
Navy, U.S.—See U.S. Navy
Naxos, 215
NBC [National Broadcasting Company], 89, 91
Neal, Gladys, 197
Neal, Idotha Bootsie, 211
Nebraska, 120, 232
Needles, Calif., 102
Negro Baptist College, 20
Negro Folk Symphony, 88, 90
Negro History Week, 171
"Negro National Anthem, The," 224
Nelson, Eliesha, 209
Nelson, Terry Van, 197
neoclassicism, 246
Nettl, Bruno, 226
Neuls-Bates, Carol, 218
New Deal, 111, 112
New England Conservatory, 244
New Mexico, 86
New Music Society, 204
New Orleans, La., 16
New York Amsterdam News, 203
New York City, ix, xvii, 33, 69, 73, 89, 90, 175, 198, 203, 216, 242, 244
New York Public Library at Lincoln Center, 193, 197, 198
New York Times, 150, 182, 198, 201, 203, 204, 218, 219, 245
New York University, xvii, 182, 203, 205, 217, 243
Newman, Lionel Hodge, 243
Nichols, David and Sharon, 200
Nickerson, Camille, 69, 217

INDEX

Nicodemus, Kans., 17
Night in Tawawa, 189, 197
Nocturne, for piano, 189, 196
Norfolk State University, 204
Normal School of North Carolina, 82
Norris, Senator George, 112
North Country Music Festival (Potsdam, N.Y.), 189
North Country New Music Performers, 189
North Platte, Nebr., 73
Northeastern University Press, 218
Northern Illinois University, 243
Northington, Julian, 198
Notes of Christmas, 163, 189
Nova Sonos, 189
Novak, Jennifer, 210
NWSA, 207
Nymph and the Farmer, The (Alexander Tcherepnin), 132

Oakland, Calif., 129
Ober, Harold, 202
Oberlin College, 85, 98, 197
Oberlin College Conservatory of Music, 82, 98, 197, 236, 245
Oberlin Community Chamber Singers, 163, 189, 210
*"O de Angels Done Bowed Down," 155, 159, 160, 161, 185, 189, 197, 198, 199, 200, 202, 204
O'Dorseys, The, 75, 76
Of Life and Love, 189
Offenbach, Jacques, 72
*"Oh, I Want Two Wings," 158
"Oh, What a Beautiful City," 91
Ohio African University, 176
Ohio Arts Council, xix, 2, 171, 176, 205
Ohio Department of Aging, 209
Ohio Educators' Association Convention, 200
Ohio General Assembly, 176, 210, 212
Ohio Humanities Council, 176, 205
Ohio Senior Citizens Hall of Fame, 183, 209, 210
Ohio State Fair Grounds, 209
Ohio State University, 120, 200, 210
Ohio Theory and Composition Teachers Association, 200
Ohio University, Athens, Ohio, 211
Ohioana Library Association, 182, 205
Ohio's Heritage, 210, 220
Ojibwa Indians, 226

Okfuskee County, Okla., 6, 30, 31, 37, 195, 216, 232
Oklahoma, viii, 1, 2, 3, 31, 61, 75, 81, 99, 100, 102, 114, 181, 195, 216, 219, 223, 231, 232, 237
Oklahoma City, Okla., 22, 60, 195, 226
Oklahoma Eagle, The, 208
Oklahoma Historical Society, ix, 219, 221
Oklahoma Jazz Hall of Fame, 208, 243
Oklahoma State Department of Health, 213, 216
[Oklahoma] State Teachers' Association, 70
Okmulgee, Okla., 22
Old Dominion University, 203, 204, 245
O Lord, Make Thy Beauty, 163, 189
Omaha, Nebr., 72, 73, 181, 232, 236
Omaha Public Library, 73
Omaha Symphony Orchestra, 202
O'Meara, Mollie, 206
Omega Psi Phi Fraternity, 205, 213
*"On a Clean Book"—See *Cycle of Songs on Poems of Paul Laurence Dunbar*
Open Meadows Foundation, x
*"O Peter, Go Ring Dem Bells," 189
Order of Eastern Star, 77, 222
Ordering of Moses, The (R. N. Dett), 82
"Organ, The," 24, 223
O'Rourke, Beatrice, ix, 137, 138, 197, 229, 230, 232, 235, 240, 242, 243, 244
Orpheus Award, 201
Orton, Paul, 202
O'Sullivan, Loretta, 203
*"O the angels done bowed"—See "O de Angels Done Bowed Down"
Otterbein College, 174, 209, 245
Out in the Fields, 90
Outlook, The, 30, 222, 230
O Whisper, O My Soul, 145, 198; see also Tawawa House

Pacific Western University, 244
Paden, Okla., 18
Paderewski, Ignacy Jan, 71, 124
Paepcke, Walter, 129
Palmer, Christopher, 242
Palomar College, 131
Paluzzi, Karen, 203
*"Pastourelle," 209; see also *Threnody*
Paxton, [Dr.], 222
Pan Africanism, 28, 49, 62, 63
Pan Indianism, 226

INDEX

paraphrases, 157
Parent-Teacher Association (PTA), Boley, Okla., 76, 77
Parham, Glover, 245
Paris, Evan, 203
Paris, France, 73, 84, 124, 127, 129, 132, 241, 242
Paris, Tex., 18
Paris Conservatory, 72, 127, 129
Park Avenue Synagogue, 47
Parker, Donald F., 225
*Pastels for orchestra, 169
PatsyLu Fund of the Open Meadows Foundation, x
Patterson, Catherine Moton, 236
Patterson, Frederick, 87, 114
Paul Laurence Dunbar House [State Memorial, Cultural & Performing Arts Center], xix, xx, 183, 201, 212
Paul Laurence Dunbar Street, Dayton Ohio, xix
Paul Robeson Cultural and Performing Arts Center [CSU], xx, 139, 192, 207
*Pavanne, 174, 189
Pawnee, Okla., 105, 181
Payne, Bishop Daniel A., 176, 177
Payne, Mike, 209, 210, 220, 231, 236
Peabody, George F., 29
Peachtree Street, Atlanta, Ga., 90
Pearl Harbor, 102, 103
Pearson, Lea, 210, 211
Pegg, Vicki D., 211
Penn State York, 213
*"Pensive," 186, 198; see also *Four Mynyms for Three Players*
Pentagon, 105, 223
Peri, Janis-Rozena [Perry], x, xv, xvi, xvii, xviii, xx, 11, 64, 78, 106, 107, 120, 132, 133, 136, 138, 139, 145, 146, 150, 169, 174, 179, 181, 182, 192, 193, 196, 197, 198, 199, 201, 202, 203, 204, 205, 206, 207, 208, 213, 216, 219, 222, 227, 228, 230, 236, 237, 238, 240, 241, 245, 245
Perry, Jimmie Rodgers, 102, 103, 104, 105, 181, 195, 238
Perry, Julia, 6, 8, 217
Perry, Lemuel Powell, 91, 100, 101, 102, 103, 104, 105, 114, 115, 117, 181, 182, 238
Petersburg, Va., 107
Petri, Egon, 69
Petrie, Ruth, ix
Peyser, Joan, 11

Phang, May, 210, 211
Phi Mu Alpha, 201, 208
Philadelphia Orchestra, 88
Philippines, 64
Phillips, Frank, 114
Phillips Petroleum Company, 114
*"Philosophy"—See *Of Life and Love*
*Philosophy, for flute, cello, and voice, 145, 190
Phoenix, The, 206
phonograph records, 33
*Piano Potpourri, 174, 185, 190, 211
*Piano Sonata no. 3, 190
*Piano Sonatina, 174, 190
Piatigorsky, Gregor, 126
Pine Bluff, Ark., 1, 29, 106, 107, 118, 119, 120, 121, 174, 195
Piston, Walter, 134
Pittenger Student Center, Ball State University, 212
Pittman, Evelyn La Rue, 6
Pittman, Portia Washington, 28, 92
Pittsburg State University, ix
Place Where the Rainbow Ends, The, 83
Plains Nations, 58, 226
"Poet, The," 15, 209
poetry, 4, 6, 14, 15, 24–25, 26, 85, 144, 145, 147, 151, 164, 169, 199, 214, 219, 237, 244
Polster, Ian, 169, 197
Pool, Betty N., ix
Pool, Jeannie Gayle, viii, xix, 203, 205, 211, 215, 216, 218, 226, 277–78
Porgy and Bess (G. Gershwin), 89, 245
Post, Wiley, 144
Potsdam, N.Y., 200
Powell, Athenea Rea, 105, 106
Powell, Birdie Lee Thompson [Jenkins], 1, 22, 23, 24, 26, 63, 72, 98, 105, 106, 138, 176, 181, 182, 222, 223
Powell, Calvin Bethel, Sr., 1, 16, 19, 20, 21, 22, 23, 24, 26, 30, 31, 34, 35, 60, 70, 77, 78, 97, 98, 101, 104, 176, 181, 195, 216, 220, 221, 222, 223, 224, 233
Powell, Calvin, Jr., 24, 26, 28, 116, 223, 233
Powell, Douglass, Jr., 105
Powell, Douglass, Sr., 24, 26, 105, 117, 223
Powell, Margaret, 105
Powell, Patricia, 105, 106
Powell [Felton], Thelma [Cleolla], 24, 26, 117, 219, 222, 223, 233
Powers, Lillian, 124
Powers, William K., 226

INDEX

powwows, 44, 226
Prairie Farms, Ala., 105, 111, 116, 117
Prairie Farms Elementary School, 116
Precious Lord, 158, 190, 200, 201
Prelude and aria, for clarinet, 190
Prelude and danse, for band, 190
*Prelude for horn and piano—See *Episodes I and II*
Prelude for organ, 174, 190
Prelude for piano, 196
Prelude in C Minor (J. S. Bach), 71
Preparatory Division, Eastman School of Music, 233, 234, 235
Presley, Elvis, 45
Price, Berkeley, x, xviii, xxii, 215
Price, Deon Nielsen, ix, xviii, xix, xxii, 205, 211, 215
Price, Florence B., xix, 7, 88, 120, 174, 186, 217, 218, 230, 244
Price Duo, The, 215
Princess Theatre (New York), 73
Prism for organ, 174, 190
Pritchett, Benny, 179, 205
Pro-Arte String Quartet, 126, 127
Promenade, 174
Protzman, Harold, 203
Puccini, Giacomo, 199

Quick, Mrs., 81
*"Quiet of Christmas, The"—See *Notes of Christmas*
quilting, 218

Raab, Alexander, 124
Rachmaninoff, Sergei, 196, 203, 236
Radano, Ronald, 48
radio broadcasts, xvii–xviii, 33, 71, 72, 82, 89, 90, 119, 125, 138, 142, 226, 257
Radio City Music Hall, 89, 90
Radtke, Anola E., 126
rags (music), 44
Rainwater, 63
rap (music), 44
Raymond, Suzanne, 209
Reagon, Bernice Johnson, 206
Reconstruction, 29, 58
Redemption, 190, 197
Reece, Cortez Donald, 1, 12, 79, 86, 93, 100, 115, 235, 237, 238, 239
Reese, James, 71
Reflets dans l'eau (Claude Debussy), 196
Reis, Claire, 129

Reisser, Marsha J., 6, 7
Republicans, 31, 60
Reynolds, Marilyn, 203
Rhapsody, for piano, 174, 190, 197
"Rhapsody" for medium voice and piano, 190
Rhyme for saxophone and piano, 190
rhythm and blues [R & B] (music), 44, 45
Richardson, Cynthia S., 7, 217
Rickelman, Melinda, 209
*"Ride, Ride, Ride King Jesus," 158–59, 191, 201
Rigoletto (Giuseppe Verdi), 70
Riley, Cleo L. "Jinx," 209
Riley Concert Hall (Otterbein College), xix
Ringo, T. R., 222
Roanoke, Va., 98
Roberson, Samuel J., 197, 198, 199
Roberts, John Storm, 226
Roberts, Randy, ix
Robeson, Paul, xx, 139, 192, 207
Robinson, Bill, 33
Robinson, Joyce, 201
Rochester, N.Y., 1, 3, 81, 82, 84, 99, 102, 181, 231
Rochester Symphony, 234
rock (music) 45, 49
Rockhold, Paula, 198
Rodgers, Bruce, 126
Roger Williams College [University], 19, 221
Rogers, Bernard, 83–84
Rogers, Paul, 208
Rogers, Treva, 216
Rogers, Will, 114
Rolfe, Rodney, 235
Rome [Italy] Jubilee Celebration, 213
Rondo Capriccioso (Felix Mendelssohn), 71
Roosevelt, Eleanor, viii, 1, 102, 106, 110, 111, 112–13, 115, 117, 181, 182, 239
Roosevelt, Franklin Delano, 111, 113
Roosevelt, Theodore, 31
Rosenberg, Donald, vii–viii, 216
Rosmond, Andrew F., 89
Rossetti, Christina Georgina, 147, 188
Rossini, Gioacchino, 198
Roth String Quartet, 126
Rothstein, Edward, 204
Royce, Edward, 84
Rusk, Okla., 220
Russell, Mr., 118
Rust College, 213
Ryan, Stephen, x

INDEX

Ryss, Olga, 245

St. Andrews Episcopal Church, 120
St. James Evangelical Lutheran Church, Wheeling, W.Va., 206
St. Louis, Mo., 78
St. Petersburg, Russia, 132
St. Philip's Episcopal Church, Dayton, Ohio, 201
Salon du Capriccii, 191
Salzano, Rachel, 200
Sam, [Chief] Alfred Charles, 30, 35–36, 225
Sampson, Carol, 212
Sampson, Janese, 206
San Diego, Calif., 102
San Diego State (College) University, 131
San Francisco, Calif., 175, 182, 193, 216
San Francisco Quartet, 197
"Sanctus," 188, 191, 197
Sandcreek/Sand Creek, Okla., 220, 237
Sanders, Wayne, 202
Sandness, Marilyn, ix
Sango, A. W., 30
Sankey, Stuart, 129
Sapulpa, Okla., 220
Saraga, Mayor John T., xviii
Saroyan, William, 128
Saudades do Brasil (D. Milhaud), 240
Saunders, Ada, 206
Scaramouche (D. Milhaud), 120, 125
Schnabel, Artur, 127
Schnauber, Louis B. Collection, UCLA, 232
Schoenberg, Arnold, 126
Schonthal, Ruth, 7, 217
Schreker, Franz, 127
Schubert, Franz, 85, 125, 126
Schumann, Clara, 108, 218
Schumann, Robert, 196
Schwartz, Elliott, 204
Schwartz, Emile, 72
Schwartz, Leslie, 201
Schwarze, Richard, 227
Scott, Inez, 70
Scriabin, Alexander, 236
Sears Recital Hall (University of Dayton), xix
Second International Congress on Women in Music, 236
Securities and Exchange Commission [SEC], 112
Seeger, Charles, 108
Seeger, Ruth Crawford, 7, 108
Segrera, Caroline, 245

Seidel, Liz, 212
Seminole Indians, 58, 59
Senrab Records, 193, 244
Sephardic Jews, 64
Sessions, Roger, 126, 127, 134
Shakespeare, 14, 69, 78
Shawnee Indians, 58
"Sheep may safely graze" (J. S. Bach), 128
Shegog, Lois, 201
Sherman, Tex., 18
Ships That Pass in the Night, 166–68, 183, 191, 206, 210
Shuffle Along, 33
sickle cell anemia, 64
"Silently," 163, 189, 210
Simmons, Beverly, iv, vii, xix, xx, xxii, 184, 194, 216
Simpson, Anne Key, ix, 82, 194, 217, 231, 234
Sinclair, Vicky, 201
Sinclair Community College, 211
Sing Unto the Lord a New Song, 163, 185, 191, 201
Singer, [Dean] Norman, 196
*"Sinner Man So Hard, Believe!," 158, 161, 191, 198, 201, 204, 243
Sinte Gleska College, 226
Sitting Bull, 229
Skidmore, William, 208
slavery, 48, 56, 57, 58, 110–11, 141, 155, 156, 229
Slonimsky, Nicolas, 216, 236, 241, 242
Small, Christopher, 48, 226, 227
Small, Levon, 199
Smith, Barbara, 197
Smith, Bessie, 33
Smith, Catherine Parsons, 7, 217
Smith, Dwayne E., 183, 212
Smith, Hale, 6
Smith, Howard, 197
Smith, Irene Britton, 217
Smith, William T., 198, 199, 200
Smithsonian Institution, 183, 206, 226
Smyth, Willie, 226
Social Security Act, 112
Society of Composers, Inc. [SCI], 210
Solfeggietto (C. P. E. Bach), 71
Solitude (Allan Willman), 124
Solomon, Izler, 196
Solomon, Maynard, 11
Somalia [Somaliland], 20, 220, 221
Sonata for clarinet and piano, 191, 197

INDEX

*Sonata for piano, 174, 191
*Sonata for violin and piano, 191
*Sonata no. 3, 191
*Sonatine for piano, 174, 191, 196
Songes, Les (D. Milhaud), 125
*Songs for Nobody, 190
"Soon Ah Will Be Done," 91
soul (music), 44
*Sound Patterns, 164, 165, 190
Southall, Geneva Handy, 207
Southern, Eileen, 41, 217, 226, 234, 236
Southern Connecticut State University, 174
Souvenirs of Brazil—See Saudades do Brasil
Spain, 64
Specht, John, 200
Speck, Frank G., 226
spirituals, 44, 82, 90, 155, 158, 161, 163, 186, 187, 188, 189, 190, 191, 192, 245
Springfield, Ohio, 138, 243
Springfield [Ohio] Symphony, 200
Spring Rose Chapter of the Order of Eastern—See Eastern Star
*Spring Song, 210; see also Cycle of Songs on Poems of Paul Laurence Dunbar
Stabat Mater (Rossini), 198
Stallworth, Dottie, 217
*"Standing in the Need of Prayer," 192
Stanley, Jerome, 199, 207
State University of New York, Potsdam, 138, 164
"Steal Away," 91
Stennett, Samuel, 145, 147
Stern, Isaac, 126
Stern-Wolfe, Mimi, 203, 204
Still, Judith Anne, 45, 217
*Still, Still, 192, 198
Still, William Grant, 7, 43, 45, 46, 47, 80, 88, 97, 155, 217, 218, 233, 234, 237, 245
Stock, Frederick, 124
Stokowski, Leopold, 90
Straight, Susan, 228
Stratton, James C., 240
Strauss, Johann, II, 69
Strauss, Richard, 199
Stravinsky, Igor, 246
Strickland, Mrs., 24
String Choir of Forest City, Ark., 175
*String Quartet no. 1, 192
Strong, Harold S., 182, 196
Studebaker, Elizabeth, 212, 213, 239
Suderburg, Robert, 163, 199
*Suite for piano, 192

*Suite for Women's Voices, 163, 185, 192
*Sunset—See Cycle of Songs on Poems of Paul Laurence Dunbar
Suthern, Orrin, 89
Swanson, Howard, 7
Swayne, Wager, 72, 73
Sweet, Jill Drayson, 226
Sweet Home, Ark., 120
*"Swing Low, Sweet Chariot," 91, 161, 173, 175, 186, 211; see also Echoes from the Journey
Switzerland, 92
"Sympathy" (F. Price), 244
*Symphonic Poem, 166, 182, 191, 192, 196
Symphony no. 5 (Ludwig van Beethoven), 70
Symphony no. 40 (W. A. Mozart), 70
Symposium in Celebration of Black American Women in Music, 183
Syracuse University, 205

Talbert, Florence Cole, 89
Tales of Hoffman (Jacques Offenbach), 72
"Talk About A Child," 91
Talladega College Choir, The, 204
Talma, Louise, 218
Tanglewood/Berkshire Music Center, 245
*Tawawa House, 2, 14, 25, 151, 158, 161, 175–79, 182, 192, 205, 206, 207
Taylor, Darryl, x, xviii, xix, xxii, 211, 215
Taylor, Hillard, 220
Taylor, Ivan George, 204
Taylor-Dunn, Corliss, 179, 198, 205
Tay-Sachs disease, 64
Tcherepnin, Alexander, 132
Teague, Maura, 204
Technology Theater, Old Dominion University, 204
*"Teeta," 210
Tempo for Wind Ensemble and Soprano, 169, 170, 183, 192, 209
Tennessee Valley Authority, 105, 112
Terry, Anna, 137, 138
Tewa Pueblo Indians, 226
Texarkana, Tex., 18
Texas, 120, 125, 223
Theisz, R. D., 226
"There Is a Balm in Gilead," 91
*"There's a Lit'l [Little] Wheel A-Turnin'," 91, 159, 192, 236
"There's a Meeting Here Tonight," 115
Thirteenth Census of the United States, 195

INDEX

Thomas, Arthur E., 243
Thompson, Artee, 23, 223
Thompson, Betty, 128
Thompson, Birdie—See Powell, Birdie Thompson
Thompson, Charlie, 55, 104, 155, 161, 185, 189, 223, 229, 230
Thompson, Clem, 23, 99, 223
Thompson, Ed, 23
Thompson, Frank, 23, 98
Thompson, Jacqueline, 217
Thompson, Johnson, 222–23
Thompson, Luticia (Lutisia), 23, 63, 69, 222, 223
Thompson, Marilyn, 234
Thompson, Merridy (Mudd), 23, 223
Thompson, Nora, 23, 223
Thompson, Neva, 23, 223
Thompson, Olibe, 223
Thompson, Sarlie, 223
Thompson, W. P., 222–23
Thomson, Virgil, 134
*Three Designs for Four Strings (Players), 175, 182, 192, 201, 203, 204
*Three Expressions for Piano, 174, 192, 199
*Three Sketches, 192
*Three Songs for Baritone and Piano, 193
*Three Songs for Christmas, 145, 193
*Threnody Song Cycle, 95, 144, 145, 146, 148, 193, 199, 204, 207, 208, 237
Thursday Music Club, 206
Tibbs, Roy, 69
Tick, Judith, 7, 217
*Times Five, 174, 193, 197
Tipton, Albert, 129
*To All of You, 193, 197
*"Toast, A," 22, 193, 197, 198; see also Life Cycle: Three Songs for Baritone and Piano
Tolliver, Patricia, 200
Tomkin Hall, Tuskegee Institute, 87
Tomlin, Elwood, 231
Topeka, Kans., 88
tornado, Greene County, Ohio (1974), 136, 139
*"Tornado"—See Narrative
Toronto, Ontario, Canada, 205
Townsend, Peter, 200
Trail of Tears, 57, 228
*Tranquility and Commotion for orchestra, 193
Trauz, Larry, 163, 199

Triangle of Mu Phi Epsilon, 205, 216
Trinity Cathedral, Cleveland, Ohio, xix, xx
Trinity School, New York, N.Y., 203
Triplett, John, ix
Trotman, LeRoy, 199
Tull, Karla, 211
Tully, James L., 167, 183, 206
Tullahassee Mission, 30
Tulsa, Okla., ix, 34, 99, 101, 104, 181, 195, 236, 237
Tulsa Civic Orchestra, 202
Turner, D. J. [David Johnson], 222
Tuskegee Hymn (Anthem), 28
Tuskegee Institute, 1, 2, 28, 29, 30, 69, 86, 87, 88, 89, 91, 92, 93, 101, 102, 103, 109, 110, 112, 113, 114, 136, 163, 174, 181, 195, 224, 233, 234, 236, 237, 243, 244
Tuskegee Institute Choir, 29, 90, 91
Twelve Days of Christmas, The, 163, 193, 203
*Two Letters, 193, 200

Uncle Jesse of Arkansas (poet), 13
Underground Railroad, 14, 25, 83, 176, 208
Unfinished Symphony (Franz Schubert), 125
United Negro College Fund, 89
United States Census, 216, 229
United States Congress, 208
United States Copyright Law, 51
United States Department of Interior, 224
Unity Feast, 210
University Conservatory of Omaha, 73
University of Akron, 207, 242
University of Arkansas, Pine Bluff, ix, 106, 122, 169, 174, 202, 217, 240
University of California, Irvine, 215
University of California, Los Angeles, x, 92
University of Dayton, Ohio, xix, 212
University of Denver, Colo., 129
University of Michigan, 199, 215, 217
University of Northern Colorado, x, 105, 238
University of Omaha, Nebr., 72
University of Pennsylvania, Philadelphia, 82
University of Southern California, Los Angeles, 86, 215, 236
University of Victoria, British Columbia, Canada, 163, 182, 199
University of Wisconsin, 127
University of Wyoming, ix, 1, 79, 106, 120, 122, 123, 124, 125, 126, 127, 128, 130,

INDEX

131, 133, 166, 167, 182, 183, 192, 195, 196, 202, 211, 234, 235, 241, 242
*"Up Over My Head," 193
U.S. Army, 125, 127
U.S. Department of Education, 110, 115
U.S. Navy, 102, 103
Usis, David A., 209

Vagner, Robert S., 126
Valentine, William de, 198, 199
Van Deusen, Nancy, x
*Variations for Piano, 196
Vennum, Thomas, Jr., 226
Verdi, Giuseppe, 70
Very, Jones, 151, 186
Viardot-Garcia, Pauline, 218
Victor record player, 72
Virginia State College, Petersburg, 107
Voelcker, Norman, 198
Voinovich, Governor George V., 209
Vorkink, Erik, x
Vronsky (Vitya) & Babin (Victor) Duo, 120, 127, 128, 241

*"Wade in the Water," 161, 186; see also Echoes from the Journey
"Wagonwheels," 90
Waites, Althea, 227
Walden College [University], 20, 221, 233
Wallace, Henry, 113
Walker, George, 6
Walker-Hill, Helen, 211, 216, 217
Wallace, Patrick, 205
Wallace, W. H., 222
Waller, "Fats," 227
Walls, Clarence, 197
Walstrum, Theodore P., 126
Walters, Gwendolyn, 243
Wanamaker Awards, 90
Ware, Peter, 205
Warne, Katherine, 242
Warren, Elinor Remick, 7, 217
Washburn College, 88
Washington, Booker T., 2, 12, 27, 28, 29, 30, 34, 62, 63, 74, 87, 88, 92, 93, 102, 163, 181, 222, 224, 243
Washington, D.C., 87–88, 92, 206, 208, 224
Washington, Diana E., 207
Watkins, Mary, 217
Watson, E. M., 222
Watson, Rev. Richard, 210
WCMH-TV, 202

WCSU Radio, 138, 202
Welch, Cheryl, 205
*"Well, Well, Well So I Can Die Easy," 173; see also Echoes from the Journey
Wesley, Charles H., 106, 122, 134, 135–36, 137, 196, 225, 243
West Memphis, Ark., 105, 118
West Virginia College, 215
West Virginia [State College] University, 2, 86, 120, 167, 169, 174, 183, 192, 205, 206, 208, 209, 213, 216, 235, 240
Western Negro Press Association, 31
Westminster Record Company, 89
Wetzel, Joseph, 125
White, Clarence Cameron, 88
White, Delores, 211
White, U. S., 75
White, Walter, 93
"White" music, 45
Whiting, Cecil, 197
Whyte, Louise, 200
Wilberforce, Ohio, xix, 1, 14, 25, 29, 106, 121, 134, 136, 138, 175, 177, 178, 182, 183, 200, 207, 209, 211, 212, 213, 219, 223, 224, 229, 232
Wilberforce, William, 175–76, 177
Wilberforce College [University], 134, 176, 178, 179, 205
Wilcox, Don, 183, 209
Wiley, Grace D., ix, 119, 136, 240
Williams, Barbara, 217
Williams, Camilla, 245
Williams, Earl, 91
Williams, John, 196
Williams, Ora, 217
Williams, Thelma, 217
Williams, Wash., 221
Willman, Allan Arthur, ix, 1, 4, 12, 79, 106, 122, 123, 124–27, 133, 182, 202, 234, 237, 240, 241, 242
Wilson, Marilyn, ix
Winograd, Arthur, 245
Winternitz, Emanuel, 244
Wise, Frederick, 203
Wisorwild, Ellen, 200
Woolf, Virginia, 238
Woman of the Year Award, 183
Women and Music: A Journal of Gender and Culture, 8
Women of Class Trio, 207
Women's Federated Arts and Reading Club, 77

INDEX

Work, John Wesley, Jr., 88, 200
Working Papers on Women in Music, 204, 252
Works Progress Administration [WPA], 75, 112
World War I, 33, 69, 88, 112
World War II, 3, 102, 129, 227, 238
Wounded Knee, 59, 229
WPA Oklahoma Slave Narratives, The, 58, 222, 229
Wright, Frank Lloyd, 114
Wright Patterson Air Force Base, 136
Wright State University, 199, 209
Writing a Woman's Life, 96, 237
*"Written at Summer's End," 193; see also *Two Letters for clarinet, violoncello, and piano*
Wyatt, Kelly, 203
Wylie, Grace D., ix, 240
Wyoming, ix, 79, 106, 120, 122, 123, 124, 125, 126, 127, 128, 130, 131, 133, 134, 166, 167, 182, 183, 192, 195, 196, 200, 202, 211, 234, 235, 241, 242
WYSO Radio, Yellow Springs, Ohio, ix, xvii–xviii, xix

Xenia, Ohio, xv, xvii, xviii, xix, xx, 107, 183, 187, 197, 201, 202, 205, 206, 207, 209, 210, 211, 212, 213, 214, 215, 224, 239, 244, 245

Xenia [Ohio] Daily Gazette, 197, 201, 209, 211, 212, 213, 214, 239, 244
Xenia Springs, Ohio, 177

Yale University, 217
Yancy, H. Miller, 94, 115
Yellowhawk, Ruth, ix
Yellow Springs, Ohio, ix, xvii, xix, 206, 207, 209, 210, 220, 223, 246
Yellow Springs Historical Society, 206
Yellow Springs News, 211
You Can Tell the World: Songs by African-American Women Composers, 193, 244
"You Got to Reap Just What You Sow," 91
*You Hear the Constant Drumming, 193
Young, [Dr.], 78
Youngstown State University, Ohio, 182, 204, 205, 244

Zabak, Steven F., 207
Zea, David, x
Zeisler, Dennis, 203
"Zenobia Perry Day," xviii
Zinsser, William, 228
"Zion's Walls," 91

About the Author

Jeannie Gayle Pool.
Photo by Elliott Barker.

Jeannie Gayle Pool is a composer, filmmaker, musicologist, film music consultant, producer, and college instructor. She lectures and writes frequently on film music history and preservation, contemporary music, and on women in music.

Dr. Pool has taught music history and appreciation, theory, and solfège at various California universities. After serving as independent music consultant for Paramount Pictures for thirteen years, she is now the Music Archivist. An award-winning radio producer, specializing in contemporary music of the Americas, she was heard weekly on KPFK-FM, Pacifica Radio in Los Angeles between 1981 and 1996. As a music historian and producer, she was executive director of the Film Music Society from 1990 to 2002. As

ABOUT THE AUTHOR

a composer, her works have been heard in California, Washington, D.C., Florida, Ohio, Canada, China, and Europe.

Since 1980, Jeannie Pool has organized many conferences and concerts, including the International Congresses on Women in Music in New York, Los Angeles, and Mexico City. She has produced recordings for Cambria Master Recordings, an independent label in California which specializes in contemporary American music. She serves as an advisor to the Board of the International Alliance for Women in Music, which she helped to establish.

In 1995, she was honored by the National Association of Composers, USA, for her work to promote American composers and music, and served on its National Board of Directors. She is currently on the Board of the American Society of Music Arrangers and Composers.

Born in Paris, Illinois, Jeannie Pool grew up in Ohio and studied music in New York City at Hunter College of the City University of New York, where she earned a B.A. in music. She also studied musicology at Columbia University, and holds a master's degree from California State University, Northridge, where she did a thesis on music in Los Angeles in the nineteenth century. She received a Ph.D. in music at the Claremont Graduate University in May 2002. Her book, *Peggy Gilbert & Her All-Girl Band*, was published by Scarecrow Press in 2008.

For more information: www.jeanniepool.org.